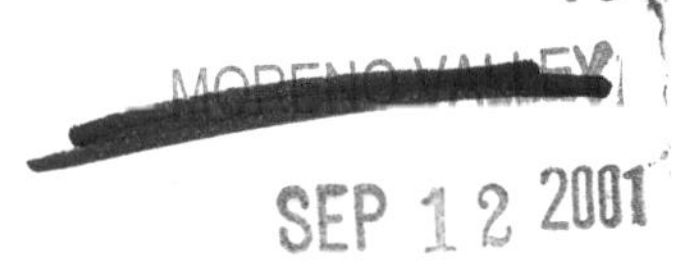

Pretense of Glory

Pretense of Glory

The Life of General Nathaniel P. Banks

James G. Hollandsworth, Jr.

Louisiana State University Press *Baton Rouge*

Manufactured in the United States of America
First Printing
07 06 05 04 03 02 01 00 99 98 5 4 3 2 1

Designer: Michele Myatt Quinn
Typeface: New Caledonia
Typesetter: Wilsted & Taylor Publishing Services

Library of Congress Cataloging-in-Publication Data

Hollandsworth, James G.
Pretense of glory : the life of General Nathaniel P. Banks / James G. Hollandsworth, Jr.
p. cm.
Includes bibliographical references and index.
ISBN 0-8071-2293-9 (cloth : alk. paper)
1. Banks, Nathaniel Prentiss, 1816–1894. 2. Generals—United States—Biography. 3. United States. Army.—Biography. I. Title.
E467.1.B23H65 1998
973.5′092—dc21
[B] 98-24709
CIP

Frontispiece courtesy National Archives.

The paper in this book meets the guidelines for permanence and durability of the Committee on Production Guidelines for Book Longevity of the Council on Library Resources. ♾

In memory of Ite

Edwin Michael Hoffman was "Uncle Mike" to most people, but he was always "Ite" (pronounced *eetay*) to me. "Ite" was short for "Ite Amaghazu" (Sioux for "Rain in the Face"), a name he adopted as director of the Indian lore program at Camp Sequoyah near Asheville, North Carolina.

Ite was a remarkable man—a musician, composer, anthropologist, botanist, writer, astrologer, and more. In particular, he was a serious student of Native American Culture, and he approached the subject with a deep reverence for its values and philosophy. In turn, he shared his respect for persons of different races and ethnic backgrounds with the campers at Sequoyah.

In the mid-1960s Ite suffered a stroke that left him partially paralyzed. His only child, a daughter living in Massachusetts, urged Ite and his wife Molly to move to Martha's Vineyard. They did, and a year or so later I received a postcard in his distinctive scrawl. He was sad, he missed the mountains of North Carolina, he regretted his failing health, and he wished to hear from former campers. I understood what he wanted. But I was in college or in the army . . . too preoccupied to appreciate the loneliness of growing old. I set the card aside and never got around to writing back. Ite died a few years later at the age of ninety-two.

I dedicate this book to you, Ite; it's the letter I never sent.

Contents

Illustrations

Photographs and Drawings

following page 133

Maps

Acknowledgments

Many persons have helped me with the research for this book. I would like to acknowledge in particular the assistance of Georgia Barnhill at the American Antiquarian Society in Worcester, Massachusetts; Alice, who works in the microfilm room of the Boston Public Library; Joan Caldwell, Director of the Louisiana Collection at Tulane University; John Barbry, Cathy Kahn, and Ann Middleton, all of whom have been associated with the Historic New Orleans Collection; Greg Potts and Michael L. Fraering at the Port Hudson State Commemorative Area; Francis Rouse at the Huntington Library in San Marino, California; Faye Phillips with the Louisiana and Lower Mississippi Valley Collection at Louisiana State University; Stuart Butler at the National Archives; Richard L. Sommers at the U.S. Army Military History Institute in Carlisle Barracks, Pennsylvania; Virginia Smith at the Massachusetts Historical Society in Boston; and Elizabeth D. Castner, Melissa Mannon, and Mary Alice Wade at the Waltham (Massachusetts) Public Library. In addition, I want to thank Ed Bearss for his close reading of the text and for his many helpful suggestions on how to improve it. I also would like to acknowledge the encouragement, support, and advice of numerous friends, students, and colleagues at the University of Southern Mississippi, especially David Bodenhamer, Lisa Boren, Evan Bradford, Crystal Campbell, Jeanne Ezell, Andrea Hinton, John Kelly (now deceased), Jan May, Paul McCarver, Lisa Moon, Henry Simmons, and Ellen Westbrook.

Abbreviations Used in Notes

AAS	American Antiquarian Society, Worcester, Mass.
CHS	Chicago Historical Society, Chicago, Ill.
HL	Huntington Library, San Marino, Calif.
HNOC	Historic New Orleans Collection, New Orleans, La.
HTML	Howard-Tilton Memorial Library, Tulane University, New Orleans, La.
ISHL	Illinois State Historical Library, Springfield, Ill.
LC	Library of Congress, Washington, D.C.
LALMVC	Louisiana and Lower Mississippi Valley Collections, LSU Libraries, Louisiana State University, Baton Rouge, La.
LMHC	Louisiana Museum Historical Center (Old Mint), New Orleans, La.
MHI	United States Army Military History Institute, Carlisle Barracks, Pa.
MAHS	Massachusetts Historical Society, Boston, Mass.
MNHS	Minnesota Historical Society, Saint Paul, Minn.
NA	National Archives, Washington, D.C.

OR	*War of the Rebellion: A Compilation of the Official Records of the Union and Confederate Armies,* 70 vols. in 127 and index. Washington, D.C.: Government Printing Office, 1880–1901.
OR (Navy)	Official Records of the Union and Confederate Navies in the War of the Rebellion. 31 vols. Washington, D.C.: Government Printing Office, 1894–1927.
SHC	Southern Historical Collection, University of North Carolina, Chapel Hill, N.C.
WDML	William D. McCain Library and Archives, University of Southern Mississippi, Hattiesburg, Miss.
WRPL	William R. Perkins Library, Duke University, Durham, N.C.
WPL	Waltham Public Library (Local History and Genealogy Room), Waltham, Mass.

Pretense of Glory

Introduction

In 1858 Nathaniel P. Banks seemed to have had as good a chance as anyone to become the next president of the United States. A two-term congressman from Massachusetts and already Speaker of the House, the forty-two-year-old Banks was an up-and-coming star of the new Republican party. Two years earlier he had contributed to John Frémont's bid for the presidency, and Frémont's strong showing had positioned the Republicans to win the White House in 1860.

Abraham Lincoln's future in 1858 did not look so bright. Debating and losing a Senate seat to Stephen A. Douglas, Lincoln stood in stark contrast to Nathaniel P. Banks. Lincoln was awkward and rough-hewn, and his plain talk seemed unrefined, even undignified, when compared to Banks's style of speaking, with its eloquent flourishes and oratorical highlights.

Despite these differences in appearance, Banks and Lincoln had much in common. Both came from working-class backgrounds; both were self-educated. Each was a pragmatic politician who understood the value of compromise. Most important, both men were against slavery. In short, Banks and Lincoln differed little in their political beliefs, but it was Lincoln who captured the presidency in 1860.

The fundamental and, as it turned out, critical difference between the two men lay beneath the surface. Although Banks and Lincoln were both skillful politicians, they had different reasons for choosing a career in politics. For Lincoln, politics provided the opportunity to realize the ideals upon which the country was founded.[1] For Banks, becoming a politician was an end in itself.

1. For example, Lincoln was steadfast in his commitment to human rights (see La-

Banks made no excuse for the way he was. "Two classes of statesmen have, at different times in the world's history, attempted to develop their ideas in its government, and clothe its institutions with a drapery of their own," he observed in one of his first speeches from the floor of the House of Representatives. "One has been willing to sacrifice nearly every opportunity and possibility of success to an artificial perfection in theory; the other has, in a more business-like manner, labored rather to attain that which was practicable than to discover or establish that which was perfect."[2]

Banks was a "practicable" man throughout his life. This book is an account of how his pragmatism, taken to extremes, prevented him from realizing the promise of what at the beginning had the prospect of becoming a remarkable career.

Wanda Cox, *Lincoln and Black Freedom: A Study in Presidential Leadership* [Columbia: University of South Carolina Press, 1981]. See also "The Republican Party" in Mark E. Neely, *The Abraham Lincoln Encyclopedia* (New York: Da Capo Books, 1982), 262–65.

2. *Congressional Globe,* 33d Cong., 1st sess., 1854, Appendix, 877. The speech was in opposition to the Kansas-Nebraska Bill.

1

Born a Talker

Nathaniel P. Banks's life began where it would end, in Waltham, Massachusetts, a factory town that grew up around a modern textile mill run by the Boston Manufacturing Company. Born in a company-owned house on River Street on January 30, 1816, Banks was the first child of Nathaniel P. Banks, Sr., and his wife of one year, Rebecca Greenwood Banks.[1]

People who knew Nat, as the young Banks was called, later remembered him as a healthy, active boy who enjoyed open, friendly relationships with the other children in his neighborhood. In time, he began his education in a crowded, one-room company school on Elm Street, where he mastered the fundamentals of reading and writing amid some seventy to eighty other pupils. His teachers considered Nat to be "bright and apt."[2]

Nat's father was a skilled worker at the mill who did better than most. Promoted to foreman, the senior Banks made as much as twelve dollars

1. Banks was entered in the records as Nathaniel Startle Prentice Banks but usually went by Nathaniel Prentice (or Prentiss) Banks, Jr. (Fred Harvey Harrington, *Fighting Politician: Major General N. P. Banks* [Philadelphia: University of Pennsylvania Press, 1948], 1, 213). A picture of the house in which Banks was born appeared in the *Illinois Central Magazine* 2 (July 1913): 15. See also Melvin T. Copeland, *The Cotton Manufacturing Industry of the United States* (New York: Augustus M. Kelley, 1966), 37–38, and Charles James Fox Binney, *The History of the Prentice, or Prentiss Family,* 2d ed. (1883; reprint, as part of John K. Prentice, "Descendants of Rev. Amos Prentice [1804–1849]" [Barrington, Ill., 1942, mimeograph]).

2. William Makepeace Thayer, *The Bobbin Boy: or, How Nat Got His Learning* (1860; reprint, Boston: Lee & Shepard, 1863), 83, 96–97; Kristen A. Petersen, *Waltham Rediscovered: An Ethnic History of Waltham, Massachusetts* (Waltham: Peter E. Ran-

a week. Although this wage was three to four times what other workers in the mill got, it did not go far with a large family to feed. Consequently, Nat's father expected him to drop out of school and go to work in the mill to help support the family.[3]

Nat did not want to quit school; he believed that he could make something of himself through education. Nevertheless, in 1830 he went to work in the Waltham Mill at the age of fourteen. His job was to remove bobbins when they were full of thread and replace them with empty spools. It was a monotonous assignment and paid only two dollars a week. Nat was also dissatisfied by the lack of respect being a mill worker brought him. "Rich men," he maintained, "were thought more of by many people, whether they were deserving or not, and [that] seemed . . . wrong." Thus at an early age, Nat acquired a determination to rise above his working-class origins.[4]

Education was the key to Nat's ambitions. In an effort to enlarge on what he had learned in school, he set up a "study" in the attic on the third floor of the family's house on the corner of Main and Common Streets. The study was a quiet place where he could go to read in the evening with Charlie, a friend who worked in the mill. Nat also began a modest library with the purchase his first book, John Locke's *Essay Concerning Human Understanding.*[5]

---

dall, 1988), 37 (a picture of the schoolhouse is on page 16); *New York Herald,* December 5, 1855. Rebecca's letters to her son referred to him as "Prentice" (Rebecca Banks to Banks, January 17, 1860, September 1, 1863, Nathaniel P. Banks Collection, LC), as did the rest of the family (numerous letters in Banks Collection, LC).

3. In 1820 Rebecca Banks bore a second son, who died in infancy, but gave birth to a third, named Miles, two years later. Susan Prentice Banks followed Miles in 1825 and another girl, Eliza, three years after that. During the 1830s, Rebecca gave birth to three more sons—Hiram, William, and Gardner. In all, there were eight children, six of whom survived to adulthood (*Vital Records of Waltham, Massachusetts, to the Year 1850* [Boston: New-England Historic Genealogical Society, 1904], 12, 112, 251). See also Victor S. Clark, *History of Manufactures in the United States,* 3 vols. (New York: McGraw-Hill, 1929), 1:395, and Walter F. Starbuck, *Picturesque Features of the History of Waltham* (Waltham, Mass.: Waltham Publishing Co., 1917), 43–44.

4. Starbuck, *Picturesque Waltham,* 43–44; Thayer, *Bobbin Boy,* 21, 59–61, 83–98, 106–9, 162–65.

5. Charles A. Nelson, *Waltham, Past and Present* (Cambridge, Mass.: Thomas Lewis, 1879), 134; Petersen, *Waltham Rediscovered,* 37; Starbuck, *Picturesque Waltham,* 43; Thayer, *Bobbin Boy,* 114, 165–79; Newspaper clipping, January [13], 1886, Banks Collection, LC.

On Saturdays, Nat and Charlie would walk the ten miles into Boston to spend the day at the Athenaeum Library, making the return trip on foot that night. Tradition has it that on one of these trips Nat stopped and peered through the gate at Harvard College, wishing that one day he would be able to study there. A college education, however, was out of reach for a mechanic's son, so Nat sought knowledge wherever he could find it.[6]

He found one such opportunity by attending lectures at the Boston Manufacturing Company's Rumford Institute, listening to some of the great speakers of the day such as Daniel Webster, Caleb Cushing, and Charles Sumner. Impressed by these displays of oratorical skill, Nat decided to form a debating society with several workers from the factory. The group met in the local schoolhouse on Tuesday evenings and provided the chance for the "Bobbin Boy" to indulge his newfound passion for rhetoric.[7]

Nat also tried his hand at acting. Inspired by seeing Edwin Booth perform in Boston, Nat decided to organize a dramatic society with some friends and took to acting with a zeal he had never demonstrated on the factory floor. By 1839 he was playing leading roles with such mastery that he was invited to perform in Boston, where he played the heroic lead in *The Lady of Lyons.*[8]

Nat liked being an actor, but in Waltham acting was not considered a "proper Christian profession." Some members of the community questioned the advisability of even having a dramatic society and called a public meeting to discuss the issue. Nat attended the meeting with his mother to defend the group. He spoke for more than twenty minutes while his mother sat in astonished silence, expecting her son to embarrass both himself and the family. But Nat spoke on, finding the right words and using his voice to good effect. The address was Nat's first

6. Thayer, *Bobbin Boy,* 174, 183–84, 235–46.

7. George F. Hoar, *Autobiography of Seventy Years* (New York: Charles Scribner's Sons, 1903), 1:223; Starbuck, *Picturesque Waltham,* 30–31; Banks to John Quincy Adams, November 1840, Banks to Theodore Parker, September 8, 1856, N. P. Banks Manuscripts, ISHL.

8. Starbuck, *Picturesque Waltham,* 44; Thayer, *Bobbin Boy,* 214–32, 252; *Boston Evening Transcript,* June 4, 1839; *New York Herald,* September 2, 1894; Banks to E. S. Walker, July 19, 1859, Banks Manuscripts, ISHL; Banks to Mary Palmer, [undated], Banks Collection, LC.

public speech, and it forecast a career in public office rather than in the theater.[9]

Another diversion for Nat during this period was a dancing school he organized. He rented space, printed programs, and issued flyers that announced "dancing to commence at 7 o'clock" with "N. P. Banks, Jr.—Manager." Tickets were $1.50.[10]

Unfortunately for Nat, dancing was another amusement that did not meet with the approval of local authorities. This time it was the Boston Manufacturing Company that objected, specifically to the late hours the young revelers kept. As one of the supervisors in the mill explained to a visitor: "We had some trouble last winter about the dancing-school. It must, of course, be held in the evening, as the young folks are in the mill all day. They are very young, many of them; and they forget the time, and everything but amusement, and dance away till two or three in the morning. Then they are unfit for their work the next day; or, if they get properly through their work, it is at the expense of their health." As an alternative, the company promised to sponsor dances itself, once every two weeks, but it stipulated that these dances "shall meet and break up early." Hoping to encourage attendance, the company posted a notice in the Waltham mill announcing that young ladies who attended Nat's dancing school would be fired.[11]

If dancing and acting were not pursuits acceptable for a young man seeking a career, Nat soon found one that was when he joined a total abstinence society. The temperate use of alcohol had become a burning issue in Massachusetts, leading the state legislature in 1838 to ban the sale of distilled liquors in quantities of less than fifteen gallons. Ostensibly, the ordinance was designed to prohibit the sale of whiskey in taverns but not to limit its use by licensed apothecaries and physicians. In reality, the measure was directed primarily at the mill workers.[12]

9. Thayer, *Bobbin Boy,* 223–24, 226, 243–45.

10. Announcement dated April 7, 1841, in Banks Collection, LC; also Banks's invitation to Mary Palmer to attend his "dancing school," March 2, 1840, Banks Manuscripts, ISHL.

11. Harriet Martineau, *Society in America,* 2 vols. (New York: Saunders & Otley, 1837), 2:139; printed invitations dated April 7, 1841, and March 1, 1844, Banks Collection, LC.

12. George Faber Clark, *History of the Temperance Reform in Massachusetts, 1813–1883* (Boston: Clarke & Carruth, 1888), 6–29; Arthur Burr Darling, *Political Changes in Massachusetts, 1824–1848: A Study of Liberal Movements in Politics* (New Haven: Yale

Opponents of the measure argued that the law was an effort on the part of the company to increase the efficiency of its workers. The temperance people, however, argued that the new law would elevate the common man by saving him from the evils of strong drink. Both sides rushed speakers to the field, and Nat became a leading spokesman for the temperance movement in Waltham. He was an effective speaker, for he believed in what he was saying. Although he sometimes drank wine with his meals and would occasionally indulge in a glass of beer, Banks avoided hard liquor throughout his life. The voters forced the repeal of the law in 1840, but Nat attracted notice and was asked to do some stump speaking for the Democrats in the 1840 presidential race.[13]

The presidential campaign of 1840 was Nat's formal introduction to politics, and he quickly attained local prominence. Encouraged by his success, Nat quit his job at the mill and tried his hand at party journalism as editor of the *Lowell Democrat.* The job came from the Reverend Eliphalet Case, who headed one of the local contingents of the Democratic party. Unfortunately, Benjamin F. Butler and other foes of the Case faction chose to launch a rival Democratic sheet, the *Vox Populi,* at the same time. Because the rival paper came out strongly for the shorter-hour movement, the more cautious *Lowell Democrat* was soon perceived to be antilabor; it folded in 1841, scarcely a year after it started.[14]

Smarting from the reversal, Nat returned to Waltham to start the *Middlesex Reporter,* which had no direct competition. But Waltham was too close to Boston to feel the need for a local press. Furthermore, Nat's second editorial effort lacked either the capital or the corporate patronage it needed to succeed. Having failed twice as a newspaper editor in a little more than two years, Nat decided to put his skills to better use by

---

University Press, 1925), 158–62; John Allen Krout, *The Origins of Prohibition* (New York: Knopf, 1925), 89–92, 263–72; Thayer, *Bobbin Boy,* 270–78.

13. Banks also did not smoke or use tobacco (Nathan Appleton, *Russian Life and Society* [Boston: Murray & Emery, 1904], 172; *Boston Globe,* February 13, 1916). See also William Stevens Robinson, *"Warrington" Pen-Portraits,* ed. Mrs. W. S. Robinson (Boston: Lee & Shepard, 1877), 20; Thayer, *Bobbin Boy,* 158–62, 266–67, 270–71; Charles Wade to Banks, May 1, 1843, M. Grant to Banks, May 4, 1843, George F. Adams to Banks, April 4, 1846, Banks Manuscripts, ISHL.

14. Charles Cowley, *History of Lowell,* 2d ed. (Boston: Lee & Shepard, 1868), 124; Harrington, *Fighting Politician,* 7; D. Hamilton Hurd, *History of Middlesex County, Massachusetts,* 4 vols. (Philadelphia: J. W. Lewis, 1890), 2:188–95.

running for political office. "I can see as far ahead as most persons of my years," Nat wrote confidently in 1844, when he ran for a seat in the Massachusetts legislature. He lost.[15]

Banks's decision to join the Democratic party made sense. The Democrats stood for the workingman against the National Republican party, or Whigs, which favored business interests. Furthermore, the Democratic leadership in Massachusetts was superior to that offered by the Whigs and included men such as Caleb Cushing, Benjamin F. Butler, and George S. Boutwell. The Democrat who caught Banks's attention and respect, however, was the brilliant and enthusiastic Robert Rantoul, Jr.[16]

One of the ablest political leaders in the state, Rantoul was fervently interested in education. Supposedly he taught himself to read at the age of three and later attended Phillips Academy at Andover and Harvard College to assuage his "unquenchable thirst for knowledge and his intellectual independence." Rantoul's many interests included progressive causes such as pacifism, temperance, the humanitarian reform of prisons and insane asylums, efforts to end capital punishment, and, most important, the abolition of slavery.[17]

Rantoul served as an attractive role model for Banks, who saw him as a politician who espoused the causes a working-class youth could endorse. By 1840 Banks had begun to imitate Rantoul's style. With practice and time, he learned to give speeches in the Rantoul manner and adopted his mentor's method of appealing to the common man.[18]

15. Banks to Mary Palmer, April 19, 1844, Banks Collection, LC; Harrington, *Fighting Politician,* 5–6; Hurd, *History of Middlesex County,* 3:737; Petersen, *Waltham Rediscovered,* 39. For one of Banks's early political speeches, see N. P. Banks, *An Oration Delivered before the Neptune and Boyden Fire Companies and the Citizens of Waltham, July 4, 1842* (Boston: H. L. Devereux, 1842).

16. *Boston Globe,* February 13, 1916; Rantoul to Banks, March 29, 1844, Banks Manuscripts, ISHL.

17. *Dictionary of American Biography,* S.V. "Rantoul, Robert"; Merle E. Curti, "Robert Rantoul, Jr., The Reformer in Politics," *New England Quarterly* 5 (April 1932): 266–67; Charles Levi Woodbury, "Some Personal Recollections of Robert Rantoul, Junior," *Historical Collections of the Essex Institute* 34 (December 1898): 206–7.

18. Harrington, *Fighting Politician,* 5. For Banks's debt to Rantoul, see George Roberts to Banks, February 14, 1856, Banks Collection, LC; also *Congressional Globe,* 33d Cong., 2d sess., 1854, Appendix, 49–50.

Like many politicians, Rantoul was not always what he appeared to be. On one hand, he was an outspoken critic of wealth and privilege. One of his greatest successes along these lines came in 1842 before the Massachusetts Supreme Court when he argued and won the case of *Commonwealth v. Hunt,* which recognized the workers' right to organize. On the other hand, Rantoul was willing to interpret his principles broadly so that on other occasions he worked energetically to promote the fortunes of the business interests he professed to hate. For example, he was instrumental in persuading the Illinois legislature to make very favorable concessions in granting the Illinois Central Railroad its charter. Rantoul defended this action by claiming that his promotion of commerce would benefit the workingman. Rantoul's pragmatism, his willingness to bend on principle when it seemed expedient, was not lost on his young protégé. Politics had become Banks's bread and butter, and he wanted to be on the winning side.[19]

Winning was particularly important in 1843 after the collapse of the *Middlesex Reporter,* when Banks found himself "not in affluence." Fortunately, he was able to get a job in the Boston customhouse, thanks to the kindness of Rantoul, who had been named collector of the port of Boston. Normally, the job fell under the federal patronage system and should have gone to a Whig because John Tyler was in the White House. But Tyler was quarreling with the Whigs in Massachusetts and favored the Democrats. Although the United States Senate rejected Rantoul's appointment as port collector, Banks was able to hold on to his newly acquired position.[20]

Financially secure for the time being, Banks consummated an engagement that had lasted more than eight years when he married Mary Theodosia Palmer on April 11, 1847. They were very much in love. "Perhaps you have heard how well satisfied I am with my girl?" he wrote to Mary several months before they were married. "Such a sweet disposition! So much energy for improving herself and gratifying the family!

19. Curti, "Robert Rantoul, Jr.," 264–80; Harrington, *Fighting Politician,* 5; Robinson, *"Warrington" Pen-Portraits,* 512–13. Also see Robert Rantoul, Jr., *Memoirs, Speeches and Writings* (Boston: John P. Jewett, 1854).

20. Harrington, *Fighting Politician,* 8; Darling, *Political Changes in Massachusetts,* 284–85, 313; *Boston Globe,* February 13, 1916; T. J. Greenwood to Banks, March 4, 1844, Banks Collection, LC. For Banks's license as a temporary weigher sworn "to prevent and detect fraud," dated May 18, 1844, see Banks Manuscripts, ISHL.

Such ambition! Such a taste for dress! Such a kind joyous heart! Such eyes! Such legs!—Oh! She's a dear!"[21]

Mary Palmer was an attractive young woman who worked in the mill. She was a strong person in her own right, quick to form opinions and reluctant to change them once they were set. She also had a temper. On one occasion, when referring to a family acquaintance known for her angry disposition, Banks remarked that "she is like my dear wife, who is occasionally very violent with those that do not treat her well." Nevertheless, theirs was a long and happy union that lasted forty-seven years and resulted in four children.[22]

Banks made another unsuccessful run for the Massachusetts legislature as a Democrat in November 1847. There were several reasons why he could not get elected. Some of the voters thought he was too young for public office. Others objected to his temperance connections. The major obstacle to Banks's success, however, was the Boston Manufacturing Company, which favored the Whigs. The company held such economic power that when it spoke, voters listened. In addition, the company used an open ballot system to force its employees to support the Whig ticket.[23]

Banks hated the Whigs because they had money. He expressed some of this resentment at the funeral of John Quincy Adams, sixth president of the United States and dean of Massachusetts politicians. Adams was buried on February 23, 1848, and his funeral was the sort of public event that someone seeking political office was expected to attend. Banks took part but found himself on foot in the funeral procession while the Whigs rode in fine carriages. The disparity irritated the aspiring politician, who at one point during the march turned to a companion and vowed, "By

21. Banks to Mary Palmer, August 17, 1846, Banks Collection, LC.

22. Mary was born in Charlestown, Massachusetts, October 26, 1817 (Harrington, *Fighting Politician,* 6, 214n). Banks to Mary Banks, June 18, 1863, Mary Banks to Banks, October 11, 1872, Banks Collection, LC; *Boston Daily Advertiser,* May 15, July 1, 1874. During the Civil War Banks had a special pocket sewn in his shirt and kept "nothing in it but the pictures of the children & their mother" (Banks to Mary ["Binney"] Banks, March 11, 1862, Banks Collection, LC).

23. George S. Boutwell, *Reminiscences of Sixty Years in Public Affairs,* 2 vols. (1902; reprint, New York: Greenwood Press, 1968), 1:110; *Boston Globe,* February 13, 1916; *New York Tribune,* August 27, 1860.

and by you and I will ride in these carriages, and those fellows will go on foot as we do now."[24]

Unseating the Whigs would not be easy, and for a time Banks became so discouraged that he considered leaving Massachusetts for new opportunities in the West. Nevertheless, he stood his ground and continued to assail the "heartless" Whigs. Democratic party chiefs played their part by focusing on voters who were not as easily controlled by the Boston Manufacturing Company—storekeepers, farmers, and mechanics not on the company payroll. The strategy began to pay off. The Whigs had failed to gain the votes needed to elect a legislator from Waltham in 1844. One year later, the town had gone Democratic in the gubernatorial campaign. Finally, Banks gained a seat in Massachusetts General Court on November 7, 1848.[25]

Banks threw himself enthusiastically into his new job as a state legislator and quickly developed a talent for accommodation. Although he had made his political debut as a temperance advocate, Banks now courted the favor of "rum cocks" by backing a liquor dealer for state senator. He also avoided offending Caleb Cushing and other conservatives in the Democratic party by playing down his advocacy of rights for the working class.[26]

Banks also held the middle ground on the slavery issue. Although he doubted the merits of the South's "peculiar institution," Banks did not share the fiery sectionalism expressed by abolitionists such as William Lloyd Garrison. For example, Banks did not oppose the annexation of Texas in 1845, even though it meant the addition of another slave state.

24. Robinson, *"Warrington" Pen-Portraits,* 436.

25. Benjamin F. Butler, *Butler's Book: Autobiography and Personal Reminiscences of Major-General Benj. F. Butler* (Boston: A. M. Thayer, 1892), 98–100; Charles T. Congdon, *Reminiscences of a Journalist* (Boston: James R. Osgood, 1880), 151; Darling, *Political Changes in Massachusetts,* 171; Harrington, *Fighting Politician,* 7; Hurd, *History of Middlesex County,* 3:714, 718–19, 731; Robinson, *"Warrington" Pen-Portraits,* 436; Thayer, *Bobbin Boy,* 122; *Boston Daily Journal,* November 11, 1845, November 10, 1846, November 14, 1848; *New York Tribune,* August 27, 1860; J. Frank Simonds to Banks, November 10, 1874, Banks Collection, LC. The General Court is a bicameral legislative body similar to those in other states (Louis Adams Frothingham, *A Brief History of the Constitution and Government of Massachusetts* [Cambridge, Mass.: Harvard University Press, 1916], 51–59).

26. Darling, *Political Changes in Massachusetts,* 322; Harrington, *Fighting Politician,* 8.

And although initially he supported the Wilmot Proviso, which was intended to bar slavery from newly acquired territories, Banks changed his position when the national Democratic party rejected the provision.[27]

Banks's moderate stand on slavery was grounded in part in his strong sense of nationalism. He was "willing to maintain an extension of slavery, northward or southward, whenever such an act may subserve all our various national interests." Antislavery sentiment, however, was on the rise in New England as the decade of the 1850s opened. Some New Englanders objected to it as a moral issue, while others were concerned with the shift of power in the U.S. Congress as the result of the admission of slave territories as states. A politician in Massachusetts could not ignore the changing sentiment, and Banks began to qualify his expansionist talk with antislavery comments. He referred to the Democratic party as the "friend of absolute freedom" and said that Andrew Jackson's strong stand in 1833 in response to South Carolina's attempt to nullify federal laws had dug slavery's grave. Banks also strengthened his connections with the new Free-Soil party in his district, which had given him the votes he needed to win by a slim margin in his election to the Massachusetts legislature.[28]

Banks's skill in handling controversial issues resulted in his playing an important role in a movement that brought the young politician his first experience of national attention—the Massachusetts Coalition of 1849–1853. Although he was not yet ready to embrace the antislavery cause, Banks saw the benefit of aligning the forces of Massachusetts Democrats with Free-Soilers to combat the powerful Whigs in the state. Such an alliance could help both parties. The Free-Soilers would be in a better position to push their fight against slavery; the Democrats could do more for the working class.[29]

27. See Banks's speech, *Congressional Globe,* 33d Cong., 1st sess., 1854, Appendix, 77–81; *Boston Post,* March 7, 1849; Free Soiler from the Start, *A Review of Mr. Banks's Political History: Designed for the Information of the People of Mass.* (N.p., 1855), 2. Rantoul advised Banks to support the annexation of Texas (Rantoul to Banks, August 9, 1844, Banks Collection, LC).

28. John Savage, *Our Living Representative Men* (Philadelphia: Childs & Peterson, 1860), 20; *Boston Post,* March 7, 1849; *Boston Daily Journal,* June 10, 1854; *Boston Daily Evening Traveller,* August 29, 1857. The Free-Soil party was made up of northern abolitionists as well as those who desired to restrict the spread of slavery to new states and territories, thus its name.

29. Harrington, *Fighting Politician,* 9–11.

Making the coalition work was not easy. Political egos and jealousies, not to mention mutual suspicion of each other's goals, kept the leaders of the two factions at arm's length. In addition, many leading Democrats, such as Caleb Cushing, were afraid that lending support to the Free-Soilers would hasten the day when the Union would be split apart. Nevertheless, Banks, Rantoul, and Boutwell set out to organize voters "with liberal notions under their caps."[30]

Their hard work paid off in the November 1850 elections, which saw a victory for the coalition that went "far beyond the anticipation of those most sanguine in its behalf." On New Year's Day 1851, the coalition organized the Massachusetts legislature, placing men of lowly origins in high places that once were monopolized by the mighty Whigs. Henry Wilson, a cobbler by trade, was elected president of the state senate, Boutwell was elected governor, and Rantoul was sent to Washington to serve the remainder of an unexpired term in the U.S. Senate. Most important, the Bobbin Boy was elected as Speaker of the House.[31]

Having beaten the Whigs handily, members of the coalition soon began to fight among themselves. Since the post of governor went to the Democrats, they agreed to let the Free-Soilers choose the successor to the seat in the U.S. Senate once held by the old Whig Daniel Webster. Although it took one hundred days and twenty-six ballots, the legislature eventually gave the nod to a staunch abolitionist, Charles Sumner.[32]

Sumner's election further alienated the Democrats from the Free-Soilers. Caleb Cushing was convinced that Sumner's election would der-

30. Harrington, *Fighting Politician,* 10; Robinson, *"Warrington" Pen-Portraits,* 405. For background, see John Bigelow, *Retrospections of an Active Life* (New York: Baker & Taylor, 1909), 4 vols., 1:101; Boutwell, *Reminiscences,* 1:114–15; Henry Wilson, *History of the Rise and Fall of the Slave Power in America,* 4 vols. (Boston: J. R. Osgood, 1875–77), 2:338–39; Robert Charles Winthrop, *A Memoir of Robert C. Winthrop* (Boston: Little, Brown, 1897), 141. Also see Claude M. Fuess, *The Life of Caleb Cushing,* 2 vols. (New York: Harcourt, Brace, 1923), 2:98; and Oscar Handlin, *Boston's Immigrants: A Study in Acculturation* (Cambridge, Mass.: Harvard University Press, 1959), 194–95.

31. Handlin, *Boston's Immigrants,* 200–201; J. G. Whittier to Henry Wilson, November 18, 1850, quoted in Harrington, *Fighting Politician,* 10; Winthrop, *Memoir,* 143; Wilson, *Rise and Fall of the Slave Power,* 2:342–51; *Boston Post,* May 28, 1851. Banks was elected to both branches of the legislature in 1850 but chose to serve in the House.

32. David Donald, *Charles Sumner and the Coming of the Civil War* (New York: Knopf, 1960), 195–202; *Boston Daily Journal,* January 14, March 13, 1851; *Boston Post,* April 25, 1851. U.S. senators were not popularly elected until passage of the Seventeenth Amendment in 1913.

ogate the honor of Massachusetts and prove a disaster to the Union. Initially, Banks had also opposed Sumner's appointment. He never would like the man. "With all his high qualities," Banks confided to Mary many years later, "he is destitute of the power of reason." Banks also considered him to be a "bitter agent" and "not a harmonizer." But a deal was a deal, and Banks did what he could to see that the Free-Soilers' candidate won.[33]

In helping elect Sumner, Banks had done two things that were to hurt him in the future: he had offended important Democratic leaders and helped a candidate whose views he disapproved. Unlike Banks, Sumner would not compromise his convictions for political expediency, and Banks soon found that his support of the new senator from Massachusetts would come back to haunt him.[34]

Although some conservative Democrats believed that Banks had prostituted Democratic principles by joining a "shameless abolition coalition," the young politician from Waltham had become a major political figure. His position with the antislavery forces was secure and would serve him well in the days to come. His role as presiding officer throughout the legislative session also had helped his standing. He looked good in the Speaker's chair and performed his duties brilliantly. He was attentive, tactful, and firm and ruled quickly and with precision. His clear voice cut through the hum of conversation and the babble of confused debate. In appreciation, the House unanimously passed a resolution of thanks for the "eminent ability, impartiality, and courtesy with which the duties of the chair have been administered during the session by Hon. Nathaniel P. Banks, speaker of the house."[35]

Banks's success came at a good time, for both he and Mary were liberal spenders, and finding enough money to support their family was a constant concern. Ever since he had been dropped from the customhouse in 1849, Banks had to support his family on his salary of three dollars per day during sessions of the General Court. At first he supplemented this income by serving on a special sanitary commission headed by Lemuel Shattuck. When that position ended, Banks took a job as a

33. *Boston Daily Journal,* March 13, 1851; Banks to Mary Banks, May 7, 1869, March 24, 1871, Banks Collection, LC.

34. Harrington, *Fighting Politician,* 13.

35. *Boston Daily Journal,* January 11, 1851; *Boston Post,* May 25, 1851.

publicist with the Massachusetts Board of Education, of which Rantoul was a member. The assignment provided additional income and allowed him to travel around the state promoting various projects being undertaken by the board. This opportunity gave Banks greater visibility outside his home district and would be an important part of his goal of achieving a political office on the state level. Banks also picked up some extra income by working for the Massachusetts Census and Valuation Commission.[36]

Although Banks obtained extra pay as Speaker of the House during 1851 and 1852, he still sought ways to supplement his income, a goal that was particularly important after his wife gave birth to their first daughter, Maude, on February 3, 1852. To that end, Banks became a lobbyist in Washington for the state of Massachusetts—for an old claim for money the state had spent on fortifications during the War of 1812—and traveled to Philadelphia to help plan a monument to be erected in Independence Square. He also took another short-lived stab at journalism with the aborted *Rumford Journal.* His brief flirtation with the law at this time was equally unsuccessful, although he won admission to the Suffolk County (Boston) bar after scanning a few law books in Rantoul's office. Lacking connections as well as an interest in dealing with the paperwork inherent to the profession, Banks abandoned plans for a law practice when the good accounts eluded him. Years later he would say, "I am no lawyer, I thank heaven." An observer who knew him agreed: "He was born for a talker, not a writer."[37]

His success as Massachusetts Speaker of the House made Banks decide to run for a seat in the U.S. House of Representatives. The Democratic candidate for president in 1852, Franklin Pierce, disapproved of

36. Harrington, *Fighting Politician,* 14; Savage, *Our Living Representative Men,* 20. For Shattuck's sanitary commission, see George Chandler Whipple, *State Sanitation: A Review of the Work of the Massachusetts State Board of Health* (Cambridge, Mass.: Harvard University Press, 1917). For examples of the couple's spending habits, see Mary Banks to Banks, January 13, 1858, Banks to Mary Banks, August 27, 1863, and misc. bills, Banks Collection, LC; and J. W. Horton to Banks, January 19, 1846, Banks Manuscripts, ISHL.

37. Banks to Mary Banks, June 29, 1852, Banks Collection, LC. Hurd, *History of Middlesex County,* 3:737; Robinson, *"Warrington" Pen-Portraits,* 438; Starbuck, *Picturesque Waltham,* 45; Woodbury, "Some Personal Recollections," 206–7; *Boston Globe,* April 24, 1874; *New York Herald,* July 7, 1852; *New York Tribune,* August 27, 1860.

political alliances with antislavery advocates. Although Banks won the regular Democratic nomination by accepting the national party platform, some Cushing Democrats insisted that he show his loyalty to Pierce by publicly denouncing the antislavery cause as well. Banks refused so the Democratic party withdrew his name and put forward another candidate. It was a close race, but Banks won by three hundred votes out of nine thousand cast after the Free-Soil nominee in his district withdrew. The victory foreshadowed Banks's eventual break with the Democratic party, for if it were not for the support of the antislavery bloc, Banks would have lost the election.[38]

Despite his elevation to a national office, Banks had one more opportunity to curtail the power of the privileged Whigs when a convention was called to rework the constitution of Massachusetts. Banks was elected president of the body and once again displayed great ability in conducting a meeting. Whereas Henry Wilson, the president pro tem, was "clumsy and forgetful and undecided," Banks was skillful, attentive, and energetic. As president, Banks also had the advantage of not having to state his position on the points under debate. Although he did speak once in favor of the militia and defended the Commonwealth's ancient but inequitable system of town representation, the Bobbin Boy chose to keep a safe distance above the political fray.[39]

The constitutional convention began on May 4, 1853, and immediately set out to shift the balance of power away from the wealthy men of Boston. Working through committees appointed by Banks, the convention voted to scrap property requirements for voting and holding office, to provide for popular election of many state and county officials, and to reduce the term of office for judges. Banks was pleased, for the new con-

38. Harrington, *Fighting Politician,* 15; *Boston Post,* November 4, December 10, 14, 15, 16, 1852.

39. Handlin, *Boston's Immigrants,* 202–3; Banks to Mary P. Banks, May 4, 1853, Banks Collection, LC, in which he claims much of the credit for getting the convention called. For a record of the convention, see Charles Francis Adams, *Richard Henry Dana: A Biography,* 2 vols. (Boston: Houghton Mifflin, 1891), 1:233–61; Massachusetts, *Journal of the Constitutional Convention of the Commonwealth of Massachusetts, 1853* (Boston: White & Potter, 1853), 3–5; Massachusetts, *Official Report of the Debates and Proceedings in the State Convention Assembled May 4th, 1853, to Revise and Amend the Constitution of the Commonwealth of Massachusetts,* 3 vols. (Boston: White & Potter, 1853), 2:12–14, 250–53, 3:598–99, 728–29.

stitution afforded a chance to end aristocratic rule in Massachusetts. With the hyperbole that characterized so many of his pronouncements throughout his life, Banks ended the convention on August 1 with lavish praise for its members. "For patient investigation, assiduous, unremitting, and conscientious devotion to laborious duties, in a most oppressive season," he intoned, "I believe no representative assembly ever surpassed that whose labors are now about to close."[40]

Apparently, a majority of voters in the Bay State disagreed with Banks's assessment, for they rejected the document when it was submitted to them in November 1853. Not only were the Whigs in strong opposition, but many anticoalition Democrats and Free-Soilers spoke against it. Its final undoing came a few weeks before the election, when Caleb Cushing, who was now the attorney general in Pierce's cabinet, issued a strongly worded letter in which he denounced the alliance between Massachusetts Democrats and Free-Soilers.[41]

With the constitution defeated, the coalition lay in ruins, but the new congressman from Massachusetts was not distressed. Banks was by nature an optimist, and with his seat in the U.S. House secure until March 1855, he had plenty of time to work out new strategies for a political career that had been remarkable to that point for its quicksilver success.[42]

40. Albert Bushnell Hart, *Commonwealth History of Massachusetts,* 5 vols. (New York: States History Co., 1930), 4:482–84; Boutwell, *Reminiscences,* 1:219–20; *Boston Post,* September 23, 1853; Massachusetts, *Official Report,* 3:729.

41. In spite of its rejection, the convention had not been a total waste of time and effort, for many of its propositions were adopted later as separate amendments to the earlier document. See Frothingham, *Brief History,* 51–59; Fuess, *Life of Caleb Cushing,* 2:139–40; Roy Franklin Nichols, *The Democratic Machine, 1850–1854,* Studies in History, Economics, and Public Law, Whole Number 248 (New York: Columbia University, 1923), 216–17.

42. See Mary Banks to Banks, January 13, 1858, Banks Collection, LC.

2

A Genius for Being Looked At

There was much to like about the new congressman from Massachusetts. A mechanic's son who had quit school to help support his family, Banks was an industrious, personable, and articulate spokesman for his district. Furthermore, he understood the plight of the worker and appreciated the enduring struggle of working-class men and women seeking to survive in a world of privilege. This outlook alone gave the young Banks an immediate set of issues around which to organize his emerging political career.[1]

Banks may have identified himself with the workers, but he was determined to rise above his working-class origins. The key to his appetite for upward mobility was education, which he thought "better than a fortune" for securing his future. Although his formal schooling was cut short, Banks taught himself law, studied foreign languages, and maintained an active interest in history, economics, and "the science of government." Throughout his adult life he recorded pertinent pieces of information almost daily in little notebooks or pocket diaries he carried with him. He used these notes in his speeches, for although Banks was known for his ability to stir the emotions of a crowd, his orations were replete with facts, figures, and other information. It was not unusual, therefore, for his audience to assume that he possessed more formal education than was actually the case. This misperception pleased the

1. *Boston Globe*, February 13, 1916.

young politician from Waltham, who liked to boast that he had graduated "from a college with a water-wheel in the basement."[2]

Perhaps Banks tried too hard. He never clipped his words by saying, "I don't" for "I do not" or "I can't" instead of "I cannot," making his speech a bit wooden and giving the impression of arrogance. At least one observer concluded that Banks was "not a warm-hearted person, and was never known to go out of his way an inch to confer a favor on a friend or supporter, unless another and a greater favor was expected at a future period." Another colleague thought that Banks was arrogant and called his "appearance of sagacity and greatness" mere "pretentious humbug," for no man could be as wise as Banks looked.[3]

But Banks was an attractive man; some said that he had "a genius for being looked at." Standing five feet, eight inches tall, the Bobbin Boy was "rather below the ordinary size" but "what you would call a *prompt* man—stands up square, and looks you square in the face, with full, round, pleasant grey eyes," a newspaper correspondent noted. "His presence was stately and attractive," George Boutwell observed, "his voice was agreeable, far reaching and commanding, and his control of an audience was absolute." This impression was not by chance, for Banks strove to combine the image of a born aristocrat with the impression of personal charm. Much of his flair came naturally, but the rest he developed on his own, knowing that through these efforts lay his only hope of avoiding a lifetime of manual labor.[4]

2. Appleton, *Russian Life and Society,* 172; John Sherman, *Recollections of Forty Years in the House, Senate and Cabinet: An Autobiography,* 2 vols. (Chicago: Werner, 1895), 1:133; Starbuck, *Picturesque Waltham,* 44; Banks to Mary Banks, August 1852, April 26, 1862; also see Banks's letter in French to Maude Banks, December 5, 1872, and notebooks and diaries, 1861–93, Banks Collection, LC. Banks eventually fulfilled his dream of becoming part of a prestigious academic community when he was appointed to one of the governance committees for Harvard College (printed copy of the *Report to the Board of Overseers, Harvard College,* March 21, 1853, ibid.).

3. Congdon, *Reminiscences,* 152; Robinson, *"Warrington" Pen-Portraits,* 437–38; Winthrop, *Memoir,* 198; *Boston Globe,* February 13, 1916.

4. Boutwell, *Reminiscences,* 1:109–10; Newspaper clipping, [1857], Banks Collection, LC. For other descriptions of Banks, see Hoar, *Autobiography,* 1:222–25; Robinson, *"Warrington" Pen-Portraits,* 435–39; Laura Stedman and George M. Gould, *Life and Letters of Edmund Clarence Stedman,* 2 vols. (New York: Moffat, Yard, 1910), 1:239; and *Boston Globe,* February 13, 1916. See also Congdon, *Reminiscences,* 152; Harring-

• • •

Banks traveled to Washington in December 1853 to assume his new position as a Democratic representative from Massachusetts. Once in office, Banks was attentive to his duties. A member of the Committee on Military Affairs, he worked to serve his constituents by presenting memorials, pressing pension claims, and seeking a pay raise for the workers in the patronage-packed Charlestown Navy Yard. Although slavery and its spread to the new territories were becoming the major topics of the day, Banks avoided controversy by reaffirming his loyalty to the national Democratic party with public praise for President Franklin Pierce and by flattering Massachusetts's ranking Democrat in Congress, Caleb Cushing. More important, he cast his votes along the lines favored by the Pierce administration.[5]

As a leader of the Massachusetts Coalition, Banks had hedged on the slavery issue by opposing antislavery agitation while maintaining his contacts with Free-Soilers and their spokesmen, including Charles Sumner. The Kansas-Nebraska Bill, which stated that the voters in each territory were to decide whether they would have slavery, "popular sovereignty," made it necessary that he take a stand. Banks was in a bind because the Democratic party insisted that Democrats show party loyalty by voting for the bill. Most voters in the Bay State, however, including a majority in Banks's district, expected their representatives to oppose the measure.[6]

Deciding that he could not safely oppose the weight of opinion in his home district, Banks voted against the Kansas-Nebraska Bill when it came before the House in March 1854. The debate over the measure raged for another three months, and Banks was one of the few Democrats to speak against the measure. But in the end the Democratic party prevailed, and the House finally passed the bill on May 22. Three days later, it sailed through the Senate and was sent to President Pierce for his signature.

Banks's decision to vote against the Kansas-Nebraska Bill was proba-

---

ton, *Fighting Politician,* 2–4; George Washington Julian, *Political Recollections, 1840 to 1872* (Chicago: Jansen, McClurg, 1884), 364.

5. Harrington, *Fighting Politician,* 18; *Boston Post,* October 13, 1853; *Congressional Globe,* 33d Cong., 1st sess., 1853, 2.

6. Roy Franklin Nichols, *Franklin Pierce: Young Hickory of the Granite Hills,* 2d ed. (Philadelphia: University of Pennsylvania Press, 1958), 333–38.

bly the most courageous step he took during his half-century in politics, for with that vote, he defied the Democrats, for whom he had worked fifteen years. He also broke with the party whose positions on other issues, such as the transcontinental railroad and America's "Manifest Destiny," Banks approved. Finally, such a vote meant accepting the antislavery doctrine, which he had been reluctant to do up to this point.[7]

Fortunately, the voters in Banks's district supported his position, which encouraged him to begin to cultivate his role as an antislavery advocate. For the first time Banks openly began to denounce the South and "southern principles" based on slavery. "By the eternal God," he proclaimed in his solemn and impressive way, "I will never yield to those principles or give those persons one moment's support."[8]

Banks's defection from the Democrats over the Kansas-Nebraska Bill and his public endorsement of the antislavery cause made it apparent that he would have to leave the party and seek reelection on some other ticket. But Banks was still popular in Massachusetts, and a large majority of the 250 delegates at the Democratic nominating convention in October favored him. Those who were against his nomination reminded the other delegates of his opposition to the Kansas-Nebraska Bill. But their cries were drowned out when the convention nominated Banks by acclamation. In addition, he picked up an endorsement from the antislavery faction of the Whig party, as well as a nomination from the old Free-Soil party. Most important, he gathered the backing of the antiforeign, anti-Catholic movement that hit Massachusetts in 1854.[9]

Dislike for Catholics and foreigners was not new to New England, but nothing compared to the nativist uprising of the 1850s. At the heart of the new movement were American workers who felt the pinch of economic competition from Irish immigrants streaming into the eastern United States following the potato famine of 1846. Joining the native workers were aggressive Protestants who objected to Roman Catholics in general. Both groups viewed foreigners as "inferior, unsanitary, in-

7. Harrington, *Fighting Politician*, 19.

8. *Boston Daily Journal*, June 10, 1854.

9. William G. Bean, "Puritan versus Celt, 1850–1860," *New England Quarterly* 7 (March 1934): 78–79; Harrington, *Fighting Politician*, 21–22, 218 n. 76; *Boston Daily Evening Traveller*, October 17, 1854. Initially, the new party was called "Republican," but it should not be confused with the permanent Republican party of Massachusetts, which was created in 1855.

temperate, and as spreaders of discord." The new movement's strength was a network of lodges, called "Wigwams," that sprang up across the region. Its secret ritual and elaborate signals also attracted attention. Although the movement was officially known as the American party, its secrecy resulted in the more familiar name Know-Nothings, for when questioned by outsiders about their activities, these nativists responded, "We know nothing."[10]

Like other politicians in Massachusetts, Banks was concerned over the growing strength of the immigrant vote and its potential for disrupting the existing balance of political power. Speaking as a U.S. congressman in favor of extending the length of the residency requirement for voting, Banks pointed out that "the foreign vote and the Catholic influence in this country is comparatively weak, and the figures cited prove it to be true. But weak in numbers, as they are," he continued, "they are not so weak but their opponents may *divide*, and American citizens and Protestants, dividing upon minor questions of policy, can easily give a balance of power to a party of diminutive numbers that eschews division."[11]

Until the local elections of 1854, Banks had avoided antiforeign, anti-Catholic agitation, just as he initially had avoided the antislavery rhetoric of the Free-Soilers. In fact, Banks had actively attempted to win the foreign vote. But with the success of the Know-Nothing party, he sought to cover that front as well. Hastily, he joined a lodge in the District of Columbia and launched a strong campaign in the newspaper under the heading "The Americanism of Mr. Banks." Banks then used the national password to get into the lodge in Waltham, where he was able to gain control through its president, Samuel O. Upham, who had admired him for many years.[12]

10. Boutwell, *Reminiscences,* 1:238; Harry J. Carman and Reinhard H. Luthin, "Some Aspects of the Know-Nothing Movement Reconsidered," *South Atlantic Quarterly* 39 (April 1940): 215–26; Ray Allen Billington, *The Protestant Crusade, 1800–1860: A Study of the Origins of American Nativism* (New York: Macmillan, 1938), 380–97; William E. Gienapp, *Origins of the Republican Party, 1852–1856* (New York: Oxford University Press, 1987), 92–93.

11. *Congressional Globe,* 33d Cong., 2d sess., 1854, Appendix, 52.

12. George H. Haynes, "The Causes of Know-Nothing Success in Massachusetts," *American Historical Review* 3 (October 1897): 67–82; Robinson, *"Warrington" Pen-Portraits,* 428, 43. See also *Boston Daily Journal,* February 2, 14, 1856, August, 31, 1857.

Although the Waltham Lodge supported Banks for Congress, other lodges in the district thought that he was using them for political gain. Consequently, the Know-Nothing organization in his congressional district nominated a Protestant preacher, the Reverend Lyman Whiting, for Congress in 1854. To make matters worse, Whiting was endorsed by the Whigs. Fortunately for Banks, Whiting decided that politics would compromise his piety, and he withdrew from the race. Banks now had three nominations—Democrat, Free-Soil, and American—which gave him an easy victory.[13]

Although he had been reelected to the U.S. House of Representatives for a second term, Banks continued to be involved in the local politics of his state. It was good that he did, for his flirtation with the American party soon caused him trouble. Banks could work with Henry Wilson, who was elected to the U.S. Senate by the Know-Nothing legislature in 1855, but neither of them could work effectively with the new American party governor of Massachusetts, Henry J. Gardner, with whom they disagreed over such issues as slavery, foreigners, business, and international affairs.[14]

By the summer of 1855, Senator Wilson was ready for a showdown. Deemphasizing his nativism and concentrating on the slavery issue, he set out to form a coalition of Massachusetts Know-Nothings with Free-Soilers, anti-Nebraska Democrats, and antislavery Whigs. Banks wanted to subordinate the antiforeign issue in favor of a general antislavery platform but did not want to risk an open break with the governor. But when it became clear that Gardner was interested in joining the new movement, Banks agreed to accept the presidency of the "Fusion" or Republi-

---

Banks also opposed aid to parochial schools (Hart, *Commonwealth History of Massachusetts*, 4:20).

13. Robert M. Taylor, "Reverend Lyman Whiting's Test of Faith," *Historical Journal of Massachusetts* 12 (June 1984): 95–100; Robinson, *"Warrington" Pen-Portraits*, 436–37; *Boston Post*, November 9, 1854; *Boston Daily Journal*, August 31, September 2, 3, 1857. Banks also enjoyed the support of many Whigs. The vote totals were 9,656 for Banks, 2,767 for Bell (a Whig), 715 for Buckman (a Pierce Democrat), and 75 scattered (Harrington, *Fighting Politician*, 218 n. 95).

14. Gienapp, *Origins of the Republican Party*, 136; Gardner in the *New York Evening Post*, August 31, 1857.

can convention in Worcester for the purpose of nominating a slate of officers for the state elections in November.[15]

The convention itself was wild. The Gardnerites demanded that the Fusion party give the gubernatorial nomination to their man. The Wilsonites and delegates who were not lodge members insisted on excluding the governor. As president of the convention, Banks could not stop the noise in spite of his experience as a parliamentarian. Nevertheless, he did get things done by using his considerable tact. Wilson's group won, and Julius Rockwell, an antislavery Whig, was named as candidate for governor. Banks praised the nomination and hoped a victory at the polls would lead to an antislavery organization on the national level.[16]

Banks's hopes were not realized. Whipped at Worcester, Gardner reconsidered his support of the Fusion party and declared himself to be the straight nativist candidate for governor. Gardner's announcement put Banks in a difficult position. He was committed to Rockwell and felt that his own future was tied to the antislavery cause. At the same time, he needed nativist support. Trying to walk the fence during the campaign, Banks let the Fusion party use his name but dropped some of his speaking dates. When he did appear, he talked primarily about the Kansas question and was careful not to denounce Gardner.[17]

The nativists in Massachusetts were firmly in control and elected Gardner governor for a second term. Had Gardner lost, it is possible that Banks would have quit the lodges to concentrate on the antislavery cause. But Gardner won, and Banks had to mix nativism with his opposition to slavery. This strategy would eventually make him Speaker of the U.S. House of Representatives and later governor of Massachusetts.[18]

Meanwhile, Banks's reputation as an effective antislavery speaker

15. *Boston Daily Journal,* August 31, 1857; Gienapp, *Origins of the Republican Party,* 221. A national Republican party did not exist at this time, although there were numerous political factions in the North that identified with the basic principles around which a national movement was organized. The first national Republican convention met in Philadelphia on June 17, 1856, and nominated John C. Frémont for president (Francis Curtis, *The Republican Party: A History of Its Fifty Years' Existence and a Record of Its Measures and Leaders,* 2 vols. [New York: G. P. Putnam's Sons, 1904], 1:172–229, 255, 260).

16. Gienapp, *Origins of the Republican Party,* 219; Harrington, *Fighting Politician,* 25; Wilson, *Rise and Fall of the Slave Power,* 2:417; *Boston Daily Journal,* September 20, 21, 22, 1855.

17. Harrington, *Fighting Politician,* 25; *Boston Daily Journal,* August 31, 1857.

18. Harrington, *Fighting Politician,* 25–26.

continued to grow. When the foes of slavery held a rally during the summer of 1855 in Portland, Maine, they asked Banks to address the crowd. This invitation afforded Banks his first chance to make a major campaign speech outside of Massachusetts. The crowd responded with wild enthusiasm as he regaled it with magnificent oratory. Thomas B. "Czar" Reed, who later became a major political figure, was a high-school student when he saw Banks in action. He never forgot the scene. "Banks that day was in the prime of figure and personal comeliness," Reed wrote many years later. "Dressed in blue, with closely buttoned coat, his well-chosen language, his graceful figure and gesture, and his aggressive way carried with him the whole audience; and when he declared that if the country was to be ruled in the interest of slavery he was ready to let the *Union slide,* the huge round of applause made it clear that the audience and the occasion were both with him."[19]

Banks's words of disunion were surprising, coming from a man who usually preferred the middle ground. The remark also proved to be a political liability, for it was thrown back at him numerous times by opponents who desired to discredit Banks as a disunionist. The only approval came from the abolitionist Garrison, whom Banks disliked. Nevertheless, the commotion caused by his speech made it clear that Banks was getting noticed. Throughout New England he had become known as a presiding officer of unsurpassed skill, a compelling speaker, and a politician with a bright future.[20]

Nathaniel P. Banks was immediately thrust onto center stage when he returned to Washington, D.C., in December 1855 to begin his second term as a congressman from Massachusetts. Antislavery forces had gained strength in the Thirty-fourth Congress and needed someone skilled in handling complex political issues to represent their interests. Three members of the House seemed to fit the bill—Lewis D. Campbell of Ohio, A. C. M. Pennington of New Jersey, and Nathaniel P. Banks of Massachusetts. All three were political moderates who hoped to strengthen the ties between the Republicans and the northern branch of the Know-Nothing party in Congress. Campbell had the best credentials on antislavery issues. Banks's credentials in this regard were sus-

19. Samuel W. McCall, *The Life of Thomas Brackett Reed* (Boston: Houghton Mifflin, 1914), 13, emphasis added.

20. Harrington, *Fighting Politician,* 26–27.

pect, as was his commitment to nativist beliefs. But his personal charm obscured these weaknesses, and his skill as a parliamentarian strengthened his appeal. Pennington was a compromise candidate should both Campbell and Banks falter.[21]

The contest between the pro- and antislavery forces grew nasty when voting for the Speaker of the House began in December. Horace Greeley, who was covering the contest for the *New York Daily Tribune,* was beaten up by an Arkansas congressman, Albert Rust. Northern representatives came to the Capitol armed, and one of Banks's supporters estimated that there were three hundred loaded weapons in the House and galleries on a typical day.[22]

Before long it was apparent that Campbell could not make the grade. His contentious personality offended many potential supporters, and his erratic stance on slavery alienated pro- and antislavery forces alike. In the balloting on December 8, Banks gained 100 votes; two days later he had 107. But there he stuck, short of victory for want of support from a handful of House members who disliked him personally. The stalemate opened the door for Pennington, but he was voted down in caucus by those who thought it best to stay with Banks. "My counsel has been to stick with Banks," advised Charles Sumner, the antislavery advocate from Massachusetts, "and leave the future to care for itself." Balloting continued through December into January 1856. Banks held on to a bloc of votes as other candidates were proposed and rejected.[23]

Banks possessed the coolness and dignity needed for the long contest. He was quick to aid backers who were under fire and to offer statements calculated to attract as many members as possible. In addition, he repudiated the speech he had given in Maine the previous summer in which he had called for the dissolution of the Union if slavery were allowed to survive. Now he said, "I am for the Union as it is, and not for its dissolution under any circumstances. I will meet its enemies in the field for the Union, to fight for the Union . . . and trust that its existence will be per-

21. Gienapp, *Origins of the Republican Party,* 241–43; *New York Tribune,* December 1, 3, 4, 1855; *New York Herald,* December 5, 1855.

22. William B. Parker, *Life and Public Service of Justin Smith Morrill* (1924; reprint, New York: Da Capo Press, 1971), 63.

23. Gienapp, *Origins of the Republican Party,* 242; Harrington, *Fighting Politician,* 28–31; Savage, *Our Living Representative Men,* 31; *Congressional Globe,* 34th Cong., 1st sess., 1855, 28, 31–32; Charles Sumner to Theodore Parker, January 20, 1856, Theodore Parker Papers, MAHS.

petual." When antislavery forces charged that this reversal meant that he was soft on slavery, Banks claimed that he represented the "strongest antislavery district in the United States." He did slip once, when he made a statement that sounded as though he favored miscegenation. Southern congressmen flew into a frenzy, but Banks hastened to "utterly disclaim" his approval of interracial marriage and added that he felt "that there was an inequality of capacity and the condition of the races." To be certain that everyone knew where he stood in regard to blacks, Banks added, "I have never asserted their equality."[24]

The deadlock was finally broken when the House adopted a resolution to allow election by plurality rather than majority. Banks's victory was narrow. He had 103 votes on the final (133d) ballot against 100 for William Aiken, a South Carolinian, for whom the Democrats and proslavery representatives combined at the last moment. Eleven votes were scattered, meaning that Banks did not have a majority. But under the plurality rule, he won.[25]

Banks moved directly to the Speaker's desk as soon as the results were announced. The sergeant at arms elevated the mace, and John Forney, the retiring clerk, passed the gavel. The representative with the longest service, Joshua Giddings, gave Banks the oath. Charles Sumner witnessed the scene. "It was a proud, historic moment," he wrote. "For the first time during years there seems to be a North. I fancied I saw the star glittering over his head. His appearance, voice, and manner were at admirable harmony with the occasion." Although Alexander H. Stephens, future vice-president of the Confederate States, called the victory a purely sectional triumph, Banks did not mind. He was gratified that "freedom had triumphed."[26]

24. Harrington, *Fighting Politician,* 29; *Congressional Globe,* 34th Cong., 1st sess., 1855, 75; 1856, 234, 253; also 1855, 31–32; 1856, 224.

25. Gienapp, *Origins of the Republican Party,* 245–46; *Congressional Globe,* 34th Cong., 1st sess., 1856, 335–36; *New York Herald,* December 8, 11, 1855; Boutwell to Banks, February 5, 1856, Banks Collection, LC.

26. Bigelow, *Retrospections,* 1:141; Arthur Charles Cole, *The Era of the Civil War, 1848–1870* (Springfield, Ill.: Illinois Centennial Commission, 1919), 142; John W. Forney, *Anecdotes of Public Men,* 2 vols. (New York: Harper & Brothers, 1873), 1:379–81; Parker, *Life and Public Service of Justin Smith Morrill,* 75; Edward L. Pierce, *Memoir and Letters of Charles Sumner,* 2d ed., 4 vols. (1894; reprint, New York: Arno Press, 1969), 3:431; *Congressional Globe,* 34th Cong., 1st sess., 1856, 342–43; *Boston Daily Journal,* October 10, 1857; *New York Times,* February 4, 1856; *Liberator,* February 8, 1856.

Banks did his best as Speaker to please everyone. He assigned each party and region its precisely correct percentage of committee posts. As a result, there was a proslavery majority in the committees on military affairs and naval affairs. Yet Banks did not forget that antislavery votes had gotten him elected, and he supported the cause in various ways. Thus he appointed a majority of antislavery men to the committees on territories and elections and voted twice favoring Kansas as a free state. Although he was a minority Speaker, every decision Banks made throughout his entire term was upheld.[27]

Banks became one of the best Speakers the House had ever had. "The best . . . since the time of Henry Clay," proclaimed one veteran of that body who recalled Banks's voice and appearance, knowledge of parliamentary procedure, "ever-ready tact," and unfailing courtesy. Supporters and opponents alike gave him high praise. Stephens of Georgia, who had seen Banks's victory as evidence of sectional enmity, thought him "one of the ablest if not the ablest Speakers I ever saw in the chair." Another southerner and former Speaker, Howell Cobb, said that "Banks was in all respects the best presiding officer he had ever seen." Although a few said the Speaker was too kind to slaveholders, and although some antislavery representatives felt that he neglected them in the distribution of committee posts, all seemed to agree that Banks was "a just and honest presiding officer."[28]

Banks's position as Speaker of the House of Representatives would have made him an attractive candidate for president in the fall of 1856 had he

27. Joel H. Sibley, "'The First Northern Victory': The Republican Party Comes to Congress, 1855–1856," *Journal of Interdisciplinary History* 20 (Summer 1989): 9–12; Harrington, *Fighting Politician,* 31–33; Eli Thayer to Banks, January 29, 1856, and Thomas Webb to Banks, January 29, 1856, Banks Collection, LC. For one reversal, later rescinded, see *Congressional Globe,* 34th Cong., 1st sess., 1856, 1017–18, 1029–38, 1046–48.

28. Ulrich Bonnell Phillips, ed., *The Correspondence of Robert Toombs, Alexander H. Stephens, and Howell Cobb* (1913; reprint, New York: Da Capo Press, 1970), 460; Forney, *Anecdotes,* 1:379; Horace Greeley, *Recollections of a Busy Life* (1868; reprint, New York: Arno Press, 1970), 352; Sherman, *Recollections,* 1:133; Mary Parker Follett, *The Speaker of the House of Representatives* (New York: Longmans, Green, 1896), 94; Petition praising Banks as Speaker with 108 signatures, Boston, April 7, 1857, Nathaniel P. Banks Correspondence, AAS.

chosen to run. Not only did his election as Speaker signal the first Republican victory at the national level, but his competent handling of the position made friends and influenced important people. But Banks decided to sit out the race; he had committed to supporting John Charles Frémont for president.[29]

The son-in-law of Thomas H. Benton, a popular and influential senator from Missouri, Frémont had gained national fame through his exploration of the Rocky Mountains. Banks was attracted to Frémont's candidacy for two reasons. With no previous experience in politics, Frémont was free of both political debts and liabilities. In addition, Frémont could counter the growing popularity of Salmon P. Chase, governor of Ohio and a staunch antislavery advocate. Chase was too radical to suit Banks's taste, and the attractive and charismatic Frémont was a perfect figurehead around whom Banks could rally the moderate elements of the Republican party. Banks lobbied energetically for his nominee, and thanks, in part, to his support, Frémont was tapped as leader of the party when the Republicans met in Pittsburgh in February 1856.[30]

The Republican party owed much of its strength to the split that tore the American party apart. Antislavery advocates in the North hoped to use the Know-Nothing movement to further their cause. Thus when the American party met in Philadelphia on February 22, 1856, for its national convention, slavery quickly became an issue. Party leaders attempted to present a united front, but the delegates voted down a motion that would have put the American party on record as opposing the extension of slavery. After the vote, several northern Americans with antislavery convictions adjourned to Pittsburgh, where they formed an alliance with the Republicans. As defections from the Know-Nothing ranks increased, the Republicans rejoiced. "The American Party are no longer united," a telegram from a group of defectors proclaimed. "Raise the Re-

29. Sibley, "'The First Northern Victory,'" 1; Gienapp, *Origins of the Republican Party,* 318; Harrington, *Fighting Politician,* 33–34; also see J. L. Richardson to Banks, December 9, 1859, Isaac Sherman to Banks, February 14, 1860, Banks Manuscripts, ISHL.

30. Dick Johnson, "The Role of Salmon P. Chase in the Formation of the Republican Party," *Old Northwest* 3 (March 1977): 32–35; Ruhl Jacob Bartlett, *John C. Frémont and the Republican Party* (Columbus: Ohio State University Press, 1930), 14–15; Bigelow, *Retrospections,* 1:141–42; Congdon, *Reminiscences,* 152–53; Allan Nevins, *Frémont: Pathmaker of the West* (Lincoln: University of Nebraska Press, 1992), 425–27.

publican banner! Let there be no further extension of slavery! The Americans are with you!"[31]

By joining the Republican party, the antislavery faction of the Know-Nothing movement, or North Americans as they were now called, hoped to dictate the choice of the presidential nominee for the fall elections. To that end, they set the date of their convention in New York City for June 12, five days before the Republicans were to meet in Philadelphia. The situation was delicate. If the North Americans spurned Frémont and the Republicans nominated him, there would be two antislavery tickets in the field. But if the North Americans chose Frémont, the Republicans might reject him lest they seem to be yielding to Know-Nothing pressure. A Banks supporter, Isaac Sherman, came up with a solution. Emphasizing Banks's popularity and strong standing with the nativists, he suggested that Banks could seek and gain the presidential nomination at the North American convention. Banks could then yield to Frémont at the Republican convention a week later.[32]

The pro-Banks forces had the situation fairly well in hand by the time the North Americans convened. After some negotiating and arm-twisting, the delegates nominated Banks on June 16 and named William F. Johnston as the vice-presidential nominee. The news strengthened Frémont's position with Republicans in Philadelphia because insiders were sure that Banks would refuse the North American nomination at the proper time. After all, Banks was already in Philadelphia urging Frémont's candidacy.[33]

The Republicans nominated Frémont for president as expected, but then the plan went awry. They refused to accept William Johnston as Frémont's running mate and passed over the Know-Nothings altogether by picking an old Whig, William Drake, for vice-president. In addition,

31. Carman and Luthin, "Some Aspects of the Know-Nothing Movement Reconsidered," 215–27; Bean, "Puritan versus Celt," 82–85; Reinhard H. Luthin, *The First Lincoln Campaign* (Cambridge, Mass.: Harvard University Press, 1944), 107. Also see Fred Harvey Harrington, "Frémont and the North Americans," *American Historical Review* 44 (July 1939): 842–48.

32. Gienapp, *Origins of the Republican Party,* 331–32; Harrington, *Fighting Politician,* 36–37.

33. *New York Tribune,* June 18, 1856; *Boston Daily Journal,* June 17, 1856; J. W. Stone to Banks, June 14, 1856, Banks Collection, LC.

when Banks rejected the North American nomination in favor of Frémont, the Know-Nothing leaders considered nominating Millard Fillmore, the old Whig with nativist leanings who had been Zachary Taylor's vice-president and later president of the United States following Taylor's death. In the end, the plan was salvaged when the North Americans accepted Banks's withdrawal and nominated Frémont on June 20. Frémont was now the presidential nominee of two antislavery parties.[34]

Banks immediately threw himself into the presidential campaign. He stumped for Frémont throughout the North, addressing large crowds from New England to Illinois. Banks began each speech by attacking the South; the rest of the oration depended on the audience. If the crowd was strongly opposed to slavery, Banks called southern leaders "ruffians" who had broken promises and ignored the Constitution by plunging Kansas into a bloody civil conflict. If the crowd was composed of nativists, Banks called Frémont a "true American" and blamed Catholics and foreigners for blocking important reforms. Banks always ended his orations with a promise that Frémont's victory would mean four years of peace and prosperity.[35]

Banks delivered one of his most important speeches of the campaign on September 25, 1856, when he addressed a large crowd from the balcony of the Merchants Exchange on Wall Street. Banks proposed that the best way to achieve national prosperity would be to diminish the political strength of the agricultural South by giving control to the commercial-industrial North. Part of this strategy included building a railroad that would run from coast to coast by a northern route. Planter "imperialism" would yield to Yankee trade and industry, while northern manufacturers, freed from economic shackles forged by southerners, could go full speed ahead. Banks insisted that Republicans would not try to destroy slavery where it existed but hoped that a restructuring of the national economy following Frémont's election would lead the South to abandon it on its own accord.[36]

34. Nevins, *Frémont,* 431–35.

35. Harrington, *Fighting Politician,* 38–39; Nevins, *Frémont,* 441. For an example of one of Banks's campaign speeches, see *New York Herald,* October 24, 1856.

36. Philip S. Foner, *Business and Slavery: The New York Merchants and the Irrepressible Conflict* (Chapel Hill: University of North Carolina Press, 1941), 127–33; James Shepherd Pike, *First Blows of the Civil War* (New York: American News Co.,

Banks's effort to persuade big business to join the Republican camp was unsuccessful. By mid-October businessmen were moving to the Democratic candidate, James Buchanan. Sensing defeat, Banks blamed antislavery advocates, whom he believed lacked a "spirit of manly concession" and thus drove away voters of a more moderate bent. Whatever the case, James Buchanan was elected as fifteenth president of the United States on November 4, 1856. In addition, the Democrats regained control of the U.S. Congress, which meant that Banks, who had won a third term in Congress, would not be reelected Speaker. But this turn of events did not bother the Bobbin Boy, for, as Charles A. Dana sagely noted at the time, Banks was "greasing his legs for 1860."[37]

1879), 350; D. G. Brinton Thompson, *Ruggles of New York: A Life of Samuel B. Ruggles* (New York: Columbia University Press, 1946), 123–24; John Weiss, *Letters and Correspondence of Theodore Parker*, 2 vols. (1864; reprint, New York: Da Capo Press, 1970), 2:191; *Boston Daily Journal*, September 27, 1856; *New York Herald*, September 26, 27, October 24, 1856; Bigelow to Banks, October 1, 1856, Banks Collection, LC.

37. *New York Evening Post*, September 9, 1857; Pike, *First Blows of the Civil War*, 349. The vote in Banks's district was 10,814 for the incumbent (Banks, a Republican and Frémont American), 4,593 for I. H. Wright (a Democrat), and 2,059 for Isaac Story (a Fillmore American) (Harrington, *Fighting Politician*, 222 n. 111).

3

Success Is a Duty

Nathaniel P. Banks won reelection to the U.S. House of Representatives in 1858 by carrying his congressional district two to one. But with the Democrats in control it was clear that his tenure as Speaker was over. Stopping to consider his political future, Banks decided that the best chance of grooming himself for a seat in the Senate or even for the presidency lay in gaining experience as the chief executive of his home state.[1]

In the race for the Republican nomination for governor, Banks attempted to avoid taking an extreme position against slavery, but that stance was becoming increasingly difficult. Republicans in Massachusetts were divided into two distinct camps. One faction, which was centered around a political clique called the Bird Club, was extremist, abolitionist, and hostile to those who did not share its radical views. The Bird Club took its name from Francis W. Bird, an ardent disunionist. Among its members were George L. Starnes, who had been a financial backer of John Brown; John A. Andrew, who later raised funds for Brown's trial; and Charles Sumner, the abolitionist whom Banks had reluctantly helped get elected to the Senate. Members of the Bird Club believed that slavery was morally wrong and should be fought unceasingly without compromise. Banks headed a second faction, known as the Banks Club, which was moderate, willing to compromise, and practical in its approach. Although Banks's faction also opposed slavery, its members

1. Harrington, *Fighting Politician*, 42. The term of office for Massachusetts governors during this period was one year.

rejected abolitionism and subordinated moral justification of their cause to attain political and economic ends. The Banks Club counted among its members many of the powerful nativists in the state.[2]

Open conflict between the two factions came to a head at the Republican nominating convention on June 24, 1857. There the radicals expressed their disapproval with shouts of "no! no!" when Banks's name was placed in nomination. But the moderates pressed ahead and requested that he be nominated by acclamation. "Trimmer," the opposition shouted. He was a "facile, pliant, flexible man." Banks offered a compromise. He agreed to yield to radical demands by softening his stand on nativism and by denouncing the *Dred Scott* decision. Satisfied with these pronouncements and preferring Banks to the reactionary incumbent Know-Nothing governor, Henry Gardner, most of the radicals voted for the man from Waltham.[3]

Banks's chief opponent in the campaign was Governor Gardner. Gardner was dull, unattractive, and a dreary speaker, but he knew how to get votes. Because of his strongly nativist background, Gardner was able to appeal to many of the ordinary people of Massachusetts. He also continued to defend the American party by opposing antislavery agitation on the grounds that it was bad for manufacturing and commercial interests.[4]

The campaign became heated when Gardner supporters went after Banks with all the tricks at their command. Hecklers were sent to Banks meetings to mock the Republican nominee and accuse him of dodging the issues. "Solemn, pretentious humbug," declared his detractors when he juggled phrases to please both moderate and radical antislavery factions. Fighting back, Banks stumped the state and organized over two dozen "Ironsides Clubs," borrowing a title from Oliver Cromwell's veter-

2. Dale Baum, *The Civil War Party System: The Case of Massachusetts, 1848–1876* (Chapel Hill: University of North Carolina Press, 1984), 103; Donald, *Charles Sumner and the Coming of the Civil War,* 321–22; Harrington, *Fighting Politician,* 40–45, Robinson, *"Warrington" Pen-Portraits,* 401, 425–27; Frank Preston Stearns, *The Life and Public Services of George Luther Stearns* (Philadelphia: J. B. Lippincott, 1907), 156–59.

3. Lorenzo Sears, *Wendell Phillips: Orator and Agitator* (1909; reprint, New York: Benjamin Bloom, 1967), 186; *New York Evening Post,* August 20, September 9, 1857; *Boston Daily Journal,* June 18, 24, 25, 1857. A trimmer is someone who charts a cautious course between opposing points of view as expediency dictates.

4. See Banks's speech in the *New York Evening Post,* September 9, 1857.

ans. Banks adopted "Little Iron Man" as his campaign nickname, although Gardner quipped that Banks was really a "Little Lead Man." The campaign slogan that Banks picked referred to the halt of slavery's spread to the territories: "Success is a duty." Indeed, Banks's energy brought success. When the final vote was in, Banks led Gardner three to two.[5]

Banks was sworn in as governor of Massachusetts in January 1858. One of the first issues over which the new governor and the radicals clashed involved Edward G. Loring, United States commissioner and Massachusetts judge of probate. The radicals had been after Loring since 1855 because of his willingness to enforce the fugitive slave law. Banks had hoped to dodge the issue by consolidating the state probate and chancery courts and thereby squeeze Loring out of a job, but the radicals wanted the satisfaction of having the judge fired and insisted that Banks remove Loring before the consolidation.[6]

The Loring controversy afforded Banks an opportunity to rally Republican moderates, but he bowed to radical pressure and dismissed Loring. Moderates felt that Banks had gone too far, and conservatives outside of Massachusetts were sharply critical. "The 'grossest' attack on the independence of the judiciary ever witnessed in the United States' " they cried. Even the *Boston Daily Journal* advised the governor to be wary since the "fanaticism which now gloats over its triumph . . . will become still more bold in its requirements, will inevitably lead the party on to destruction." But the average voter did not blame Banks for removing Loring, which led one commentator to note that Banks could "do what-

5. Free Soiler, *Review of Mr. Banks's Political History,* 1, 8; Winthrop, *Memoir,* 198–99; *Boston Daily Journal,* September 26, 1857; *Boston Daily Evening Traveller,* August 29, October, 16, 17, 30, 1857; George S. Boutwell to Banks, June 22, 1857, Banks Manuscripts, ISHL. The campaign slogan is from Banks's Republican acceptance speech published in the *Boston Daily Journal,* June 30, 1857.

6. Nathaniel P. Banks, *Address of His Excellency Nathaniel P. Banks, to the Two Branches of the Legislature of Massachusetts, January 7, 1858* (Boston: William White, 1858), 5–6; Harrington, *Fighting Politician,* 44; Henry Greenleaf Pearson, *The Life of John A. Andrew: Governor of Massachusetts, 1861–1865,* 2 vols. (Boston: Houghton Mifflin, 1904), 1:70–82; Laura E. Richards, ed., *Letters and Journals of Samuel Gridley Howe,* 2 vols. (Boston: Dana Estes, 1909), 2:474; Eben F. Stone, "Sketch of John Albion Andrew," *Essex Institute Historical Collections* 27 (1890): 5–7; *Boston Daily Journal,* June 20, 1857; *New York Tribune,* March 25, April 9, 23, May 8, 1858; *New York Evening Post,* September 9, 1857.

ever he may be pleased to do, without incurring any unpopularity." He was right. Banks captured the Republican nomination for governor again in 1858 and was reelected by a clear majority that fall.[7]

Banks's successful entry into politics had provided a steady income and enabled him to purchase a fine frame house on upper Main Street in Waltham. The family, which now included two girls, Maude and Binney, and a little boy, Joseph Frémont, also spent a good bit of time at the farm Banks had purchased in 1855, complete with a spacious white wood-frame house shaded by two large elm trees and two sycamores.[8]

A correspondent for the *New York Evening Post* sought out the former Speaker of the House at the farm during his first race for governor. The modest library Banks had begun twenty-five years before had grown. "The first thing that strikes the visitor on entering the house," the newspaperman reported, "is the large number of books, books of law, of Parliamentary rules, geographies, histories, Political Philosophy, the English poets, books of German and French, among which he will see excellent copies of Helvetius, of Machiavel, of the Bible, and of the writings of Martin Luther." The report leaves the impression that at least some of the books in Banks's library had been purchased primarily for show. "Even the Dutch are tributary," the reporter continued, "in whose language I observed several ponderous folios, illustrated with curious and rare engravings on subjects of theology, travels, and natural history." Whatever the reason for Banks's effort to enlarge his library, he was serious. "As I entered, two huge bundles more of books came from the Boston publishers, Little & Brown," the reporter observed. "At the rate at which the library increases, the wonder is where they, the speaker, will find room for them, unless he builds another house to accommodate them."[9]

Banks's practical bent is also notable from the correspondent's report.

7. *Boston Daily Journal,* March 19, 20, 1858; *New York Times,* June 23, 1858; *Boston Post,* March 24, 1858.

8. Petersen, *Waltham Rediscovered,* 39–40. Banks's second son, Joseph Frémont, was born on August 19, 1855, and his second daughter, Mary, on February 15, 1857. Their firstborn, Harry, died in childhood. The family lived with his parents until they moved to the Gale mansion on Main Street (personal communication from Elizabeth D. Castner, WPL).

9. *New York Evening Post,* August 20, 1857.

> Pictures or engravings, however, on the wall there were none—or at least none to speak of—if we except the portrait of Mr. Banks's father, a thin, rather stern-faced old man, with an expression of austere kindliness, who died recently at an advanced age. This absence of paintings and objects of art, amid so many treasures of literature and science, is characteristic of the training of Mr. Banks, who has been so much absorbed in the education of his intellect and the practice of affairs of government, as to leave little time for the collection of works of art, and the cultivation of those luxurious amenities which sometimes occupy the attention of men of hereditary wealth and elegant leisure.[10]

The correspondent went on to note that Banks's political duties away from home were such that he had not yet had time to furnish the house to his satisfaction. When he was there, Banks was "engrossed in the cultivation and improvement of [its] forty acres." Helping him were three "laboring assistants," who worked in the fields, weeding the corn and potatoes and growing vegetables. In addition, Banks could boast of a nursery with seven hundred young fruit trees, as well as a stable full of coal-black horses, a healthy litter of little white pigs, and more than fifty barnyard fowls. In his farming theories, he was "somewhat of a conservative." For example, Banks continued to favor the "old-fashioned barnyard dressing for the soil, though he acknowledges the efficacy of the more modern fertilizers—guano and blood manure—in corn." Nevertheless, by 1857 his farming enterprise had succeeded to the point that in August he won a second prize at the Waltham Fair for his breeding sows and third prize for his pumpkins.[11]

Nor did Banks forget to mend his political fences. Although the American party was not as powerful as it used to be, Banks looked after his constituents with nativist leanings while in office. Wanting their support for another run at the governorship in 1859, Banks threw his weight behind the effort to pass a constitutional amendment that barred immigrants from voting until two years after naturalization. Banks supported the

10. Ibid. Nathaniel P. Banks, Sr., died April 24, 1857, at the age of seventy-four.

11. Ibid.; *Report of the Industrial Exhibition Held in the Town of Waltham, Massachusetts, September 24, 1857* (Boston, 1857), cited in Harrington, *Fighting Politician*, 42.

measure, he told the legislature, "to maintain the purity of elections and to protect the rights of American citizens."[12]

The problem with his position was that Republican leaders in Wisconsin, Iowa, Illinois, and Ohio needed the votes of newly naturalized German immigrants. This reality placed Banks in a bind, which he handled with customary evasion. First, the governor tried to backtrack by suggesting that the two-year period be cut to ninety days. Failing in that, he conveniently left the state two days before the Massachusetts electorate went to the polls and approved the amendment. Banks had gone to New York for a legitimate reason, to confer with Republican leaders, but his evasiveness hurt him in the Know-Nothing lodges without attracting favor elsewhere. "Everybody says Banks won't do," concluded Horace Greeley. It was a case of "the odor of Americanism without the support of Americans."[13]

Despite the criticism, Banks was elected to a third term as governor in 1859. Ironically, a crucial ingredient in his victory was an incident over which he had no control. On October 16, 1859, the violent abolitionist John Brown made his abortive raid into Virginia. Although the radical element praised "Old Brown" and set about raising money for his defense, Massachusetts as a whole was not ready to endorse armed insurrection. Moderates quickly condemned Brown as a madman and threw their support to the moderate Nathaniel P. Banks.[14]

Banks's third term was a success. Among others, New England's intellectuals were impressed. They were particularly grateful for Banks's support of education. In a brief speech at the installation of C. C. Felton as president of Harvard, Banks earned the admiration of the audience with his talk of how poor boys longed for a college education. Banks noted that "the education of the young is one of the noblest prerogatives that can fall to the lot of man." More than sixty years later, one speaker re-

12. Banks, *Address of January 7, 1858*, 9–11, 17, 19–20.

13. Luthin, *First Lincoln Campaign*, 109; Greeley to Colfax, February 3, 1860, quoted in Harrington, *Fighting Politician*, 45; *New York Tribune*, March 4, December 21, 1859. See Edward Everett to Banks, February 15, 1859, also H. Kreismann to Banks, April 2, 1859, Banks Collection, LC; William Wade to Banks, March 8, 1859, N. C. Bryant to Banks, April 25, 1859, Banks Manuscripts, ISHL.

14. Harrington, *Fighting Politician*, 46; Pearson, *Life of John A. Andrew*, 1:96–110; Stearns, *Life of George Luther Stearns*, 105–6, 118, 135, 187–88; *Boston Daily Journal*, December 3, 1859.

called that "upon the same platform with the graduates of Harvard stood and spoke the graduate of the Waltham factory and that as a speaker he did not suffer in comparison with any of them."[15]

The crowning event of his third term occurred in October 1860, when he entertained the Prince of Wales (later Edward VII) at the start of a four-day visit to New England. Everyone celebrated the event. At the music hall in Boston, twelve hundred schoolchildren serenaded the prince with selections from Mendelssohn and Mozart. The visit was climaxed by a grand ball for which almost three thousand tickets were sold. The prince paid the governor and his lady every courtesy, and Mary Banks looked splendid as she danced with the prince in the second round of the evening. Hobnobbing with royalty was not bad, Banks thought, especially considering his origins as a Bobbin Boy.[16]

The presidential campaign of 1860 heated up in the waning months of Banks's third and final term as governor of Massachusetts. The degree to which the country had become divided over the issue of slavery was evident from the start. In April, the Democrats convened in Charleston, South Carolina, to select their nominee. Stephen A. Douglas was the strongest candidate. Although his endorsement of popular sovereignty did not threaten slavery where it already existed, the mere thought that the institution might be prohibited from expanding into new states sent the southern delegates into a frenzy. Disorganized and frustrated by enmity and procedural disputes arising from the controversial issue, the convention adjourned with a resolution to reconvene early that summer in Baltimore.

If anything, the distance between the northern and southern factions

15. *Addresses at the Inauguration of Cornelius Conway Felton, LL.D., as President of Harvard College* (Cambridge, Mass.: Sever & Francis, 1860), 21; Bigelow, *Retrospections,* 1:298–99; Hoar, *Autobiography,* 2:222–25. Banks's reputation in intellectual circles was so high that luminaries such as Oliver Wendell Holmes, Ralph Waldo Emerson, Henry Wadsworth Longfellow, and James Russell Lowell gave him a testimonial dinner (Oration of John Q. A. Brackett, in *Celebration of the Centennial of the Birth of General Nathaniel Prentice Banks: Waltham, Massachusetts, January 30, 1916* [Waltham, Mass.: Waltham Publishing Co., (1916)], 16; *New York Tribune,* August 27, 1860). See also C. C. Felton to Banks, July 25, October 24, 1860, Banks Collection, LC; G. and C. Merriam to Banks, December 23, 1856, Banks Correspondence, AAS; Horace Mann to Banks, June 24, 1859, Banks Manuscripts, ISHL.

16. *New York Tribune,* October 18, 20, 23, 1860.

of the Democratic party increased during the six weeks between the conventions. A dispute over the seating of delegations from several states resulted in another walkout. Although Douglas eventually won the party nomination, the dissenting delegates met in a rump convention and nominated John C. Breckinridge to oppose him. The Democrats thus entered the election with two candidates for president.

Unlike the Democrats, the Republican party was united for the 1860 election. The unifying factor was the party's position on slavery—no extension of slavery into the territories but no interference where the institution already existed.[17]

Banks roamed the North to promote his candidacy for the Republican presidential nomination, but his clash with the radicals in Massachusetts had damaged his standing in the party. To help him obtain the nomination, a special plan was concocted by Samuel Bowles and Anson Burlingame. The strategy involved supporting William H. Seward for president in hopes that the convention would become deadlocked, in which case Banks's name could be brought forward as a compromise candidate. It was the same tactic that had resulted in his election as Speaker of the House.[18]

Feelings ran high as the Republican nominating convention approached. "Somebody must *smash* the '*snake head*' or pull the teeth out of them and organize your strength," Burlingame wrote to Banks, "or all will be lost." For Burlingame's plan to work, Banks knew that he must have the Massachusetts delegation. But the radicals controlled the state convention that named four delegates at large. On top of that, Francis W. Bird, leader of the club that bore his name, headed the Committee on Credentials. The result was a split that gave Banks two of the four delegates. Banks's attempt to garner enough district delegates fared even worse. Although he enjoyed some support from Boston, where friends controlled the Republican machinery, only one delegate from the rural

17. Albert J. Beveridge, *Abraham Lincoln, 1809–1858,* 2 vols. (Boston: Houghton Mifflin, 1928), 2:708–12.

18. William Eldon Baringer, *Lincoln's Rise to Power* (1937; reprint, St. Clair Shores, Mich.: Scholarly Press, 1971), 218; Cole, *Era of the Civil War,* 161 n. 20; Luthin, *First Lincoln Campaign,* 106–11; George Fort Milton, *Eve of Conflict: Stephen A. Douglas and the Needless War* (1934; reprint, New York: Octagon Books, 1963), 281–82; Thurlow Weed, *Life of Thurlow Weed, Including His Autobiography and a Memoir,* ed. T. W. Barnes, 2 vols. (Boston: Houghton Mifflin, 1883–84), 2:260.

districts was enthusiastic about the governor. Banks was unable even to swing his old congressional district, and the radicals claimed nineteen of the twenty-six spots. Banks had lost his own state.[19]

Under these circumstances Banks decided not to go to Chicago, which was just as well because he was never really in the running. Abraham Lincoln received the presidential nomination on the third ballot. Banks did stand fifth for vice-president on the first round, but after that his supporters switched to Hannibal Hamlin of Maine. Banks would have to wait until 1864 for a chance to be president.[20]

The political divisiveness of the 1860 presidential campaign was still evident as the November election approached. Remnants of the American party in the North that had not gone over to the Republicans and its adherents in the South who had balked at joining the Democrats organized a fourth political bloc, the National Constitutional Union party. This faction nominated John Bell of Tennessee for president. The 1860 presidential race was now composed of four nominees, which almost assured that the next president would win with less than a majority of the vote.[21]

The split among the Democrats meant that neither Douglas nor Breckinridge could win the election, and Bell was siphoning votes from both. The only hope for southern Democrats was for the election to be thrown into the House of Representatives. It never happened. Although Lincoln won only 40 percent of the popular vote, he swept the free states and gained a clear victory in the electoral college.[22]

Banks's failure to garner support from his own state during the presidential contest was an indication of the degree to which Massachusetts had

19. Boutwell, *Reminiscences,* 1:110; Edith Ellen Ware, *Political Opinion in Massachusetts during Civil War and Reconstruction,* Studies in History, Economics and Public Law, Vol. 74 (New York: Columbia University, 1916), 26–27; *New York Tribune,* April 5, 1860; Anson Burlingame to Banks, February 18, March 4, 1860, Banks Collection, LC.

20. See, for example, *New York Evening Post,* August 20, 1857. Banks received numerous invitations to speak in behalf of the Republican ticket at various functions during August and September (Banks Manuscripts, ISHL).

21. Carman and Luthin, "Know-Nothing Movement Reconsidered," 232; Mary Lilla McLure, "The Elections of 1860 in Louisiana," *Louisiana Historical Quarterly* 9 (October 1926): 661.

22. The popular vote in the election of 1860 was 1,857,610 for Lincoln; 1,365,976 for Douglas; 847,953 for Breckinridge; and 590,631 for Bell.

moved toward the radical end of the Republican spectrum. The shift was further evidenced by the election of a radical, John A. Andrew, to succeed Banks as governor.[23]

Disappointed by the repudiation of his leadership and needing a steady source of income to support his family, Banks decided to leave politics for a while. Although he had begun his career by taking a stand against big business, that was exactly where he went to parlay his political connections into a lucrative position.

As governor, Banks had supported several measures that favored a stable business economy, and his probusiness image was enhanced further when he broke with the radical faction of the Republican party. His new stance did not mean that Banks had become an agent of the wealthy, but since the mid-1850s he had drifted away from his strong support of labor and had become more of an advocate for corporate interests. It was not surprising, therefore, when he received a business offer at the end of his term as governor.[24]

Banks had always been interested in railroads, and this interest soared in the summer of 1860, when William H. Osborn, president of the Illinois Central Railroad, made him a lucrative job offer. Osborn resided in New York and needed someone to handle the railroad's affairs in Chicago. George B. McClellan had done this work for a time but had gone on to something else. Osborn turned to Banks, who accepted the position with the rank of resident director effective January 1861 at the salary of $7,000 a year, double what he had received as governor of Massachusetts. Osborn also gave Banks $2,000 for studying railroad problems in the last months of his term and promised him a house rent-free for the first year.[25]

Banks delivered his farewell address to the General Court of Massachusetts on January 3, 1861, and left the Bay State for his new job. By the time he reached Chicago, seven southern states had seceded from the Union. In the meantime, representatives from the seceded states had

23. Harrington, *Fighting Politician*, 51.

24. *Congressional Globe*, 35th Cong., 1st sess., 1857, 106–7, 129–30; Banks to W. C. Bryant et al., May 1, 1860, Banks Manuscripts, ISHL; Clippings, Banks Collection, LC.

25. Charles F. Fletcher to Banks, September 16, October 9, 1859, A. E. Burnside to Banks, November 21, 1860, Banks Manuscripts, ISHL; Osborn to Banks, September 1, 1860, Banks Collection, LC.

met in Montgomery, Alabama, and adopted a provisional constitution for the Confederate States of America.[26]

Banks favored a compromise between the two regions, and privately he complained that Lincoln was missing a chance to be a peacemaker. But there was a personal motive behind his criticism of the new administration. Banks wanted and had even expected to get a cabinet appointment. Several Republican leaders, including Andrew, Boutwell, and Bowles, suggested that he was the logical cabinet member from New England. Lincoln, however, had decided to let Vice-President Hannibal Hamlin name the "New England member." Lincoln actually favored Banks, whom he thought was "able, well known and might make a capable executive." But Hamlin objected to Banks on the grounds that he was a "trimmer in politics." Although he believed that Banks had ability, Hamlin did not like the "theatrical" way he presented himself. Instead, the vice-president recommended Gideon Welles for secretary of the navy, the post that Lincoln had thought appropriate for Banks.[27]

To soothe Banks's feelings, Lincoln suggested that his move to Chicago had worked against his appointment. More specifically, Lincoln instructed Boutwell to tell Banks that "had you remained in New England there would be no second man thought of, that your name was in the first list that he [Lincoln] ever made, that previous to his own election, he did not feel at liberty to make any suggestion concerning your removal from Massachusetts, but that the change put it out of his power to do what he should otherwise have done without suggestion from anyone."[28]

In reality, being passed over for a cabinet post kept Banks out of an embarrassing situation, for in accepting the job with the Illinois Central

26. Harrington, *Fighting Politician,* 52; Dwight Lowell Dumond, *The Secession Movement, 1860–1861* (New York: Macmillan, 1931), 210. Banks auctioned off his farm in Waltham on December 18, 1860, in anticipation of his move to Chicago (handbill dated December 12, 1860, Banks Collection, LC).

27. William Eldon Baringer, *A House Dividing: Lincoln as President Elect* (Springfield, Ill.: Abraham Lincoln Association, 1945), 76–77; Harry James Carman and Reinhard Harry Luthin, *Lincoln and the Patronage* (New York: Columbia University Press, 1943), 12–15, 48; Charles Eugene Hamlin, *Life and Times of Hannibal Hamlin* (1899; reprint, Port Washington, N.Y.: Kennikat Press, 1971), 369–70; John A. Andrew to Lincoln, January 20, 1861, John A. Andrew Papers, MAHS; also see G. P. Burnham to Banks, February 26, 1861, Boutwell to Banks, March 8, 1861, Banks Collection, LC.

28. Boutwell to Banks, March 8, 1861, Banks Collection, LC.

he had agreed to retire from political life "for three or four years at least." Thus Banks swallowed his disappointment and got down to work as the railroad's resident director in Chicago.[29]

Banks was in charge of the Illinois Central's extensive freight and passenger business. He was also expected to act as a public relations officer and salesman for railroad lands, which would yield cash and generate new freight revenue. To that end, Banks attempted to attract buyers based on information furnished by Osborn and the company's marketing experts. He also contacted several Massachusetts businessmen in an attempt to persuade them to buy thousands of acres of railroad land for the purposes of colonization.[30]

Banks had scarcely settled into his new duties when the South fired on Fort Sumter. Eager to gain political backing for the war he was about to wage, Lincoln offered Banks a commission as major general in the new army. Osborn, a patriotic Republican, gave Banks a full release, which allowed him to accept a commission dated May 16, 1861. In just over five months, Banks had gone from governor to businessman to major general.[31]

29. Osborn to Banks, September 1, 1860, ibid.

30. Paul W. Gates, *The Illinois Central Railroad and Its Colonization Work* (Cambridge, Mass.: Harvard University Press, 1934), 186; "General Banks," *Illinois Central Magazine* 2 (July 1913): 13–22; "The Story of the Illinois Central Lines during the Civil Conflict 1861–5: General Banks," *Illinois Central Magazine* 2 (August 1913): 13–18; Osborn to Banks, November 13, 1860, February 11, 13, 1861, Banks Collection, LC.

31. William K. Ackerman, *Historical Sketch of the Illinois-Central Railroad* (Chicago: Fergus Printing Co., 1890), 94. Although Banks received his rank in May, he did not join the army until June.

4

Faultless-Looking Soldier

The new major general was woefully lacking in military experience and knowledge. Banks had served on the Military Affairs Committee during his first term in Congress, but he had used that assignment primarily to attract labor votes by demanding civilian administration for the Springfield Armory. As governor, Banks had commanded the armed forces of the commonwealth of Massachusetts and actually took to the field during the first encampment in the state's history. But leading the militia was more an exercise in flashy display than hard-nosed instruction. As one observer noted, "The Massachusetts militia, I have no doubt, are as good as any other. Certainly, their uniforms are quite as brilliant."[1]

Before his appointment as major general of United States Volunteers, Banks sought to deemphasize his military experience. He had even gone on record as saying that he was "not acquainted with details of military matters, and personally have no pride in them." Yet Banks became a ranking Union general overnight. Only Winfield Scott, John C. Frémont, and George McClellan outranked him at the beginning of the war. Because all three of these officers dropped out after the first two years of the conflict, Banks remained one of the highest-ranking generals in the U.S. Army, even outranking Ulysses S. Grant until 1864.[2]

1. James M. McPherson, *Abraham Lincoln and the Second American Revolution* (New York: Oxford University Press, 1991), 71; *Congressional Globe,* 33d Cong., 1st sess., 1853, Appendix, 1137–41; *New York Herald,* September 12, 1859; *New York Tribune,* September 12, 1859; William Schouler to Banks, May 6, 1845, Banks Collection, LC.

2. Massachusetts, *Official Report, 1853,* 2:12–14. Banks did not hesitate to use his

Banks's lack of experience led some observers to criticize Lincoln for having made the appointment. But offering Banks a commission brought popular support to an administration that needed it badly during the early months of the struggle. Furthermore, Banks's lack of military experience was not a serious handicap for his first assignment as commander of the Department of Annapolis in Maryland.[3]

Baltimore, where Banks was headquartered, by tradition and preference identified with the South. Prosouthern feelings ran so high that Lincoln had decided to slip through the city secretly on the way to his inauguration in March, and a Baltimore mob attacked a Union regiment en route to Virginia a month later. Banks realized that "in the event of the establishment and recognition of a Southern Confederacy, the destinies of Maryland would incline her to join that section," but given its strategic location, Federal control of the city was vitally important to the Union cause.[4]

The first response of the Lincoln administration to the situation in Baltimore had been to follow a policy of conciliation. The president ordered troop trains to go around the city after the April riot and would not allow Union regiments to camp in the metropolis. When the first military commander of the district, Benjamin F. Butler, exacerbated the situation with his confrontational manner, Lincoln replaced him.[5]

Banks continued the administration's policy of cooperation. He set up a commission to assess property losses caused by the Union occupation and even allowed the Confederate flag to be displayed. Many Baltimor-

---

new position to lobby for the promotion of his brother Gardner, who had raised a company of infantry (Banks to William Schouler, July 10, 1861, William Schouler Papers, MAHS).

3. Herman Hattaway and Archer Jones, *How the North Won: A Military History of the Civil War* (Urbana: University of Illinois Press, 1983), 695; Charles Richard Williams, *The Life of Rutherford B. Hayes, Nineteenth President of the United States,* 2 vols. (Boston: Houghton Mifflin, 1914), 1:192; *New York Herald,* June 2, 4, 1861; Samuel Hooper to Banks, May 30, 1862, Banks Collection, LC.

4. *OR,* 2:690 (references to *OR* are to Series 1 unless otherwise indicated); *New York Herald,* June 28, 1861. For a detailed account of the period, see George William Brown, *Baltimore and the Nineteenth of April, 1861: A Study of the War,* Studies in Historical and Political Science, Vol. 3 (Baltimore: Johns Hopkins University, 1887).

5. *OR,* 2:681, Ser. 2, 1:585–86. For Butler's heavy-handed seizure of Baltimore, see Hans L. Trefousse, *Ben Butler: The South Called Him BEAST!* (New York: Twayne, 1957), 72–75, and Richard S. West, *Lincoln's Scapegoat General: A Life of Benjamin F. Butler, 1818–1893* (Boston: Houghton Mifflin, 1965), 64–75.

eans praised Banks for his tolerance, and a newspaper correspondent noted that "if any military commander from the North can be popular in this southern Department, Major General Banks is that commander."[6]

Although Banks's policies did much to boost his popularity, they also gave comfort to the enemy. Marylanders sneaked across the lines and operated Confederate enlistment centers in the city. Baltimore's papers continued to be as anti-Union as they could, and there were numerous public gatherings at which citizens openly aired secessionist sentiments. When Banks came to realize that his policy was not working, he moved gradually from conciliation to coercion by restricting the movement of civilians in and out of the city and allowing Union troops to make more of a public presence. An order from his superiors, however, forced a showdown. Late in June, Banks was told to arrest Baltimore's police chief, George P. Kane, along with the four police commissioners. The police were openly prosouthern and had even attempted to keep Unionists from giving food and water to northern troops in the Baltimore railroad depots.[7]

Banks decided to arrest only Kane and detailed eighteen hundred soldiers for the task. Moving silently after midnight on June 27, the contingent entered the city, roused the irritable police chief from his bed, and sent him in a carriage to Fort McHenry. Banks turned over Baltimore's four hundred policemen to the temporary command of John R. Kenly of the First Maryland (Union) Infantry. But the crisis was not over. The four police commissioners met the next morning and ordered the entire police force to disband in protest. Colonel Kenly quickly swore in a new pro-Union force, and three days later Banks finished the job by arresting the commissioners, even though there were no charges against them. Even then, Banks did not feel that it was necessary to impose martial law, nor did he interfere further with the state or city authorities. All in all, it might be said that Banks had dealt with the situation with some skill. Certainly, he was able to solve a difficult situation with more tact than Butler would have used.[8]

6. *New York Herald*, June 28, 1861; Harrington, *Fighting Politician*, 57.

7. Elihu S. Riley, *"The Ancient City": A History of Annapolis in Maryland, 1649–1887* (Annapolis: Record Printing Office, 1887), 296–97; William H. Eastman to his sister, August 12, 1861, and to his mother, August 25, 1861, William H. Eastman Letters, MAHS; *OR*, 2:138–39. See also "Union Policy of Repression in Maryland," in *OR*, Ser. 2, 1:563–748.

8. *OR*, 2:141–43, 724, Ser. 2, 1:586–87, 622–26, 632–33; Charles Camper and J. W.

Following his success in Baltimore, Banks was ordered to take command of the Department of the Shenandoah with headquarters in Harpers Ferry, Virginia. The department embraced much of Maryland, including the temporary state capital at Frederick. Banks's primary mission was to prevent Maryland from seceding from the Union when the legislature met in special session on September 17, even if that meant arresting those legislators who sided with the South. "Exercise your own judgment as to the time and manner," the secretary of war directed, "but do the work effectively."[9]

Banks called for Lieutenant Colonel Thomas Ruger of the Third Wisconsin Infantry and ordered his regiment to Frederick. Ruger's troops drifted into the city as if on leave and then formed into details to carry out their mission. Before the legislature knew what was happening, nine of its members had been arrested. At the same time, the new commander in Baltimore, John A. Dix, detained other members as they passed through his department. Other prosouthern representatives heard what was happening and avoided traveling to Frederick.[10]

Banks's prompt action may have prevented Maryland from seceding, but the danger of secession remained unless a pro-Union legislature could be elected in November. Consequently, Lincoln wanted "a killing majority rolled up against secession." To make certain that this would happen, the administration ordered Banks to furlough Maryland soldiers so that they could vote, to use other troops to protect loyal voters at the polls, and to arrest "suspected persons," notably men just back from the Confederacy. The result was a Unionist sweep.[11]

Kirkley, *Historical Record of the First Regiment Maryland Infantry* (1871; reprint, Baltimore: Butternut & Blue, 1990), 14–18; Bernard C. Steiner, "James Alfred Pearce," *Maryland Historical Magazine* 19 (March 1924): 25.

9. *OR*, 5:193, Ser. 2, 1:679, 681–85; *New York Herald*, July 31, 1861.

10. *OR*, Ser. 2, 1:667–85; Edwin E. Bryant, *History of the Third Regiment of Wisconsin Veteran Volunteer Infantry* (Madison: Veteran Association, 1891), 26–28; J. Thomas Scharf, *The Chronicles of Baltimore* (Baltimore: Turnbull Brothers, 1874), 651–59; S. Teackle Wallis, *Correspondence between S. Teackle Wallis, Esq. of Baltimore, and the Hon. John Sherman Of the U.S. Senate, concerning the Arrest of Members of the Maryland Legislature* (Baltimore: N.p., 1863), 3–7, 15–31; William H. Eastman to his sister, September 13, 1861, Eastman Letters, MAHS; for Banks's defense, see the *Boston Daily Journal*, November 1, 1864.

11. Wallis, *Correspondence*, 8–14. See McClellan's orders, October 29, 1861, in *OR*, Ser. 2, 1:608.

Banks's success in Maryland led him to recognize the political importance of disfranchising disloyal citizens and placing legislative power in the hands of those who could be counted on to support the "Old Flag." He predicted that "what occurred there [in Maryland] would occur in North Carolina, South Carolina, in Georgia, in Alabama, and Mississippi. If . . . those states shall be controlled by men that are loyal . . . we shall then have loyal populations and loyal governments." The strategy was to become a model for Lincoln's attempt to reconstruct Louisiana.[12]

That Banks's interference with the Maryland legislature went against the democratic principles upon which he had placed so much faith did not seem to concern him much. The administration was happy, and Banks still hoped that he might serve in Lincoln's cabinet. In fact, Seward brought Lincoln out to Harpers Ferry in early October to discuss this possibility further. The meeting was pleasant, and Lincoln, who was feeling pressure from radical Republicans to move faster than he desired to go, liked Banks's cautious approach, which contrasted sharply with the hasty and ill-advised actions of several other Union commanders, such as Frémont in Missouri, who had issued an emancipation proclamation of his own, and Butler in Virginia, who had begun to put escaped slaves to work for the Union army around Fort Monroe. But Lincoln did not offer Banks a spot in his cabinet because he preferred to keep the new major general busy in the army.[13]

12. *Boston Semi-Weekly Journal,* October 31, 1865, quoted in Harrington, *Fighting Politician,* 60.

13. Edward Bates, *Diary of Edward Bates, 1859–66,* ed. Howard Kennedy Beale (Washington, D.C.: U.S. Government Printing Office, 1933), 228; Howard P. Nash, *Stormy Petrel: The Life and Times of General Benjamin F. Butler, 1818–1893* (Rutherford, N.J.: Fairleigh Dickinson University Press, 1969), 102–11; Theodore Calvin Pease and James G. Randall, eds., *The Diary of Orville Hickman Browning,* 2 vols., Collections of the Illinois State Historical Library, Vol. 20 (Springfield, Ill.: Illinois State Historical Library, 1925), 1:601–3; J. G. Randall, *Lincoln, the President,* 2 vols. (New York: Dodd, Mead, 1945), 2:242; Samuel M. Quincy, "General Halleck's Military Administration in the Summer of 1862," in *Papers of the Military Historical Society of Massachusetts,* Vol. 2, ed. Theodore F. Dwight (Boston: Houghton Mifflin, 1895), 23, 38; Charles H. T. Collis to Banks, July 3, 1862, Banks Collection, LC. In late summer it had been rumored that Banks was to be made secretary of war (Richard Cary to his wife, August 27, 1861, Richard Cary Letters, MAHS). Evidence of Banks's adeptness at walking the political tightrope during this period can be found in R. Morris Copeland's uncomplimentary *Statement of R. Morris Copeland* (Boston: Prentiss & Deland, 1864), 8–9.

Fortunately, Banks liked being in the army. He enjoyed the trappings of command, not to mention the respect and admiration shown by his troops. On one occasion, he personally drilled his men after a review near Little Washington, Virginia. It was his first experience giving commands on the field, and he was astonished by his ability to direct ten thousand men. "I felt as if I had been doing it all my life, & I think the officers were surprised," he confided in a letter to his wife the next day.[14]

Like many commissioned politicians, Banks was impressive in uniform—"one of the finest appearing and best looking officers in the army," one civilian remarked. To enhance his image further, Banks surrounded himself with a bodyguard of colorful Zouaves, outfitted with scarlet trousers, white leather leggings, and red fezzes. A correspondent wrote to his wife that Banks was "by all odds the most impressive man, in countenance, language and demeanor, whom I have seen since the war commenced." Even David Dixon Porter, who was later one of his greatest detractors, admitted after the war that he "never saw a more faultless-looking soldier."[15]

Although he looked the part, Banks was not an effective commander. One problem was that his discipline was inconsistent. For example, when a subordinate officer ordered a private strung up by his thumbs, Banks rescinded the order when objections were voiced. An officer in his command observed that Banks "means well, but I fear that he lacks a little either of education or confidence to push things through."[16]

The lack of discipline contributed to an outbreak of venereal disease, and prostitutes became so numerous that Banks had them rounded up and sent back to Washington by the wagon load. Consumption of alcohol was also a major problem. One night during a terrific thunderstorm, some soldiers from the Fifth Connecticut Infantry got drunk on liquor they had smuggled into camp. The *New York Herald* reported that "one

14. Banks to Mary P. Banks, July 29, 1862, February 26, 1863, Banks Collection, LC.

15. Cornelia McDonald, *A Diary with Reminiscences of the War and Refugee Life* (Nashville: Hunter McDonald, 1934), 42; David Dixon Porter, *Incidents and Anecdotes of the Civil War* (New York: D. Appleton, 1885), 218–19; Newspaper clipping, [1857], Banks Collection, LC.

16. Henry Hall and James Hall, *Cayuga in Field: A Record of the Nineteenth N.Y. Volunteers and Third New York Artillery* (Auburn, N.Y.: Truair, Smith, 1873), 70–93; Wilder Dwight, *Life and Letters of William Dwight*, ed. Elizabeth Amelia Dwight (1868; 2d ed., Boston: Little, Brown, 1891), 91–94; Richard Cary to his wife, September 6, 1861, Richard Cary Letters, MAHS.

citizen was killed, two or three wounded, and several cattle and horses shot" in the melee that followed. In reality, the unfortunate victim was one of the regiment's own, Private John Gallagher, who had turned on a colleague in a drunken fury. Although Banks responded to this and other disturbances by ordering all liquor in the camp destroyed, he never was able to prevent his troops from getting hold of it.[17]

Looting was another problem. Banks's soldiers supplemented army rations by plundering nearby farms. It was said that "stock and poultry joined the Union side" and that "the officers shut their eyes whenever a rooster crowed." One officer observed matter-of-factly that "everywhere that soldiers marched a great mortality prevailed among poultry, pigs, and sheep." Banks issued orders to try to stop the looting, but the men generally ignored his directives.[18]

Banks added to his difficulties as a commander by failing to assemble a competent staff. Not only were his appointees lacking in professional experience, they tended to be tactless and arrogant. "His staff officers seem to be very unpopular everywhere, supercilious as the Devil," wrote an officer in a New York regiment.[19]

Banks's authority was weakened further by the resentment of West Pointers in his command who disliked serving under a political general. They often undercut respect for Banks among the men by grousing that a "political education" meant incompetence for war. One regular army officer confided to a citizen that service of the Union forces was "most

17. *New York Herald*, August 3, September 27, October 9, 11, 12, 17, 1861; Charles William Boyce, *A Brief History of the Twenty-Eighth Regiment, New York State Volunteers* (Buffalo: Matthews-Northup, 1896), 97; Edwin E. Marvin, *The Fifth Connecticut Volunteers* (Hartford: Wiley, Waterman & Eaton, 1889), 41.

18. *OR*, 5:747, 12, pt. 3:61–62; Bryant, *History of the Third Wisconsin*, 40–41; Frank Freidel, "General Orders 100 and Military Government," *Mississippi Valley Historical Review* 32 (March 1946): 548; George H. Gordon, *From Brook Farm to Cedar Mountain: In the War of the Great Rebellion, 1861–62* (Boston: James R. Osgood, 1883), 102, 118–19; Henry R. Pyne, *The History of the First New Jersey Cavalry (Sixteenth Regiment, New Jersey Volunteers)* (Trenton, N.J.: J. A. Beecher, 1871), 70; Alonzo Hall Quint, *The Potomac and the Rapidan* (Boston: Crosby & Nichols, 1864), 168.

19. Willoughby M. Babcock, *Selections from the Letters and Diaries of Brevet-Brigadier General Willoughby Babcock of the Seventy-Fifth New York Volunteers* (Albany: University of the State of New York, 1922), 74; Robert S. Denison to Chase, January 8, February 12, 1863, in Salmon P. Chase, "Diary and Correspondence of Salmon P. Chase," *Annual Report of the American Historical Association, the Year 1902* (Washington, D.C.: U.S. Government Printing Office, 1903), 346, 359.

distasteful to him, that belonging as he did to the regular army, he could not help being disgusted at the mismanagement mistakes of civilians who were in high and responsible positions, placed there by political influence, and who could only lead their armies to disgrace and defeat."[20]

Because Banks was given an elevated rank at the very beginning of the conflict, he never had the opportunity to learn the basics of military command from the ground up. Furthermore, because he surrounded himself with a staff that was as inexperienced as he, Banks had little opportunity to benefit from the advice of competent professionals. The situation was exacerbated by the resentment generated by his appointment, which kept professional military men under his command at a distance. It is likely that Banks would have been a capable regimental commander had he been given the opportunity. But he was cursed with too much rank too soon and never had the chance to go back and acquire the skills that his hasty promotion forced him to lead without.[21]

Nathaniel P. Banks crossed the Potomac into Virginia in mid-February. Moving cautiously up the Shenandoah Valley, he reached Strasburg and set up headquarters. The Valley was not a good avenue for a Federal offensive because it veered to the southwest, away from Richmond. Yet it did provide a route by which southern troops could move to disrupt lines of communication between Washington and the midwestern states. Banks was not particularly pleased with his assignment. Other generals were advancing on Richmond while he was guarding lines of communication and protecting routes to Washington.[22]

20. A. J. H. Duganne, *Camps and Prisons: Twenty Months in the Department of the Gulf* (New York: J. P. Robens, 1865), 364–65; McDonald, *Diary with Reminiscences,* 67; also Porter, *Incidents and Anecdotes,* 219; *OR,* 34, pt. 2:61.

21. For an assessment of Banks's promise as a regimental commander, see George H. Gordon, *History of the Campaign of the Army of Virginia* (Boston: Houghton, Osgood, 1880), 453–57. Lincoln's secretary of the navy, Gideon Welles, recorded in his diary on December 29, 1862, that "Banks has some ready qualities for civil administration and if not employed in the field or active military operations will be likely to acquit himself respectably as a provisional or military governor" (Welles, *Diary of Gideon Welles: Secretary of the Navy under Lincoln and Johnson,* ed. Howard K. Beale, 3 vols. [New York: Norton, 1960], 1:210). Also see a critical editorial regarding political generals during the war, with a favorable comment about Banks's administrative ability, in the *New York Herald,* January 11, 1865.

22. Gordon, *From Brook Farm to Cedar Mountain,* 172–74; Quint, *The Potomac and the Rapidan,* 134.

Major General George B. McClellan, commander of the Army of the Potomac, planned to strike Richmond from the southeast via the James River peninsula. Because that line of advance would leave Washington partially uncovered, Secretary of War Edwin M. Stanton ordered Banks to drive the Confederates from the Shenandoah Valley. Banks advanced, and the Confederate commander, Thomas J. "Stonewall" Jackson, fell back beyond Woodstock to Mount Jackson, leading Banks to assume, prematurely, that Jackson was abandoning the area. Thinking that he had accomplished his mission, Banks turned east and crossed the Blue Ridge to join the advance on Richmond. Jackson was pleased to see him go. Doubling back, Stonewall approached Winchester on the day Banks departed and found ten thousand northern troops left behind under one of Banks's subordinates, Brigadier General James Shields. Jackson hurled his forces against the Union troops at Kernstown on March 23, 1862, but Shields, who was a soldier-politician like Banks, handled his small army well and turned back Jackson's assault.[23]

Tactically, Kernstown was a Union victory. Strategically, it was a Confederate success. Lincoln became concerned for the safety of Washington, and, just when McClellan needed heavy reinforcements for his peninsular campaign, the chief executive retained Irvin McDowell's thirty thousand troops to defend the capital city and hastened another division to help hold western Virginia. Lincoln also ordered Banks back to the Shenandoah Valley and directed him to chase Jackson out of the Valley entirely this time. Following orders, Banks crept from Winchester to Strasburg and then past New Market to Harrisonburg. Turner Ashby, Jackson's chief of cavalry, did everything he could to slow the Federal advance. In addition, the roads were made terrible by recent rains. Nevertheless, the desultory movement of the Union army suggested that Banks had not yet learned how to handle troops in the field.[24]

23. *OR,* 12, pt. 3:4, 16, 43–44, 5:18, 725–66; Douglas Southall Freeman, *Lee's Lieutenants: A Study in Command,* 3 vols. (New York: Charles Scribner's Sons, 1942–44), 1:329–46; Robert G. Tanner, *Stonewall Jackson in the Valley: Thomas J. "Stonewall" Jackson's Shenandoah Valley Campaign, Spring 1862* (Garden City, N.Y.: Doubleday, 1976), 114.

24. *OR,* 12, pt. 3:15, 16, 27, 32, 48–51, 113, 118–19, 126–27, 136–37; Gordon, *From Brook Farm to Cedar Mountain,* 136–37; David G. Martin, *Jackson's Valley Campaign: November 1861–June 1862* (New York: W. H. Smith, 1988), 47–62, 3–25; Tanner, *Stonewall Jackson in the Valley,* 136–61; Quint, *The Potomac and the Rapidan,* 145–48; Banks to Colfax, May 4, 1862, Banks Collection, LC.

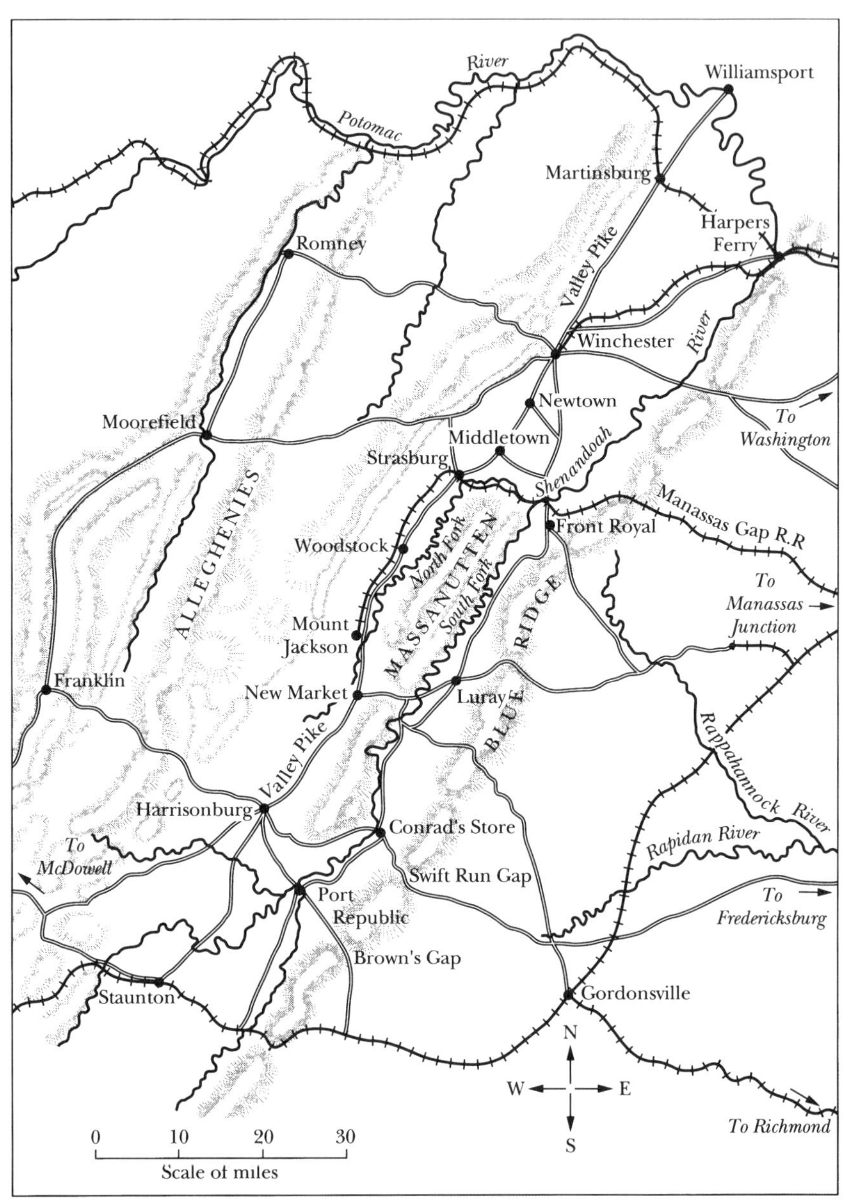

The Shenandoah Valley in 1862

Banks's spies informed him in late April that Jackson had left the Valley. His confidence soared. Stonewall's army was "much demoralized by defeat, desertion," he reported, and it was suffering a "general depression of spirits" and was "not in condition to attack, neither to make strong resistance." Upon receiving his report, the War Department ordered Banks to fall back to Strasburg with one of his two divisions and send the other (Shields's) to eastern Virginia to assist in putting pressure on Richmond. Banks did not object because there was "nothing more to be done by us in the valley." Even so, Banks was dissatisfied with having to remain at Strasburg while others got all the glory in capturing the Rebel capital.[25]

Hoping to improve his prospects, Banks suggested to Washington in early May that his command could be shifted across the mountains into the area around Manassas Junction, leaving two or three regiments (approximately one thousand men) in Strasburg. According to Banks, this relocation would retain a presence in the Valley and protect lines of communication while allowing him to join the march on Richmond with the bulk of his troops. Banks's proposal came too late and was not accepted. But his disappointment over being left out of the action did not last long, for new reports indicated that Jackson had been reinforced by Richard Ewell and Edward Johnson and was on his way back to the Valley. Banks was well informed. Using the reports of prisoners, Confederate deserters, and Virginia Unionists, he estimated that Ewell had at least eight thousand troops and Johnson half that many, which gave Jackson a total of twenty thousand men against Banks's nine thousand. If these reports were true, there was good reason for expecting "unfortunate results."[26]

Banks's best defensive position was the triangle of roads linking Winchester, Strasburg, and Front Royal. If he moved further up the Valley

25. *OR,* 12, pt. 3:51, 106–7, 118–19, 122; Harrington, *Fighting Politician,* 67; Martin, *Jackson's Valley Campaign,* 63–86; Richard Cary to his wife (Helen), May 9, 1862, Cary Letters, MAHS. For evidence that Jackson was aware of Banks's overconfidence, see Archie P. McDonald, ed., *Make Me a Map of the Valley: The Civil War Journal of Stonewall Jackson's Topographer* (Dallas: Southern Methodist University Press, 1973), 25.

26. *OR,* 12, pt. 3:106, 112, 126–27, 118–19, 136–37, 140; Harrington, *Fighting Politician,* 68; Quint, *The Potomac to the Rapidan,* 77–78; Banks to Stanton, April 26, May 6, 1862, Banks to Colfax, May 4, 1862, Banks Collection, LC. Jackson's force was slightly smaller; see William Allan, *History of the Campaign of Gen. T. J. (Stonewall) Jackson in the Shenandoah Valley of Virginia* (1912; reprint, Dayton, Ohio: Morningside, 1987), 92.

toward New Market, he would have to guard two avenues of approach. If he retreated too far north toward Harpers Ferry, he would have to extend his flanks across the entire width of the northern plain. Of the three towns, Winchester presented the best defensive possibility. Troops stationed at Strasburg or Front Royal could be flanked by a Confederate advance up either side of the Massanutten Mountain range. Unfortunately, both Strasburg and Front Royal were on the Manassas Gap Railroad, which was the major line of communication to eastern Virginia. Consequently, Stanton sent word for Banks to locate in "Strasburg or its vicinity."[27]

Banks took up a position in Strasburg, but Stanton ordered him to send a detachment toward Front Royal to protect the Manassas Gap Railroad. Although he did as he was ordered, Banks did not like the idea. Such a move would "reduce my force greatly, which is already too small to defend Strasburg if attacked." Furthermore, he argued, dividing his small army would make his position "hopelessly indefensible" because he would be "compelled to defend two points, both equally accessible to the enemy."[28]

Banks made a bad situation worse by failing to increase the number of patrols along the routes that led to his exposed position. He also failed to prepare for the eventuality of a Confederate advance by sending his sick, wounded, and surplus stores from Strasburg to Winchester in the rear. These were not his only mistakes. Banks assumed that Jackson would not attack Front Royal, although he had already observed that it and Strasburg were "equally accessible." Instead, he chose to dig in at Strasburg to guard the approach from New Market. To protect his left flank, Banks stationed Colonel John R. Kenly with one thousand men from the First Maryland (Union) Infantry at Front Royal. This deployment left Banks with slightly less than seven thousand effectives in Strasburg.[29]

The mistake was fairly obvious because Front Royal was an important communications point on the railroad. Furthermore, Banks was aware of the mountainous road from New Market to Luray that Jackson could use to advance on Front Royal, for Banks had sent a reconnaissance party

27. *OR*, 12, pt. 3:122, 150.

28. *OR*, 12, pt. 1:522, 524–25; David Hunter Strother, "Personal Recollections of the War," *Harper's New Monthly Magazine* 34 (March 1867): 436–37.

29. Quint, *The Potomac and the Rapidan*, 144–46; *OR*, 12, pt. 3:524, 536–37; Tanner, *Stonewall Jackson in the Valley*, 206.

across the same road when he fell back on Strasburg. Nevertheless, he was sure that Jackson would march, as he had before, by way of the Harrisonburg–New Market–Strasburg Turnpike.[30]

All was quiet for the time being. "Nothing to write you about from here," Captain Richard Cary in the Second Massachusetts Infantry wrote his wife from Strasburg on Wednesday, May 21. "Everything is perfectly stagnant." But even as Cary penned those words, Major Hector Tyndale of the Twenty-eighth Pennsylvania captured a Rebel soldier south of Front Royal. When Tyndale informed Banks, confirming that the Confederate army was in the Luray Valley, Banks ignored his report. Banks preferred to believe that Jackson was still at New Market.[31]

Another day passed. Union troops in Strasburg heard rumors of a Confederate advance but generally disregarded them. A traveling minstrel show was in town, and Banks's men roared with laughter at each performance. On May 23, a Union soldier wrote his mother to complain about the lack of reading matter and to assure her that they were "leading the most lazy life imaginable." Little did he know that an excited sergeant had just arrived at headquarters with news that the Rebels were attacking Kenly at Front Royal. Banks dismissed the report as just another cavalry raid designed to throw him off track.[32]

Stonewall Jackson had been in camp near New Market until Wednesday, May 21, but that morning he directed his men to march northward along the Valley Turnpike toward Strasburg. After traveling a short distance, Jackson ordered the column to turn eastward and proceed through the gap in Massanutten Mountain to Luray. There, Jackson's men rejoined Ewell's division, which had marched directly from Swift Run Gap. Jack-

30. Evidence that Banks had access to an accurate map of the area can be found in the papers of one of his brigade commanders (Military records folder for April 1862, George H. Gordon Papers, MAHS).

31. *OR,* 12, pt. 1:523–35, 554–55, pt. 3:65–66, 135; Richard Cary to his wife (Helen), May 21, 1862, Cary Letters, MAHS.

32. Gordon, *From Brook Farm to Cedar Mountain,* 191–92; G. F. R. Henderson, *Stonewall Jackson and the American Civil War* (1898; reprint, New York: Longmans, Green, 1961), 241; David Hunter Strother, *A Virginia Yankee in the Civil War: The Diaries of David Hunter Strother,* ed. Cecil D. Eby (Chapel Hill: University of North Carolina Press, 1961), 38–39; Richard C. Goodwin to his mother, May 23, 1862, Goodwin Family Papers, MAHS.

son's army was reunited and ready to make its move against Kenly's men at Front Royal.[33]

Jackson's march continued northward on Thursday, over a miserable road down the Luray Valley. At nightfall, the troops halted and made camp ten miles south of Front Royal. As they bedded down, Jackson's hard-riding cavalry under Turner Ashby moved north to disrupt Federal communications by attacking the Union outpost at Buckton Station four miles east of Strasburg on the Manassas Gap Railroad. By early Friday afternoon, Ashby's troopers struck the outpost and drove 150 Union soldiers from their positions in the depot, which had been fortified and loopholed with sandbags. As the Federal troops retreated toward Strasburg, Ashby burned the depot and slashed the telegraph wires before rejoining Jackson's army near Front Royal. In the meantime, two regiments of Rebel cavalry struck the Manassas Gap Railroad east of Front Royal, cutting Kenly's communications in that direction.[34]

Jackson's army marched the remaining ten miles to Front Royal by noon on Friday and moved into position to attack. The first word Kenly received of the Confederate approach was from a black man who dashed into the Union camp shouting that the Rebels were coming in great numbers. "They will surround you and cut you off," he cried. Some of Kenly's men greeted his warning with laughter, but Kenly knew better and ordered the drummer to sound a long roll. The First Maryland (Union) Infantry formed in line and threw out pickets to the south, but the Confederates swarmed over the pickets before they knew what hit them. The few that got away fell back to Front Royal to join their comrades now under arms.[35]

As the Confederates poured into Front Royal, the Federals retreated in confusion. Although Kenly could have saved his command by a quick withdrawal down the road to Winchester, he decided to make a stand, hoping that a delaying action might save the main Union force at Strasburg. Several miles north of town he ordered his troops to turn and face their kinsmen in the Confederate First Maryland. Twice Kenly's troops

33. Freeman, *Lee's Lieutenants,* 1:373; Richard Taylor, *Destruction and Reconstruction: Personal Experiences of the Late War,* ed. Richard Harwell (New York: Longmans, Green, 1955), 52–53.

34. *OR,* 12, pt. 1:560–61, 702–3.

35. Thomas A. Ashby, *The Valley Campaigns* (New York: Neale, 1914), 115–21; *New York Tribune,* May 30, 1862.

reformed to blunt the Confederate advance, but they could not stop the Rebel assault. Behind them, Ashby's men cut through the fields and forest, threatening all lines of retreat. Kenly's chief of cavalry screamed for the troops to run for their lives, and the bluecoats quickly sought safety in disordered flight. The Confederate cavalry pursued the fleeing soldiers through meadows and wheat fields so effectively that only one in five escaped. Colonel Kenly himself became a casualty when he was wounded and taken prisoner.[36]

Although Ashby had cut the road to Strasburg early Friday morning, at least one of Kenly's couriers got through to Banks's headquarters. He was followed shortly thereafter by the first telegraph reports from survivors who had managed to reach Winchester. At last Banks had definite news of Jackson's whereabouts; Front Royal was taken, Kenly's command was "cut to pieces," and the Confederates were pressing northward toward Winchester in full force.[37]

Banks refused to consider a retreat. He was still convinced that the affair at Front Royal was just another raid. Part of the reason was that Captain G. W. Myers with a small detachment of Confederate cavalry had boldly attacked Banks's forces in front of Strasburg the evening before. Occupying a hill just outside the town, Myers's troopers dug in as darkness fell. The feint was timed perfectly, for it contributed to Banks's conviction that the main force of Jackson's army was still south of Strasburg. Thus Banks waited while a Confederate army that numbered some sixteen thousand men devoured Kenly's small force of one thousand.[38]

Banks finally decided to send reinforcements to Front Royal in midafternoon but recalled them when he discovered that the garrison had ceased to exist. As darkness fell, Banks still thought that the major portion of Jackson's army was south of Strasburg. Furthermore, he dis-

36. *OR,* 12, pt. 1:564–65; Rosamond Randall Beirne, ed., "Three War Letters," *Maryland Historical Magazine* 40 (December 1945): 290–92; Robert L. Dabney, *Life and Campaigns of Lieut.-Gen. Thomas J. Jackson* (New York: Blelock, 1866), 364–68; Camper and Kirkley, *Historical Record of the First Regiment Maryland Infantry,* 27–46; Taylor, *Destruction and Reconstruction,* 57. Banks had high praise for Kenly. See his notation on a letter from Kenly dated February 28, 1867, Banks Collection, LC.

37. *New York Tribune,* June 3, 6, 1862.

38. *OR,* 12, pt. 1:702; Gordon, *From Brook Farm to Cedar Mountain,* 191–93; William N. McDonald, *A History of the Laurel Brigade* (Baltimore: Sun Job Printing Office, 1907), 53.

counted the news from Front Royal that Jackson's force was "15,000 or 20,000," believing that the numbers were "much overestimated." But there was another reason why he hesitated. Banks was well aware of the political implications of ordering a retreat that might turn out to be premature. "We have more to fear from the opinions of our friends than from the bayonets of our enemies," he told Colonel George H. Gordon when he conferred with his brigade commanders at eleven o'clock that night.[39]

Banks's army was in a precarious position. It was scattered, and scarcely seven thousand troops were available for duty in and around Strasburg. Jackson's sixteen thousand men were poised on his left flank less than a dozen miles away. More important, the road from Front Royal to Winchester lay open to Jackson's army. If Jackson got to Winchester before Banks, or if Confederate troops were able to cut the road between the two points, Banks's army would be trapped. Confused by the contradictory reports from Front Royal, Banks lost confidence. Although he preserved the outward appearance of dignity and calm, aides found Banks dispirited and downcast. Unable to find out what had happened, he finally went to bed without deciding whether to stand and fight or to retreat.[40]

News from Front Royal continued to trickle in. Finally, around 3:00 A.M. on Saturday, Banks decided to order the sick and wounded to the rear. Portions of his wagon train began moving northward toward Winchester at 4:30 A.M. Banks directed units stationed south and east of Strasburg to pull back at the same time. He hesitated to do anything more because he still believed that his position was strategically sound. By 6:00 Banks had revised his calculations of the size of the Confederate army upward to "not less than 6,000 to 10,000" men, about half of what Jackson really had. Noting that "our information this morning shows that the enemy . . . will not now at the least attempt our rear," Banks ordered Colonel Gordon to hold his positions around Strasburg.[41]

Banks had four courses of action open to him. One was to retreat across Little North Mountain to the west and possibly link up with Fré-

39. *OR,* 12, pt. 1:526; Bryant, *History of the Third Wisconsin,* 58; Gordon, *From Brook Farm to Cedar Mountain,* 196.

40. Strother, *Virginia Yankee,* 39.

41. *OR,* 12, pt. 1:525–27, 546–47, 594–95, 614.

mont's army on the other side of the Alleghenies. A second option was to attack Jackson at Front Royal and hope to interrupt his lines of communication with Richmond. The third alternative was to march to Winchester before Jackson got there. This option would maintain open lines of communication with his own base of supply and reinforcements at Harpers Ferry. A fourth alternative, to dig in at Strasburg, would have been an invitation to disaster. Banks ruled out the first two options, the first because to move over the Alleghenies would mean abandoning his large wagon train and the second because Jackson's force was larger than his own. As Banks eventually came to realize, an immediate withdrawal to Winchester was the only realistic course of action open to him.[42]

Waiting for Jackson to play his hand, Banks sat down at eight o'clock Saturday morning and wrote a letter to his mother. "Yesterday our troops were badly beaten at Front Royal," he reported. "Thus they mass their men upon us, while our govt. separates its forces in little powerless squads, without power ever to crush the foe—anywhere." Banks was more right than he wanted to be, for scouts returned with information that the Confederates held all the roads running north and west out of Front Royal. Realizing the threat to his line of retreat, Banks finally ordered a total withdrawal. Although Banks claimed later that he completed preparations for the move to Winchester with "incredible celerity," the main body of his army was not in motion until midmorning Saturday, almost twenty-four hours after Jackson's assault on Front Royal.[43]

42. *OR*, 12, pt. 1:546.

43. Banks to Mrs. Banks, Sr., May 24, [1863], Banks Collection, LC. See also Bryant, *History of the Third Wisconsin*, 57–58; Gordon, *From Brook Farm to Cedar Mountain*, 196–97; Strother, *Virginia Yankee*, 39; George L. Andrews to his wife, May 28, 1862, George L. Andrews Papers, MHI.

5

The Most Remarkable Movement of the War

Knowing that his men were exhausted by the rapid marches and fighting, Stonewall Jackson halted his column Friday evening near Cedarville, several miles north of Front Royal. From that point he could move west to cut the Valley Turnpike or northwest to capture Winchester. Early the next morning, Jackson ordered a brigade from Ewell's division to probe the road toward Winchester. He also dispatched Brigadier General George Steuart with the Second and Sixth Virginia Cavalry to Newtown on the Valley Turnpike nine miles south of Winchester. Ashby, with a few companies of cavalry, scouted in the direction of the Valley Turnpike along a road that connected Cedarville to Middletown.[1]

About eleven o'clock Saturday morning, a panting, hatless courier arrived at Jackson's headquarters to report that Steuart had reached Newtown an hour earlier to find the pike crowded with Union trains. Finally, Jackson had the information he needed. Hoping to catch most of Banks's army before it passed through Middletown, Jackson ordered his troops forward with Major Roberdeau Wheat's Louisiana Tigers and two long-range rifled guns from Captain Robert Chew's Rockbridge Artillery leading the way.[2]

The Union withdrawal from Strasburg had begun smoothly but soon turned chaotic. Civilians, slaves, sutlers, and camp followers jammed the turnpike. Some were mounted, others rode in wagons, carts, and bug-

1. Tanner, *Stonewall Jackson in the Valley*, 217–20.
2. Ibid., 219–20.

gies, while still others fled on foot. The confused mass of refugees clogged the road and made it difficult for the Union troops to maintain their formations as they trudged toward Winchester less than twenty miles away.[3]

In spite of the obstacles, Banks kept his men moving. "General Banks (God bless him!) was here, there, everywhere," one soldier recalled, "urging the men on, and determined to fight the cruel foe until the last." By the time Jackson reached Middletown, the bulk of the Federal army had already passed through. Jackson immediately ordered Richard Taylor's Louisiana brigade to race toward Winchester in an effort to overtake the rest of Banks's command, but the debris of retreat was Banks's salvation. Abandoned wagons littered the road for miles. Some had overturned in the rush to get away, scattering their contents. Muskets, rain capes, ornate footlockers stuffed with gaudy uniforms, and sutlers' stores were thrown about. Bibles, playing cards, photographs, songbooks, and cooking utensils littered the ground. Confederate soldiers, who had not eaten since breakfast, stopped to rummage through the abandoned wagons and knapsacks. Ashby's ill-disciplined cavalry, which should have spearheaded the pursuit, lost its cohesion while plundering the trains. Although Taylor's troops attempted to keep up the pressure on the retreating Federals, the new Union rear guard formed by Colonel Gordon offered stiff resistance. Near Newtown, a Union battery swung around to confront the small force of Confederates pursuing them, and an artillery duel continued until Jackson arrived at the head of the infantry several hours later. This action plus the delay caused by plundering enabled Banks to get away.[4]

Banks arrived at Winchester around five o'clock Saturday afternoon. The major portion of his command had escaped, and he thought he was safe for the time being. Unfortunately for his army, Banks persisted in the misguided belief that the Rebels would not attack him in Winchester. Colonel Gordon urged Banks to withdraw because Jackson held numerical superiority. Thinking again of how such a movement would be

3. *New York Tribune,* June 6, 1862; *New York World,* May 28, 1862.

4. *OR,* 12, pt. 1:704; Dabney, *Life of Jackson,* 369–70; Henry Kyd Douglas, *I Rode with Stonewall* (Chapel Hill: University of North Carolina Press, 1940), 54–55, 60, 70–71; Gordon, *From Brook Farm to Cedar Mountain,* 206–7; Tanner, *Stonewall Jackson in the Valley,* 223–24; Taylor, *Destruction and Reconstruction,* 58–59; *New York Tribune,* June 6, 1862; *New York World,* May 28, 1862.

portrayed in the newspapers, Banks resisted the idea: "No sir! the enemy is not as remorseless as the public!" Hoping that he could reoccupy Strasburg when Jackson turned south, Banks sent a confident telegram to Washington announcing that he had reached Winchester "with all our trains and stores in safety." Then, exhausted by the day's events, he retired to his room to take a bath.[5]

Banks's second in command, Brigadier General Alpheus S. Williams, positioned the Federal troops south of the town. In the darkness and excitement, Williams placed the Union brigades in positions that could be flanked if the enemy gained control of the high ground farther to the south. He also failed to use his cavalry to gather information of the Confederate advance.[6]

Early Sunday morning, Banks awoke to realize how precarious his situation had become. Information from scouts, prisoners, and fugitives indicated that the Confederates were coming. When they arrived, he would be outnumbered two to one. Banks ordered his military trains to continue moving north toward the Potomac River. Just as the wagons cleared the town, Confederate troops drove in the pickets through the mist that still clung to the ground as Union soldiers prepared to receive the assault.[7]

The key to Winchester was a series of hills overlooking the town and running west of the Valley Turnpike. Jackson ordered Charles S. Winder, who commanded the Stonewall Brigade, to take possession of a small hill just west of the road and somewhat south of the others. Winder's men moved forward and gained possession without a fight, securing the mid-

5. *OR,* 12, pt. 1:527, 546; Gordon, *From Brook Farm to Cedar Mountain,* 225; Richard Cary to his wife (Helen), June 18, 1862, Cary Letters, MAHS. Colonel Gordon became thoroughly disgusted with Banks and nurtured a hostility toward his commanding officer that lasted throughout the war and beyond (see Gordon to Benjamin F. Butler, April 5, 1865, in Benjamin Franklin Butler, *Private and Official Correspondence of Gen. Benjamin F. Butler during a Period of the Civil War,* ed. Jessie Ames Marshall, 5 vols. [Norwood, Mass.: Plimpton Press, 1917], 5:588–89).

6. *OR,* 12, pt. 1:595–96, 704; Dabney, *Life of Jackson,* 376; James E. Hall, *Diary of a Confederate Soldier,* ed. Ruth Woods Dayton (Phillipi, W.Va.: Editor, 1961), 58.

7. *OR,* 12, pt. 1:549, 595; Marvin, *Fifth Connecticut,* 99–101; *New York World,* May 30, 1862.

dle of Jackson's line. From this vantage point, Jackson could see that Banks had positioned his troops on the high ground to his front with the Federal left flank anchored in the town itself.[8]

The artillery opened up on both sides. Enjoying the advantage of being emplaced on high ground, the northern guns maintained a brisk and damaging fire that drove Winder's troops back from the crest of the hill they had just taken. Jackson ordered Ewell's division to probe the Federal left. The Union infantry conducted themselves well and put up such a stiff resistance that the Confederate assault stalled. In the meantime, the Federal artillery continued to provide effective counterfire to the Confederate guns trying to drive the Union troops back from their positions behind the stone walls that snaked along the ridge line.[9]

Jackson extended his line to the west, hoping to turn the Federal right flank, but the Union artillery kept the Confederate troops pinned down. Winder sought out Jackson and yelled above the din of battle that the Federal right flank must be turned. "I shall send you up Taylor," Stonewall replied as he spurred his horse to deliver the order personally.[10]

Earlier that morning Taylor had roused his troops and moved them to a position three miles south of Winchester. As they approached the town, they heard artillery and musket fire in the distance. Jackson rode up to Taylor and pointed out the hill that anchored the right flank of the Federal line. "General, can your brigade charge a battery?" "It can try," Taylor replied. "Very good, you must carry it," Jackson ordered.[11]

Taylor saw what had to be done. A small stream known as Abraham's Creek ran in a northwesterly direction from the turnpike. Taylor started his men in motion along the streambed, which afforded some shelter from Federal fire. It was a mile to the foot of the hill, from which their advance would encounter a moderate ascent interrupted only by two

8. Douglas, *I Rode with Stonewall*, 56–57; Tanner, *Stonewall Jackson in the Valley*, 236.

9. Tanner, *Stonewall Jackson in the Valley*, 226–29.

10. *OR*, 12, pt. 1:764; McHenry Howard, *Recollections of a Maryland Confederate Soldier and Staff Officer under Johnston, Jackson and Lee* (1914; reprint, Dayton, Ohio: Morningside Bookshop, 1975), 110; Tanner, *Stonewall Jackson in the Valley*, 229; John H. Worsham, *One of Jackson's Foot Cavalry* (New York: Neale, 1912), 86.

11. This conversation is a combination of the accounts by Douglas, *I Rode with Stonewall*, 58, and Taylor, *Destruction and Reconstruction*, 61–62.

fencerows. The real test would come beyond the fences, for then the Confederates would be exposed to the combined fire of Federal infantry and artillery on the crest of the hill.[12]

Federal guns began to drop shells around Taylor's men as they marched along the streambed to the base of the hill. After a brief halt, Taylor ordered his men to advance. A haze covered the battlefield, but a breeze sprang up as they approached the ridge, dispersing the smoke and the last tatters of the morning fog. A bluebird with a worm in its beak swooped along the ranks of advancing men. The Louisianians came into full view of both armies. One of Jackson's staff, who observed the charge from Winder's position in the center of the line, wrote that the brigade presented an impressive sight "with a line of glistening bayonets bright in the morning sun, its formation straight and compact, its tread quick and easy as it pushed on through the clover and up the hill."[13]

The Federal troops fired into the oncoming ranks but did not slow their advance. A great cheer rose from the Confederates viewing the scene from below as the Louisianians swarmed over the Union right. To the east, Ewell ordered a brigade forward to encircle the Federal left flank. Regiments from Mississippi and Alabama rushed toward Union troops from Pennsylvania, New York, and Connecticut and drove them into the outskirts of the town. Winder, who was still holding the center, ordered the Stonewall Brigade forward. The whole Confederate line from left to right advanced, "yelling like demons." Suddenly, panic seized the Union troops as they beat a hasty retreat through Winchester and north along the road to Martinsburg.[14]

Hopes for an orderly withdrawal were dashed when Banks's beaten and bewildered soldiers streamed back through Winchester "like a muddy torrent with the sunlight glittering on its turbid waves." Southern sympathizers fired on the disorganized troops from windows and passageways, adding to the chaos. Some Federal troops attempted to erect a barricade at an intersection, but Confederate infantry were on

12. Tanner, *Stonewall Jackson in the Valley,* 230.

13. *OR,* 12, pt. 1:800–801; Douglas, *I Rode with Stonewall,* 58; Taylor, *Destruction and Reconstruction,* 63–64.

14. *OR,* 12, pt. 1:800–801; Allan, *History of the Campaign,* 114; Henderson, *Stonewall Jackson,* 259–62; Tanner, *Stonewall Jackson in the Valley,* 231; Taylor, *Destruction and Reconstruction,* 61–65; entry for May 25, 1862, George A. Brooks Journal, SHC.

top of them before they could resist. A charge by a fragment of northern cavalry in an effort to stem the Rebel advance ended in failure. The retreat turned into a rout, leaving no time to finish destroying supplies or to take off the wounded. Many of the Federal troops dropped their guns as they raced out of town, feeling themselves lucky to escape at all. Banks rode among his shattered command and attempted to reform the broken ranks. "My God, men, don't you love your country?" he pleaded. "Yes," came a reply, "and I am trying to get to it as fast as I can."[15]

Banks finally rounded up a few small units of cavalry and some infantry to form a rear guard north of the town. Fortunately for the small band, Jackson's infantry was tired and his cavalry disorganized. Against orders, Ashby had taken his troopers on a ride around the Federal left flank and was not in position to pursue the remnants of Banks's army. The Confederates slackened their pace and gave up the pursuit. Even then, Banks could not reform his lines. By night the disorganized mass reached the Potomac River thirty-five miles from Strasburg. Crossing the river took another half day before the last of the beaten soldiers reached the safety of the Maryland shore.[16]

In Winchester, Jackson collected his exhausted army. Surgeons worked feverishly on the Confederate and Federal wounded while burial parties labored throughout the day burying the dead. Confederate casualties for the three days of running battles from Front Royal to Winchester had been some four hundred killed and wounded. Banks, however, had lost almost twenty-eight hundred men, of which some twenty-four hundred were prisoners. In addition, he had been driven from the Valley, leaving behind nine thousand small arms, two pieces of artillery, droves of sheep and cattle, and tons of food. What pleased Jackson's quartermaster, John Harman, even more was the vast amount of

15. *OR,* 12, pt. 1:617, 624–25; Bryant, *History of the Third Wisconsin,* 67–69; Marvin, *Fifth Connecticut,* 71, 99–100; Quint, *The Potomac and the Rapidan,* 140, 155, 159; Strother, *Virginia Yankee,* 42–43; Strother, "Personal Recollections," 445; *New York Tribune,* June 3, 6, 1862; *New York World,* May 31, 1862; Richard Cary to his wife (Helen), May 27, 1862, Cary Letters, MAHS; Richard C. Goodwin to his mother, May 30, 1862, Goodwin Papers, MAHS.

16. *OR,* 12, pt. 1:578–81, 596–98, 600–607, 705–7, 761–62; Dabney, *Life of Jackson,* 376–83; Strother, "Personal Recollections," 445–46; *New York World,* May 31, 1862; entry for May 25, 1862, Brooks Journal, SHC.

badly needed medical supplies that fell into Confederate hands. There were "more medical stores than you ever heard of," he reported. From that day forth, the major general from Massachusetts was known to Rebels and Yankees alike as "Commissary Banks."[17]

Licking his wounds north of the Potomac, Banks tried to minimize the extent of his defeat by reporting that "although serious," his losses had been "much less than might have been anticipated, considering the very great disparity of forces engaged and the long-matured plans of the enemy, which aimed at nothing less than entire capture of our force." Banks estimated that his casualties, including dead, wounded, and missing, did not exceed seven hundred. In reality, his losses were four times that number. Similarly, Banks also reported that he had saved all but fifty-five of his five hundred wagons, when the actual loss in government property was much greater. Banks also failed to mention the five hundred mules and horses that had been lost to his command and the destruction of stores that had been accumulated in Front Royal, Strasburg, and Winchester. The latter may have been worth almost half a million dollars.[18]

Banks's supporters defended the Bobbin Boy. "Plainly Gen. Banks was not to blame for the failure of his expedition," one newspaper argued. Supposedly, he had been sacrificed by the inept War Department. Banks's friends and even his wife urged him to criticize the administration openly for not having provided him with sufficient men. But Banks did not want to attack his superiors publicly or resign his commission in protest because that would mean lining up with the Republican radicals. Banks took pride in being able to do his duty "without grumbling" and kept his silence, hoping for the best.[19]

17. The actual figures for Union casualties were 62 dead, 243 wounded, and 1,714 captured or missing, which omits most of 750 hospitalized northerners taken in Front Royal and Strasburg. Jackson claimed to have taken 3,500 prisoners in his Valley campaign, mostly from Banks's command. Confederate losses for the campaign were 68 killed, 329 wounded, and 3 missing (*OR*, 12, pt. 1:530, 551–54, 570–71, 581, 707–8, 720–24, pt. 3:251–52). Banks indicated even larger losses on the back of a note dispatch to Banks from Franz Sigel, June 4, 1862, Banks Collection, LC.

18. *New York Tribune*, June 3, 6, 1862.

19. *Boston Daily Evening Traveller*, May 31, 1862; John A. Goodwin to Banks, June 6, 1862, Stephen Hoyt to Banks, June 8, 1862, Samuel O. Upham to Banks, June 16, 1862, Samuel Hooper to Banks, May 30, 1862, Banks to Mary Banks, May 28–29, June 6, 1862,

His strategy paid off, for Stanton said that Banks's retreat would actually help his reputation because "on this occasion as at all other times Gen. Banks has obeyed the orders from the War Department without one selfish complaint and was the only General of his rank of whom it could be said." At a time when the administration was trying to deal with McClellan, who had political ambitions of his own, Lincoln appreciated Banks's willingness to be a team player. But the officers and men in his command were not impressed. "I never complain at the hardships of war," wrote one officer to his wife, "but I cannot but complain when my life & the lives of those about me [are] placed in the hands of such a general as Banks."[20]

For his part, Banks continued to insist that he had not done poorly. "Whatever may be said of our recent movement," he declared in a letter to Mary on May 28, "I can assure you that it is one of the most remarkable that has occurred or will occur during the war. It is miraculous almost that my entire command and its train should escape without harm the long matured plans of an enemy five times our number." In truth, the statement was just another indication of Banks's unwillingness to learn from his mistakes, a defect that would become even more obvious two years later in the Red River Valley when Banks demonstrated conclusively that he had not learned the lessons the disastrous campaign in the Shenandoah Valley could have taught him.[21]

---

all in Banks Collection, LC. For a favorable assessment of Banks's generalship during the Shenandoah Valley campaign, see Colin R. Ballard, *The Military Genius of Abraham Lincoln* (Cleveland: World, 1965), 89.

20. Adam Gurowski, *Diary*, 3 vols. (Boston: Lea & Shepard, 1862–66), 1:212–13; Richard Cary to his wife (Helen), June 18, 1862, Cary Letters, MAHS; Irvin McDowell to Banks, June 5, 1862, Banks Collection, LC.

21. Banks to Mary Banks, May 28, 1862, Banks Collection, LC.

6

We Have Backed Out Enough

While Jackson parried with 70,000 Union troops in and around the Shenandoah Valley, George B. McClellan with an army of 110,000 well-supplied and well-trained men moved closer to the Confederate capital. On May 31, the Confederate commander of the army defending Richmond, Joseph E. Johnston, attempted to halt the Union advance at a place called Fair Oaks. The battle was a draw, but Johnston was wounded and had to step down from command. He was replaced by Robert E. Lee, who promptly drew up a new plan for defeating McClellan. Part of the plan involved recalling Jackson's army from the Valley and using it to fall on McClellan's exposed right flank northeast of the capital.

This audacious strategy was possible because the Federal armies in the Shenandoah Valley had had enough of Stonewall Jackson for a while. Following the battle of Port Republic, Frémont had retreated eighty miles down the Valley to Strasburg and beyond. Meanwhile, Banks had slowly inched his way back up the Valley, regaining the ground lost in his hasty retreat. Eventually, Banks, Frémont, and Shields linked up at Middletown, where they established a strong defensive line and waited for Jackson's next move. But Jackson had other plans. After allowing his army a week for rest and recuperation, he slipped away to join Lee and the newly designated Army of Northern Virginia.[1]

1. *OR,* 12, pt. 1:26, pt. 3:434, 583; Freeman, *Lee's Lieutenants,* 1:465–69, 490–91. Banks reoccupied Winchester on June 9, the same day Jackson bloodied Shields's nose at Port Republic.

As Jackson deployed his troops before Richmond, Lincoln reorganized Union troops in northern Virginia to form the Army of Virginia. Banks's command became the II Corps of the new army. Frémont and his troops from the Mountain Department constituted the I Corps, while Major General Irvin McDowell was named to command the III Corps, which was stationed just south of Washington. The army's new commander was Major General John Pope, fresh and confident from Union victories in the western theater. Although the reorganization of Union troops in northeastern Virginia was needed, there was a problem with Pope. All three of his corps commanders outranked their new commander. Frémont was furious and resigned his commission in protest. The two others, Banks and McDowell, chose to stay.[2]

John Pope was as arrogant as he was confident. A peacock from West Point, Pope openly expressed his dislike for political generals. This attitude did not mean that he disliked politicians, for Pope was a darling of the radical Republicans in Congress. But politicians in Washington and politicians in the field were two different things, and Pope was quick to blame Banks for the condition of the Union forces in the vicinity of Strasburg, which he described to McClellan as "much demoralized and broken down, and unfit for active service for the present." In addition, Pope did not like Banks's tendency to assume the defensive. "Dismiss any idea that there is any purpose whatever to retreat from the positions which you are instructed to take up," he admonished Banks, "or that there is any design whatever to await any attack of the enemy." Pope was trying to shame Banks into being an aggressive commander.[3]

Having pushed McClellan's huge army back down the peninsula in a series of hard-fought battles over a period of seven days, Lee turned his attention to the threat posed by Pope's new army to the north. On July 13, Lee ordered Jackson to start his men toward Gordonsville. Lee knew that Jackson did not have enough men to defeat Pope's army in open combat, but he promised to send A. P. Hill's strong division of six brigades from Richmond to Jackson's assistance. Even then, Jackson would

2. *OR*, 12, pt. 1:169; Mary Banks to Banks, June 27, 29, 30, 1862, Banks Collection, LC; Strother, "Personal Recollections," 733–34.

3. *OR*, 11, pt. 3:295, 12, pt. 3:472–74; T. Harry Williams, *Lincoln and the Radicals* (Madison: University of Wisconsin Press, 1941), 141–42.

not have more than half the troops that Pope had in the Army of Virginia. To be successful, Jackson had to find an opening for the sort of hard, quick offensive thrust that was his trademark. Recalling the success he had enjoyed the month before at Cross Keys and Port Republic, Jackson decided to move rapidly to Culpeper and place himself between two of the new Union army's three corps, hoping to defeat each separately.[4]

Jackson's offensive came at a time when Banks was not feeling very well. Bothered by ear trouble, diarrhea, and general exhaustion, he was also depressed over the prospects for a Union victory. Referring to the string of recent defeats in a letter to Mary, he wrote, "It was not strange that the People should feel sad. It does not seem that our affairs could be much worse."[5]

Banks's comment was more prophetic than he realized. Lincoln's new general in chief, Henry W. Halleck, decided to terminate the Peninsula Campaign and ordered McClellan's troops transferred to the Washington area to approach the Confederate capital from that direction. While McClellan's army was being repositioned, Pope decided to take the initiative and ordered Banks's corps to Culpeper, which put it on a collision course with Jackson. If Pope had concentrated all of his forces east of the Blue Ridge to meet Jackson, things might have turned out differently. As it was, Pope underestimated Jackson's strength while at the same time overestimating the number of men in Banks's command.[6]

Jackson reached Orange ahead of Banks and took up a position north of the town on August 4. During the next several days, the two sides maneuvered in a blistering summer heat that sent temperatures to the nineties. A lieutenant in the Fifty-second Virginia Infantry noted in his diary, "The weather's so hot men faint and die on the march." One of Banks's

4. *OR*, 12, pt. 2:176–77, 181, pt. 3:915; William Allan, *The Army of Northern Virginia in 1862* (Boston: Houghton Mifflin, 1892), 165–66; Daniel A. Grimsley, *Battles in Culpeper County, Virginia, 1861–1865* (Culpeper, Va.: Raleigh Travers Green, 1900), 26.

5. Banks to Mary Banks, July 22, 1862, Banks Collection, LC. A third corps of the Army of Virginia under Major General Franz Sigel remained in the Shenandoah Valley to guard against a Confederate advance along that corridor, but by early August had crossed the Blue Ridge and gone into camp at Sperryville.

6. *OR*, 12, pt. 1:186, 201, pt. 2:20–26, pt. 3:434, 498–99, 504, 527, 780, but see 488; Gordon, *From Brook Farm to Cedar Mountain*, 264, 286; William Allan, "Strength of the Forces under Pope and Lee," in *Papers of the Military Historical Society of Massachusetts*, Vol. 2 (Boston: Houghton Mifflin, 1895), 197–202.

brigade commanders recorded that "the atmosphere . . . was like that of a pest-house, from the number of dead animals lying about." In some regiments as many as eight or ten men died each day, which led the officer to remark sarcastically, "If we were not conforming to Pope's order to live on the country, we were doing the next thing to it,—we were dying on it."[7]

By the night of August 8, lead elements of Jackson's army were in position just south of Cedar Mountain, a low but distinctive prominence some ten miles north of Orange that rises suddenly out of the gentle landscape. In front of them were some Federal cavalry under Brigadier General George D. Bayard and a brigade of infantry commanded by Samuel W. Crawford. During the morning of August 9, the rest of Banks's corps moved south through Culpeper and closed on Crawford's position. Pope was confident. The day would see "the greatest battle of the season," he told a group of admirers at his headquarters; Pope planned "to ride right over him [Jackson] into Richmond," he assured them.[8]

In spite of Pope's confidence, Jackson was in a position to wield the upper hand. He had twenty thousand men as compared to some eight thousand troops under Banks, although another seven thousand Union reinforcements from McDowell were on their way. Once again, Banks found himself not only outgeneraled but also outnumbered.[9]

At 9:45 on the morning of August 9, Banks received an order from Pope. The order, which was delivered orally by Colonel Louis Marshall of Pope's staff, seemed to indicate that Banks should attack Jackson as he advanced. Realizing the importance of the directive, Banks had a member of his staff write it down, word for word, as Marshall dictated it: "General Banks to move to the front immediately, assume command of all forces in the front, deploy his skirmishers if the enemy advances, and

7. Gordon, *From Brook Farm to Cedar Mountain,* 277; Grimsley, *Battles in Culpeper County,* 26–27; Summer's diary quoted in Robert K. Krick, *Stonewall Jackson at Cedar Mountain* (Chapel Hill: University of North Carolina Press, 1990), 18.

8. Grimsley, *Battles in Culpeper County,* 26–27; *New York Tribune,* August 13, 1862.

9. William Allan, "Relative Numbers and Losses at Slaughter's Mountain," *Southern Historical Society Papers* 8 (April 1880): 178–83; Krick, *Stonewall Jackson at Cedar Mountain,* 45.

attack him immediately as he approaches, and be reenforced from here."[10]

The order was ambiguous, particularly since it directed Banks to assault a formidable enemy regardless of his strength or position. Banks sought out Pope for clarification. Pope would not elaborate but indicated that he had sent one of his staff officers who knew the Cedar Mountain area well to "designate the ground you are to hold, and will give you any instructions he may deem necessary." Although the word *hold* might have suggested that Pope's order to attack had been modified, Banks did not request clarification and rode to the front eager to redeem his reputation.[11]

The staff officer, Brigadier General Benjamin S. Roberts, was waiting. Possibly because he was a West Pointer who disliked political generals, Roberts goaded Banks as he pointed out the positions his men were to occupy. "There must be no backing out this day," he taunted. Then, for emphasis, he repeated the sentence half a dozen times: "No backing out this day; no backing out this day." Banks was offended by Roberts's remark, although he said nothing about it at the time. "I knew that my command did not want to back out," he testified later, "we had backed out enough."[12]

Roberts may have been familiar with the countryside, but the positions he selected for Banks's men were not the best on the field. In fact, Jackson had the advantage of position by being posted on Cedar Mountain with artillery and two infantry divisions hidden in the woods on the west side of the mountain. Although Banks reported that his troops "panted for a fight," Jackson's men were ready, too. When Hunter McGuire, Jackson's trusted physician and staff member, asked on the morning of August 9 whether he expected a battle that day, Jackson smiled and

10. U.S. Congress, Joint Committee, *Report of the Joint Committee on the Conduct of the War, at the Second Session Thirty-Eighth Congress (Miscellaneous)* (Washington, D.C.: U.S. Government Printing Office, 1865), 45; Freeman, *Lee's Lieutenants*, 2:21.

11. *OR*, 12, pt. 2:25–27, 133–35; W. W. Rowley to Banks, May 1, 1865, Banks Collection, LC. For Banks's view, see U.S. Congress, *Report of the Joint Committee on the Conduct of the War*, 44–46; for Pope's view, see ibid., 47–51. Also see George Leonard Andrews, "The Battle of Cedar Mountain," *Papers of the Military Historical Society of Massachusetts*, Vol. 2 (Boston: Houghton Mifflin, 1895), 405–14; and Kenneth P. Williams, *Lincoln Finds a General: A Military Study of the Civil War*, 5 vols. (New York: Macmillan, 1949–59), 1:267, 424.

12. *OR*, 12, pt. 3:547; U.S. Congress, *Report of the Joint Committee on the Conduct of the War*, 46, 48.

responded, "Banks is in our front and he is generally willing to fight. And," he added slowly, almost to himself, "he generally gets whipped."[13]

After some skirmishing, artillery on both sides opened a hot and furious barrage around two o'clock in the afternoon. The southern guns were in a better position and could either support a Confederate advance or check an attack by sweeping Federal units with a strong crossfire. Given the strength of the Confederate position, Banks should have been more cautious. He knew nothing of Jackson's strength and little about the terrain, and his reinforcements were still far in the rear. In addition, there was little cover for advancing troops between him and the enemy.[14]

Around four o'clock, Banks saw gray-coated soldiers creeping up, looking to pick off Union gunners in their exposed position. In response, he ordered his infantry to advance. Finding Jackson stronger than he anticipated, Banks continued to commit his troops until the entire center of his line, essentially the bulk of his command, was engaged. The Confederate line began stretching to the left as more troops arrived on the field. In front of them, a Federal division of three brigades under Christopher C. Augur formed into a battle line as the Confederate and Union artillery continued to duel.[15]

With the heavy line of skirmishers in front, the Union troops advanced against the Confederate position just before six o'clock. Banks did not realize when he ordered Augur to attack that he was outnumbered. But Banks had been stung by Pope's intimation that he would not fight, and Roberts's chiding had only served to goad him further. As it turned out, even though he was attacking a stronger opponent, Banks almost won.[16]

The brigades under Henry Prince and John W. Geary ran into a withering fire as they worked their way across a cornfield. Southern muskets

13. U.S. Congress, *Report of the Joint Committee on the Conduct of the War,* 46, 51–53; Gordon, *From Brook Farm to Cedar Mountain,* 282; Hunter H. McGuire, *Address by Dr. Hunter McGuire . . . on 23rd day of June, 1897* (Lynchburg, Va.: J. P. Bell, Co. for the Virginia Military Institute, 1897), 6.

14. *OR,* 12, pt. 2:146–47, 161, 163–64, 237–38; *New York World,* August 12, 15, 1862.

15. U.S. Congress, *Report of the Joint Committee on the Conduct of the War,* 46; Philip Slaughter, *A Sketch of the Life of Randolph Fairfax,* 2d ed. (Richmond: Tyler, Allegre & McDaniel, Enquirer Job Office, 1864), 30.

16. Krick, *Stonewall Jackson at Cedar Mountain,* 117–41.

cut into the lines as Stonewall's artillery found its range. Prince was taken prisoner, and Geary and Augur were wounded. The center of the Union advance soon became bogged down in a bitter fight. Banks then ordered Crawford's brigade to hit the Confederate left. The decision was aggressive, even foolhardy, because Crawford's brigade was outnumbered by the force holding the position it was ordered to attack. Nevertheless, Crawford sent his troops forward and found that a combination of surprise and luck enabled his relatively small unit to roll up the Confederate flank. In quick succession, the Union troops drove back a half dozen Confederate regiments in confusion.[17]

Crawford's brigade continued to move down the Confederate line, and within thirty minutes two more Confederate brigades were driven from their positions. For a moment, it seemed as if Crawford's assault would carry the day. Onward they charged, reforming when their lines broke under fire and striking hard. "Our troops never fought better," exulted Banks as Crawford's dwindling force slashed down the Confederate left flank.[18]

The tide appeared to have turned in favor of the boys in blue as the southern troops gave way. But the further it pressed the attack, the weaker Crawford's brigade became, while in its wake the Confederate troops it had scattered began to rally. The catalyst for the Confederate counterattack was Jackson himself. In a highly unusual display, Stonewall rode among his men attempting to draw his sword to inspire them. Unfortunately, the sword had rusted in its scabbard. Undaunted, Stonewall unbuckled the scabbard and waved it over his head with the sword still sheathed. Dropping his reins, he grabbed a Confederate battle flag with his other hand. With sword and flag held high, he yelled above the cacophony of battle: "Rally, brave men, and press forward. Your general will lead you. Jackson will lead you. Follow me!"[19]

This episode was possibly the most heroic moment of Jackson's life, and its effect was electric. Confederate soldiers who had been heading to

17. *OR,* 12, pt. 2:157–61, 167–70; Krick, *Stonewall Jackson at Cedar Mountain,* 142–201.

18. *OR,* 12, pt. 2:181–85, 214–16, 221–23; U.S. Congress, *Report of the Joint Committee on the Conduct of the War,* 46; Gordon, *From Brook Farm to Cedar Mountain,* 294–95; Worsham, *One of Jackson's Foot Cavalry,* 109–15.

19. Charles Minor Blackford, *Letters from Lee's Army* (New York: Charles Scribner's Sons, 1947), 105; Krick, *Stonewall Jackson at Cedar Mountain,* 202–7; Jedediah Hotchkiss to G. F. R. Henderson, September 5, 1896, Jedediah Hotchkiss Papers, LC.

the rear moments before turned to counterattack. Even more important than Jackson's gesture, however, was the timely arrival of reinforcements, fresh brigades from A. P. Hill's division, which swung into action to fill the void caused by Crawford's brave charge. Their arrival was particularly timely because Crawford's attack had lost its momentum. Banks had failed to follow up the initial success with reinforcements, and now these exhausted troops had to retreat along a course that would take them directly in front of the lowered muskets of the fresh Rebel brigades. The result was a maelstrom of crossfire that inflicted more damage than the brigade had yet endured. "The slaughter was fearful," Crawford recorded in his report. Two-thirds of his officers and half of his men were killed, wounded, or captured in fifteen minutes. Colonel Dudley Donnelly fell mortally wounded at the head of his regiment. The fire was so devastating that all of the field officers in three of his four regiments were either killed or wounded, and one regiment, the Twenty-eighth New York, lost all of its company officers as well.[20]

Banks sat on his horse at the edge of the woods, watching Crawford's attack dissolve. He had already diminished the chances for success by withholding one of the brigade's largest regiments, the Tenth Maine, to support a Federal battery that was some distance to the rear. These men would have done much to help carry Crawford's attack through to the end had they been allowed to move forward with their comrades. Now that it was too late, Banks decided to send this unit into battle alone.

The Tenth Maine closed ranks and marched forward, stopping on the crest of the hillock in the middle of a wheat field, where its men stood silhouetted as targets along the skyline for fresh Confederate troops positioned in the relative safety of woods some 150 yards away. What followed was unmitigated carnage. Bullets slammed into the men, knocking them over or causing "a sudden jump or shudder." One officer of the ill-fated regiment reported that so many men were hit that "it looked as if we had a crowd of howling dervishes dancing and kicking around in our ranks." In a matter of minutes 173 men in the Tenth Maine fell, killed or wounded. That was more than 40 percent of the men the regiment took into battle.[21]

20. *OR,* 12, pt. 2:146–47, 150–52; Krick, *Stonewall Jackson at Cedar Mountain,* 209–21.

21. John M. Gould, *History of the First-Tenth-Twenty-ninth Maine Regiments* (Portland, Me.: Stephen Berry, 1871), 174–76; Krick, *Stonewall Jackson at Cedar Mountain,* 220–31.

Unfortunately, Banks's piecemeal use of his limited troops was not over. As the survivors of the Tenth Maine stumbled back across the wheat field, Banks ordered a small squadron of 164 cavalrymen to charge the Confederate line. Ostensibly, Banks ordered the ill-judged charge to save some Union artillery that was exposed by the collapse of the Federal attack. Just before seven o'clock a small four-company battalion from the First Pennsylvania Cavalry under Major Richard Falls galloped forward into the waiting rifles of the Confederate line.[22]

The mounted men were no match for the Confederate infantry in the woods. Horses and men went down like so many ducks in a shooting gallery. The Pennsylvanians had scarcely gotten to the Confederate lines before they recoiled in every direction. One group that survived turned to the right and ran the gauntlet in front of James J. Archer's Confederate brigade. As the survivors headed for their own lines, they mixed with remnants of Crawford's brigade making their way back to safety. Only 71 of the 164 men who participated in the futile charge were present for duty the next day.[23]

As the survivors of the First Pennsylvania Cavalry regained the shelter of the woods east of the wheat field, common sense called for Banks to fall back while there was still time. Yet Banks continued to hurry forward every Federal soldier he could find. He ordered George S. Greene's brigade to advance over the ground that had been gained and then lost by Prince and Geary. Southern guns were still in command and littered the field with dead and dying. Banks also ordered Gordon's brigade forward on the right to regain the sector that Crawford had been forced to yield.[24]

Gordon's brigade was the only fresh Federal unit on the entire battlefield, but it was no match for the Confederates and quickly gave way. Meanwhile, Brigadier General Lawrence O'Bryan Branch's brigade of North Carolinians from A. P. Hill's division struck the remnants of Augur's shattered command. As the victorious Confederates swarmed in and around the disintegrating Federal units, chaos and darkness de-

22. Krick, *Stonewall Jackson at Cedar Mountain,* 232–50.

23. *OR,* 12, pt. 2:139, 141.

24. *OR,* 12, pt. 2:147–49, 153–57; Allan, *Army of Northern Virginia,* 174–75; Gordon, *From Brook Farm to Cedar Mountain,* 303–12; Pyne, *History of the First New Jersey Cavalry,* 86–87; *Boston Morning Journal,* August 28, 1886; *New York Tribune,* August 19, 1862; *New York World,* August 12, 15, 1862.

scended on the battlefield. For good measure, Jackson threw two more brigades from Ewell's division into the fight from their positions on Cedar Mountain. As the Confederates advanced, many Federal soldiers found themselves surrounded and threw up their hands to surrender. Banks did what he could to stem an impending rout. On several occasions he exposed himself by taking positions along the skirmish line at points where he refused to allow his staff to follow because of the danger. Nevertheless, the odds were too great and his coordination of the Federal attacks too poor to allow for victory that day.[25]

Banks finally gave the order to withdraw as dusk settled, leaving the Confederates in possession of the field of battle. Union casualties numbered twenty-four hundred, almost a third of Banks's command. Although it was clearly a Confederate victory, this was no Front Royal or Winchester. Even after the last repulse, the Union soldiers withdrew only as far as their positions of that morning. Reinforced by James B. Rickett's division from McDowell's corps that night, they yielded no more ground.[26]

Pope joined Banks on the field of battle after dark. The two men and several other high-ranking Union officers had dismounted and were seated on the ground under some trees, discussing the day's events, when they heard a trampling sound in the woods about forty yards away. It was Confederate cavalry under William E. "Grumble" Jones probing behind Federal lines in the bright moonlight. Spotting the prize, the Rebels charged as the Union officers jumped to their feet and raced for their horses. Bullets flew, and an orderly took a mortal wound. His horse, struck by a stray shot, reared in terror, striking Banks on the left hip with its forefoot. Banks went down but got to his feet and painfully mounted his own horse to escape in the confusion.[27]

25. Krick, *Stonewall Jackson at Cedar Mountain,* 283–98.

26. Allan, *Army of Northern Virginia,* 177; Quint, *The Potomac and the Rapidan,* 192. Banks lost over 500 killed, 400 captured, the rest wounded; Jackson's losses were 250 killed and missing, 1,000 wounded (*OR,* 12, pt. 2:28, 136–39, 145–49, 179–80, 184–85).

27. English Combatant, *Battle-fields of the South: From Bull Run to Fredericksburg* (New York: J. Bradburn, 1864), 429–30; Gordon, *From Brook Farm to Cedar Mountain,* 320–23; Strother, *Virginia Yankee,* 77; Banks to Mary Banks, August 16, 1862, "How Banks was injured at the time of the Battle of Cedar Mountain" (undated [189?] MSS), Banks Collection, LC; also entry for August 12, 1862, in George H. Gordon Diary, 1862–63, Gordon Papers, MAHS.

The battle at Cedar Mountain made it clear that the Yankees had learned to fight. In addition, it could not be denied that Banks had been courageous under fire. Pope, who was no fan of the major general from Massachusetts, wrote Halleck a few days after the battle in praise of his corps commander. "I cannot speak too highly of the intrepidity and coolness of General Banks himself during the whole of the engagement," Pope wrote. "He was in the front and exposed as much as any man in his command. His example was of the greatest benefit to his troops, and he merits and should receive the commendation of his Government." Even Stonewall Jackson had been impressed. "I think General Banks a better officer than his people think he is," Jackson remarked to Jeb Stuart after the battle. "I always found he fought well." Stuart, ever the joker, quipped in response, "Well, General, you at least have no reason to complain; indeed it would be ungrateful if you did, for he has been the best commissary and quartermaster you ever had!"[28]

In Washington, praise and criticism for Banks's showing at Cedar Mountain was divided along political lines. Halleck and the administration felt that Banks had accomplished a "hard earned but brilliant success against superior numbers." The radicals, however, claimed that he had muffed his chances by disobeying Pope in attacking before support was near. The moderates responded by blaming Pope for ordering Banks to fight and then failing to send reinforcements.[29]

In reality, those from whom Banks won respect were applauding his courage more than his skill. His attacks on Jackson's position had been uncoordinated and piecemeal. Furthermore, he had ordered his troops forward with little understanding or knowledge of the force he was facing or how the enemy was positioned. Even then, Banks almost pulled off a remarkable victory when Crawford's brigade unexpectedly rolled up the Confederate left flank. But he had failed to exploit Crawford's initial success, which withered in the face of stiffening Confederate resistance. The men who had fought at Cedar Mountain knew this to be the case. "The action was totally unnecessary," George L. Andrews, who later served as Banks's chief of staff in Louisiana, wrote his wife. It was,

28. *OR,* 12, pt. 2:134; Douglas, *I Rode with Stonewall,* 50.

29. *OR,* 12, pt. 2:135. See T. Harry Williams, "General Banks and the Radical Republicans in the Civil War," *New England Quarterly* 12 (June 1939): 268–80, for an extended discussion of this dispute.

he added, "about as great a piece of folly as I have ever witnessed on the part of an incompetent general."[30]

As it turned out, there was blame enough for all. Pope's instructions had been vague, and his staff work had been shoddy. Furthermore, Pope failed to capitalize on the slight advantage Banks did gain by blocking Jackson at Cedar Mountain, for he neglected to move against the Confederates while they stood still before him for two days. This failure allowed Jackson's army to slip away on August 11 and soon march on Pope's supply base at Manassas Junction, which it plundered and destroyed.[31]

The remainder of Pope's army finally caught up with Jackson on August 28. Waiting for Lee and the rest of the Army of Northern Virginia to join him, Jackson beat off numerous stubborn attempts by Pope to crush his isolated force. After much savage fighting, Lee's army arrived and combined with Jackson to send the erstwhile Union Army of Virginia reeling back toward the defenses of Washington. Traveling painfully toward the capital by ambulance, Banks received news of the second battle of Bull Run from his brother, Captain Gardner Banks, who met him en route. Gardner had more bad news; their brother Hiram, a second lieutenant in the Sixteenth Massachusetts Infantry, had been killed in the fighting on August 29.[32]

News reached the capital on September 1 that Lee was moving north and possibly would cross the Potomac. Lincoln quickly put McClellan back in command of all Union forces in Virginia. He appointed Banks commander of Union troops stationed in Washington and ordered him

30. U.S. Congress, *Report of the Joint Committee on the Conduct of the War,* 53; *New York Tribune,* August 11, 1862; George L. Andrews to his wife, August 12, 1863, Andrews Papers, MHI.

31. *OR,* 12, pt. 2:11. Both Henderson (*Stonewall Jackson,* 416–17) and Freeman (*Lee's Lieutenants,* 2:44–46) criticize Jackson's tactics and management of this portion of the campaign.

32. "How Banks was injured," Banks Collection, LC; Gardner Banks to his wife, September 1, 1862, in the *Waltham Sentinel,* September 5, 1862; Banks family marker in the Waltham cemetery, Waltham, Massachusetts; *Official Army Register of the Volunteer Force of the United States Army for the Year 1861, '62, '63, '64, '65,* 8 vols. (1865; reprint, Gaithersburg, Md.: Ron R. Van Sickle Military Books, 1987), 1:170. Another brother, William, succumbed to fever and died the following month (Susan P. Banks [Banks's sister] to Banks, September 28, 1862, Banks Collection, LC). For a complete account of the campaign, see John J. Hennessy, *Return to Bull Run: The Campaign and Battle of Second Manassas* (New York: Simon & Schuster, 1993).

to organize the defense of the capital. Anxiously, McClellan and Banks waited to see what Lee would do next.

On September 13, McClellan received an exceptional piece of good luck. A careless Confederate aide had dropped a copy of Lee's marching orders, and a Union officer picked it up. This windfall gave McClellan all the information he needed, and he moved quickly toward Lee's widely scattered army. McClellan caught up with Lee on September 15 at the town of Sharpsburg on the Potomac River. Lee was outnumbered, but in the battle two days later McClellan sent his men forward in uncoordinated and desperate attacks. Lee countered these moves skillfully and defended his position. Although fresh Union troops arrived to join in the battle on September 18, McClellan refused to renew the contest, and Lee recrossed the Potomac into Virginia later that night.[33]

33. *OR*, 19, pt. 2:202, 214.

7

Even Thieves Take Off Their Hats

After the Battle of Antietam the war in the East settled into a stalemate when McClellan decided not to advance further until better weather in the spring. In the western theater, however, the situation looked considerably brighter for the North. After taking New Orleans in April, David G. Farragut had proceeded up the Mississippi River. Defenseless against the guns of his fleet, both Baton Rouge and Natchez had surrendered. Farragut then ran past the incomplete Confederate fortifications at Vicksburg to link up with the Union flotilla south of Memphis. Had more Federal troops been available at the time, Vicksburg could have been taken and held. But the opportunity was missed, and the Confederates quickly strengthened their fortifications both at Vicksburg and further down the river at Port Hudson, some sixteen miles north of Baton Rouge. Nevertheless, Federal forces were in control of a large portion of Tennessee down to Memphis and well positioned in New Orleans near the mouth of the Mississippi River. The year 1863 promised to bring the opportunity for concerted movement of Union armies both up and down the great waterway.

In preparation for these operations, Lincoln ordered John A. McClernand, a politician-general from Illinois, to organize troops for an advance on Vicksburg from Memphis. This movement would coincide with a parallel thrust by Ulysses S. Grant overland from northern Mississippi toward Vicksburg. At the same time, Lincoln decided to send a force from New Orleans up the river. Not only would this offensive cause a diversion and draw off Confederate forces that otherwise would oppose Grant and McClernand, but it would also increase the amount of territory under Union control. Lincoln picked Nathaniel P. Banks for the job on November 9, 1862, and ordered him to New York to organize troops for a campaign against Vicksburg in the spring.[1]

Banks was to replace Benjamin F. Butler as commander of the Department of the Gulf. Lincoln decided to remove Butler from command in part because Butler had caused problems for the administration by his hostile treatment of foreign consuls in the Crescent City, thereby increasing the prospect of foreign intervention. In addition, many northerners felt that Butler's aggressive antislavery tactics, which included accepting black soldiers into the Union army, had been too extreme. Most important, Lincoln believed that Butler's no-nonsense approach and blunt manner had impeded the emergence of Unionist sentiment among the citizens of New Orleans.[2]

Banks's assignment to New Orleans was a reflection of Lincoln's appreciation of his loyalty to the administration as well as his ability to avoid the political intrigues that had sidetracked such of his fellow officers as Frémont and McClellan. Lincoln was also aware that Banks was popular in the North, despite the two thrashings he had suffered at the hands of Stonewall Jackson, and the president counted on Banks's continued popularity to strengthen the war effort. But there was more to Lincoln's decision to send Banks to New Orleans than party loyalty and personal popularity. Lincoln had plans for Louisiana, for it was there that he would experiment with a strategy to coax seceded states back into the Union. Thus the assignment was a vote of confidence in Banks's political

1. *OR,* 15:590–91.

2. Thomas Ewing Dabney, "The Butler Regime in Louisiana," *Louisiana Historical Quarterly* 27 (April 1944): 487–526; Howard Palmer Johnson, "New Orleans under General Butler," *Louisiana Historical Quarterly* 24 (April 1941): 507–16; Trefousse, *Ben Butler,* 130–32; West, *Lincoln's Scapegoat General,* 192–204; T. Harry Williams, *Lincoln and His Generals* (New York: Knopf, 1952), 188–89. For Banks's view that concern over foreign intervention was a factor in deciding to organize his expedition, see *Boston Daily Evening Traveller,* December 4, 1862, and his letter to Mary Banks, February 26, 1863, Banks Collection, LC. Also see *OR,* 15:590–91, 619–21, 53:545–46; Butler, *Private and Official Correspondence,* 2:584; Denison to Chase, December 17, 1862, in Chase, "Diary and Correspondence," 340–41; Moncure Daniel Conway, *Autobiography, Memories and Experiences of Moncure Daniel Conway,* 2 vols. (Boston: Houghton Mifflin, 1904), 1:375–76; Charles A. Peabody, "United States Provisional Court for the State of Louisiana, 1862–1865," *Annual Report of the American Historical Association, 1892* (Washington, D.C.: U.S. Government Printing Office, 1893), 199–210; *New Orleans Daily True Delta,* December 27, 1862; *New York Herald,* July 25, 1863.

expertise and the skill with which he had handled the Department of Annapolis more than a year before.[3]

Banks established the headquarters for his Louisiana expedition in New York. To confuse the enemy and silence the radicals who supported Butler, Lincoln decided to keep Banks's destination secret, although rumors that Banks was to replace Butler had begun to circulate even before the decision was made. Only Banks, President Lincoln, Secretary of War Stanton, Secretary of State Seward, General in Chief Halleck, and Cornelius Vanderbilt (who chartered vessels for the operation) knew where he was going. Even the secretary of the navy, Gideon Welles, was kept in the dark, as were the governors of New York and the New England states, although they were asked to provide troops for the expedition. The need for secrecy called for political dexterity as Banks toured the Northeast, conferring with the governors and gaining their cooperation without providing details of the plan.[4]

By the end of November, Banks had assembled the men for his expeditionary force, but there were still problems that had to be resolved before he was ready to get under way. The troops consisted entirely of new recruits who were yet to be trained. There were also serious logistical problems. Supplies and equipment were delayed, and when they arrived, they proved to be more than the transports could handle. To make matters worse, Banks left the matter of organizing the expedition to subordinates who did not understand its objective. Given the confusion, Banks wanted to delay his departure as long as possible, but Lincoln pressed him to move. He needed Banks in Louisiana before the Emancipation Proclamation took effect on New Year's Day 1863.[5]

Banks finally agreed to leave on December 4, 1862, and boarded a

3. Cox, *Lincoln and Black Freedom,* 52; Alvin M. Josephy, *The Civil War in the American West* (New York: Knopf, 1991), 161; George S. Merriam, *The Life and Times of Samuel Bowles,* 2 vols. (New York: Century, 1885), 1:303. For the definitive account of Lincoln's use of Louisiana as an experiment, see Peyton McCrary, *Abraham Lincoln and Reconstruction: The Louisiana Experiment* (Princeton: Princeton University Press, 1978).

4. *OR,* Ser. 3, 2:691–92, 705–6, 712–13; Robert S. Holzman, *Stormy Ben Butler* (New York: Macmillan, 1954), 103; Richard B. Irwin, *History of the Nineteenth Army Corps* (1892; reprint, Baton Rouge: Elliott's Book Shop Press, 1985), 56; George Winston Smith, "The Banks Expedition of 1862," *Louisiana Historical Quarterly* 26 (April 1943): 353–54; Welles, *Diary,* 1:209–10; Robert S. Denison to Chase, November 28, 1862, in Chase, "Diary and Correspondence," 332.

5. Harrington, *Fighting Politician,* 87; Williams, *Lincoln and His Generals,* 189–90.

steamer at three o'clock that afternoon for the short trip to the flotilla in the East River. He was joined by the mayor of New York, Commodore Cornelius Vanderbilt, and a dozen other officers and dignitaries. Once the steamer was under way, the party retired to the salon on the boat to drink a toast to the success of the expedition. Praising the men in his new command, Banks proclaimed, "We go to uphold the flag of the Union and sustain the constitution, and may God grant that we may be successful." The party drank another toast with much cheering and the cry for Banks to "go on; go on." Banks rose again. "There is a point where I shall stop talking," he declared. "I have now reached that point," he announced as he resumed his seat amid much laughter. At seven o'clock in the evening, Banks boarded the *North Star* and ordered the expedition out to sea.[6]

It was fortunate that the fifty transports chartered by the government reached their destination. Many were old, unseaworthy vessels that had been hastily assembled for the expedition. Several were rotten, "totally unfit for transporting troops outside . . . any harbor." The *Niagara*, for example, was an old side-wheeler built in 1845 for the Great Lakes trade. She set out with 450 men of the Fiftieth Massachusetts Infantry and only one hundred life preservers. Once she reached open water, the *Niagara* listed so heavily to one side that she made only five knots in a smooth sea. When a wave knocked off a plank on the deck, an officer found the beams "so rotten that . . . I pushed my fingers into the timbers as though it was soil or mere earth, not wood at all." The *Niagara* barely made it to Philadelphia, where she was condemned by a Federal inspector.[7]

Other ships in the flotilla were suited only for inland waters even if they were in good condition, and all were seriously overloaded. Furthermore, no one bothered to set a limit on supplies or to establish standard quotas for each regiment. Nor did anyone check on storage space before it came time to load. The result was that every vessel was jammed with soldiers and piled high with quartermaster stores.[8]

A Senate committee later charged that Vanderbilt had chartered "all sorts of crazy and leaky vessels" for the expedition. Although the com-

6. *New York Herald*, December 5, 1862; S. B. Holabird to Captain Lefevre of the *North Star*, December 4, 1862, Banks Collection, LC.

7. U.S. Congress, Senate, Select Committee, *Senate Report No. 75: Vessels for the Banks Expedition*, 37th Cong., 3d sess., 7–12, 15, 27–28, 74–75.

8. Ibid., 27–30, 42; Lawrence Van Alstyne, *Diary of an Enlisted Man* (New Haven:

modore received no compensation for his efforts, one witness said that he clearly showed a "want of that skill and forecast which the government had a right to expect in those who share its confidence and accept places of responsibility." The problem was confounded because the government inspectors did not know Banks's destination and thought that perhaps he was headed for Virginia. Actually, the flotilla had to make it past the treacherous waters off Cape Hatteras and around the Florida keys on its voyage to New Orleans.[9]

One young officer from Connecticut who shipped out on the transport *Mary Bordman* described the voyage in a letter to his mother:

> The cabin where we sleep is too low for a six-footer to stand upright in except between the beams of the deck above. In this space there are three tiers of bunks made of rough boards, and each man in consequence has less than two feet in height and in width has eighteen inches; in length, four feet six inches—(I am four feet eight inches tall) and in this small space each man is expected to stow himself and all his traps. Between the two sides where the bunks are, a double row of rifle boxes is laid and on these company B sleeps—rather poor beds, but they have more room overhead. My bunk is near the end, and near a port hole usually open and once in a while a breath of pure air comes in, but the atmosphere of the place at night, with over three hundred men sleeping or trying to sleep in it, is perfectly awful.[10]

The expedition's horses were stabled on the lower decks, and the smell from below became almost unbearable as the temperature climbed during the trip south. When weather allowed, the men sprawled in groups on the decks, passing the time and playing every card game imaginable. Other diversions included making trinkets such as

---

Tuttle, Morehouse & Taylor, 1910), 68–72; Diary entries for December 28, 29, 30, 1862, in James F. Dargan, *My Experiences in Service: Or a Nine Months Man* (Los Angeles: California State University, Northridge, Libraries, for the Bibliographic Society of California State University, Northridge, 1974); *New York Herald*, December 17, 1862.

9. U.S. Congress, *Senate Report No. 75*, 1–6, 57, 62, 101; Irwin, *History of the Nineteenth Army Corps*, 57; *New York Herald*, December 5, 1862; *New York Times*, January 31, 1863; *New York Tribune*, December 23, 1862; Mary Banks to Banks, January 4, 1863, Banks Collection, LC. Also see U.S. Congress, Senate, Select Committee, *Senate Report No. 84: Employment of Transport Vessels*, 37th Cong., 3d sess.

10. *Memorial of Lt. Daniel Perkins Dewey, of the Twenty-Fifth Regiment, Connecticut Volunteers* (Hartford: Press of Cage, Lockwood, 1864), 39.

finger rings from beef bones. Finally, the lead ships put in at Ship Island in the Mississippi Sound on December 12. Banks arrived on the *North Star* the following day. After taking some sherry "to steady their sea legs & stomachs," Banks and his staff went to work to prepare the men for their new assignment. Within a week all was ready, and Banks steamed into New Orleans to replace Butler as commander of the Department of the Gulf.[11]

Not everyone was pleased to learn of Banks's arrival. The radicals had expected him to go to Texas to set up a Unionist government there. When they learned that he had relieved their champion, Butler, they cried out in protest. Butler promptly returned to the North, where he was well received at grand receptions and lauded for his strict administration of the department. "It would seem from the papers that he had been faultless in his course in New Orleans," wrote Mary Banks to her husband. "I am quite surprised that he should be removed if all the papers say of him is correct."[12]

As pressure from the radicals mounted, Lincoln agreed that Butler could return to Louisiana but asked that "the whole [matter] must be so managed as not to wrong or wound the feelings of General Banks." He thought that Banks might go on to Texas or even lead a column against Port Hudson while Butler resumed command of New Orleans. But this was not to be, for Butler realized he had little to gain by returning to Louisiana. Having made his point, Butler rejoiced in a "personal vindication" and ignored the advice of fellow radicals to accept the offer. Banks was on his own in the lower Mississippi Valley.[13]

11. Entries for December 12, 13, 1862, Henry Rust, Jr., Diary, MHI. For an interesting description of life on a transport during a voyage to Ship Island and New Orleans, see William H. Eastman to his father, May 1, 1862, Eastman Letters, MAHS. Some of the transports, such as the *Baltic,* drew so much water that they were unable to cross the bar at the mouth of the Mississippi River, which meant that the troops on these vessels had to be off-loaded onto Ship island and reboarded on lighter-draft ships after they unloaded their human cargo in the Crescent City. As a result, the expedition arrived in New Orleans over a period of several weeks (George Whitfield Powers, *Story of the Thirty-Eighth Regiment of Massachusetts Volunteers* [Cambridge, Mass.: Dankin & Metcalf, 1866], 29).

12. U.S. Congress, *Senate Report No. 75,* 20, 42, 51–52; Holzman, *Stormy Ben Butler,* 109; West, *Lincoln's Scapegoat General,* 205–16; Mary Banks to Banks, January 4, 1863, Banks Collection, LC; *Congressional Globe,* 37th Cong., 3d sess., 1863, 584–86.

13. Lincoln to Stanton, January 23, 1863, *OR,* 53:547; Butler, *Private and Official*

• • •

The remainder of Banks's expeditionary force continued to arrive throughout January and into February 1863. Union troops who had been in the city since it fell viewed the new arrivals with much skepticism and some contempt. "A greener set of men I never saw," wrote one young soldier to his mother, adding that "they gawk around like so many countrymen." Their reaction was not unusual, given the strange and uncommon sights of America's most "un-American" city. One new arrival from Rhode Island was very much impressed when he slipped away his first night and attended a masked ball. "[I] went to [a] masked ball . . . an institution that I never expected to see," he reported to his family, "but they have them every week."[14]

Banks's new appointment as commander of the Department of the Gulf was one of the most challenging assignments in the Union army. "I find . . . on arriving here," he informed Halleck, "an immense military government, embracing every form of civil administration, the assessment of taxes, fines, punishments, charities, trade, regulation of churches, confiscation of estates, and the working of plantations, in addition to the ordinary affairs of a military department." And he had to deal with another problem—widespread corruption and rampant theft. "Everybody connected with the government has been employed in stealing other people's property," Banks wrote Mary shortly after assuming command. "Sugar, silver plate, horses, carriages, everything they could lay hands on" had been confiscated.[15]

Banks began his tenure as commander by ordering members of his

---

Correspondence, 2:584, 587, 3:15, 16, 21–27, 120, 123–25; Holzman, *Stormy Ben Butler,* 108; Ludwell H. Johnson, *Red River Campaign: Politics and Cotton in the Civil War* (1958; reprint, Gaithersburg, Md.: Butternut Press, 1986), 30–31.

14. *OR,* 15:923; William H. Eastman to his mother, December 22, 1862, Eastman Letters, MAHS; William H. Stevens to "Dear Molly," William H. Stevens Papers, SHC. The masked ball the soldier referred to was probably one of the dances held in public ballrooms that were popular in New Orleans before the war (R. Randall Couch, "The Public Masked Balls of Antebellum New Orleans: A Custom of Masque Outside the Mardi Gras Tradition," *Louisiana History* 35 [Fall 1994]: 403–31). Banks forbade the observance of Mardi Gras in 1863, but many residents of the city celebrated the carnival anyway (Elisabeth Joan Doyle, "Civilian Life in Occupied New Orleans, 1862–65" [Ph.D. dissertation, Louisiana State University, 1955], 204).

15. *OR,* 15:639; Banks to Mary Banks, January 3, 15, 1863, Banks Collection, LC; Banks to W. L. Garrison, January 30, 1865, *Liberator,* February 24, 1865.

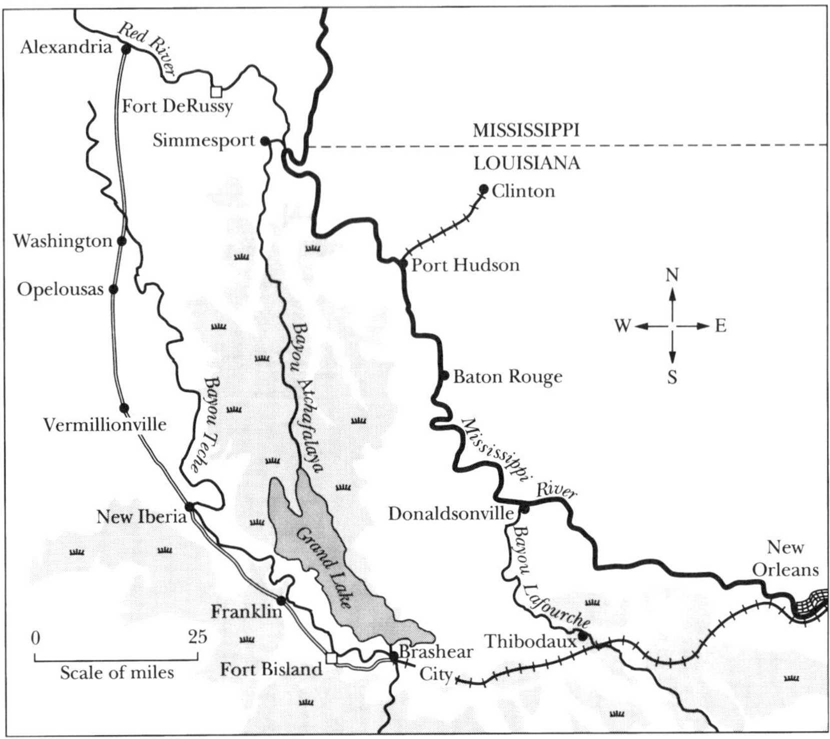

South Louisiana in 1863

staff to make an inspection of his new command. Their report was disturbing. Butler had detached his best officers for civil jobs and neglected engineering work. As a result, the fortifications built to defend the city were inadequate and ammunition for the guns was "very deficient." There were few records, and those that had been kept had disappeared. Banks could not even find out how many prisoners he was holding in the various forts or who they were. In short, the Union forces in south Louisiana were in a state of disarray after eight months of Butler's negligence, "a neglect," Banks remarked in a letter to Mary, that was "not only discreditable but almost treasonable."[16]

Adding to his problems, Banks found that his troops, most of whom had never been in the South before, fell easy prey to disease. Although

16. *OR,* 15:648–54; Banks to Mary Banks, January 22, 24, March 14, 1863, Banks Collection, LC. For an idea of the size and administrative responsibilities of Banks's staff see the *New Orleans Daily Delta,* February 5, 1863.

Butler had done a creditable job of cleaning up the city, it was difficult to protect such a large body of men from diseases that flourish in tropical climates. Banks expanded Butler's sanitary program and enforced quarantines to keep out yellow fever. He also appointed a medical commission to investigate burial procedures, tenements, and drainage. The results of these efforts were good but far from perfect. The men in one company, for example, had the dubious distinction of suffering from measles, mumps, scurvy, jaundice, typhoid fever, homesickness, and coughs of an undiagnosed origin all at the same time.[17]

Banks's officer corps was another area of concern. Some of his officers had regular army experience, but most were volunteers as poorly trained as the troops they led. Banks's inspector general reported that "the ignorance of officers is lamentable." One colonel admitted that he did not know how to give the proper commands to have his regiment pass in review, and another "executed the same movement in such a style that it was humiliating to witness it." To make matters worse, almost half of the fifty-six regiments in the department were nine-month volunteers whose enlistments were due to expire by August 1863.[18]

Banks did what he could to correct the situation by reorganizing the troops into an army corps (the XIX) consisting of four divisions. He selected Major General Christopher C. Augur to command the First Division. Augur had served with distinction as a division commander at Cedar Mountain, and Banks requested that he serve under him again in Louisiana. He assigned Brigadier General Thomas W. Sherman (no relation to William T.) to the Second Division. The Third Division was under the command of Brigadier General William H. Emory and the Fourth under Brigadier General Cuvier Grover. Banks's department stretched from Pensacola, Florida, to Baton Rouge and included some thirty-six thousand officers and men present for duty. Of these, twenty-two thou-

17. *OR,* 34, pt. 2:560–61, 48, pt. 2:745; Van Alstyne, *Diary of an Enlisted Man,* 72–77; *New York Herald,* July 11, August 13, 1864. Many residents of New Orleans believed that the unacclimated Federal troops would fall victim to the scourge of yellow fever once the hot summer weather arrived (Doyle, "Civilian Life in Occupied New Orleans," 56–58; Julia LeGrand, *The Journal of Julia LeGrand, New Orleans, 1862–63,* ed. Kate Mason Rowland and Mrs. Morris L. Croxall [Richmond: Everett Waddey, 1911], 46).

18. *OR,* 15:649, 26, pt. 1:7, 565; Harrington, *Fighting Politician,* 91–92; *New York Herald,* November 1, 1863; Banks to Mary Banks, February 24, July 6, 1863, Banks Collection, LC.

sand men were in New Orleans and the surrounding area. This force compared to the forty-seven hundred Rebel soldiers present for duty in the Confederate District of Louisiana.[19]

Slaves from plantations in the rural parishes began making their way through Union lines as soon as the Federal army occupied New Orleans. The flood of black refugees continued, and soon the presence of thousands of "contrabands," in need of food, clothing, and housing, created a major problem. As a result, one of Banks's major priorities as the new commander of the Department of the Gulf was to establish a system to put former slaves back to work.[20]

Banks had built his political career on the platform of free labor. Now he began to implement a system of noncompulsory, compensated labor in Louisiana. Just as Benjamin F. Butler eased the way for Banks to take over the civil administration of New Orleans, Butler had anticipated Banks's labor system by seizing abandoned plantations and placing former slaves to work on them. Banks took Butler's policy a step further by directing Captain Samuel W. Cozzens from his staff to lease these lands to private individuals who would operate them under contract for the government.[21]

On January 30, 1863, his birthday, Banks issued an order establishing the conditions for black employment. Although the freedmen were required to sign contracts that obligated them to work for one year, they could choose their employers and had to be compensated for their labor.

19. *OR,* 15:627, 636, 712–14, 888; Irwin, *History of the Nineteenth Army Corps,* 66–67; Ezra J. Warner, *Generals in Blue: Lives of the Union Commanders* (Baton Rouge: Louisiana State University Press, 1964), 12, 441.

20. Harrington, *Fighting Politician,* 91; Charles Kassel, "The Labor System of General Banks," *Open Court* 42 (January 1928): 37; George Gilbert Smith, *Leaves from a Soldier's Diary: The Personal Record of Lieutenant George G. Smith, Co. C, 1st Louisiana Regiment Infantry Volunteers* [*White*] (Putnam, Conn.: George G. Smith, 1906), 34–35; Banks to William Lloyd Garrison, January 30, 1865, *Liberator,* February 24, 1865. See Thomas W. Knox, *Camp-Fire and Cotton-Field: Southern Adventures in Time of War* (1865; reprint, New York: Da Capo Press, 1969), 313–22, 355–454.

21. McCrary, *Abraham Lincoln and Reconstruction,* 140–42; Charles P. Ripley, *Slaves and Freedmen in Civil War Louisiana* (Baton Rouge: Louisiana State University Press, 1976), 38–39, 52–53; West, *Lincoln's Scapegoat General,* 182–85; Howard A. White, *The Freedmen's Bureau in Louisiana* (Baton Rouge: Louisiana State University Press, 1970), 45–47, 102.

In addition, they had a right to maintain the integrity of their families, to educate their children, and to cultivate land for personal gain. The order limited the hours of labor and prohibited the use of corporal punishment. Finally, Banks's plan allowed freedmen to enroll in the militia, which was equivalent to giving them the right to bear arms. By one account, Banks's program "was one of the most comprehensive attempts made during the war to solve the problems created by the destruction of slavery."[22]

Not everything about the system favored the freedmen. Among other provisions, Banks's plan revised the pass system, allowing provost marshals to arrest blacks who lacked passes and put them to work on plantations. Banks also gave the police in New Orleans authority to arrest "any idle, destitute, or vagrant negroes who may be found in the parish, and employ such negroes on any public work." The intent was to keep "refractory blacks" from "strolling about the city." These restrictions heralded the notorious Black Codes that were reinstituted after the war by returning Confederates.[23]

Criticism of Banks's labor system immediately arose from all sides. The freedmen resented the annual contracts and limitations on their mobility. Some felt that the pay for their work was too low, while others

22. Louis S. Gerteis, *From Contraband to Freedman: Federal Policy toward Southern Blacks, 1861–1865* (Westport, Conn.: Greenwood Press, 1973), 72–73; George H. Hepworth, *Whip, Hoe, and Sword; or, The Gulf-Department in '63* (Boston: Walker, Wise, 1864), 25–27; LeGrand, *Journal,* 134; Ripley, *Slaves and Freedmen,* 48–49; *New Orleans Era,* February 19, 20, 1863; Banks to William Lloyd Garrison, January 30, 1865, *Liberator,* February 24, 1865; *OR,* 15:666–67; Williams, "General Banks and the Radical Republicans," 272. An example of a standard contract was published in the *New York Herald,* February 21, 1863.

23. Dan T. Carter, *When the War Was Over: The Failure of Self-Reconstruction in the South, 1865–1867* (Baton Rouge: Louisiana State University Press, 1985), 178; Harris H. Beecher, *Record of the 114th Regiment, N.Y.S.V.: Where It Went, What It Saw, and What It Did* (Norwich, N.Y.: J. F. Hubbard, Jr., 1866), 108; John W. Blassingame, *Black New Orleans, 1860–1880* (Chicago: University of Chicago Press, 1973), 30–31; Doyle, "Civilian Life in Occupied New Orleans," 285–86; Eric Foner, *Reconstruction: America's Unfinished Revolution, 1863–1877* (New York: Harper & Row, 1988), 135; Gerteis, *From Contraband to Freedman,* 93–94; Jean-Charles Houzeau, *My Passage at the New Orleans* Tribune: *A Memoir of the Civil War Era,* ed. David C. Rankin, trans. Gerard F. Denault (Baton Rouge: Louisiana State University Press, 1984), 37; Ripley, *Slaves and Freedmen,* 45, 58; Ted Tunnell, *Crucible of Reconstruction: War, Radicalism, and Race in Louisiana, 1862–1877* (Baton Rouge: Louisiana State University Press, 1984), 84.

found that the prohibition against corporal punishment was often ignored. Banks had gone too far in trying to please the planters, they charged, and his system "was nothing less than slavery under another name."[24]

If the laborers were unenthusiastic, so were the planters, who believed that only the whip could motivate former slaves to work. "High wages will not make a lazy negro industrious," a planter predicted in a letter to a New Orleans newspaper. "His forecast is short, and his wants few; he has no desire to accumulate, lest he should die and some one else spend the earnings of his labor."[25]

The dire predictions of the planter class regarding free labor were doubtless influenced by resentment over having to treat the former slaves as employees. George Hepworth, an antislavery advocate and aide-de-camp on Banks's staff, visited from sixty to seventy-five plantations and arrived at a different conclusion. Hepworth found that most freedmen were willing to work the same land on which they had toiled before the war as long as they were treated fairly. Rather than finding them ignorant, restless, or lazy, Hepworth described the freedmen as "far more intelligent, and better aware of the position of affairs, than I had been led to expect."[26]

Despite its shortcomings, Banks's labor system did achieve some significant results. For one, it reduced the overcrowding in the black refugee camps, which had become hellholes of hunger, unemployment, disease, and death. In addition, black men worked for wages for the first time in their lives—a crucial step in the transition of Louisiana's economic base from slave to free labor. Finally, former slaves were free to

24. *OR*, 41, pt. 2:683–84; Duganne, *Camps and Prisons*, 48; Gerteis, *From Contraband to Freedman*, 77–78, 90–91; Harrington, *Fighting Politician*, 106; George C. Rable, *But There Was No Peace: The Role of Violence in the Politics of Reconstruction* (Athens: University of Georgia Press, 1984), 92.

25. Carter, *When the War Was Over*, 153; Kassel, "Labor System of General Banks," 41–45; Ripley, *Slaves and Freedmen*, 50–51, 70–71; George S. Denison to Chase, March 14, 1863, in Chase, "Diary and Correspondence," 366–67; and see *New York Herald*, April 2, 1864; *New Orleans Times*, October 13, 15, November 22, 1864; *New Orleans Tribune*, October 22, 1864; *Liberator*, March 3, 1865; *National Anti-Slavery Standard*, July 23, 1864; Hanks to Banks, June 1, 1864, Banks Collection, LC.

26. Hepworth, *Whip, Hoe, and Sword*, 25, 49–53, 139–42, 158–62; William F. Smith and James T. Brady, *Commission on Corrupt Practices in the Gulf, Final Report, September 23, 1865*, 194, Record Group 94, Records of the Adjutant General's Office, NA.

choose a new employer at the end of the contract year, which provided an incentive for planters to treat their employees fairly.[27]

Although Banks would have welcomed the support of both the workers and the planters for his labor system, his chief desire was for a good reaction in the North. Not only did he want to be seen as the architect for a smooth transition from a slave to free economy, he also wanted northerners to appreciate that he had increased Louisiana's agricultural production at a time when there was a great demand for its products, especially cotton. But newspapers in the North did not pay much attention to Banks's labor scheme, and when they did, the radical press tended to highlight the system's abuses and failures.[28]

Having done what he could to improve the combat effectiveness of his command and having implemented a plan to put former slaves back to work, Banks turned his attention to the daunting problem of coaxing Louisiana back into the Union. From the start, Abraham Lincoln had believed that a large number of southern citizens were neutral or, at best, lukewarm about secession and that they could be induced to reassert their loyalty to the Union. The president hoped to use this group as a nucleus to reestablish loyalist governments in southern states and put the Union back together.[29]

Banks saw promise in Lincoln's strategy. "The people here in New Orleans are not hostile to the government," he insisted. Although "their instincts, sympathies and hopes" were "naturally with the South," Banks felt that they had been "taught to hate the People of the North, whom

27. McCrary, *Abraham Lincoln and Reconstruction,* 155–56. Banks revised his labor system in 1864, doubling wages and granting freedmen the right to cultivate small plots of land for personal use (*OR,* 34, pt. 2:227–31). For an unfavorable assessment of Banks's labor system, see Charles P. Roland, *Louisiana Sugar Plantations during the American Civil War* (Leiden, Netherlands: E. J. Brill, 1957), 102–10.

28. *OR,* 48, pt. 1:703–10, Ser. 3, 3:926–27; William Wells Brown, *The Negro in the American Rebellion: His Heroism and His Fidelity* (1867; reprint, New York: Johnson Reprint Corp., 1968), 184–85; Kassel, "Labor System of General Banks," 39–40; Knox, *Camp-Fire and Cotton-Field,* 371–80; Carter, *When the War Was Over,* 178; Harrington, *Fighting Politician,* 107; Ripley, *Slaves and Freedmen,* 87–88; Banks to Mary Banks, February 24, 26, March 7, June 18, 1863, Gerrit Smith to Banks, October 17, 1865 (printed circular), Banks Collection, LC; Banks to William Lloyd Garrison, January 30, 1865, *Liberator,* February 24, 1985.

29. *OR,* 15:640, Ser. 3, 3:187–90.

they do not know." He believed that the people of Louisiana would not "willingly continue a long[,] bloody and doubtful war" if treated fairly. As one of Banks's aides explained it, "There had been harsh measures enough in this department, and since Butler had stroked the cat from the tail to head, and found her full of yawl and scratch, [Banks] was determined to stroke her from head to tail, and see if she would hide her claws, and commence to purr."[30]

Banks moved quickly to provide evidence of the new approach. He ordered the immediate release of 120 of Butler's political prisoners and announced on Christmas Eve that he was reversing Butler's order that had closed churches whose pastors refused to pray for the president of the United States. Banks also issued a public proclamation stating that he would investigate illegal seizures and other forms of extortion as well as force the return of houses improperly held by Union officers.[31]

To pacify the working class, Banks set a ceiling on the price of bread and prohibited a local railway company from repudiating its blue tickets, which poor people used as a fractional currency. He also continued his predecessor's program of public charity financed by taxes on rich secessionists and expanded Butler's public works program, which added thousands of jobs to the government payroll.[32]

It did not take long for Banks to realize that, just as had happened in Baltimore, too much conciliation would be interpreted as a sign of weakness. The prosouthern press that had survived Butler's regime grew bolder under Banks's conciliatory rule. Federal defeats were headlined, and items Banks wished to have published were omitted. Eventually, Banks reprimanded several organs for their blatantly prosouthern bias and insisted that they remove certain offensive articles. Failing to get the cooperation he desired, Banks suppressed the publication of several papers. At the same time, he attempted to strengthen the Unionist newspa-

30. *OR*, 15:311; Hepworth, *Whip, Hoe, and Sword*, 27–28; Ripley, *Slaves and Freedmen*, 44; Strother, *Virginia Yankee*, 134–35; Banks to Mary Banks, January 15, 1863, Banks Collection, LC.

31. *OR*, 15:615, 619–21, 623–24; LeGrand, *Journal*, 119; White, *Freedmen's Bureau in Louisiana*, 45; *New Orleans Daily Picayune*, December 28, 1862; *New York Times*, January 3, 1863; Banks to Mary Banks, January 15, 1863, Banks Collection, LC; see also General Orders 113, 114, 117, 120, 121, December 20–28, 1862, *OR*, 15:615–26.

32. *OR*, 26, pt. 1:764–65, Ser. 3, 3:926–27; *New Orleans Era*, February 18, 1863; *New Orleans Daily Delta*, February 3, 6, 1863; *New Orleans Daily Picayune*, December 28, 30, 31, 1862; *New York Tribune*, January 14, 1863.

pers in New Orleans by distributing six hundred to eight hundred dollars a month to the *Era* (his own tabloid), the *New-Orleans Times,* and the *Daily True Delta* as payment for "government printing."[33]

Banks followed a policy of firm conciliation when he opened his office to visitors requesting favors. Although Banks received each supplicant with "frankness and courtesy," he offered persons with secessionist sentiments little sympathy. "My husband will die, sir, his health is so bad, and my relative has lost his mind in confinement," pleaded one woman who gained an audience with the major general. "We must all die, madam," Banks replied. "Prison life affects men differently; some lose their minds and some die; this we cannot help." A correspondent from the *New York Herald* informed his readers that "if people here in New Orleans imagined that the General would give the secessionists their own way they have discovered their mistake."[34]

Banks believed that his policies were beginning to work. "The merchants are doing more business every day," he wrote to Mary in February 1863, two months after his arrival. "The ladies and children are out in the street and all are feeling well. All the People seem to think well of me—even the thieves take off their hats." But in spite of these outward signs of acceptance, the Crescent City remained a Rebel city through and through. Commenting on Banks's attempt to placate the citizens of

33. *New York Tribune,* January 14, April 2, 1863; Banks to James Bowen, May 25, 1864, V. Hébert to Major Porter (Provost Marshal), June 23, 1864, Banks Collection, LC; Banks to Mayor W. W. Howe, July 18, 1864, Nathaniel P. Banks Collection, CHS; Harrington, *Fighting Politician,* 96; Houzeau, *My Passage at the New Orleans* Tribune, 23; LeGrand, *Journal,* 69–70, 128; *New Orleans Era,* May 6, 7, 1863; *New York Tribune,* February 10, 21, 23, June 4, 1863; *New York Herald,* June 23, 1863; George S. Denison to Chase, September 21, 1863, in Chase, "Diary and Correspondence," 408, 412–13; Albert G. Hills to Banks, February 28, 1864, Banks Correspondence, AAS; T. W. Conway-Banks correspondence, 1864, Banks Collection, LC. The *Era* took over the *Daily Delta* on February 15, 1863, and became the official city newspaper the next day (Charles F. Youngman, "Historic Sketches of the *Daily Delta* and the *Era* and the *New Orleans Daily Independent* from October 12, 1845 to January 19, 1865" [New Orleans: City Archives, 1939, typescript (photocopy)], 32, 35, HTML).

34. *OR,* 15:615; Wickham Hoffman, *Camp, Court and Siege: A Narrative of Personal Adventure and Observation during Two Wars, 1861–1865, 1870–71* (New York: Harper & Brothers, 1877), 63–65; LeGrand, *Journal,* 120; *New Orleans Era,* March 29, April 4, 1863; *New York Tribune,* May 8, 23, 1863; *New York Herald,* February 15, April 22, 1863; *National Anti-Slavery Standard,* January 30, 1864; Draft on back of letter from Nevil Soulé to Banks, April 7, 1863, Banks to Allen Rutherford, June 24, 1871, Banks Collection, LC.

New Orleans, one soldier noted that "they didn't bite worth a cent; they seemed to know better than Gen. Banks the kind of treatment they deserved." Another soldier expressed the same opinion two years later when he observed that the people of New Orleans had not changed "one whit for the better, or that kindness and leniency will cure them or bring them to a better mind."[35]

The failure of the citizens of New Orleans to accept Banks's fair but firm approach became evident on February 20, 1863, when some Confederate officers were being transported through the city on their way to be exchanged. Ten thousand secessionists, mostly women, turned out to wave good-bye. The Union officer in charge was disturbed by the size and spirit of the crowd and irritated at finding some contraband materials in the coats of the departing Confederates. Meanwhile, the Rebel women continued to squeal defiance and wave red handkerchiefs. Alarmed, the officer called for reinforcements to disperse the crowd. One woman was arrested, others were frightened, and most thought Banks "worse than Butler."[36]

35. A. H. Carpenter, "Military Government of Southern Territory, 1861–1865," *Annual Report of the American Historical Association, the Year 1900* (Washington, D.C.: U.S. Government Printing Office, 1901), 1:478; Percival Drayton, *Naval Letters of Captain Percival Drayton, 1861–1865* (New York: New York Public Library, 1906), 41, 48; Frank M. Flinn, *Campaigning with Banks in Louisiana, in '63 and '64, and with Sheridan in the Shenandoah Valley in '64 and '65* (Lynn, Mass.: Thos. P. Nichols, 1887), 12; John Chandler Gregg, *Life in the Army, in the Departments of Virginia, and the Gulf, Including Observations in New Orleans* (Philadelphia: Perkinpine & Higgins, 1866), 143; Hoffman, *Camp, Court and Siege,* 111; Marion Southwood, *"Beauty and Booty," the Watchword of New Orleans* (New York: M. Doolady, 1867), 275; *New York Times,* March 4, 1864; *New Orleans Daily True Delta,* December 3, 1864; *New York Herald,* January 3, 1864; *Boston Commonwealth,* March 4, 1865; Denison to Chase, January 16, February 12, 26, 1863, in Chase, "Diary and Correspondence," 350, 358–60; Shepley to Butler, February 20, 1863, in Butler, *Private and Official Correspondence,* 3:3, 14; Banks to Mary Banks, February 24, September 15, 1863, James T. Tucker to Stephen Hoyt, June 23, 1864, Banks Collection, LC.

36. Carroll Storrs Alden, *George Hamilton Perkins, Commodore, U.S.N.: His Life and Letters* (Boston: Houghton Mifflin, 1914), 149–50; Beecher, *Record of the 114th Regiment,* 174; Sarah Morgan Dawson, *A Confederate Girl's Diary* (Boston: Houghton Mifflin, 1913), 318, 403; Southwood, *"Beauty and Booty,"* 278–81; *New York Herald,* February 15, 1863; *New York Tribune,* September 21, 1863; *New York Times,* March 4, 1863. The affair became known as the Battle of the Handkerchiefs.

8

To Stir a Man's Blood

Coaxing the citizens of Louisiana back into the Union was only part of Nathaniel P. Banks's assignment. He was also expected to help wrest control of the Mississippi River from the Confederates. Both Lincoln and Halleck recognized the importance of opening the Mississippi, an accomplishment they thought would be worth "forty Richmonds." Banks, who had studied the geography of the region as a director with the Illinois Central Railroad, knew that "the freedom of the Mississippi puts an end to the rebellion so far as an independent Confederacy is concerned. There is no room for an independent government between the Mississippi and the Atlantic."[1]

The campaign to open the river had begun in November 1862, when Ulysses S. Grant began moving south with his army in northern Mississippi. William T. Sherman, who had assumed command of McClernand's expeditionary force, started his troops in motion from Memphis late the same month, taking a southward course along the river in hopes of eventually linking up with Grant. In a bold gamble just before Christmas

1. *OR*, 15:255, 726, 26, pt. 1:619. The importance of river transportation in the western theater cannot be overemphasized. Railroads were few and far between, while the distances between population centers were great. A medical officer with an Ohio regiment that served in the Mississippi Valley kept a record of the distances it traveled during the war and calculated that of the almost ten thousand miles covered, more than 75 percent was by water as compared to approximately 5 percent by rail and 20 percent on foot (Thomas B. Marshall, *History of the Eighty-Third Ohio Volunteer Infantry, the Greyhound Regiment* [Cincinnati: Eighty-Third Ohio Volunteer Infantry Association, 1912], 245–47).

Day, Confederate general Earl Van Dorn smashed Grant's supply base at Holly Springs, halting Grant in his tracks. A few days later, Sherman's advance on Vicksburg was severely repulsed at Chickasaw Bayou just above the city. Both of these developments signaled the end of Union attempts to capture Vicksburg via an overland route.[2]

Rebuffed on land, Grant had decided to join forces with Sherman. Once the two forces were united, Grant switched to the west bank of the river, where he marched southward until his troops were directly across from the Confederate citadel. The problem was getting the army back across the river to the dry land south of Vicksburg where Grant could maneuver against the Confederate defenders. The transports needed to accomplish this objective were blocked by the Confederate batteries at Vicksburg. At the same time, the Federal navy was prevented from steaming upriver from Baton Rouge by the Confederate guns at Port Hudson.[3]

Given the stalemate at Vicksburg, Banks and Farragut decided to do what they could to help by demonstrating against Port Hudson. They began planning the operation during a meeting at the St. Charles Hotel in New Orleans in late February. Because the Confederate garrison depended on supplies from the Red River Valley, the fortress might fall if Banks could help Farragut get his warships on the Mississippi River north of Port Hudson to plug the mouth of the Red. In addition, such a move would allow Union gunboats to establish contact with Grant, as well as disrupt Rebel supply and communication routes between the Trans-Mississippi Department and the rest of the Confederacy.[4]

Banks had tried to bypass Port Hudson in mid-February by reaching the Atchafalaya River through a labyrinth of small bayous across from

2. Steven E. Woodworth, *Jefferson Davis and His Generals: The Failure of Confederate Command in the West* (Lawrence: University of Kansas Press, 1990), 109–24. Unlike Banks's expeditionary force, McClernand's troops had been sent south piecemeal. By the time he returned from an extended trip to Illinois to assume command, McClernand found that his men had been absorbed into an existing Union army under Sherman (see Edwin Cole Bearss, *The Campaign for Vicksburg,* Vol. 1, *Vicksburg Is the Key* [Dayton, Ohio: Morningside, 1985], 26–28; Williams, *Lincoln and His Generals,* 191–94, 217–18).

3. *OR,* 15:240–42, 661–62, 1109–11; U.S. Congress, *Report of the Joint Committee on the Conduct of the War,* 2:306; Loyall Farragut, *The Life of David Glasgow Farragut, First Admiral of the United States Navy* (New York: D. Appleton, 1907), 345–46.

4. *OR,* 15:255.

Baton Rouge. Gaining access to the Atchafalaya would allow Banks to make his way by boat to the Red River, which entered the Mississippi between Vicksburg and Port Hudson. But the attempt failed because an accumulation of driftwood made the route impassable. Because the direct approach to the Atchafalaya through Grand Lake was blocked by a small Confederate army under Richard Taylor, Banks and Farragut decided that it would be easier to attempt a passage at Port Hudson by steaming past the Confederate guns at night. Banks's role in this operation would be to attack the garrison from the land side as Farragut and his ships made their dash.[5]

Banks began moving the XIX Corps from New Orleans to Baton Rouge once the decision was made. The plan called for Banks to leave a garrison of some three thousand men in Baton Rouge to prevent the Confederates from threatening that post and march with twelve thousand troops the sixteen-odd miles to Port Hudson. Signal officers would accompany Farragut aboard his flagship and Banks's column on the march. When all was ready, the admiral would send a message to Banks, and the major general would order an attack against the fortifications. Facing Farragut and Banks at Port Hudson were sixteen thousand Confederate soldiers under the command of Major General Franklin K. Gardner. Gardner had twenty-one big cannon, most of which were in position to fire on Federal boats attempting to force a passage.[6]

Union troops in Baton Rouge received an order to fall in on Thursday, March 12. They were eager to start. For more than a week they had

5. *OR,* 15:240–50, 298–300, 303–4, 689; *OR, (Navy),* 19:637, 640; U.S. Congress, *Report of the Joint Committee on the Conduct of the War,* 2:309, 386; David C. Edmonds, *The Guns of Port Hudson,* 2 vols. (Lafayette, La.: Acadiana Press, 1983–84), 1:1, 10–11; Harrington, *Fighting Politician,* 117–19; Irwin, *History of the Nineteenth Army Corps,* 66–71, 77–78, 85–88; John C. Palfrey, "Port Hudson," in *Papers of the Military Historical Society of Massachusetts,* Vol. 8 (Boston: Military Historical Society of Massachusetts, 1910), 28–30; Banks to Mary Banks, February 24, March 14, July 6, 1863, Banks Collection, LC; Banks to W. H. Emory, January 1863, W. H. Emory Papers, ISHL; Willoughby Babcock, "War Commentary," 2a, Vol. 9 of Willoughby Babcock and Family Papers, MNHS.

6. *OR,* 15:259–61, 692–93, 1036; Lawrence Lee Hewitt, *Port Hudson, Confederate Bastion on the Mississippi* (Baton Rouge: Louisiana State University Press, 1987), 181–83; Irwin, *History of the Nineteenth Army Corps,* 77–78. Thomas Sherman's division was left in New Orleans to guard the city.

waited to begin the campaign against the Confederate stronghold at Port Hudson. Tents had been struck and stored; superfluous baggage and clothing had been boxed and set aside. Knapsacks were packed, canteens filled, and each man had drawn one hundred rounds of ammunition. But the campaign did not begin on March 12. Instead of taking the road north to Port Hudson, the troops were marched to a large field near the state arsenal. Nathaniel P. Banks, commander of the Department of the Gulf, had decided to hold a grand review.[7]

The reviewing field was located at the edge of Baton Rouge, where a struggle for the state capital had taken place seven months earlier. Black laborers had thrown up extensive earthworks to protect the city from another Confederate attack. As the regiments made their way past these entrenchments, Banks sat at attention on a coal-black stallion named Shenandoah. His large staff was gathered behind him in mounted splendor. To his right on a prancing bobtail mare sat the first admiral of the United States Navy, David Glasgow Farragut, accompanied by the five captains of the Union fleet.[8]

After the troops were drawn up in formation, Banks motioned to Farragut, and the two commanders and their staffs rode down the long line. A military band began to play. The men broke into cheers, and Banks and Farragut waved their hats in response. At the end of the formation the procession turned and rode past the troops once more, this time at a full canter. On the return trip they came to one of the wide ditches that crisscrossed the plain. Without hesitation, Banks spurred Shenandoah forward and cleared the obstacle easily. His staff also took the ditch in stride. The navy men, who were more at home on the deck of a ship than

7. Edmonds, *Guns of Port Hudson,* 1:23–24; J. F. Moors, *History of the Fifty-Second Regiment, Massachusetts Volunteers* (Boston: George H. Ellis, 1893), 71; Diary entry for March 12, 1863, in Dargan, *My Experiences;* William E. Wilcox to his wife, March 12, 1863, William E. Wilcox Papers, WDML.

8. Edmonds, *Guns of Port Hudson,* 1:32–33; James K. Ewer, *Third Massachusetts Cavalry in the War for the Union* (Maplewood, Mass.: Wm. G. J. Perry Press for the Historical Committee of the Regimental Association, 1903), 62–63; Charles S. Foltz, *Surgeon of the Seas: The Adventurous Life of Surgeon General Jonathan M. Foltz in the Days of Wooden Ships* (Indianapolis: Bobbs-Merrill, 1931), 260; Irwin, *History of the Nineteenth Army Corps,* 77; Albert Plummer, *History of the Forty-Eighth Regiment M.V.M. during the Civil War* (Boston: New England Druggist Co., 1907), 25; Powers, *Story of the Thirty-Eighth Regiment,* 50–51; Strother, *Virginia Yankee,* 154; Entry for March 12, 1863, Samuel Gault Diary, HNOC.

on the back of a horse, pulled up short. Farragut frowned, for it was clear that Banks was testing the navy's mettle. Turning his mare to get a good start, the admiral jumped the ditch gracefully. One by one, his captains followed until all were across and navy honor was saved.[9]

The matter should have ended there, but it did not. With Banks in the lead, the army galloped across the field again, taking several ditches at their widest. The navy, not to be outdone, followed in hot pursuit. The cavalcade cleared the ditches one by one without incident until a man and horse went down. When the rider appeared from the depths of the trench, he turned out to be Captain Charles Sargent of Banks's staff. The navy men had held their own, and there was to be no more ditch jumping that day. Amused by the show, the troops marched back to their camps to continue their preparations for the impending campaign.[10]

Farragut started upriver late Friday afternoon, March 13, with the intention of running the batteries sometime Saturday night. At the same time, Banks set his men in motion toward Port Hudson. "It was a grand and imposing spectacle," the chaplain of the Fifty-second Massachusetts Infantry wrote to his wife. "The line stretched on as far as the eye could reach." The Union troops marched about eight miles before making camp by starlight. "It was a glorious evening, not very warm," the chaplain reported. "The trees are getting into full leaf, the peach-trees in full bloom, the fences covered with roses in full bloom, trumpet-flowers and a profusion of others on either side, the men in good condition, singing and joking."[11]

The XIX Corps continued the march along the Bayou Sara Road toward Port Hudson early Saturday morning. Grover's division led the way, followed by Emory and then Augur. The men marched four abreast along a sandy highway cut through the thick forest of cypress and pine. Interspersed among the brigades were batteries of artillery and canvas-covered supply wagons. Banks, accompanied by his staff, couriers, and a

9. James K. Hosmer, *The Color-Guard: Being a Corporal's Notes of Military Service in the Nineteenth Army Corps* (Boston: Walker, Wise, 1864), 80–82; Foltz, *Surgeon of the Seas*, 260.

10. Loyall Farragut, "Farragut at Port Hudson," *Putnam's Magazine* 5 (October 1908): 46–47; Strother, *Virginia Yankee*, 154; Diary entry for March 12, 1863, Henry B. Whitney Papers, WRPL.

11. Moors, *History of the Fifty-Second Regiment*, 72.

small contingent of cavalry, left Baton Rouge at seven o'clock Saturday morning and caught up with the troops on foot by midday. "Make way for the General, Make way for the General," came the cry as Banks rode along the line of marching men. Cheers rolled down the road as the men opened a path for their commander. "I have never received such compliments before," Banks wrote his wife that night. "It gave me great courage. There is nothing like the cheers of a soldier to stir a man's blood."[12]

Early Saturday afternoon, Banks dictated a message to Farragut: "My command is at Barnes' Cross-Roads, and occupies the road to Ross Landing, on the flank and rear of Rebel batteries. When will you open fire? We shall be ready this evening." Banks planned to move his men along a road that ran in a northwesterly direction to the Confederate line. This maneuver would place the Union forces behind the Confederate batteries that were aimed at the river. Unfortunately, the road proved to be nothing more than a narrow path that was virtually impassable for artillery. Federal scouts soon returned from a more extensive reconnaissance to inform Banks that his maps were hopelessly inaccurate. Some roads that appeared on the maps turned out to be little more than overgrown trails. Others did not exist at all. Union troops trying to move into position became lost and disorganized. Meanwhile, Farragut prepared to make his run upstream, thinking that Banks would be ready in time.[13]

Around five o'clock Saturday afternoon, Banks received a message from Farragut indicating that he would begin his movement at eight o'clock that evening. The communiqué came as a complete surprise, for Banks assumed that the attempt would be made "in the gray of the morning." It soon became clear that the Union infantry and artillery would not be able to get into position in time. Banks's staff tried frantically to straighten things out as the minutes slipped away, but Banks concluded that nothing more could be done and retired to his tent. "I do not mean to lead my men to a fool's fight and a dog's death," he wrote Mary

12. Hosmer, *Color-Guard,* 84–90; *Memorial of Lt. Daniel Perkins Dewey,* 67–68; Powers, *Story of the Thirty-Eighth Regiment,* 53–54; Strother, *Virginia Yankee,* 155; Luther T. Townsend, *History of the Sixteenth Regiment, New Hampshire Volunteers* (Washington, D.C.: Norman T. Elliott, 1897), 76–78; Banks to Mary Banks, March 14, 1863, Banks Collection, LC.

13. *OR,* 15:251–56, 261–62; *OR (Navy),* 19:665–66; Farragut, "Farragut at Port Hudson," 48–49; Henry T. Johns, *Life with the Forty-Ninth Massachusetts Volunteers* (Pittsfield, Mass.: C. A. Alvord, 1864), 157; Strother, *Virginia Yankee,* 156–57.

that evening. The hours passed in silence; there was no word about Farragut's fleet.[14]

At half past eleven that night, all hell broke loose. Banks's soldiers, who had fallen asleep wherever they could find a spot, were awakened by the roar of hundreds of guns firing all at once. "Crash after crash broke upon my ears like a chorus of doomsday," one young soldier recalled afterward. The sky to the west above the river was illuminated by the glow of a huge bonfire set by the Confederates and the graceful arc of hundreds of shells. "Through the trees to the westward arose the flashes, incessant, like the winking heat-lightning of a hot summer evening," another Union soldier described it. A young southern girl living on a plantation about five miles north of Port Hudson was stirred from bed. "What an awful sound," she wrote in her diary. "Such an incessant roar! And at every report the house shaking so, and we thinking of our dear soldiers, the dead and dying, and crying aloud for God's blessings on them."[15]

The firing continued for more than two hours. Banks paced; he was in a foul mood. The explosions from the river and the extent of the firing convinced him that Farragut's attempt to run the batteries must have failed. It was Farragut's fault, Banks decided. The admiral had been both "rash and headstrong" in his attempt to pass the Confederate stronghold. Even as Banks worried out loud, the entire western horizon was lit up with a red flame so vast and widespread that "night turned into day." For thirty seconds there was a breathless silence, followed by a "roar, pealing and long continued, which made the earth tremble" and rattled windows miles away. What Banks and his staff heard was the explosion of one of Farragut's largest ships, the *Mississippi*.[16]

14. *OR,* 15:253; Edmonds, *Guns of Port Hudson,* 1:91; Hewitt, *Port Hudson,* 71; Irwin, *History of the Nineteenth Army Corps,* 79; William B. Stevens, *History of the Fiftieth Regiment of Infantry, Massachusetts Volunteer Militia in the Late War of the Rebellion* (Boston: Griffith-Stillings Press, 1907), 73–75; Banks to Mary Banks, March 14, 1863, Banks Collection, LC.

15. Orton S. Clark, *The One Hundred and Sixteenth Regiment of New York State Volunteers* (Buffalo: Matthews & Warren, 1868), 56–57; diary entry for March 15, 1863, in Dargan, *My Experiences;* Dawson, *Confederate Girl's Diary,* 337; Farragut, "Farragut at Port Hudson," 50; Hosmer, *Color-Guard,* 97–98; Strother, *Virginia Yankee,* 157.

16. *OR,* 15:254–56, 262; Farragut, "Farragut at Port Hudson," 51; Plummer, *History of the Forty-Eighth Regiment,* 28–29; Strother, *Virginia Yankee,* 157–59; Diary entries for March 14, 15, 1863, James Albert Osborne Diary (typescript), MAHS.

Banks's worst fears were realized. Farragut's flotilla of seven vessels had been battered and beaten by the Rebels at Port Hudson. Although Farragut's flagship, the *Hartford,* and a gunboat lashed to her side made it through, the rest had turned back. The *Mississippi,* which had known better days as Matthew Calbraith Perry's flagship when he visited Japan, had blown up. Farragut considered the operation a disaster.[17]

The Confederates had been well prepared, and the outcome probably would have been the same even if Banks's troops had been able to get into position. Banks called his commanders together to order a countermarch to Baton Rouge. In addition, he had his adjutant issue an order to be read before each regiment, explaining the reason for the withdrawal. Banks congratulated the men on their success, mentioned that the *Hartford* and a gunboat had passed the batteries, and stated that "the object of the expedition has been accomplished." But the men in Banks's command knew a defeat when they heard one, regardless of what he called it. "Banks will never do anything," one soldier wrote. "He will conduct another campaign of glorious retreats as he did in the Shenandoah Valley." Another soldier from Massachusetts wrote his parents to ask whether they had any news of "Ben Butler coming back here again. I hope that it is so. Banks in my opinion is a Coward."[18]

The march back to Baton Rouge was horrendous for the dispirited men. Frustrated over not having accomplished anything, they went on a frenzy of looting. "This marauding went on ruthlessly and wastefully," a young soldier from Massachusetts wrote. "We left the road behind us foul with the odor of decaying carcasses," he continued. "Cattle were killed, a quarter or so taken out of them, and the remainder left to the buzzards. So with sheep and poultry. Pigs were bayoneted, sugar-houses plundered of sugar and molasses, private dwellings entered; and, if any

17. *OR (Navy),* 19:665; Farragut, *Life of Farragut,* 321–22; Hewitt, *Port Hudson,* 72–95; Farragut to his wife, April 30, 1863, David G. Farragut Collection, HL.

18. *OR,* 15:255; Edmonds, *Guns of Port Hudson,* 1:149–51, 201; *Memorial of Lt. Daniel Perkins Dewey,* 70–71; Luther T. Townsend, *History of the Sixteenth Regiment, New Hampshire Volunteers* (Washington, D.C.: Norman T. Elliott, 1897), 89; Banks to Mary Banks, March 21, [1863], Banks, Collection, LC; Peter Eltinge to his father, March 22, 1863, Eltinge-Lord Papers, WRPL; Charles H. Richardson to his mother, April 7, 1863, Lois (Wright) Richardson Davis Papers, WRPL; also William E. Wilcox to his wife, March 20, 1863, Wilcox Papers, WDML; Charles J. Paine to his father, April 8, 1863, Charles J. Paine Letters (microfilm P-384), MAHS.

resistance was offered by the owner, his arms were wrested from him, and he overmastered. To be sure, there can be no manner of doubt of sympathy of all these people with the Rebel cause."[19]

Adding to the turmoil, a major storm with heavy wind and hard rain hit the retreating column as it headed south. The road that had been so straight and smooth on the march north now became a sticky mass of mud, like a deep pudding. After stopping to camp on Sunday night, the men tried to sleep where they could but found no relief from the rising water, which stood several inches deep in places. Everything was wet, although Banks made out better than most. Five men who had been charged with cowardice before the enemy were put under armed guard and given shovels to make sure that no water entered the general's tent.[20]

Banks's detractors thought he had erred by not staying to invest the garrison at Port Hudson after Farragut's attempt to run the batteries, but doing so would have invited disaster. Gardner outnumbered Banks four to three. In addition, Gardner's troops were battle-tested veterans behind an extensive network of fortifications. In contrast, most of Banks's men were recent recruits with inadequate training and no experience in battle. It was not until the Confederate high command weakened Gardner's command to reinforce Vicksburg that the investment of Port Hudson became realistic. Even then, Banks's expanded force of twenty thousand men was unable to reduce the bastion. Banks's decision to withdraw to Baton Rouge showed good rather than poor judgment. "Had we invested Port Hudson defended by that force," Banks contended, "our army would have been certainly destroyed and probably have resulted in the loss of New Orleans."[21]

Meanwhile, Farragut tried unsuccessfully to blockade the Mississippi

19. Hosmer, *Color-Guard,* 103.

20. Hosmer, *Color-Guard,* 100–102, 104; Johns, *Life with the Forty-Ninth Massachusetts,* 170–71; *Memorial of Lt. Daniel Perkins Dewey,* 70–71; Moors, *History of the Fifty-Second Regiment,* 81–90; Plummer, *History of the Forty-eighth Regiment,* 85–86; Homer B. Sprague, *History of the 13th Infantry Regiment of Connecticut Volunteers during the Great Rebellion* (Hartford: Case, Lockwood, 1867), 104–6; Stevens, *History of the Fiftieth Regiment,* 70; Strother, *Virginia Yankee,* 159.

21. Edmonds, *Guns of Port Hudson,* 1:201–2; Hewitt, *Port Hudson,* 122, 181; Williams, *Lincoln Finds a General,* 5:24; Woodworth, *Jefferson Davis and His Generals,* 206; Letter dated June 19, [1866], Nathaniel P. Banks Papers, LALMVC.

between Port Hudson and Vicksburg with the *Hartford* and the *Albatross*. He did burn Confederate supplies stockpiled at some points along the river, but his ability to disrupt Rebel communications was impaired by the failure to get most of the fleet past the batteries at Port Hudson. Furthermore, Farragut would eventually need to reestablish contact with Federal forces to restock his own supplies. At some point the *Hartford* and the *Albatross* would have to attempt to pass Port Hudson again, a prospect Farragut did not look forward to.[22]

Banks realized that he had to make another effort to neutralize Port Hudson, and he had to do it soon. Consequently, he returned to his alternative plan of attempting to find a water route to the Red River via the Atchafalaya. Because the earlier attempt to open a passage from the Mississippi River had failed, Banks now had to turn his attention to Grand Lake. He would have to confront Richard Taylor, his old foe from the Shenandoah Valley, who had been transferred to his native state a few months before Banks's expeditionary force set sail for the Crescent City.[23]

Taylor's small army was entrenched behind the earthworks at Fort Bisland on the Bayou Teche just a few miles upstream from Berwick. The fortifications consisted of a line of simple breastworks across the narrow neck of dry land that extended between impenetrable cypress swamps and canebrakes on either side. The Bayou Teche ran down the middle of the defensive position. Taylor had approximately three thousand men available to defend the fort as well as a gunboat, the *Diana*, which had been captured after it had ventured too far up the Teche two weeks before. Alfred Mouton's brigade of fifteen hundred men held the ground between the lake and Bayou Teche, while approximately the same number of men and twelve guns manned the embankments on the other side of the stream.[24]

22. Edmonds, *Guns of Port Hudson,* 1:203–6; Hewitt, *Port Hudson,* 95.

23. *OR,* 15:251–56, 290–91, 970–71, 1117–18, 1021, 26, pt. 1:5–21, 43–45; Edmonds, *Guns of Port Hudson,* 1:202; Irwin, *History of the Nineteenth Army Corps,* 88–89; Taylor, *Destruction and Reconstruction,* 151–52; *New Orleans Daily True Delta,* August 5, 1863; Banks to Mary Banks, March 10, 14, 1863, Banks Collection, LC. T. Michael Parrish, *Richard Taylor: Soldier Prince of Dixie* (Chapel Hill: University of North Carolina Press, 1992), is a definitive biography of Taylor.

24. *OR,* 15:388–89; Morris Raphael, *The Battle in the Bayou Country* (Detroit: Morris Raphael Books, 1975), 79–84; John G. Walker, "The War of Secession West of the Mississippi River during the Years 1863–4– & 5," [1866], typescript, 24, MHI; John D. Win-

Banks began shifting his troops from Baton Rouge to Donaldsonville on March 28 for a march to Thibodaux, from where they would march to Brashear City. He moved his headquarters to Brashear City on April 8 and assumed command of the two and a half divisions from the XIX Corps involved in the operation. Brigadier General Godfrey Weitzel's brigade occupied a position at Brashear City, while Emory's division remained in bivouac at Bayou Ramos five miles to the rear. Grover was four miles behind Emory with his division at Bayou Boeuf.[25]

Banks assembled a fleet of transports, flatboats, and small steamers at Brashear City for the campaign. His strategy, suggested initially by Weitzel, was to engage the Confederate army at Fort Bisland while a large force under Grover moved by boat across Grand Lake to land in Taylor's rear, cutting off his retreat.[26]

Weitzel's brigade from Augur's division crossed the narrow stretch of water that separated Brashear City from Berwick on the morning of April 9, driving away a small detachment of Confederates who were posted there. Before darkness fell, Emory's division had also crossed safely to Berwick. Grover's division took up a position along the wharves at Brashear City so as to board boats for their part of the operation.[27]

Over the next few days, Weitzel and Emory advanced cautiously up the Teche. By nightfall of April 11, they reached the vicinity of Pattersonville. With eight thousand men, Weitzel and Emory enjoyed a large numerical advantage over Taylor. Nevertheless, Taylor continued to strengthen Fort Bisland, using slaves from nearby plantations to work through the night until the fortifications could be completed.[28]

Meanwhile, Grover's force of eight thousand men with horses, ammunition, and artillery had boarded transports and steamed into Grand

---

ters, *The Civil War in Louisiana* (Baton Rouge: Louisiana State University Press, 1963), 223–24.

25. Duganne, *Camps and Prisons*, 157; Irwin, *History of the Nineteenth Army Corps*, 89; William H. Root, "The Experiences of a Federal Soldier in Louisiana in 1863," *Louisiana Historical Quarterly* 19 (July 1936): 639; William F. Tiemann, *The 159th Regiment Infantry, New-York State Volunteers* (Brooklyn: Author, 1891), 27.

26. *OR*, 15:294, 676–77; Irwin, *History of the Nineteenth Army Corps*, 90–91.

27. *OR*, 15:294; Beecher, *Record of the 114th Regiment*, 134–35.

28. *OR*, 15:396–97; William Arceneaux, *Acadian General: Alfred Mouton and the Civil War* (Lafayette, La.: Center for Louisiana Studies, 1981), 74–75; Flinn, *Campaigning with Banks*, 35; Raphael, *Battle in the Bayou Country*, 93–100; Donald S. Frazier, "Texans on the Teche: The Texas Brigade at the Battle of Bisland and Irish Bend, April 12–14, 1863," *Louisiana History* 32 (Fall 1991): 419–20.

Lake. Weitzel and Emory continued their slow progress, holding back to give Grover time to land behind Taylor's army. The Union advance was slowed further by broad fields of unharvested sugarcane so high that a soldier could see only half a dozen or so of his comrades at one time. The labyrinth of stalks and rows was interrupted at intervals by deep drainage ditches. A soldier in the 114th New York wrote later, "Jumping from cane row to cane row, leaping over ditches, crowding between stiff cane stalks, wading through mud-holes, beneath the scalding sun, the boys toiled on." Not surprisingly, Union regiments entering a field on one side would emerge from the other disorganized and exhausted. It was slow going.[29]

Finally, at five o'clock on the afternoon of April 12, the Union troops came within range of the guns at Fort Bisland. The *Diana* held the center of the Confederate line, where she could discharge her powerful guns and then be pulled out of sight around a bend in the bayou to reload. Learning that a fleet of Federal vessels had entered Grand Lake, Taylor dispatched Colonel William G. Vincent with the Second Louisiana Cavalry to Verdun's Landing about a mile and a half north of Centerville and approximately four miles behind the fortifications at Fort Bisland.[30]

At Fort Bisland, the artillery on both sides opened fire, providing the Union infantry huddled in the ditches a close-up view of the severest artillery duel of the campaign. "The air was rent with solid shot and a haze filled the atmosphere from the smoke of discharged guns and bursting shells," one soldier wrote. The firing continued until sunset, at which time the Federals fell back about a mile for the night. Taylor detached Colonel James Reily's regiment from Henry H. Sibley's brigade of Texas cavalry to assist Vincent in preventing a Union landing from the lake. At this stage of the campaign, Taylor's only reinforcements were Major Franklin H. Clack's ninety-man battalion, which had been stationed in New Iberia to guard the salt mines. Despite the threat of Grover's force in Grand Lake and the Union strength arrayed before Fort Bisland, the Confederates had held the Federals in check during the first day of

29. Beecher, *Record of the 114th Regiment,* 140; John William De Forest, *A Volunteer's Adventures: A Union Captain's Record of the Civil War,* ed. James H. Croushore (New Haven: Yale University Press, 1946), 87; Frazier, "Texans on the Teche," 424–25.

30. *OR,* 15:388; Flinn, *Campaigning with Banks,* 42.

fighting. As darkness fell, a Confederate band struck up a favorite tune, the "Bonnie Blue Flag."[31]

Grover's flotilla put several scouting parties ashore at various places during the early morning hours of April 13 as they moved up Grand Lake. A detachment from the Sixth New York Infantry landed at Magee's Point just before daybreak and found a plantation road practicable for movement of men, horses, and wagons. At daylight, troops from William Dwight's brigade began to disembark. Although the deep draft of the vessels prevented them from coming any closer than one hundred yards from the shoreline, Dwight got his men in the water and established a foothold on the shore after a spirited fight with Vincent's troopers.[32]

Getting Grover's infantry ashore did not pose a problem, for they simply scrambled to the bank in the shallow water. Unloading the horses, artillery pieces, and wagons was more difficult and took some time. Grover was not eager to engage the Confederates prematurely because he did not know how many of the enemy he was facing. By midday, most of the division was ashore, ready to begin its march toward Franklin. Vincent and some artillery attempted to slow the advance and burned several bridges to impede its progress.[33]

As Grover labored to land his division, Banks ordered a general assault against Fort Bisland. The Confederates put up stiff resistance and halted the Union charge. The *Diana* offered effective counterfire to the Union batteries from its protected position in the bayou, but a Confederate defeat was only a matter of time. The *Diana* was beginning to run short of ammunition, and the Federals would soon make the weight of their numbers felt.[34]

Firing began again in earnest as Banks attempted to extend his line to

31. *OR,* 15:388–89; Beecher, *Record of the 114th Regiment,* 141; Frazier, "Texans on the Teche," 428–29; Henry Hall and James Hall, *Cayuga in the Field: A Record of the 75th N.Y. Volunteers* (Auburn, N.Y.: Truair, Smith, 1873), 92; Babcock, "War Commentary," 5, MNHS; Banks to Mary Banks, April 13, 1863, Banks Collection, LC; William E. Wilcox to his wife, April 18, 1863, Wilcox Papers, WDML.

32. *OR,* 15:358–59, 371, 377; Irwin, *History of the Nineteenth Army Corps,* 105–6.

33. *OR,* 15:371. Some Union officers believed that Grover's failure to strike aggressively at Taylor's rear constituted gross negligence (Babcock, "War Commentary," 9, MNHS).

34. *OR,* 15:390, 53:463; Taylor, *Destruction and Reconstruction,* 154–59.

the left in order to outflank the Confederate position. Colonel Tom Green, who held the extreme right with his regiment of Texas cavalry, reported that the Federal fire was becoming so fierce that he did not know how much longer he could hold his position. A well-placed shot from a Federal battery just before noon added to the precariousness of the Confederate situation when it penetrated the iron plating on the front of the *Diana* and exploded near the gunboat's boilers. Two men were killed and five wounded, and the *Diana* had to be withdrawn for repairs.[35]

The Federal attempt to turn the Confederate flank was foiled after a fierce struggle, and the fighting continued throughout the afternoon. Not only were the Confederate fortifications strong, but Banks was waiting until he was sure that Grover was in position to block Taylor's retreat. Around four o'clock, a nine-inch shell hurtled from behind the Federal lines and burst over Fort Bisland. The shot announced the arrival of the Union gunboat *Clifton*, which had left Grand Lake and steamed up the Teche with a message from Grover reporting that he had landed successfully. Thankful, Banks ordered his tired troops to pull back to rest for the night. The following day he would advance and crush Taylor between his two commands.[36]

A few miles away, the vanguard of Grover's column under Dwight reached the Teche and extinguished a fire Vincent had set to a bridge across the bayou. Having secured his objective, Dwight waited for further instructions from Grover, who was attempting to get the last of his division ashore. Vincent continued his retreat to Franklin, where he met Reily, who was on his way with a regiment to reinforce the beleaguered cavalry commander.[37]

Although Dwight had reached the Teche, he had failed to cut a road that would allow Taylor's army to escape. The bayou swings back to the east at Franklin toward Grand Lake, where it makes a wide arc before turning west again to resume its normal course. At this point, the Teche resembles a large letter "U" lying on its side with the top or open end facing west. The area inside the "U" was known as Irish Bend, named after Alexander Porter, an Irishman and former U.S. senator who owned sev-

35. *OR*, 15:390.

36. Irwin, *History of the Nineteenth Army Corps*, 99–101.

37. *OR*, 15:371, 53:466.

eral thousand acres of land in the area. As was usual in the lower Mississippi valley, the main road followed the bayou along its circuitous path, but a cutoff road had been built across the open end of the "U," making travel from Franklin to New Iberia quicker and more convenient. With the lead elements of Grover's division across the Teche north of Franklin, Taylor needed to hold the cutoff road to allow for his retreat.[38]

By four o'clock in the afternoon, the last of Grover's troops had landed. After spending two hours issuing food and ammunition, Grover began moving forward around six o'clock, reaching Dwight's position at the bridge over the Teche a short while later. Crossing the bayou, Grover proceeded along the west bank toward Franklin before stopping to bivouac for the night at Madam Porter's plantation, Oaklawn Manor. He was still two miles short of Franklin, and although his troops were in possession of the road along the bayou, the cutoff road was still in Confederate hands.[39]

Around nine o'clock that evening, Taylor received news from Reily that Grover was in control of the road north of Franklin. Realizing that he had not a minute to spare, Taylor ordered Mouton quietly to start his withdrawal and Sibley to hold his position in front of Weitzel.[40]

Grover ordered his men forward on Tuesday morning, April 14. The Confederate troops hidden in the edge of the woods across a large field of sugarcane were no match for Grover's division, but they put up a stiff fight, knowing that Taylor's army would be trapped should Grover reach the cutoff road. At seven o'clock, Taylor heard "the peculiar whistle of a Parrot shell," which told him that the *Diana* had arrived to lend a hand. The Twenty-eighth Louisiana Infantry and some Louisiana militia arrived to strengthen Vincent and Reily about the same time. Mouton reached the field about an hour later and quickly deployed his brigade. The sun rose higher and the temperature increased. Casualties mounted on both sides. Still, the Confederates would not give and countercharged with a shout. Dwight attempted to bring his entire brigade into action, but he was flanked by a Confederate regiment that sent the Union troops reeling back to their lines.[41]

38. Raphael, *Battle in the Bayou Country,* 107.

39. Arceneaux, *Acadian General,* 80–81; Raphael, *Battle in the Bayou Country,* 107–9.

40. Taylor, *Destruction and Reconstruction,* 157–58.

41. *OR,* 15:372, 383–84; Hosmer, *Color-Guard,* 133–34; Sprague, *History of the 13th*

Seeing that Grover's advance had been checked, Taylor hastened to Franklin to supervise the withdrawal. The Confederates had pulled back from Fort Bisland during the night, leaving Tom Green with the Fifth Texas Cavalry to form a rear guard. Banks's men were up at dawn and in the abandoned works shortly after daylight, but Green deployed his troops at Centerville, halfway between Pattersonville and Franklin, and slowed the Federal pursuit.[42]

As soon as Sibley arrived with his brigade from Fort Bisland, Taylor ordered him to burn the bridge over Bayou Yokely after the last of the Confederate forces had crossed. Unfortunately for Mouton, because Sibley assumed that the troops still fighting at Irish Bend had already withdrawn, he set fire to the structure prematurely. Mouton with the Confederate forces contesting Grover's advance continued to withdraw with the *Diana* covering his retreat. Using bypaths, Mouton's troops reached the Yokely bridge to find it almost consumed by fire. There was still time, however, and the men hurried across, scorched and singed by the ordeal. They realized that the *Diana* would soon fall into enemy hands, so she was set on fire and "blown to atoms."[43]

When Grover's men reached the bridge over Yokely Bayou, they found it impassable. Banks arrived at the bridge around two o'clock that afternoon and saw that he could go no further. Deciding against the long detour along the bayou road to the north, he ordered his men to bivouac for the night. Meanwhile, Taylor's men continued their retreat until they reached Jeanerette some fifteen miles above Franklin.[44]

Losses had been heavy on both sides. Grover's casualties amounted to 353 men, of whom 49 were killed and 30 missing. Banks's casualties at Fort Bisland had totaled 224, with 40 dead. Federal losses together came to almost 600 men. Taylor was unable to determine how many casualties his little army had suffered. In the confusion that accompanied the hasty retreat, many of the conscripts that Taylor had recently brought into the ranks dropped by the way to return home. Straggling was not limited to the conscripts, for a considerable number of men from Sibley's brigade

---

Infantry, 113–16; Taylor, *Destruction and Reconstruction,* 159; Tiemann, *159th Regiment,* 29–31.

42. *OR,* 15:392, 53:464–65; Irwin, *History of the Nineteenth Army Corps,* 115–16; Root, "Experiences of a Federal Soldier," 643.

43. *OR,* 15:392; Beecher, *Record of the 114th Regiment,* 152.

44. *OR,* 15:678; Irwin, *History of the Nineteenth Army Corps,* 103, 115–17.

also left their units without permission. In his report to Richmond, the commander of the Trans-Mississippi Department, Lieutenant General E. Kirby Smith, estimated that Taylor's force had been reduced by one-third, or approximately thirteen hundred men, as a result of casualties and desertion. Although many of these men would eventually return to their units, Taylor's battered force was in no condition to contest Banks's larger army as it continued its advance up the Teche.[45]

Union troops entered New Iberia on April 16 after Taylor withdrew. From there, Banks dispatched a brigade of infantry to destroy the salt-works on Avery Island. Meanwhile, Taylor's small army continued its retreat, burning bridges over the many bayous that crisscrossed the region and slowing the Federal pursuit. Advance units of the Sixth New York Infantry caught up with the tail end of Taylor's column at the bridge over Vermillion Bayou on April 17, but the Confederates destroyed the bridge, delaying the Union advance for two days. Taylor continued to move northward, passing through Opelousas on April 18 and reaching Washington the following day.[46]

The Union incursion up the Teche was a serious blow to Confederate strength in the area. Transports and barges loaded with food, supplies, and ammunition had to be scuttled to prevent them from falling into enemy hands. Also left behind were more than a thousand barrels of corn, much of which Banks ordered distributed to poor families in the area. In addition, Banks's army grabbed up $3 million worth of spoils—ten thousand bales of cotton, quantities of sugar and molasses, ten thousand head of cattle, and nearly as many horses and mules. Thousands of slaves (one report estimated six thousand contrabands seeking their freedom in six hundred wagons) were swept up with the advancing army.[47]

There was also widespread looting. "Boys are getting fat," commented one observer, while another noted that Union soldiers had taken watches, dishes, earrings, Bibles, portraits, and women's clothing. One

45. *OR*, 15:319, 387, 393–94; Babcock, "War Commentary," 10, MNHS; De Forest, *Volunteer's Adventures*, 92; Frazier, "Texans on the Teche," 432–33.

46. *OR*, 15:373–74, 382; Irwin, *History of the Nineteenth Army Corps*, 128.

47. *OR*, 15:343–44; U.S. Congress, *Report of the Joint Committee on the Conduct of the War: Red River Expedition*, 345; Robert S. Denison to Chase, May 9, 1863, in Chase, "Diary and Correspondence," 386–87; Flinn, *Campaigning with Banks*, 65–71; Irwin, *History of the Nineteenth Army Corps*, 123; Ripley, *Slaves and Freedmen*, 20–21; Root, "Experiences of a Federal Soldier," 654; *New Orleans Era*, May 30, 1863.

of Banks's staff passed Captain Ormand F. Nims's battery and reported that "every man had at least three chickens." He was right, for one of their number wrote his mother that "they generally have 3 meals a day & chicken broth at every meal." Another soldier reported that "men of such reckless dispositions are frequently guilty of the most horrible destructions, and have been seen, in one of their 'raids,' dressed in full robes of a Catholic priest, or ornamented with the regalia of a Free Mason, while they marched through the dust with guns on their backs." "The scenes of disorder and pillage on those two days of march were disgraceful to civilized war," Dwight noted in his report. "Houses were entered and all in them destroyed in the most wanton manner. Ladies were frightened into delivering their jewels and valuables into the hands of soldiers by threats of violence toward their husbands. Negro women were ravished in the presence of white women and children. These disgusting scenes were due to the want of discipline in this army, and to the utter incompetency of regimental officers."[48]

Banks tried not contribute to the destruction. When he and his staff boarded at an elegant plantation house called Shadows on the Teche in New Iberia, they tried to make certain that the household would not be disturbed during their stay. The most serious casualty was the flower garden, which was destroyed by the constant coming and going of couriers, commanders, and staff. Nevertheless, neither his example nor the stringent orders Banks issued at the beginning of the campaign against straggling and looting made much difference.[49]

Onward the Union army pressed; the Confederates continued to retreat. With little opposition, Banks's army entered Opelousas, "the Rebel Capital of Louisiana," on April 20. With the help of gunboats operating

48. *OR*, 15:292–400, 703–32, 1041–85, 1115–16, 26, pt. 1:9–12; Beecher, *Record of the 114th Regiment*, 149; Taylor, *Destruction and Reconstruction*, 131–76; Van Alstyne, *Diary of an Enlisted Man*, 119–20; *New York Herald*, December 7, 1863; William H. Eastman to his mother, May 8, 1863, Eastman Letters, MAHS; also Smith, *Leaves from a Soldier's Diary*, 31, 46–47. A good bit of the looting was attributable to former slaves who had attached themselves to the Union army and served as servants to officers and men (De Forest, *Volunteer's Adventures*, 97–98).

49. Irwin, *History of the Nineteenth Army Corps*, 132; Raphael, *Battle in the Bayou Country*, 139–40. Banks's staff did avail themselves of the spoils of war by replacing their worn-out mounts with superior animals captured with Confederate prisoners (Babcock, "War Commentary," 11, MNHS).

from Grand Lake, Banks assumed control of the Atchafalaya on the same day by taking the Confederate position at Butte-a-la-Rose. This opened the safe water route from New Orleans to the Red River that Banks had wanted. A Federal gunboat located Farragut near the mouth of the Red River on May 1. Farragut promptly returned to New Orleans, leaving Commodore James S. Palmer in command of the *Hartford*. Meanwhile, Banks continued his march to Alexandria, occupying the city on May 7. Banks was delighted with his conquest. "Our success has been splendid," he wrote to Mary. "All say it is the cleanest, the best conceived and best executed campaign of the war."[50]

Although Banks proclaimed that "the Rebellion is broken," he had overestimated the importance of his drive up the Bayou Teche. "The *opening of the Mississippi River* has been continually presented as the *first* and *most important* object to be attained," General in Chief Halleck informed Banks in a dispatch. "Operations up the Red River, toward Texas, or toward Alabama, are only of secondary importance, to be undertaken *after* we get possession of the river." Halleck went on to say that he was "exceedingly disappointed" to see the commander of the Department of the Gulf pursuing "these eccentric movements," which cost six hundred casualties and diverted soldiers who were needed elsewhere. The Confederates, however, were delighted. Kirby Smith called Banks's digression "one of the most desirable events of the campaign." Both Kirby Smith and Richard Taylor knew that "the decisive battle of the West must soon be fought near Vicksburg . . . and Banks, by operating here [the valley of the Red River], is thrown out of the campaign on the Mississippi."[51]

50. *OR*, 15:240–50, 298–300, 303–4; *OR (Navy)*, 20:153–55; U.S. Congress, *Report of the Joint Committee on the Conduct of the War: Red River Expedition*, 309; Edmonds, *Guns of Port Hudson*, 1:219, 224; Foltz, *Surgeon of the Seas*, 283–85; Irwin, *History of the Nineteenth Army Corps*, 126, 128–29; Banks to Mrs. Banks, Sr., April 21, 1863, Banks to Mary Banks, April 23, May 3, 1863, Banks Collection, LC.

51. Banks to Mary Banks, May 4, 1863, also see Banks to Mary Banks, April 29, May 4, 6, 8, 1863, Banks Collection, LC; *New York Herald*, May 6, 1863; *OR*, 22, pt. 2:839–40, 26, pt. 1:500.

9

Pound Him at Your Will

Farragut carried a letter from Nathaniel P. Banks to Ulysses S. Grant with him when he fought his way past the Confederate batteries at Port Hudson during the early morning hours of March 15. Banks suggested in the letter several ways by which the two armies might cooperate in the attempt to open the Mississippi River. Grant was pleased to learn that Banks had moved against Port Hudson because the movement would divert Confederate troops away from Vicksburg. In fact, Grant was so pleased that he considered sending an army corps to help Banks reduce Port Hudson if Banks could move upriver to link up with Grant in front of Vicksburg afterward.[1]

Although the two Federal armies were less than 120 miles apart as the crow flies, the delay caused by Grant's having to send his reply through Confederate lines meant that Banks did not hear from Grant for several weeks. Finally, Farragut's secretary, Edward C. Gabaudan, memorized Grant's message to Banks and floated past the Confederate sentries at Port Hudson in a skiff disguised as a tree. By then, Banks had withdrawn from Port Hudson and had begun his effort to open an all-water route to the Mississippi through the Atchafalaya basin. He would not be in position to invest Port Hudson before May 10, Banks told Farragut's secretary when he arrived.[2]

Gabaudan headed back north, making his way overland to deliver

1. *OR*, 15:300–301, 692–93; Hewitt, *Port Hudson*, 108–9; Irwin, *History of the Nineteenth Army Corps*, 129–30.

2. Hewitt, *Port Hudson*, 109–10.

Banks's response to Grant. This time, it was Grant's turn to change his mind. On April 22, Grant had ordered the navy under Rear Admiral David Dixon Porter to run transports past the batteries at Vicksburg. Although one transport was lost, eleven vessels got through, bringing supplies to Grant's troops on the west bank and, most important, providing Grant with a means of getting his army to the east side of the river. Grant landed near Grand Gulf, Mississippi, on May 1 and shattered Confederate resistance at Port Gibson before pushing inland. These developments meant that Grant could not afford to send troops to reinforce Banks, but he could spare a few gunboats now that he was across the river. Leaving Grand Gulf with a small flotilla on May 4, Porter steamed up the Red River and joined Banks in Alexandria three days later.[3]

Grant's decision not to send troops left Banks in a predicament. He had counted on reinforcements before attempting to capture Port Hudson. Now he was not sure what to do. Several options were open to him. One was to retreat down the Teche and return to New Orleans. Another was to move from Alexandria down the Red River to the Mississippi and link up with Grant below Vicksburg. Finally, Banks could march directly to Port Hudson and attempt to reduce the fortress by himself.[4]

Banks sat in Alexandria for several days, trying to decide what to do. The problem was that there was no one with whom to explore his options. His generals, mostly professional soldiers, still kept their distance from the politician from Massachusetts. On May 14, Banks decided to evacuate Alexandria and proceeded with his troops down the Red River to Simmesport, from which he could move north to join Grant or south toward Port Hudson. But when he reached Simmesport, Banks was still uncertain which direction to take. Boarding a steamer, he returned to New Orleans via the Atchafalaya for a conference with Farragut. "Did you ever see such vacillation?" Commodore Palmer wrote to Farragut on May 14 from the *Hartford,* which continued to patrol the Mississippi River between Vicksburg and Port Hudson. "I do not know what to make of this army," he added. "They have got the whole of them down at Simmesport, and the commanding general seems to be loitering at New Orleans."[5]

3. *OR,* 15:311–13; Irwin, *History of the Nineteenth Army Corps,* 136–38.

4. *OR,* 15:590, 729–32; Farragut, *Life of Farragut,* 357–66; Irwin, *History of the Nineteenth Army Corps,* 138–40.

5. *OR,* 15:312, 729–32; *OR (Navy),* 20:187, 203; Irwin, *History of the Nineteenth*

Banks's chief of staff, Brigadier General George L. Andrews, urged him to return "at the earliest possible moment," while Halleck in Washington continued to seethe. "These operations are too eccentric to be pursued," he wrote to Banks on May 19. "I must again urge that you cooperate as soon as possible with General Grant. . . . Your forces must be united at the earliest possible moment." Four days later Halleck wrote Banks again: "I assure you that the Government is exceedingly disappointed that you and General Grant are not acting in conjunction." But Halleck's prodding was too late, for by the time his dispatches arrived, Banks had made up his mind. He had decided to take Port Hudson.[6]

Banks's decision to attack Port Hudson was probably the best of the three alternatives open to him. A retrograde movement down the Teche was unnecessary. Furthermore, such a retreat would not have looked very good in the press and certainly would have demoralized the troops, just as his withdrawal from Port Hudson had done two months earlier. Linking up with Grant was questionable at best. Grant had abandoned established lines of communication by marching into Mississippi. Banks was not even sure where Grant was. Port Hudson was the only viable option. A move on that post would prevent troops there from reinforcing the Confederate army facing Grant. In addition, it would prevent the Rebels from moving on New Orleans and thereby threatening Banks's own base of supply.

Transports that had entered the Mississippi River by taking a circuitous route up the Atchafalaya began to ferry Banks's men from the west bank to Bayou Sara north of Port Hudson on May 19. In the meantime, Augur had moved his division from Baton Rouge, and Thomas Sherman, who was in charge of the defenses of New Orleans, transported his division by boat up the river. The XIX Army Corps was reunited by May 21, and after a sharp skirmish, Augur's men cut the last remaining road out of Port Hudson. On the river, Farragut's ships closed that avenue of escape. By May 23, Banks's investment of the fortress was complete.[7]

Although most of his troops were committed to the siege of Port Hud

---

Army Corps, 149–51; Palfrey, "Port Hudson," 37; Richard B. Irwin to Banks, May 17, 1863, Gregory A. Coco Collection, MHI.

6. *OR*, 26, pt. 1:494–95, 500–501.

7. *OR*, 15:313, 316–17, 1084, 26, pt. 1:5–21; Edmonds, *Guns of Port Hudson*, 2:15; Taylor, *Destruction and Reconstruction*, 163.

son, Banks directed Colonel Thomas E. Chickering, the Federal commander in the Bayou Teche region, to collect as much booty as possible for shipment to New Orleans. Wagon trains guarded by Union troops snaked across the region gathering supplies. Steamers navigated as far up the Teche as obstructions would allow and picked up the wagons for transshipment to the Crescent City. Banks estimated the value of the cotton and sugar "confiscated" in the region at $10 million. When the spoliation was complete, Chickering gathered his troops and returned to Berwick, accompanied by six thousand slaves who were abandoning their lives on the plantation for whatever freedom following the Union army held in store.[8]

Grant continued his lightning-swift strike into Mississippi while Banks was debating his next move. After defeating a Confederate force at Raymond near Jackson on May 12, Grant swung back to the west and routed the Rebel army at Champion's Hill and Big Black River. Arriving before Vicksburg on May 18, Grant ordered an assault on the city's defenses. The first attack on May 19 failed. Regrouping his troops, Grant ordered a second all-out attempt to overrun the garrison on May 22. The second assault failed as well, and Grant was forced to settle for a long siege.

Banks's chances of taking Port Hudson improved considerably as a result of Grant's success, for the garrison at Port Hudson was substantially smaller in May than it had been in March. Banks now had many advantages over the Confederate commander, Franklin Gardner. For one thing, Banks had twenty-eight thousand troops as opposed to Gardner's seven thousand, as well as plenty of cavalry to guard his rear. Banks's artillery was also first-rate, and he could count on an unlimited quantity of ammunition and rations via a supply line that extended from Baton Rouge to New Orleans. In addition, the Union navy controlled the Mississippi River both north and south of Port Hudson and, by controlling the Atchafalaya, it could prevent Taylor from attacking from the west. Gardner, in contrast, had inferior guns and a limited supply of food and ammunition. In addition, the four and a half miles of Confederate

8. Arceneaux, *Acadian General*, 92–93; Beecher, *Record of the 114th Regiment*, 182–83; Ewer, *Third Massachusetts Cavalry*, 77–78, 81–83; Irwin, *History of the Nineteenth Army Corps*, 156–57; Moors, *History of the 52nd Regiment*, 134–37.

breastworks at Port Hudson had been designed for a force that was three times the number of defenders Gardner had available.[9]

Nevertheless, the Confederate situation was far from hopeless. Gardner's defenses were complete when the siege began, and he enjoyed the advantage of topography. His interior lines of communication would allow him to concentrate his forces to beat off any attack unless it was coordinated so that the Federal assaults came from several directions at the same time. In addition, the ground in front of the Rebel fortifications was covered with a dense undergrowth and crisscrossed by harsh ravines. Gardner could also count on John L. Logan's cavalry, operating out of Clinton, Louisiana, to pester Banks's army and limit its ability to forage off the countryside. Finally, Banks's concentration of troops at Port Hudson left New Orleans open to a diversionary attack by Richard Taylor's small army in west Louisiana.[10]

On Tuesday evening, May 26, Banks held a conference with his commanders to consider their options. Banks was in favor of an immediate assault, arguing that it was imperative for the XIX Corps to reduce Port Hudson quickly so they could steam upriver to join Grant. Augur disagreed. It would be folly, he said, to order troops to attack over unknown terrain. Furthermore, they should weaken the Confederate fortifications with a prolonged artillery bombardment before the assault. Thomas Sherman agreed with Augur, noting that the Federal army could starve the Confederates out of their strong positions. Banks countered by reminding his generals that more than half of the army was made up of nine-month men whose terms of service would begin to expire in a few weeks. Furthermore, Taylor was stirring up trouble and might risk an attack on New Orleans, cutting the Union troops off from their base of supply. Sherman persisted, pointing out that a frontal assault would be too costly. Banks replied hotly, "The people of the North

9. *New Orleans Daily True Delta*, August 2, 8, 1863. Gardner surrendered 6,340 officers and men, to which must be added losses (623 total) during the siege (*OR*, 26, pt. 1:144, 642). The Confederate forces under Logan at Clinton amounted to some twelve hundred men (*OR*, 26, pt. 1:180). Union strength is based on Irwin's estimate (*History of the Nineteenth Army Corps*, 216–17) and reports in *OR*, 26, pt. 1:13, 14, 511, 526–28, 572–73. To this must be added the Union cavalry under Grierson (*OR*, 26, pt. 1:135) and naval forces under Farragut.

10. *OR*, 26, pt. 1:44, 511–12, 53:873; Clark, *One Hundred and Sixteenth Regiment*, 82–92.

demand blood, sir." With that comment, the meeting ended, and Banks issued orders for a general assault the next day.[11]

The battle plan called for Farragut to open the assault with a bombardment at daybreak. Banks's artillery, consisting of some ninety pieces, would open fire at the same time. The artillery barrage would be the signal for Augur in the center and Sherman on the left to advance their skirmishers and "place their troops in position to take instant advantage of any favorable opportunity, and will, if possible, force the enemy works at the earliest moment." Weitzel was expected to exert pressure on the right of the Union line as soon as he heard Augur's and Sherman's men begin firing. Grover with four regiments was held in reserve.[12]

It did not take long for these plans to go awry. During the night, artillery assigned to support Weitzel could not get into position because of the rough terrain and uncertainty regarding the nature of the Confederate positions. Nevertheless, at 5:45 Wednesday morning, Farragut and the fleet opened up with a furious barrage. The guns supporting Augur and Sherman joined in, and "the ball was opened."[13]

Without waiting for signs of an advance in any of the other sectors of the Union line, Weitzel ordered his men forward. They immediately ran into a hailstorm of fire from the Confederate defensive line. As Weitzel's attack floundered, Banks waited for sounds of firing that would announce the advance of Sherman and Augur. By noon there still was no evidence of an attack. Banks mounted Shenandoah and rode to Sherman's headquarters a short distance away. There, he found the division commander and his staff seated for lunch, horses unsaddled and wine bottles set out on a linen-covered table. Banks was furious. Pointing to Slaughter's field, the ground with an unfortunate name over which his troops were to charge, Sherman argued that it would be suicidal to attack. In a rage that was as uncharacteristic as it was furious, Banks re-

11. *OR,* 26, pt. 1:507–9; Edmonds, *Guns of Port Hudson,* 2:33–34; Hoffman, *Camp, Court and Siege,* 70; Irwin, *History of the Nineteenth Army Corps,* 158, 166–69; Palfrey, "Port Hudson," 39. The expiration of enlistments was a serious problem. During the move from Alexandria to Port Hudson in May 1863, for example, the Sixth New York Infantry abruptly quit the army and left for home, having served the two years for which it enlisted.

12. *OR,* 26, pt. 1:508–9.

13. *OR (Navy),* 20:211, 212, 769.

lieved Sherman of command and ordered his own chief of staff, George L. Andrews, to take charge of the division.[14]

Andrews had to be summoned from Banks's headquarters. By the time he reached the field, Sherman was drunk, mounted on his horse, and preparing to lead his men into battle. Andrews informed Sherman that he was relieved. Sherman refused to relinquish command and insisted on riding in front of the division during the charge. Uncertain what to do, Andrews retired a short distance to witness the spectacle.

Sherman's men moved forward at a trot across Slaughter's field. The Confederates were ready and waiting, hidden behind the parapet of their defensive line. When the Federal troops came within range, the defenders rose as one and let loose a terrible volley. The front line of Sherman's division simply melted away. Sherman's horse went down, falling into a ditch and pinning the general underneath. A Union officer ran to the division commander and got him out from beneath his horse with difficulty. Dusting the dirt from his uniform, Sherman started forward on foot, only to take a rifle ball through the left thigh. Sherman was carried off the field, but still the Union attack pressed on until it broke like a great wave on the fortifications and flowed back to the rear.[15]

Situated between Sherman and Weitzel, Augur's division waited for their assault. When Augur heard the sound of firing to the south, he assumed that Sherman had begun his attack but waited for a direct order from Banks. Distracted by his difficulties with Sherman, Banks failed to give the word, although he was in direct communication with Augur via a series of semaphore stations perched atop trees. Realizing that Sherman's assault had failed, Banks finally ordered Augur to "advance at once." By the time Augur got his men in motion, Sherman's division was already falling back across Slaughter's field.[16]

14. *OR*, 26, pt. 1:509–10; Hoffman, *Camp, Court and Siege*, 66–67; Irwin, *History of the Nineteenth Army Corps*, 175–77. For Thomas Sherman's version of these events, see his "unofficial" report (p. 18) written on February 20, 1877, Banks Manuscripts, ISHL.

15. Edward Bacon, *Among the Cotton Thieves* (1867; reprint, Bossier City, La.: Everett, 1989), 138–40; Neal Dow, *The Reminiscences of Neal Dow: Recollections of Eighty Years* (Portland, Me.: Evening Press Publishing Co., 1898), 694–95; Hoffman, *Camp, Court and Siege*, 71; John Smith Kendall, "Recollections of a Confederate Officer," *Louisiana Historical Quarterly* 29 (October 1946): 1113–17; Van Alstyne, *Diary of an Enlisted Man*, 115.

16. Edmonds, *Guns of Port Hudson*, 2:79; Plummer, *History of the Forty-eighth Regiment*, 37–39.

With Weitzel and Sherman out of the fight, Gardner shifted troops from their original positions to strengthen those facing Augur. By the time Augur's men began to move forward, the Confederates had concentrated almost as many men as the attackers. The division never had a chance. Augur's troops were soon pinned down by a furious Confederate fire.[17]

The only Federal troops on the field that Banks had not committed were Grover's small force of reserves. On several occasions during the morning Grover had conferred with Weitzel over whether he could add his troops to the latter's attack. But both waited, expecting to learn the outcome of Sherman's and Augur's assaults before committing the reserves. As a result, Grover's men remained far in the rear and were not ready when orders came from Banks at 2:30 in the afternoon to attack. It was a classic case of too little, too late. By three o'clock Grover's men were in position, at which time the order to charge was given and the men moved forward. It was a repetition of what had happened too often that day. Grover's attack, like the others, was an "ill-advised, unsupported, heroic, and hopeless effort."[18]

The fighting went on until 5:30 that evening, when someone had the good sense to raise a white flag and call a temporary cease-fire so that the wounded could be attended to. Union casualties on May 27 exceeded 450 dead and missing and over 1,500 wounded. The Confederate losses numbered no more than several hundred. Banks had many excuses for the defeat. He felt that his superiors had left his force "too weak for the work it has to do." Banks also blamed his subordinates, for "had they not failed me here we should have carried the works." Finally, he blamed the defenses, which he considered "perhaps the strongest in the country, and garrisoned by determined men."[19]

The problem was essentially the lack of coordination, for which Banks

17. Edmonds, *Guns of Port Hudson,* 2:80–88; Kendall, "Recollections of a Confederate Officer," 1117–19.

18. *OR,* 26, pt. 1:509–10; Clark, *One Hundred and Sixteenth Regiment,* 89–91; DeForest, *Volunteer's Adventures,* 113; Edmonds, *Guns of Port Hudson,* 2:89–95; Powers, *Story of the Thirty-eighth Regiment,* 92–95; Sprague, *History of the 13th Infantry,* 139–40; entry for May 27, 1863, Osborne Diary, MAHS.

19. *OR,* 26, pt. 1:47, 144, 526–27, 546–49, 554–55. Banks indicated in a letter to Mary (May 30, 1863, Banks Collection, LC) that he had but 11,000 men available for an assault. Yet his monthly report for May included 28,822 "present for duty" at Port Hudson, although not all of these would be available for a general assault on the works.

was responsible. Banks's vague instructions had left his generals confused, and the difficult terrain made good communication between them difficult. Nevertheless, Banks blamed Thomas Sherman as the primary culprit for many of these failures. Had Sherman moved at dawn as ordered, Augur would have attacked too and Weitzel could have received the assistance he needed. Instead, Sherman "failed utterly and criminally to bring his men into the field." Had not Banks found him at noon eating dinner with "his staff officers all with their horses unsaddled, and none knowing where to find their command?" Sherman retorted that it was only then, when he became aware of Banks's "anxious manner," that he realized that Banks intended for him to set his division in motion. By then, it was too late. Although Sherman clearly played a role in the debacle, it was Banks's responsibility to see that his commanders followed their instructions. As he had failed to do at Cedar Mountain, Banks did not employ his forces on May 27 in a coordinated manner.[20]

In planning for a second assault for June 14, Banks gave detailed written orders that specified the hour and minute of each advance and the way in which each column was to be formed. He also ordered his staff to make a thorough reconnaissance of the ground and placed his men in positions closer to Rebel lines.[21]

At precisely 11:45 A.M. on June 13, the Federals opened a furious bombardment in preparation for an assault the next day. Banks followed up with an ultimatum to Gardner. In a lengthy demand for the garrison to surrender, Banks complimented the Confederates on their gallant defense and expressed the desire "to avoid unnecessary sacrifice of life." After reminding Gardner that he was faced by dwindling supplies, desertions, and being cut off from all help, Banks added a threat: "I have at my command a train of artillery seldom equalled in extent and efficiency, which no ordinary fortress can successfully resist, and an infantry force of greatly superior numbers, and most determined purpose, that cannot fail to place Port Hudson in my possession at my will." Gardner laughed out loud when he read the message. He knew that many of

20. *OR*, 26, pt. 1:507–10; *New Orleans Daily True Delta*, August 2, 1863; Sherman's report, 18, Banks Manuscripts, ISHL; also see Edward Cunningham, *The Port Hudson Campaign, 1862–1863* (Baton Rouge: Louisiana State University Press, 1963), 66–67.

21. Bacon, *Among the Cotton Thieves*, 151–52.

Banks's nine-month men were counting the days before they could go home and that Banks's previous attempt to overwhelm the garrison had met with complete failure. "I decline to surrender," Gardner stated in his brief reply, and the Federal artillery opened fire once again.[22]

By now Banks's men were beginning to lose faith in their commander. The situation had become so bad that some officers were reluctant to lead their men into battle, and many nine-month privates actively avoided duty that would place them in the line of fire. In particular, the troops were angry that Banks had given Gardner advance notice of the impending assault. One of Banks's brigade commanders, William Dwight, complained that the pattern of following up an artillery bombardment with an infantry assault let the Rebels anticipate each attempt to take Port Hudson by storm.[23]

Dwight was right. Gardner and virtually everyone else in the fortress were certain that an all-out assault was imminent. They were not disappointed, for on Sunday morning, June 14, Banks made a second attempt to overwhelm the garrison. The results were much the same as on May 27. During the two weeks between attacks, the Confederates had continued to strengthen their fortifications, and although Union coordination and preparation were better, the defenders were too strong. "How do you like it?" a Rebel with a boyish voice taunted as the Union troops huddled behind tree stumps and in ravines, pinned down by the murderous fire. "Why don't you come on?" another Confederate called out from behind a parapet. There would be no triumph of Union arms that

22. *OR*, 26, pt. 1:552–53; Crawford M. Jackson, "An Account of the Occupation of Fort [*sic*] Hudson," *Alabama Historical Quarterly* 18 (Winter 1956): 475; Cunningham, *Port Hudson Campaign*, 79; M. J. Smith and James Freret, "Fortifications and Siege of Port Hudson," *Southern Historical Society Papers* 14 (1886): 327. For a typical "short-timer's" letter home during this period, see William H. Hayward to "My Dear Sisters," April 4, 1863, William H. Hayward Letters, MHI.

23. Bacon, *Among the Cotton Thieves*, 148; G. G. Benedict, *A History of the Part Taken by the Vermont Soldiers and Sailors in the War for the Union, 1861–65* (Burlington, Vt.: Free Press Association, 1888), 129; Clark, *One Hundred and Sixteenth Regiment*, 94–99; Plummer, *History of the Forty-Eighth Regiment*, 44; William Dwight to Banks, June 24, 1863, Banks to F[rank] P. Blair, July 8, 1863, Banks to Mary Banks, June 18, 1863, Banks Collection, LC. After Port Hudson fell, some nine-month soldiers mutinied and had to be detained under arrest in the penitentiary at Baton Rouge (William E. Wilcox to his wife, July 16, 1863, Wilcox Papers, WDML; also Irwin, *History of the Nineteenth Army Corps*, 257; and Babcock, "War Commentary," 48, MNHS).

day. The assault on June 14 resulted in another four hundred dead and missing and fourteen hundred wounded. Together, the assaults of May 27 and June 14 had generated more than four thousand casualties, or one man in seven.[24]

Banks was not about to give up. On the day following his defeat, he issued a call for one thousand volunteers to form a special storming party "to vindicate the flag of the Union and the memory of the defenders who have fallen." The major general promised recognition, promotion, and a medal to those who would volunteer. They were to be called the "Forlorn Hope," and more than thirteen hundred men came forward, including volunteers from two black regiments that had participated in the assault of May 27.[25]

Still outfitted in heavy woolen blue uniforms, the Union soldiers investing Port Hudson found the summer heat oppressive. Nevertheless, they had plenty of food, and the rotation of front-line units allowed troops periodic breaks during which they foraged on the nearby farms for items to supplement their diet.[26]

The Confederates had a rougher time of it. Although there was an ample supply of molasses, salt, and sugar, as well as a large quantity of cow-beans until they spoiled in the hot, damp weather, there was no beef, no pork, and little corn. By July 1 the men had begun slaughtering mules and found the meat to be "quite tender and juicy." Horses also proved to be "good eating, but not equal to mule." Snakes and rats also found their way on to the mess plates of many a hungry Rebel, the latter considered "quite a luxury—superior . . . to spring chicken." Water was in short supply, but the Port Hudson defenders were able to drink a

24. *OR,* 26, pt. 1:14; Bacon, *Among the Cotton Thieves,* 178. For accounts of the assault, see Babcock, "War Commentary," 37–41, MNHS; De Forest, *Volunteer's Adventures,* 133–44; Diary entry for June 15, 1863, Dargan, *My Experiences;* Irwin, *History of the Nineteenth Army Corps,* 185–208; Root, "Experiences of a Federal Soldier," 666–67.

25. *OR,* 26, pt. 1:56–61; Dudley Taylor Cornish, *The Sable Arm: Negro Troops in the Union Army, 1861–1865* (New York: Norton, 1966), 143; Irwin, *History of the Nineteenth Army Corps,* 212–13, 488–506; Van Alstyne, *Diary of an Enlisted Man,* 132–33. Most of these volunteers came from regiments that had suffered light losses up to that point in the campaign (Cunningham, *Port Hudson Campaign,* 95).

26. Smith, *Leaves from a Soldier's Diary,* 57–79; Van Alstyne, *Diary of an Enlisted Man,* 119–44.

sugar-beer, and when tobacco ran out, the Confederates found sumac leaves "tolerably good." The one thing that a substitute could not be provided for was medicine, which forced southern surgeons to operate without chloroform.[27]

On the Union side there was no shortage of ordnance, and Yankee guns boomed day and night. The Confederates had to conserve their missiles and spaced their shots accordingly. With cannonballs and canister in short supply, the Rebels stuffed their half-disabled batteries with nails, horseshoes, chains, and pieces of Union shot and shell that fell within the lines. Although the Confederates could make cartridges, there was a scarcity of percussion caps, so marksmen had to make each shot count.[28]

With the opposing lines in such close proximity, it was not surprising that soldiers on both sides began to fraternize. Despite the disapproval of the officers, a brisk trade thrived as erstwhile enemies swapped sugar and molasses for coffee, smokes, and news. The pleasure of this break in monotony was such that the enlisted men went to lengths to continue it in spite of orders to the contrary. "Get under cover now, Johnny," a Yank would yell out when officers appeared. "Look out Yank, we're going to fire," was the corresponding warning from the other side.[29]

Banks became more and more impatient as the siege extended. "I swear terribly," he wrote Mary. "I lay down my knife and fork at breakfast, I wake up at night and swear. We have great trials—so many poor

27. *OR*, 26, pt. 1:536–37, 557, 613–14, 617; Bacon, *Among the Cotton Thieves*, 293; Smith and Freret, "Fortifications and Siege of Port Hudson," 327; Linn Tanner, "Port Hudson Calamities—Mule Meat," *Confederate Veteran* 17 (October 1909): 512; *New Orleans Daily True Delta*, August 4, 8, 14, 1863; also *New York Herald*, July 23, 1863; C. P. Stone to Banks, March 4, 1886, Banks Collection, LC.

28. *OR*, 26, pt. 1:147, 536–39, 551; Flinn, *Campaigning with Banks*, 76; C. P. Stone to Banks, March 4, 1886, Banks Collection, LC; *New York Herald*, June 27, 1863; *New Orleans Daily True Delta*, August 8, 14, 1863. One of the unusual wounds resulting from the Confederate practice of using scrap iron for ammunition was suffered by a Union soldier who had "an old piece of a French bayonet three inches long" strike him in his mouth, knocking out his front teeth and splitting his tongue down the middle before lodging in the roof of his mouth. Remarkably, the soldier survived (Plummer, *History of the Forty-Eighth Regiment*, 65–66).

29. *OR*, 26, pt. 1:513–18; Bacon, *Among the Cotton Thieves*, 214; Edmonds, *Guns of Port Hudson*, 2:284–85; Hoffman, *Camp, Court and Siege*, 72; Van Alstyne, *Diary of an Enlisted Man*, 134; *New Orleans Daily True Delta*, August 13, 1863.

men." To pass the time he walked through the trenches and visited with the enlisted men. He found them to be as "tough as grain-fed horses" and holding up well under the blistering summer sun and soaking summer rains. Banks was aware that defeat here would mean "death to all his political aspirations," but his luck held. Confederate general Joe Johnston near Vernon, Mississippi, continued to hesitate and did not move against either Grant at Vicksburg or Banks at Port Hudson. Inside the fortress, the Confederates grew discouraged, and the number of deserters sneaking off at night to the Union lines increased.[30]

The Forlorn Hope under the command of Colonel Henry Birge was divided into two battalions and began training at their new campsite at Carter's Plantation near Banks's headquarters. The officers instructed the men in the use of their weapons, briefed them on the terrain over which they would attack, and drilled the volunteers in new tactics to be used in the assault. Unlike most of the troops in the Union lines before Port Hudson, the morale of the Forlorn Hope was high.[31]

Banks paid a visit to his elite command on June 30. Stepping up on a crude platform constructed for his visit, Banks delivered an oration as if he were back on the floor of the House of Representatives. "A little more than a month ago you found the enemy in the open country far away from these scenes," he proclaimed. "Now he is hemmed in and surrounded. What remains is to close upon him and secure him within our grasp. We want the close hug! When you get an enemy's head under your arm, you can pound him at your will. . . . The hug he will never recover from until the Devil, the arch Rebel, gives him his own!" Many of the soldiers who witnessed the speech felt inspired. "Remarkably eloquent!" declared one bystander, while another described it as "moving." But not everyone was impressed. Some of the men listened "in cold silence, responding with cheers only at the call of their officers," a Union colonel

30. Hosmer, *Color-Guard,* 210; Van Alstyne, *Diary of an Enlisted Man,* 122; *New Orleans Era,* June 23, 1863; Banks to Mary Banks, May 30, 1863, Banks Collection, LC; Entry for June 1, 1863, Osborne Diary, MAHS. In spite of the trials and tribulations, Banks's health was excellent during the siege. He even put on some extra weight (167 pounds on his 5′ 8″ frame), "a high figure for me," he admitted to Mary (June 4, 1863, Banks Collection, LC).

31. Townsend, *History of the Sixteenth Regiment,* 244–46.

wrote. "They were tired and worn out, and had a full appreciation of the bravery of the besieged, if General Banks had not."[32]

To be successful, the Forlorn Hope had to get closer to the earthworks of the fortress. Earlier assaults had failed because the Union troops had to advance over a wide expanse of open ground before reaching the parapet. Consequently, during the last two weeks of June and the first week in July, Federal troops at several points along the line spent their time digging deep trenches or saps toward the Confederate works. The Confederates did not stand by idly as the Federals tunneled toward their position. They rolled unexploded mortar shells from Farragut's fleet down the embankments into the Federal trenches and sunk countermines in which they planted explosives to collapse the walls of Union tunnels. The countermeasures were so successful that the Fourth of July came and went without another attempt to take the fortress by storm.[33]

The same was not true in Vicksburg. The Confederate commander, Lieutenant General John C. Pemberton, called it quits on July 4, 1863, and three days later, news of Vicksburg's fall arrived at Port Hudson. The Rebel troops first became aware of it from the cheers of Banks's men, who were wild with joy. Why the cheers, the Confederates asked. Vicksburg has surrendered, came the reply. At first the Rebels thought it was a Yankee trick, but when Banks sent an official confirmation, Gardner knew that it was time to quit, too. It would be just a matter of time before reinforcements from Grant's army would float down the river to join Banks in a final overwhelming assault.[34]

Representatives from both sides met in a grove of shade trees on July 8. The meeting took longer than expected, but the delegations finally decided that the surrender would take place the next morning at seven o'clock. During the night a thunderstorm drenched the troops, but the

32. Henry A. Willis, *The Fifty-third Regiment Massachusetts Volunteers* (Fitchburg, Mass.: Blanchard & Brown, 1889), 144–46; entry for July 2, 1863, Osborne Diary, MAHS; Babcock, "War Commentary," 48, MNHS.

33. Edmonds, *Guns of Port Hudson*, 2:322–43; Smith and Freret, "Fortifications and Siege of Port Hudson," 336–38.

34. *OR*, 26, pt. 1:52–56, 177; *New Orleans Daily True Delta*, August 16, 1863; *New York Herald*, July 11, 1863. Gardner told one of Banks's staff officers after the surrender ceremony that he had decided to capitulate because of the dwindling rations even before he received news of Vicksburg's fall (C. P. Stone to Banks, March 4, 1886, Banks Collection, LC).

morning of July 9 dawned fair and cool. At the appointed hour, the band from the Thirteenth Connecticut struck up "Yankee Doodle" as a long column of Union troops marched through the Jackson Road sally port into the Confederate fortress. The first unit was the Forlorn Hope, which had never had the chance to see whether its training would have accomplished what others had been unable to do. Banks made Andrews commander of the newly acquired Union post and ordered him to accept Gardner's surrender. The Confederate troops, thin and worn out from weeks of privation, stood at attention in a long line facing the Union regiments. Gardner gave the order to ground arms and offered his sword to Andrews, hilt first. The band broke into the "Star Spangled Banner," after which it played a rousing rendition of "Dixie." A Union soldier ran the Stars and Stripes up the Port Hudson flagpole. Interestingly, no one cheered.[35]

The surrender netted the Union army sixty-three hundred prisoners, fifty-one pieces of artillery, five thousand stands of small arms, twenty-one tons of cannon powder, 150,000 rounds of ammunition, and two steamers. The "absolute necessities of the situation" forced Banks to parole all the prisoners except commissioned officers, which his superiors later criticized because they feared that the Confederate prisoners would quickly break their paroles.[36]

The price of victory was dear. It had cost the Union at least two men dead, wounded, or struck down by illness for every defender who marched out of Port Hudson on July 9 to lay down his arms. Ironically, Banks could have had the fortress without the loss of a single life. Johnston had ordered Gardner to abandon the post just as Banks shut the back door on the Confederate garrison in late May. Nevertheless, Banks

35. *OR,* 26, pt. 1:620–28; Clark, *One Hundred and Sixteenth Regiment,* 106–7; Irwin, *History of the Nineteenth Army Corps,* 229–33; Johns, *Life with the Forty-Ninth Massachusetts,* 322–23; Kendall, "Recollections of a Confederate Officer," 1131; Plummer, *History of the Forty-Eighth Regiment,* 50; Sprague, *History of the 13th Infantry,* 171; Van Alstyne, *Diary of an Enlisted Man,* 146–47; George Andrews to his wife, July 8, 12, 1863, George Leonard Andrews Papers, LALMVC.

36. *OR,* 26, pt. 1:55–56, 631, Ser. 2, 6:209, 223–24, 248–49; Williams, *Lincoln Finds a General,* 5:64–66; John A. Rawlins to Ulysses S. Grant, July 30, 1863, John A. Rawlins Collection, CHS. Cunningham asserts in *The Port Hudson Campaign,* 120, that the enlisted men captured at Port Hudson were quickly reintegrated into the Confederate army. For Benjamin F. Butler's criticism of Banks's decision to parole his Confederate prisoners, see *Butler's Book,* 584.

had bottled up a sizable contingent of reinforcements for Johnston's army. This accomplishment was particularly important in early June when the combined Rebel forces around Jackson and Vicksburg was equal in numbers to Grant's army. The addition of Gardner's troops might have tipped the balance, perhaps allowing Johnston to lift the siege. Yet if the strategic value of investing Port Hudson was in pinning down Gardner's men, the assaults of May 27 and June 14 were unnecessary. But Banks could not rely on hindsight, and, like Grant, he did not appreciate the difficulty of taking well-constructed fortifications defended by determined men. If one is to criticize Banks at Port Hudson, one must also criticize Grant for his assaults against the fortifications at Vicksburg on May 19 and 22.[37]

As he customarily did, Banks overstated the accomplishments of the campaign. "The siege will be remembered not only for its important results, but also for the manner in which it has been conducted." Although he expected that the taking of Port Hudson would bring him great recognition, he failed to realize that other headlines would attract more attention. Vicksburg, Gettysburg, and the draft riots in New York provided ample news for July 1863. Those who did notice were inclined to give Grant the credit, saying that "the fall of Vicksburg necessarily carries with it the surrender of Port Hudson." Much to Banks's disappointment, the public would continue to remember him more for his unfortunate confrontation with Stonewall Jackson in the Shenandoah Valley than for his victory at Port Hudson.[38]

37. *OR*, 26, pt. 1:16–17; Edmonds, *Guns of Port Hudson*, 2:370; Hewitt, *Port Hudson*, 22, 44; Williams, *Lincoln Finds a General*, 5:23; Woodworth, *Jefferson Davis and His Generals*, 208–21; *New Orleans Daily True Delta*, August 6, 1863.

38. *New Orleans Daily True Delta*, July 11, 1863; Banks to Mary Banks, July 6, 8, 17, 1863, Banks Collection, LC.

Nathaniel P. Banks, Speaker of the House. *From the author's collection.*

Major General Banks in 1861. *From the author's collection.*

Nathaniel P. Banks late in the war. *Courtesy National Archives.*

"The General," ca. 1890. *Courtesy MASS MOLLUS & USAMHI.*

Mary Theodosia Palmer Banks. *Courtesy Library of Congress.*

Nathaniel P. Banks and his family in New Orleans, 1863. From left to right: "Binney," Joseph Frémont, Mary Palmer, and Maude. Mary and the children arrived in October 1863 and stayed until early August 1864. *Courtesy MASS MOLLUS & USAMHI.*

"Exciting scene in the House at Washington in 1856, following the election of N. P. Banks as Speaker after nine weeks of balloting." *From* Leslie's Weekly Illustrated Newspaper, *February 16, 1856.*

"General Banks addressing the Louisiana planters in the parlor of the St. Charles Hotel, New Orleans." *From* Leslie's Illustrated Newspaper, *March 28, 1863.*

Banks's residence on Coliseum Place in New Orleans. *Courtesy the Louisiana and Lower Mississippi Valley Collections, LSU Libraries, Louisiana State University.*

Major General Banks with his staff in New York prior to embarking on their expedition to New Orleans.
Courtesy National Archives.

McLaflin's Battery, First Indiana Heavy Artillery, at Port Hudson. The men have taken off their coats because of the heat. The man sitting in the center is sheltered by canvas stretched over a framework of limbs attached to the inside of the parapet. The artillery piece on the left is a thirty-pound rifled Parrott cannon. *Courtesy Port Hudson State Commemorative Area.*

Cox's Battery, First Indiana Heavy Artillery, at Port Hudson. One of the cotton bales used by the Union Army in its fortifications around Port Hudson can be seen behind the barrel at left. Loose cotton from bales struck by Confederate counterfire is scattered on the ground. *Courtesy Port Hudson State Commemorative Area.*

This caricature of Nathaniel P. Banks by Thomas Nast appeared in the December 28, 1872, issue of *Harper's Weekly,* shortly after Banks had lost his seat in Congress. Nast's skill as a cartoonist is evident when his sketch is compared with this photograph of Banks, taken during this period.
Photograph courtesy National Archives.

10

The Sensation of Deliverance

Once the Mississippi River was opened, Banks believed that Mobile, Alabama, was the next logical military objective in the Department of the Gulf. Although a naval blockade had been fairly effective in reducing the flow of traffic, Mobile was one of the few remaining deepwater ports under Confederate control. In addition, several rail lines converged on the city, which made it an important transportation and distribution center. Furthermore, with the capture of New Orleans, Memphis, and Nashville, Mobile, Charleston, and Richmond were the only cities of any size still in Confederate hands. Nevertheless, Halleck ordered Banks to turn his attention in another direction. There was a need to establish a Union presence in Texas for "reasons other than military."[1]

Lincoln had been interested in Texas for some time and had seriously considered using Banks's expeditionary force to occupy portions of that state in 1862. Local elections that fall in Ohio, Indiana, and Lincoln's home state of Illinois had gone badly for the Republican party, however, because of the economic hardship of the closing of the Mississippi River to commercial traffic. Consequently, Lincoln had ordered Banks to the Crescent City. But now that the great artery and outlet of all western commerce had been opened, Lincoln could turn his attention once again to the Lone Star State.[2]

1. *OR*, 26, pt. 1:18, 661–62, 652–53, 666, 673–75; Johnson, *Red River Campaign*, 36–37. For an excellent account of the overland portion of this campaign, see Richard Lowe, *The Texas Overland Expedition of 1863* (Fort Worth: Ryan Place Publishers, 1996).

2. William Dudley Foulke, *Life of Oliver P. Morton, Including His Important*

The main reason Lincoln wanted to show the flag in Texas was to block the ambitions of Louis Napoleon, emperor of France, who had recently taken a possessive interest in Mexico. With the United States distracted by the Civil War, French troops had occupied Mexico City on June 7, 1863, and quickly set up a puppet government under one of Louis Napoleon's distant relatives, Archduke Maximilian of Austria. Lincoln feared that having gained a foothold, Louis Napoleon would attempt to reestablish Mexico's traditional boundaries by incorporating Texas as part of his new empire.[3]

A second reason for the renewed interest in Texas was its status as the only Confederate state completely free of Federal control. Important Republicans in Washington wanted a Federal presence there so that a loyalist government could be formed to bring Texas back into the Union. Among the strongest backers of such a plan were antislavery advocates who expected the support of a large number of nonslaveholding German immigrants in the state. The immigrants' success in producing cheap cotton with free labor was seen as a model for a new southern economy to follow the cessation of hostilities. Together, the growing pressure from influential radicals in Washington and the French presence in Mexico prompted Lincoln to have Halleck advise Banks in mid-August 1863 that the "flag of the United States should be again raised [in Texas] and sustained somewhere."[4]

To occupy even a small part of such a large state would take considerably more men than Banks had at his command. Although the surrender of Port Hudson had freed thousands of troops for duty elsewhere, Banks's strength had been diminished by the departure of his nine-month men. During the summer and early fall of 1863, more than thirty regiments claimed that their time was up, packed their bags, and were shipped north to be mustered out. Furthermore, the Confederate com-

---

Speeches, 2 vols. (Indianapolis: Bowen-Merrill, 1899), 1:206; Johnson, *Red River Campaign,* 22–23.

3. *OR,* 26, pt. 1:664, 672–73, 693; Lincoln to Banks, August 5, 1863, in Roy P. Basler, ed., *The Collected Works of Abraham Lincoln,* 9 vols. (New Brunswick, N.J.: Rutgers University Press for the Abraham Lincoln Association, 1953–55), 6:364; Johnson, *Red River Campaign,* 35; Robert L. Kerby, *Kirby Smith's Confederacy: The Trans-Mississippi South, 1863–1865* (New York: Columbia University Press, 1972), 187.

4. U.S. Congress, *Report of the Joint Committee on the Conduct of the War: Red River Expedition,* 21; *OR,* 26, pt. 1:673; Johnson, *Red River Campaign,* 6; Smith, "Banks Expedition of 1862," 340–43, 348.

mander of the District of Texas, Major General John B. Magruder, still had considerable resources with which to oppose such an operation.[5]

To prepare his forces for their new objective, Banks reorganized the XIX Corps, whose strength had been cut by more than a third with the loss of the nine-month soldiers. Thomas Sherman's Second Division was broken up, and its remaining regiments were distributed among the other three divisions. Emory and Grover retained their commands (the Third and Fourth Divisions, respectively), while Major General William B. Franklin, who had just arrived from service with the Army of the Potomac, replaced an ailing Augur as commander of the First.[6]

Banks also continued to seek and finally got reinforcements from Grant's army. During the siege of Vicksburg, thousands of fresh troops had been sent down the Mississippi River to bolster Union forces in Mississippi. The relative ease with which these reinforcements reached Grant contrasted with the difficulty of reinforcing Banks via the long and hazardous ocean route down the Atlantic coast, around the Florida keys, and across the Gulf of Mexico. Consequently, Grant's army had received many thousands of fresh men during the summer of 1863, while Banks's department had received none. Now that Vicksburg had fallen, Halleck ordered Grant to share some of his men with Banks.[7]

The lead units from the XIII Corps under the command of Major General Cadwalader C. Washburn began to arrive at New Orleans from Vicksburg by mid-August. The XIII Corps was composed of midwesterners and offered an interesting contrast to the New Englanders who made up the majority of Banks's original expeditionary force. From a different part of the country and with different attitudes and accents, the men of the XIII Corps were looked upon as outsiders by the veterans of the XIX Corps. "The western men were strangers in this army, and attracted considerable attention from their peculiar habits and singular style of doing duty," one of Banks's men from New York noted. "They were, evidently, excellent fighting men, and were very proficient in drill; but they had a wonderful disregard of personal appearance, wearing all manner of dirty

5. David C. Edmonds, *Yankee Autumn in Acadiana: A Narrative of the Great Texas Overland Expedition through Southeastern Louisiana, October–December 1863* (Lafayette, La.: Acadiana Press, 1979), 16.

6. Irwin, *History of the Nineteenth Army Corps*, 250, 257–61. Thomas Sherman was recuperating from the wound he received while leading his men at Port Hudson.

7. *OR*, 24, pt. 3:58; Grant to Halleck, August 31, 1863, U. S. Grant Collection, CHS.

and outlandish costumes. They also took a special delight in destroying every species of Rebel property that came within their reach, whether serviceable to them or not."[8]

The arrival of the XIII Corps gave Banks more than fifty thousand men in and around New Orleans. Now that there were two army corps under his command, and with the formation of the Corps d'Afrique as a third major unit, Banks relinquished command of the XIX Corps and named Franklin in his place. Brigadier General Godfrey Weitzel replaced Franklin as commander of the First Division.[9]

Having completed the reorganization of his troops, Banks turned his attention to carrying out Halleck's directive in regard to Texas. The place at which Banks established a Federal presence was not important. Initially, Halleck suggested either of two seaports, Indianola or Galveston. Upon further consideration, the general in chief wrote that he might prefer an advance by land via southwest or northwest Louisiana. Nevertheless, he left it up to Banks to decide.[10]

Banks had been up the Bayou Teche before and knew that the route through southwest Louisiana would be short of potable water and difficult to traverse. Furthermore, the region had been systematically stripped of its produce, livestock, and supplies during the campaign earlier that spring. An alternative route followed a northwestern approach up the Red River to Shreveport, from which the army could move into Texas by way of Marshall and Tyler. The latter was an important arsenal, supply depot, and site of Camp Ford, the largest Confederate prisoner-of-war camp in the Trans-Mississippi Department. The problem with the northwestern approach was that it depended on the water level in the Red River, which needed to be high enough for steamboats and gunboats in support of the ground troops as far as Shreveport. Banks believed that predicting the water level of the Red River was more risky than steaming through the Gulf of Mexico and therefore decided to land at Galveston, from which Union forces could move down the coast or drive inward to Magruder's base at Houston. Banks placed Franklin in command of the expedition, which consisted of units from the First and

8. Edmonds, *Yankee Autumn in Acadiana,* 18–19; Irwin, *History of the Nineteenth Army Corps,* 258; Albert O. Marshall, *Army Life; From a Soldier's Journal* (Joliet, Ill.: Author, 1883), 284–86; Beecher, *Record of the 114th Regiment,* 255.

9. Irwin, *History of the Nineteenth Army Corps,* 259–60.

10. *OR,* 26, pt. 1:672–73, 742, 834–35.

Third Divisions of the XIX Corps. Banks remained in New Orleans to await the outcome.[11]

Franklin's expedition to Galveston was not the first time the Union army had attempted to occupy the port city during the war. In December 1862, just before Banks reached New Orleans, a small detachment of Federal troops had landed there. On the advice of Farragut, Banks reinforced the outpost with three companies of the Forty-second Massachusetts Infantry. But Magruder made a bold bid to retake the city on New Year's Day 1863 and captured the contingent. This time, the Rebels were not likely to let the city fall into Union hands without a fight.[12]

Knowing that the Confederates were expecting an attack from the sea, Banks directed Franklin to land his men at the mouth of the Sabine River and march by way of Houston to strike Galveston from the land side. Although the strategy was sound, the campaign was botched by bad planning, a lack of cooperation between the army and navy, and a series of incredible mistakes. On September 8, four Federal gunboats made an ill-advised frontal assault on the Rebel batteries at Sabine Pass. In the meantime, the army under Franklin waited on the transports rather than going ashore to assist the navy. In one of the most remarkable actions of the war, four dozen Texans commanded by an Irish tavern owner, Dick Dowling, used their heavy guns to batter the Union fleet into submission. Two of the gunboats, the *Sachem* and the *Clifton*, surrendered. The remaining two gunboats retreated in haste. Although the five thousand soldiers on the transports still could have landed up the coast and flanked the tiny garrison, Franklin decided to give up and returned to New Orleans.[13]

After the debacle at Sabine Pass, Banks decided to take matters into his own hands. He started by positioning Franklin and his men, along with two divisions from the XIII Corps and a division of cavalry under

11. *OR*, 26, pt. 1:18–20, 683, 696–97, 767–68, 871–72; Irwin, *History of the Nineteenth Army Corps*, 267.

12. *OR*, 15:199–227; Irwin, *History of the Nineteenth Army Corps*, 62–65; Johnson, *Red River Campaign*, 28; Smith, "Banks Expedition of 1862," 357–58; Banks to William Lloyd Garrison, January 30, 1865, *Liberator*, February 24, 1865.

13. *OR*, 26, pt. 1:18–19, 285–312, 683; Clark, *One Hundred and Sixteenth Regiment*, 124–27; Irwin, *History of the Nineteenth Army Corps*, 268–72; Kerby, *Kirby Smith's Confederacy*, 189; Welles, *Diary*, 1:441–42; Banks to Mary Banks, September 22, 1863, Banks to Lincoln, September 23, 1863 (finished but not sent), Banks Collection, LC.

Brigadier General Albert E. Lee, at Berwick Bay with orders to drive up the Teche toward Alexandria. Banks wanted Franklin to distract the Rebels in Louisiana and prevent them from reinforcing Magruder in Texas. If all went well, Franklin might push into Texas. But the major effort would be along the coast under the direction of Banks himself.[14]

Franklin began moving his troops up the Bayou Teche on October 3. Opposing the Union force was small army under the command of Richard Taylor, who set fire to the bridge over the Vermillion Bayou. Franklin's men swept across the fields but encountered no hostile fire from the opposite shore. The burning of the bridge had been meant to delay, not stop, the Union invaders. Just as the smoke cleared from the bloodless assault, Banks arrived by steamer from New Orleans to see how things were going. Sitting down to a sumptuous breakfast under the outspread branches of a great China tree, Banks conferred with his commander in the field. Satisfied with the progress so far, Banks ordered Franklin to continue his advance and then started back to the Crescent City. Stopping at New Iberia, Banks telegraphed Halleck to inform him that "as soon as we cross the Vermillion Bayou . . . no time will be lost in raising the flag [in Texas], as directed."[15]

Franklin pushed the men from the XIX Corps a dozen miles north of Vermillionville until he reached Carencro on Bayou Bourbeau, where he paused. Finally, they pushed on to Opelousas and then to the town of Washington, forcing the Confederates to retire before them. Taylor tempted the Federals to engage in combat, but Franklin was not eager to do battle. He was hampered by the thorough work of Chickering and his men the previous spring, for the area around Opelousas had been stripped of fodder and grain, sugar and cotton, and livestock of all kinds. There was hardly anything left to feed the inhabitants, much less the army. The lack of food and provisions forced Franklin to rely on a long and exposed supply route from Berwick Bay. A season of heavy rains had also contributed to the difficulty of bringing up supplies. Concerned, Franklin telegraphed Banks in New Orleans on October 23 to report that

14. Edmonds, *Yankee Autumn in Acadiana,* 405–9.

15. *OR,* 26, pt. 1:380–88, 756–57; Beecher, *Record of the 114th Regiment,* 260; Edmonds, *Yankee Autumn in Acadiana,* 82–88. Also see dispatches in the *New York Herald,* September 31, November 1, 1863; B. F. Stevenson, *Letters from the Army* (Cincinnati: W. E. Dibble, 1884), 262.

forage was very scarce and that he depended on supply boats to continue the campaign.[16]

But Banks had other matters on his mind, for he was preparing to set sail for the Texas coast in a few days. Although he expected Franklin to keep the pressure on Taylor, Banks failed to issue explicit orders and left Franklin to decide for himself what his next step should be. Under these circumstances, Franklin decided that a further advance toward Texas in the bad weather and with exposed supply lines would be ill-advised and ordered his men to retreat back down the Teche.[17]

Seeing the Union army fall back, Taylor ordered Brigadier General Tom Green and his cavalry to attack. Green struck the Federal rear guard at Bayou Bourbeau near Grand Couteau below Opelousas on November 3. Green had two brigades, one of cavalry and the other infantry, to throw against Brigadier General Stephen G. Burbridge's detachment of seventeen hundred men. When Green's brigade of Texas cavalry swept around the Federal left flank, the fight soon turned into a rout. The Sixty-seventh Indiana Infantry surrendered en masse, and other Federal units dissolved before the onslaught. Washburn rushed reinforcements from the XIII Corps to sound of the firing, and their counterattack stopped the rout and temporarily disorganized Green's troops. For a short time both sides traded shots until Green withdrew. The Confederates lost fewer than two hundred men while more than seven hundred Federals were killed, wounded, or taken prisoner.[18]

Following the embarrassment at Bayou Bourbeau, Franklin continued his retreat down the Teche to New Iberia, where the XIX Corps went into camp toward the end of November. As units from the XIII Corps were gradually drawn off to garrison the outposts that Banks was establishing along the coast of Texas, Franklin was left with little more than five thousand men from the XIX Corps and Lee's division of cavalry

16. *OR*, 26, pt. 1:388–89; *New Orleans Times*, September 23, 1863; Edmonds, *Yankee Autumn in Acadiana*, 109–49, 225, 263; Joseph Orville Jackson, ed., *"Some of the Boys . . .": The Civil War Letters of Isaac Jackson, 1862–1865* (Carbondale: Southern Illinois University Press, 1960), 143.

17. *OR*, 26, pt. 1:341, 354, 779.

18. *OR*, 26, pt. 1:356–59, 394, pt. 2:411–12, 433–34, 449–50, 508, 518; Edmonds, *Yankee Autumn in Acadiana*, 272–95; Alwyn Barr, "The Battle of Bayou Bourbeau, November 3, 1863: Colonel Oran M. Roberts' Report," *Louisiana History* 6 (Winter 1965): 83–91; Jackson, *"Some of the Boys,"* 144–48.

to hold the region along the Bayou Teche. His effective force was reduced even more by an outbreak of smallpox, which forced him to retire further down the Teche, where Franklin finally settled into a winter camp near the town that bore his name.[19]

While Franklin fumbled along the Bayou Teche, Banks probed the Texas coast. His initial objective was Brownsville at the mouth of the Rio Grande. The Confederate garrison there numbered only a few hundred men, and planting the Union flag on the Texas shore just north of its boundary with Mexico would make the desired impression on Louis Napoleon. In addition, Brownsville was one of the South's most active ports, sending out cotton to both Mexico and Europe and importing arms and ammunition in a steady stream.[20]

Banks's force consisted primarily of one division from the XIII Corps, which landed at Brazos Island near Brownsville on November 2. Once again, the mission was mishandled. Banks failed to arrange effective cooperation with his navy escort, and the leaky transports containing four thousand soldiers proved bothersome. Fortunately for Banks, the Rebels did not contest the landing. Nevertheless, it took three days to get the men ashore, during which time the Union force's situation was so precarious that bad weather alone would have defeated the entire operation.[21]

Banks's successful landing meant that at least part of his mission had been achieved. The fall of Brownsville forced the Confederates to move their contact point with the outside world up the Rio Grande to Eagle Pass, while the presence of Union troops in the city improved contacts with Mexican leaders in the northern provinces who continued to resist the presence of French forces in their country.[22]

Setting up a state government loyal to the Union did not go as

19. Irwin, *History of the Nineteenth Army Corps,* 278–79.

20. *New Orleans Times,* December 31, 1863; Banks to Mary Banks, September 25, 1863, Banks Collection, LC.

21. *OR,* 26, pt. 1:396, 399, 434–35, 796–98, 876–77; Irwin, *History of the Nineteenth Army Corps,* 275; Banks to Mary Banks, November 3, 4, 1863, Banks Collection, LC.

22. U.S. Congress, *Report of the Joint Committee on the Conduct of the War: Red River Expedition,* 19; *New Orleans Times,* November 29, 1863; Banks to Mrs. Banks, September 25, 1863, Banks to Mary Banks, November 3, 4, [1863], Banks Collection, LC.

smoothly. The leader of the Texas Unionists and would-be governor was Andrew Jackson Hamilton, who had accompanied Banks with a small group of exiled Texans when he sailed out of New York Harbor in December 1862. The secrecy surrounding the voyage led Hamilton to conclude that Banks's force was bound for Texas. When Banks stopped in New Orleans, Hamilton was wild with rage.[23]

Banks did not think that Hamilton was a bad man, "but he does not manifest great force of character, and is surrounded by men who come here on the government transports, unknown to me, for base, speculative purposes, and nothing else." When Banks set off for Brownsville, he advised Hamilton to stay in New Orleans. But Hamilton hastened to Brownsville as soon as Banks secured a foothold and announced that he was setting up a government for those parts of Texas under Union occupation. To this end, Hamilton established what he termed the "Executive Department, State of Texas," and made it clear that he intended to assume control of extradition, judicial, and taxation powers. When Banks's staff officers told him to exercise a little caution, Hamilton attributed their complaints to jealousy and declared that only force could make him yield his authority.[24]

Banks did not want to use his position as commander of the Department of the Gulf to strip Hamilton of his power. He had already offended radical Republicans by telling Salmon P. Chase's treasury agents that they could not operate in Texas. Consequently, Banks determined to limit rather than eliminate the "governor" by making it clear that Hamilton would not be in control of the Union occupation along the Texas coast.[25]

Encouraged by having taken Brownsville, Banks decided in mid-November to expand the Federal presence in Texas by seizing all the ports and passes between the Rio Grande and the Sabine. Once this had been accomplished, he could press on to Houston or advance up the Rio

23. *OR*, 26, pt. 1:680, 832, 865–67; Harrington, *Fighting Politician*, 133; Johnson, *Red River Campaign*, 15; *New Orleans Times*, December 2, 1863.

24. Banks to Halleck, January 7, 1863, *OR*, 15:201; also 26, pt. 1:842–44, 846, 856–59, 865–67; Johnson, *Red River Campaign*, 27–28; Smith, "Banks Expedition of 1862," 348–50, 357–59.

25. *OR*, 26, pt. 1:832–33, 34, pt. 2:223, Ser. 3, 2:782–83; Harrington, *Fighting Politician*, 133–34. A brief biography of Hamilton can be found in Harold B. Simpson and Marcus J. Wright, *Texas in the War, 1861–1865* (Hillsboro, Tex.: Hill Junior College Press, 1965), 140.

Grande valley to link up with the Federal commander in New Mexico and thus reestablish Union control of the entire Southwest. Banks was convinced that such a move would be the finest campaign of the war. So it seemed, as his troops quickly took Point Isabel, Aransas Pass, and Pass Cavallo. Banks was in a boastful mood. "We have been very fortunate," he wrote to Mary on November 15. "I have always known that there was a protecting Hand above us but I never *felt* it till now. I have experienced the sensation of deliverance. I may say for the first time in my life, I believe our success to have one of great importance to the Country."[26]

Despite his enthusiasm, Banks's Texas operation brought few significant results. The Confederates retained possession of Galveston and the Sabine River. There was no drive on Houston, nor could Union troops in New Mexico link up with Banks's men along the Rio Grande. Although the capture of Brownsville had a nuisance value by disrupting Confederate trade, the other posts were of little value. Halleck saw the uselessness of the positions, and Grant, when he became the commanding general of Union army in 1864, ordered that all of the outposts be abandoned with the exception of Brownsville.[27]

26. *OR,* 26, pt. 1:410, 785, 788; Banks to Mary Banks, September 5, November 4, 15, 1863, Banks Collection, LC.

27. *OR,* 26, pt. 1:879, 34, pt. 3:190–91; U.S. Congress, *Report of the Joint Committee on the Conduct of the War: Red River Expedition,* 22–23; Johnson, *Red River Campaign,* 40–41; Kerby, *Kirby Smith's Confederacy,* 194.

11

Unsuited for This Duty

Port Hudson had the distinction of being one of the first battles of the Civil War in which black troops engaged Rebel soldiers in combat. Many of these soldiers were free men of color who had offered their services to Louisiana at the outbreak of the war. Confederate governor Thomas O. Moore made them part of the state militia but left them behind when the Confederates abandoned New Orleans. After Federal troops occupied the city, some of the black officers volunteered to serve under Benjamin F. Butler.[1]

Butler promptly offered them commissions with the authority to reorganize their regiment for service in the Union army. "By accepting a regiment which had already been in Confederate Service," Treasury Agent George S. Denison reported to Salmon P. Chase, "he [Butler] left no room for complaint (by the Rebels) that the government were arming the negroes." With the exception of the black officers, Butler's black troops were primarily former slaves who had fled into Union lines. In all, Butler organized three regiments of black soldiers before being replaced by Banks in December 1862. Banks continued Butler's policy of recruit

1. James G. Hollandsworth, Jr., *The Louisiana Native Guards: The Black Military Experience during the Civil War* (Baton Rouge: Louisiana State University Press, 1995), 1–11; Mary F. Berry, "Negro Troops in Blue and Gray: The Louisiana Native Guards, 1861–1863," *Louisiana History* 8 (Spring 1967): 168–70; Brown, *The Negro in the American Rebellion,* 82–90; Charles H. Wesley, "The Employment of Negroes as Soldiers in the Confederate Army," *Journal of Negro History* 4 (July 1919): 243–45; Winters, *Civil War in Louisiana,* 143–45, 208–9.

ing black troops and had enough inductees for a fourth regiment within three months of his arrival.[2]

Discipline in the military not only can be harsh, it can be brutal, excessive, and inhumane. Too often this was the case in Banks's fourth regiment of black soldiers, for its lieutenant colonel, Augustus W. Benedict, was a tactless and unstable man prone to foul language and callous treatment of his troops. While stationed at Baton Rouge, a black enlisted man in the fourth regiment whose brass buckle did not shine brightly enough or whose boots were not polished risked a punch or a kick from the malevolent Benedict. On one occasion, the lieutenant colonel wrested a sword from a sergeant who was standing nearby and struck a soldier in the face for being out of uniform. But this abuse paled in comparison to the punishment he meted out in early August 1863 to two men he caught stealing corn. Benedict ordered the officer of the guard to remove the men's shoes and stockings and "lay them on the ground, straighten their legs and arms out, and stake them—tie them down." Benedict then told the officer "to go to the commissary and get some molasses, and cover their faces, feet, and hands with molasses. He told me to keep them there during the day and night, and said he did not care if I kept them there until they died."[3]

2. *OR,* 15:556–57, 559; George S. Denison to Chase, September 9, 1862, in Chase, "Diary and Correspondence," 313; James Franklin Fitts, "The Negro in Blue," *Galaxy* 3 (February 1867): 252–53; Handon B. Hargrove, *Black Union Soldiers in the Civil War* (Jefferson, N.C.: McFarland, 1988), 62–69, 86, 99; James M. McPherson, *The Negro's Civil War: How American Negroes Felt and Acted during the War for the Union* (New York: Pantheon Books, 1965), 23–24; James Parton, *General Butler in New Orleans: History of the Administration of the Department of the Gulf in the Year 1862* (New York: Mason Brothers, 1864), 517. Banks expressed an interest in recruiting an "armed working corps of blacks" in November 1862 while organizing his expedition to Louisiana (Banks to Francis Lieber, November 23, 1862, Francis Lieber Papers, HL).

3. *OR,* 26, pt. 1:471, 473; Fitts, "Negro in Blue," 251; Joseph T. Glatthaar, *Forged in Battle: The Civil War Alliance of Black Soldiers and White Officers* (New York: Free Press, 1990), 87–88, 107–8; Thomas Wentworth Higginson, *Army Life in a Black Regiment* (Boston: Fields, Osgood, 1870), 259–60; Norwood P. Howell, "The Negro as a Soldier in the War of the Rebellion," in *Papers of the Military Historical Society of Massachusetts,* Vol. 13 (January 1892): 297; Root, "Experiences of a Federal Soldier," 657; *New York Times,* March 8, 1863; Bell Irvin Wiley, *Southern Negroes, 1861–1865* (New Haven: Yale University Press, 1965), 315–18; Samuel M. Quincy to his mother, November 30, 1863, and to Josiah Quincy (grandfather), December 8, 1863, Quincy, Wendell, Holmes, and Upham Family Papers, LC.

Later that month, the regiment was transferred from Baton Rouge to Fort Jackson on the Mississippi River below New Orleans, where Benedict's cruel treatment continued. At the new post he again ordered a soldier staked spread-eagle on the ground for two days in the summer heat. These indignities continued throughout the fall until things came to a head on the evening of December 9, 1863. About five o'clock, Benedict caught two members of the regimental band, Harry Williams and Munroe Miller, attempting to leave the grounds of the fort without permission. Picking up a rawhide teamster's whip, he flogged both men unmercifully, striking Williams fifteen to twenty times. The sound of the lashes and the pleas of the two soldiers attracted a crowd. Benedict ordered the onlookers to disperse, which they did grudgingly. Upon returning to their quarters, the black soldiers who had witnessed the incident decided they had had enough and gathered again on the parade ground to protest Benedict's cruel treatment. Soon more than 250 men, over half the regiment, joined them. "Give us Colonel Benedict; we did not come here to be whipped by him," and "Kill Colonel Benedict; shoot him," they shouted.

The mutineers fired their rifles in the air as the white officers attempted to break up the assembly. Colonel James R. Drew, the Fourth Regiment's commander, tried without success to restore order. One group of soldiers rushed the guardhouse, where they forced the release of the prisoners held there. Another group went to the levee, thinking that Benedict had made his way to a steamer lying in the river near the fort. More shots were fired. Afraid that his boat was about to be taken, the captain of the steamer cast off and moved upriver. The captain docked at the quarantine station above the fort and sent an urgent telegram to New Orleans informing Banks of the uprising. Banks ordered two gunboats from the city to proceed as rapidly as possible to Fort Jackson and dispatched a regiment of white infantry to the post. These precautions proved unnecessary, however, for Colonel Drew and the other officers eventually persuaded the men to disband and return to their quarters.[4]

Banks summoned Benedict to New Orleans, where the lieutenant colonel offered to resign. Banks refused to accept his resignation and appointed a court of inquiry to meet at Fort Jackson. Although some of

4. *OR*, 26, pt. 1:456–59; *New York Herald*, December 21, 1863.

Banks's staff urged him to try Benedict for "conduct unbecoming of an officer and a gentleman," Banks insisted on the stronger charge of "inflicting cruel and unusual punishment, to the prejudice of good order and military discipline." The appropriateness of the charge became evident when officers of the regiment came before the court to tell of Benedict's record of brutal treatment of black soldiers. After two days of testimony, the court found Benedict guilty and sentenced him to be dismissed from the service.[5]

The court of inquiry was also responsible for determining the fate of the thirteen soldiers from the Fourth Regiment who had been the ringleaders of the uprising. Although the court found four of the thirteen men not guilty, it sentenced two to die before a firing squad and six to spend prison terms with hard labor of from one to twenty years. In addition, the court ordered that one soldier, Private James H. Moore, be confined for one month in the guardhouse.

Although Banks approved the court's sentence of Benedict, he was more sympathetic toward the black prisoners. In his report to Halleck he noted that "the punishments to which the men were subjected for a considerable length of time before the revolt was contrary to the rules of war, and contrary to the orders constantly given in this department. They may justly be classed as among the cruel and unusual punishments interdicted by the Constitution." Yet he could not condone insubordination and armed insurrection no matter what may have precipitated it. "The conduct of the soldiers is inexcusable," Banks concluded, "and [it] must be punished with such severity as to prevent its recurrence." He confirmed the six prison sentences and had the offenders shipped to Fort Jefferson in the Florida keys to serve their time, but he suspended the two death sentences and ordered both men to serve a sentence of hard labor instead. Banks also refused to approve Private Moore's sentence because of conflicting evidence and ordered him released from the guardhouse and returned to duty.[6]

The experience of the black soldiers in the fourth regiment was not out of the ordinary. Many of the white officers who were placed in charge of

5. Banks to Charles P. Stone, December 29, 1863, quoted in Harrington, *Fighting Politician,* 111; *OR,* 26, pt. 1:476–79.

6. *OR,* 26, pt. 1:457, 476–79.

black troops in the Department of the Gulf were inferior to those commanding white soldiers. Competent white officers, who could expect promotion and advancement in their own regiments, refused assignment to the black units. Many of those who did volunteer were incompetents who were dissatisfied with their current situation. Furthermore, it was widely known that white commanders unloaded their troublemakers on black companies.[7]

Banks compounded the problem of finding good officers for black regiments by terminating Butler's practice of giving commissions to black men. Banks felt that black officers were a source of "constant embarrassment and annoyance" because their use "demoralizes both the white troops and the negroes." Furthermore, he complained that the "arrogance and self-assertion" of the black officers goaded his white officers and men to violence. As Banks put it to Lincoln, they were simply "unsuited for this duty."[8]

It was true that many Union soldiers, particularly the nine-month men, objected to having to "salute a negro." In fact, some of Banks's white troops threatened to go home if reenlisting meant that they had to submit themselves to this "indignity." As one lieutenant told a newspaper correspondent, if a black man was allowed to hold a commission, then "I must not only obey him, I must politely touch my cap when I approach him. I must stand while he sits, unless his captainship should condescendingly ask me to be seated. Negro soldiers are all very well," he continued, "but let us have white officers, whom we can receive and treat as equals everywhere, and whom we may treat as superiors without humiliation."[9]

Having decided not to commission black officers, Banks had to find a way to get rid of those Butler had commissioned before he arrived. To

7. *OR,* 15:716–17, 26, pt. 1:457, 688–89, 41, pt. 2:118, 351. For examples of the misconduct of white officers in black regiments in the Department of the Gulf, see Wiley, *Southern Negroes,* 311–12, 341–42; Glatthaar, *Forged in Battle,* 91–92; *New Orleans Times,* March 23, 1864.

8. Banks to Lincoln, August 16, 1863, *OR,* 26, pt. 1:689; also see Ira Berlin, Joseph P. Reidy, and Leslie S. Rowland, *Freedom: A Documentary History of Emancipation, 1861–1867,* Ser. 2: *The Black Military Experience* (New York: Cambridge University Press, 1982), 305–6.

9. *OR,* Ser. 3, 3:46; *New York Herald,* February 4, May 24, 1863; John W. Blassingame, "The Selection of Officers and Non-Commissioned Officers of Negro Troops in the Union Army, 1863–1865," *Negro History Bulletin* 30 (January 1967): 10.

this end, Banks used a newly created Board of Examiners to determine the qualifications of Butler's appointees. Although the board generally did a creditable job of improving the caliber of the white officers assigned to black regiments, it did not intend to approve the commissions of black officers. Some of the black officers resigned in protest, others came before the board and were dismissed. Even then, a few black officers remained. Captain André Cailloux retained his commission and was killed leading his company during the assault of May 27 at Port Hudson. Pinckney Pinchback, who was later to serve as a U.S. senator from Louisiana during Reconstruction, held on to his commission until September 1863. By then, white officers in his regiment expressed so much dissatisfaction over Pinchback's presence that he was forced to resign.[10]

Banks's decision not to commission black officers not only prevented him from using an important and available pool of talent, it also undercut the dignity, pride, and morale of the black troops under his command. Realizing from his home in Lowell that black officers were being stripped of their rank, Butler reacted in anger. "The negro, whether the equal to the white man or not, knows when he is treated fairly, and appreciates an injustice quite as endearingly as if of a lighter color." Rhetorically, Butler asked, "How can we expect the Black man to stand up against the White rebel when we allow him to be insulted by our own soldier because he [the Union soldier] is White?"[11]

Despite the incompetence of many of their white officers, black sol-

10. *OR,* 26, pt. 1:688–89; Berlin, Reidy, and Rowland, *Freedom,* 19; Blassingame, *Black New Orleans,* 44; Blassingame, "Selection of Officers," 8–11; Glatthaar, *Forged in Battle,* 35–59; Agnes Smith Grosz, "The Political Career of Pinckney Benton Stewart Pinchback," *Louisiana Historical Quarterly* 27 (April 1944): 529–610; Benjamin Quarles, *The Negro in the Civil War* (Boston: Little, Brown, 1963), 209; Ripley, *Slaves and Freedmen,* 116–17. For a detailed account of Captain Cailloux's funeral in New Orleans on July 11, 1863, see *New York Times,* August 8, 1863.

11. *OR,* Ser. 3, 3:36; Brown, *The Negro in the American Rebellion,* 168–69; Butler to Chase, February 28, 1863, in Butler, *Private and Official Correspondence,* 3:24; Blassingame, *Black New Orleans,* 39; Irwin, *History of the Nineteenth Army Corps,* 49–50, 174; Emily Hazen Reed, *Life of A. P. Dostie; or, The Conflict in New Orleans* (New York: Wm. P. Tomlinson, 1868), 129–32; *New Orleans Tribune,* May 14, 1865. Although one-fifth the size of New York, New Orleans in 1860 had almost as many free blacks as the nation's largest city—10,689 as compared to 12,472 (McPherson, *Negro's Civil War,* 319). In addition, there were almost as many blacks in the Crescent City who enjoyed the status of free men and women as there were slaves (10,689 as compared to 13,385). Consequently, Banks had a sizable pool of talent from which to draw had he decided to do so.

diers acquitted themselves well. A newspaper correspondent who observed black troops in Banks's department for nearly a year concluded that, in spite of his initial reservations, "at least two-thirds of the men slaves would make brave and effective soldiers." Another Union soldier wrote his sister that freedmen made "excellent soldiers[,] learn very quick[,] & at the recent fight at Port Hudson I have it from eye witnesses[,] Troops never fought better." Banks agreed with this assessment. After their assault at Port Hudson on May 27, Banks wrote Mary, "They fought splendidly!, splendidly! Every body is delighted that they did so well! Their charges upon the rebel works, of which they made three, exhibited the greatest bravery and caused them to suffer great losses."[12]

There were essentially two schools of thought in the Federal army regarding black troops. Some soldiers had no problem with their enlistment, noting that "the niggers had as good a right to be shot as anybody." But many white officers and enlisted men could not "bear to have the United States uniform so degraded as it is when worn by 'niggers.'"[13]

In response to these objections, Banks had briefly halted the enlistment of black troops after he arrived in Louisiana. But it did not take him

12. *OR*, 26, pt. 1:45, 689; *Conduct of the War: Red River Expedition*, 314; Babcock, *Selections from the Letters and Diaries*, 80; Irwin, *History of the Nineteenth Army Corps*, 172–74; Randall C. Jimerson, *The Private Civil War: Popular Thought during the Sectional Conflict* (Baton Rouge: Louisiana State University Press, 1988), 106–9; *New York Times*, March 9, 1863; William H. Eastman to his sister, June 8, 1863, Eastman Letters, MAHS; Banks to Mary Banks, May 30, 1863, Banks Collection, LC. Northern newspaper reports generally praised the bravery of black troops under fire (e.g., *New York Times*, June 13, 1863). For a Union soldier's view of black courage, see Benjamin F. Stevens to his mother, August 12, 1863, in Richard N. Ellis, ed., "The Civil War Letters of an Iowa Family," *Annals of Iowa* Ser. 3, 39 (Spring 1969): 582. This perspective should be compared with that of a Confederate soldier printed in the *New Orleans Daily True Delta*, August 9, 1863.

13. Onley Andrus to Mary Andrus, November 22, 1862, June 28, 1864, in Onley Andrus, *The Civil War Letters of Sergeant Onley Andrus*, Illinois Studies in the Social Sciences, ed. Fred Albert Shannon, Vol. 28, no. 4 (Urbana: University of Illinois Press, 1947), 115–16, 128; Jimerson, *Private Civil War*, 97–100; Ripley, *Slaves and Freedmen*, 124–25; *New York Herald*, February 4, 1863. This sentiment among Union troops was far from unanimous (e.g., Richard C. Goodwin to his mother, April 7[8], 1862, Goodwin Papers, MAHS), although it was prevalent (e.g., William E. Wilcox to his wife, February 20, May 21, 1863, Wilcox Papers, WDML).

long to reverse his field when President Lincoln announced that former slaves were "the great available, and yet unavailed of, force for restoring the Union." Chiding those who resented this reality, Lincoln wrote a prominent member of the Republican party in Illinois who accused the president of having given in to the radicals. "You say you will not fight to free negroes," Lincoln responded; "some of them seem willing to fight for you."[14]

To emphasize his point, Lincoln ordered Brigadier General Daniel Ullmann to the Department of the Gulf with two hundred officers recruited largely from the Army of the Potomac and with authority to raise a black brigade. Ullmann had made his biggest splash as the Know-Nothing candidate for governor of New York in 1854 before becoming a functionary in the Republican party. He was familiar with the commander of the Department of the Gulf, for he had served under Banks in Virginia. Captured during the retreat from Cedar Mountain, Ullmann had been imprisoned in Richmond until he was released on parole in October 1862.[15]

Banks was upset by Ullmann's mission for two reasons. First, if black troops were to be raised in his department, he wanted to be in charge of their recruitment. Second, Banks had little use for Ullmann, whom he termed "a poor man . . . [who] will make all the trouble he can." Although Banks's objections may have been motivated by jealousy, he was not far off the mark, for Ullmann's exaggerated sense of self-importance could make working with him difficult.[16]

To head off this intrusion on his authority, Banks stepped up his own enlistment program before Ullmann arrived. On May 1, 1863, Banks announced the organization "a corps d'armée of colored troops, to be des-

14. *OR*, 26, pt. 1:688–89, 34, pt. 2:115–16, Ser. 3, 5:118–24; Basler, ed. *Collected Works of Abraham Lincoln*, 6:408–10; George S. Denison to Salmon P. Chase, August 26, 1862, March 21, 1863, in Chase, "Diary and Correspondence," 311–12, 377; *New York Times*, February 23, 1863; *New York Tribune*, February 21, 1863.

15. *OR*, Ser. 3, 3:14, 100–103; George S. Denison to Chase, December 23, 1862, in Chase, "Diary and Correspondence," 341; George W. Williams, *A History of the Negro Troops in the War of the Rebellion, 1861–1865* (1888; reprint, New York: Kraus Reprint Co., 1969), 102; Warner, *Generals in Blue*, 517–18; Carman and Luthin, "Some Aspects of the Know-Nothing Movement Reconsidered," 218.

16. Banks to Mary Banks, May 30, 1863, Banks Collection, LC; *OR*, Ser. 3, 3:17. For George L. Andrews' derogatory assessment of Ullmann, see Andrews to his wife, June 26, 1865, Andrews Papers, LALMVC.

ignated as the 'Corps d'Afrique.'" To ease the transition of the former slaves into soldiers, Banks limited the new regiments to five hundred men, half their normal size, while retaining the full number of commissioned and noncommissioned officers.[17] Nowhere in the lengthy order authorizing the Corps d'Afrique did Banks mention Ullmann's name, nor did he hint of cooperating with Ullmann's efforts to raise a black brigade. Consequently, Ullmann found himself beset with numerous difficulties in finding recruits. Although he did raise five regiments of infantry by relying on impressment gangs that often dragged men unwillingly from their families, Banks stole his thunder by absorbing Ullmann's troops into the Corps d'Afrique.[18] The final blow occurred on September 3, 1863, when the War Department revoked his special orders and assigned him to General Banks.[19]

Life for the black soldiers in the Corps d'Afrique was rough. Most army officers believed that if the black soldier was good for anything, it was performing guard or fatigue duty such as "throwing up defensive earthworks, a kind of labor always unwillingly performed by white troops." Thus, while white troops cleaned their equipment and drilled, the black soldiers were busy digging ditches and latrines, loading and unloading supplies, throwing up defensive earthworks, and standing guard. One of Banks's aides noted just before the ill-fated Union diver-

17. *OR,* 26, pt. 1:539; John G. Nicolay and John Hay, *Abraham Lincoln: A History,* 10 vols. (New York: Century, 1914), 6:455; Banks to Mary Banks, April 12, 1863, Banks Collection, LC. Butler's Native Guard was incorporated into the Corps d'Afrique.

18. *OR,* 15:716–17, 26, pt. 1:539, 684, 688–89, 726, 733, 740–41, 803, Ser. 3, 3:766; Berlin, Reidy, and Rowland, *Freedom,* 118–20, 161–63; Cornish, *Sable Arm,* 126–28; *New York Herald,* June 4, 1863; *New Orleans Era,* May 26, 1863. For further discussion of the forced enlistment of black soldiers, see McCrary, *Abraham Lincoln and Reconstruction,* 142–43, and Ripley, *Slaves and Freedmen,* 107–13. Banks was not above impressing men to fill his black regiments as well. See *OR,* 26, pt. 1:737–38; Babcock, "War Commentary," 63, MNHS.

19. Ullmann's brigade remained at Port Hudson for the remainder of 1863 and for most of 1864, guarding this strategic point on the Mississippi River and preventing Confederate attempts to disrupt traffic. Ullmann was eventually assigned to Morganza, some thirty miles north of Port Hudson, where he remained until a fondness for the bottle made it difficult for him "to give highest attention to the duties devolving upon him." The officer who brought the order relieving Ullmann of his command reported that he "is full of whiskey all of the time—so much so tonight that he cannot walk steady" (*OR,* 48, pt. 1:677, 984, 986).

sion before Port Hudson in March 1863 that "the white soldiers won't do anything now except make Negroes work for them." The tendency to use black troops primarily for fatigue duty became so widespread that Ullmann wrote Senator Henry Wilson of Massachusetts to complain that "many high officials outside of Washington have no other intention than that these men shall be used as diggers and drudges." Following an incident when a group of drunken New Yorkers assaulted some black troops, Ullmann observed that the white soldiers "are more exacting and brutal than the masters were originally."[20]

To his credit, Banks tried to correct the situation. On August 5, 1864, he issued General Orders No. 108, which directed that "requiring these [black] troops to perform most of the labor on fortifications, and the labor and fatigue duties on permanent stations and camps, will cease, and they will only be required to take their fair share of fatigue duty, with the white troops."[21]

Neither fatigue duty, racism, nor incompetent commanders prevented black soldiers from becoming an important part of the Union war effort. More than 185,000 black men served in the Federal ranks; by the end of the war, about 12 percent of the one million men in the Union army were black. When Banks left for Washington in the fall of 1864, there were more than twenty-eight regiments of black troops in the Department of the Gulf, and Banks had enrolled more black soldiers than any other departmental commander during the entire war.[22]

20. *OR,* Ser. 3, 3:1127; Babcock, *Selections from the Letters and Diaries,* 104; Jimerson, *Private Civil War,* 93; Ripley, *Slaves and Freedmen,* 118–19; Strother, *Virginia Yankee,* 154; Samuel M. Quincy to his mother, April 25, 1864, Quincy, Wendell, Holmes, and Upham Family Papers, LC.

21. Smith and Brady, *Commission on Corrupt Practices in the South, Final Report,* 52, 54; General Orders No. 108 (printed), August 5, 1864, Banks Collection, LC.

22. *OR,* Ser. 3, 5:137–40, 660–62; *Official Army Register,* 8:331–42; Frederick Henry Dyer, *A Compendium of the War of the Rebellion* (1908; reprint, New York: Thomas Yoseloff, 1959), 11, 18. In all, there were 120 regiments of infantry, 12 regiments of heavy artillery, 10 batteries of light artillery, and 7 regiments of cavalry designated as United States Colored Troops. More than a sixth of the enlisted men in these units died during their term of service (2,751 in battle and the balance as a result of disease or wounds).

12

No Desire for Dishonest Gains

Denied fame for his military ventures, Banks decided to pursue another stratagem to capture the nation's attention. Although it is apparent today that Union victories at Gettysburg and Vicksburg constituted the decisive turning point of the war, Banks had no way of knowing that at the time, and although things looked promising from the Union side, the war was far from over. Consequently, the idea of a negotiated peace to end the bloodshed was a remote possibility that Banks knew many people hoped for during the late summer and early fall of 1863.

Banks thought that he might succeed where others had failed. If he could encourage the South to reenter the Union under generous terms, perhaps a program of gradual emancipation with compensation for the loss of slave property, the North might agree to a peace settlement. Not only would the country as a whole benefit from a peaceful termination of the debilitating struggle if he were successful, but Banks would emerge as a peacemaker and statesman of great note. An accomplishment of this magnitude would be of particular importance for someone who had his eye on the presidential election just over a year away.[1]

The first man Banks chose to assist him in his attempt to initiate a dialogue between the United and Confederate States was a successful cotton broker in New Orleans, Martin Gordon. As a registered enemy of the United States, Gordon could travel safely in the Confederacy to act as

1. For an overview of the peace movement during the last full year of the war, see Edward Chase Kirkland, *The Peacemakers of 1864* (1927; reprint, New York: AMS Press, 1969).

Banks's emissary. Banks sent Gordon through the lines in early July 1863, just before the capture of Port Hudson.[2]

Gordon went to Richmond, where he talked to President Jefferson Davis and other leading officials of the Confederate government. Although he found that Davis favored continued resistance, Gordon also discovered that many southerners wanted peace, even if it meant emancipation, provided owners would be compensated for their liberated slaves.[3]

Banks was encouraged by Gordon's report and decided to follow up the initial contact with a second peace emissary, Dr. Issachar Zacharie, an ardent promoter of Banks's aspirations for president in 1864. Zacharie was a native of New York and a onetime grocer who had developed some fame as a chiropodist after pirating a popular book on the subject. Banks had brought him to New Orleans late in 1862 to act as a spy and informant. In this capacity, Zacharie was reasonably successful. He established many good contacts and gathered valuable information. He also was able to gain the confidence of the powerful Jewish community in New Orleans by performing minor favors for persons of his own Jewish faith.[4]

Not everyone appreciated Zacharie's presence in New Orleans. George S. Denison, an abolitionist from Vermont and confidant of the most radical member of Lincoln's cabinet, Salmon P. Chase, considered Zacharie to be just another of the "host of speculators, Jews and camp-followers, [who] came hither in the track of Banks's expedition." Denison wanted as little to do as possible with Zacharie and his "Israelite friends." Brigadier General George F. Shepley, military governor of Louisiana and a native of Maine, was even more outspoken. Commenting on Zacharie's position regarding Banks's administration, Shepley

2. Banks to W. H. Emory, July 2, 1863, Gordon to Banks, January 1, 1864, Banks Collection, LC; George S. Denison to Chase, September 21, 1863, in Chase, "Diary and Correspondence," 408–9.

3. Harrington, *Fighting Politician,* 125–26.

4. Banks to Zacharie, January 1, 1863, Zacharie's reports, January–February 1863, Banks Collection, LC; also *New York Herald,* May 6, 1863. Harrington (*Fighting Politician,* 247) reports that the text of Zacharie's book, *Surgical and Practical Observations on the Diseases of the Human Foot* (New York, 1860), was taken without acknowledgment from John Eisenberg's book of the same title (London, 1845). The correspondence between Banks and Zacharie has been printed by Fred Harvey Harrington, "A Peace Mission of 1863," *American Historical Review* 46 (October 1940): 76–86.

complained to Butler that "the Christ killers, as Andrew [Butler's brother] calls them, have it all their own way."[5]

Given these anti-Semitic remarks from high-ranking Union officials with impeccable abolitionist credentials, there is some irony to that fact that the man Banks directed Zacharie to contact, Judah P. Benjamin, was both a Louisiana Jew and the highest-ranking member of the Confederate cabinet. But first Zacharie had to seek an appointment with Lincoln in Washington to inform the president of Banks's plan for peace. Banks gave Zacharie $2,000 in Confederate money and a letter of introduction to William H. Seward. Zacharie immediately set out for Washington, where he impressed both Seward and Lincoln with the possibilities for a negotiated peace. But the radicals caught wind of the initiative and opposed any proposal that the war be stopped before the South was completely crushed. When Lincoln raised the matter with some of his cabinet officials on July 26, Chase disapproved of giving Zacharie a pass through the Confederate lines. Zacharie wrote Banks in Louisiana that the radicals feared his peace mission and were "unwilling to give you credit for anything."[6]

Lincoln was more open-minded than the radicals and allowed Zacharie to pass on a flag of truce to Richmond in September. Later that month, Zacharie met Benjamin, James A. Seddon, the Confederate secretary of war, and Stephen R. Mallory, secretary of the navy, at City Point, Virginia. The conversation was friendly and convinced Zacharie that, if given the authority, Banks could "make peace in 24 hours, satisfactory to the North and without humiliating the South."[7]

Although Lincoln was initially pleased with the opening Zacharie had created, he decided not to follow up with further inquiries. The recent Confederate reversals of July made such negotiation less pressing, and

5. George S. Denison to Chase, February 5, 12, 1863, in Chase, "Diary and Correspondence"; Shepley to Butler, February 20, 1863, in Butler, *Private and Official Correspondence,* 3:3, 9, 14. For another scathing denunciation of Zacharie by a Union colonel, see Babcock, "War Commentary," 54–58, MNHS.

6. George S. Denison to Chase, September 21, 1863, in Chase, "Diary and Correspondence," 353, 355–56; Harrington, *Fighting Politician,* 126; Hoffman, *Camp, Court and Siege,* 60–61; U.S. Congress, House, *Executive Document No. 101: Funds Seized at New Orleans during the Late Civil War,* 49th Cong., 1st sess., 24; Banks to S. B. Holabird, July 2, 1863, Banks to Seward, July 2, 1863, and Zacharie to Banks, July 4, 30, September 8, December 28, 1863, Banks Collection, LC.

7. Zacharie to Banks, September 8, October 9, 16, 24, 1863, Banks Collection, LC.

the radicals continued to voice their strong opposition. Furthermore, Lincoln was aware that within the year he would have to mount his re-election campaign, and he did not want to improve Banks's presidential chances. Consequently, Lincoln told Zacharie to "lay quiet" for a while; the president would call him when it was time. Zacharie knew what that meant and wrote Banks that Lincoln resembled "the man that won the elephant at a raffle, he doesn't know what to do with it." As he expected, the call never came, and Zacharie returned to New York to pursue his profitable business of fixing feet. Banks never got another chance to be a peacemaker.[8]

Even after the fall of Port Hudson, Banks could ill afford the distractions of an aborted peace mission in Washington. He had his hands full where he was.

Perhaps the most imposing nonmilitary challenge facing Banks in 1863 was corruption growing out of the lure of quick wealth for the hundreds of speculators who flocked to Louisiana. The fuel that fired the engine of corruption was cotton. Cotton mills in the Northeast, with their one hundred thousand looms and more than five million spindles, created a yearly demand for seven hundred thousand bales of the staple. By the late spring of 1862, a mere thirty-six hundred bales had been shipped from Nashville to northern mills. New Orleans, which had exported as many as two million bales annually before the war, ended the year by sending only thirty-eight thousand bales to northern ports. By July 1862, at least 80 percent of the cotton mills in New England had closed down. The huge demand for cotton in both the North and Europe had enabled speculators to establish an extremely lucrative trade in the commodity with the connivance of local authorities.[9]

Speculators had offered to share their profits with the new commander almost as soon as Banks arrived in December 1862. "Dear Sir," Andrew J. Butler (Benjamin's brother) wrote Banks through his agent, C. A. Weed. "If you will allow our commercial program to be [carried] out as projected previous to your arrival in the department[,] giving the same support and facilites [*sic*] as your predecessor I am authorized on

8. Zacharie to Banks, October 9, 24, December 28, 1863, Banks Collection, LC.

9. A. Sellew Roberts, "The Federal Government and Confederate Cotton," *American Historical Review* 32 (January 1927): 262–75; Johnson, *Red River Campaign*, 13; Smith, "Banks Expedition of 1862," 346–47; Banks to Mary Banks, January 15, 1863, Banks Collection, LC.

obtaining your assent to place at your disposal $100,000." Banks passed up the offer. "I thank God every night that I have no desire for dishonest gains," he wrote Mary a few days later. "I had one hundred thousand dollars offered me the other day to allow the people to 'continue' the commercial enterprises, but it was no temptation for me." Failing to obtain Banks's support, Andrew Butler left Louisiana, possibly because he had already made his fortune or perhaps because he was ill with tuberculosis. When he died in February 1864, his estate was estimated to be worth $200,000, which suggests that the nine months of brother Ben's rule had been profitable for the older sibling.[10]

As the war progressed and the demand for cotton increased, even more speculators arrived, including Gardner Banks, the major general's younger brother, who had resigned his commission in the Sixteenth Massachusetts Infantry because of a bad knee. With little to do in Waltham, Gardner decided to deal in sutlers' goods (commodities sold to troops) and hoped to do a booming business in the Department of the Gulf. "Of course I should not allow my name to be used as a *sutlers,*" Gardner assured his brother. "But if I could do anything whereby I could make a little money *honestly,* I should like to do so." Whether for reasons of honesty or ineptitude, Gardner never did very well in New Orleans. His letters to Banks were filled with requests for money to tide him and his family over. Banks was disinclined to accede, although occasionally he did send something Gardner's way, such as an inspection tour of plantations operating under Banks's labor system. Generally, Gardner was an embarrassment to Banks, and his presence in the department strained their relationship.[11]

One way enterprising individuals could make an honest profit was to take advantage of Banks's policy of leasing abandoned plantations to grow cotton. This policy, however, never came close to satisfying the demand for several reasons. First, the amount of land available for cultiva-

10. Holzman, *Stormy Ben Butler,* 143; Nash, *Stormy Petrel,* 21; *New Orleans Era,* November 29, 1864; C. A. Weed (for A. J. Butler) to Banks, December 27, 1862, Banks to Mary Banks, January 16, [1863], Banks to Brig. Gen. Emory, July 22, 1863, Banks to Cuthbert Bullitt, July 22, 1863, Banks to Halleck, August 29, 1863, Banks Collection, LC.

11. Doyle, "Civilian Life in Occupied New Orleans," 167–68; *Official Army Register,* 1:169; Gardner Banks to Banks, October 5, 1863, Banks to Mary Banks, August 14, 1864, Banks Collection, LC.

tion was small; most cotton-producing acreage remained within Confederate lines. Second, the turmoil and displacement caused by the fighting and the siphoning off of the best field hands into the Union army made it difficult for the lessees to obtain a dependable labor force. Finally, the Confederates did everything they could to disrupt cotton production on these "government" plantations. Periodic forays by Confederate raiders effectively limited the supply of cotton from this source throughout the war.[12]

Because of the failure of the lease system, "the cotton mania rages with unabated fury," and its corruptive influence affected Federals and Confederates alike. A correspondent for the *New York Herald* quoted Richard Taylor, the Confederate commander in Louisiana, as stating that cotton made "more damn rascals on both sides than everything else." With prices ranging up to a dollar a pound, the margin of profit was very great, and traders were able to hand large sums of money to military men who permitted shipments to slip across the lines. Soon visitors were remarking that the treasury agencies that had been established to regulate the buying and selling of cotton "proved little else than schools of dishonesty."[13]

Realizing that the widespread acceptance of bribes was "a discredit to the service," Banks had tried in January 1863 to take some of the profit out of the trade by legalizing it within Federal lines. "All products of the country sent to the city of New Orleans in good faith may be sold at market prices by the proprietors or their factors, for legal currency of the United States, without restriction or confiscation," he proclaimed in General Orders No. 8. "Planters will find it for their interest to forward

12. *OR*, 24, pt. 2:466, 34, pt. 2:955; Winters, *Civil War in Louisiana,* 310–11, 392–94.

13. *OR*, 34, pt. 2:16–17, 823–26, Ser. 3, 4:68; Knox, *Camp-Fire and Cotton-Field,* 401–5; George Hamilton Perkins, *Letters of Geo. Hamilton Perkins, U.S.N.*, ed. George E. Belknap (Concord, N.H.: Rumford Press, 1901), 114; Francis Winthrop Palfrey, *Memoir of William Francis Bartlett* (Boston: Houghton Mifflin, 1881), 86; *New York Tribune,* April 9, May 8, 1863; *New Orleans Daily True Delta,* June 21, 24, 1863; *New York Herald,* October 29, 1863, June 11, 1864; Andrew Jackson Butler to Banks, January 30, 1863, Banks to Lincoln, December 16, 1863, J. S. Brisbin to Banks, June 17, 1864, Banks Collection, LC; Andrew Butler to Benjamin Butler, February 6, 1863, P. R. George to Benjamin Butler, March 23, 1863, in Butler, *Private and Official Correspondence,* 3:4, 36; George S. Denison to Chase, January 15, 1863, in Chase, "Diary and Correspondence," 349.

their crops to New Orleans rather than to dispose of them on the plantations," he assured them.[14]

The response to the scheme was gratifying, and in May 1863 Banks urged his superiors to extend the open-market system to cotton owned by private individuals who lived in areas held by the Confederacy. Banks proposed letting the crop come across the lines, provided Union officials held half the sale price as a guarantee that the profit would not be used to aid the secessionist state government in Shreveport. Banks saw several advantages to his scheme. First, the legalized trade in cotton would help northern manufacturers who needed it, including those in his home state of Massachusetts. In addition, such trade would undercut the speculators and reduce their ability to tempt Union army officers. Finally, the restoration of a limited trade might convince southerners that it was advantageous for Louisiana to rejoin the Union. Whatever the case, Banks's plan never got a chance, for the Treasury Department vetoed it. Secretary Chase did not want the military interfering with the work of his officials.[15]

Banks was not discouraged, however, for he had thought of another way to get all the cotton he needed. He could seize it. Owners would be compensated for their loss if they could prove that they were either Unionists or foreigners. But if the cotton belonged to secessionists or the Rebel government, Banks could simply confiscate the crop.[16]

Banks had tried this approach during the spring of 1863 along the Bayou Teche when Chickering's men seized $10 million worth of the staple before returning to their base in New Orleans. Despite orders from the War Department in late March directing military commanders to turn over all captured and abandoned property to treasury agents, Banks continued to sell captured cotton and used the proceeds to meet the expenses of the Department of the Gulf. But for his seizure scheme to work, he had to prevent Confederate authorities from destroying cotton before it could be confiscated. To encourage their cooperation, Banks

14. *OR,* 15:616, 643–45; U.S. Congress, *Report of the Joint Committee on the Conduct of the War: Red River Expedition,* 344–57.

15. *OR,* 15:310, 26, pt. 1:715, Ser. 3, 3:229–31, 1174; U.S. Congress, *Report of the Joint Committee on the Conduct of the War,* 2:350–51, 356–57.

16. *OR,* 15:697–98; U.S. Congress, House, *Executive Document No. 3: Report of the Secretary of the Treasury on the State of Finances for the Year Ending June 30, 1863,* 38th Cong., 1st sess., 436–37; Johnson, *Red River Campaign,* 55; Banks to Maj. Gen. Dana, October 15, 1863, Banks Collection, LC.

proposed to bribe them. He summarized his plan in a letter to Lincoln: "The state of the rebellion and the impoverished condition of its officers west of the Mississippi is such that they are willing to take measures for the preservation of this cotton wherever it may be found, and allow it to be taken and sold by the officer of the Government, appropriating the proceeds, except 18 cents a pound to be reserved for their use in the hands of the chief quartermaster, until satisfactory guarantees are given that it is not to be used by any person in hostile acts against the United States."[17]

Banks saw important advantages to such a program. Money would flow into the treasury (through the Department of the Gulf), and the Confederate government would gain supplies or cash. Furthermore, the scheme would hasten the breakup of the Confederacy by indirectly making Confederate officials employees of the Union army. In other words, Banks thought that he could transfer the blight of corruption from the Union to the Confederate side.[18]

Banks's plan might have worked had more Confederate officials been interested in the proposition. But Richard Taylor had no intention of giving the Union army such a windfall. Although initially he had objected to the policy of burning cotton because it would hurt private citizens, Taylor changed his mind when he realized that Banks could get all the cotton he needed through seizure. Taylor also had come to appreciate the corrupting influence of a staple with so much potential for a quick profit. "The possession of any large amount of cotton will in time destroy the patriotism of the best citizen as surely as water will in time wear away stone," he wrote to Kirby Smith. Reluctantly, Taylor ordered its destruction whenever it was "likely to fall into the hands of the enemy."[19]

17. *OR*, Ser. 3, 4:68; U.S. Congress, *Report of the Joint Committee on the Conduct of the War: Red River Expedition*, 345; Harrington, *Fighting Politician*, 136; *New York Herald*, July 1, 1863; Banks to Col. Beckwith, July 22, 1863, Banks to Flanders, March 21, 1864, Banks to Stanton, February 2, 1864, Banks Collection, LC; *OR*, Ser. 3, 4:68–70.

18. E. Kirby Smith, "The Defense of the Red River," in *Battles and Leaders of the Civil War*, ed. Robert U. Johnson and Clarence C. Buel, 5 vols. (1884–88; reprint, Secaucus, N.J.: Castle, 1987), 4:369–74.

19. *OR*, 34, pt. 2:818, 853, 878, 911, 972, 978; U.S. Congress, *Report of the Joint Committee on the Conduct of the War: Red River Expedition*, 208–9, 225, 270–71; Sarah A. Dorsey, *Recollections of Henry Watkins Allen: Brigadier General, Confederate States Army; Ex-Governor of Louisiana* (New York: M. Doolady, 1866), 282–83; Banks to Flanders, March 21, 1864, quoted in Harrington, *Fighting Politician*, 139; Joseph H. Parks, *General Edmund Kirby Smith, C.S.A.* (Baton Rouge: Louisiana State University Press,

. . .

Military operations in Louisiana in 1864 were a sideshow to more important campaigns elsewhere. Yet other events in the Pelican State that year were of even greater importance. Although Lincoln's plan for Reconstruction was initiated simultaneously in the several states occupied by Union forces, nowhere did it progress as far or have as much chance for success as in Louisiana. It was in Louisiana that the first efforts were made to enfranchise the black man, to provide him with an education, and to set up a civil government that was responsive to the needs of all of its citizens.[20]

The first attempt to reconstruct Louisiana had occurred in December 1862, when Lincoln asked the military governor, George F. Shepley, to hold elections in the two congressional districts then under Union control. The turnout was remarkably high inasmuch as most of the electorate was off fighting in the Rebel army or living as refugees behind Confederate lines. The two victorious candidates, Michael Hahn and Benjamin F. Flanders, traveled to Washington to claim their seats in the Thirty-seventh Congress. Banks arrived in New Orleans close on the heels of the election. Heartened by evidence that Unionist sentiment was on the rise, Banks set out to establish a loyalist regime for the state as a whole.[21]

Given his working-class background, it was not surprising that Banks looked to the "humble and honest farmer, the poor mechanic, the hard working classes, the bone and sinew of the land" as a basis for the new government. Banks had good reason to place his hopes in the workingman. Since his days as a young politician in Massachusetts, Banks had used the tactic of playing on class divisions for political gain. Like many northerners, he believed that the stratified society of the South made it vulnerable to class conflict and predicted that poor southern whites would rise against the wealthy planters if provided the opportunity. Assuming that secession was the work of the rich planter class, Banks believed that "a clear majority of the people . . . were opposed to the war

---

1954), 354; P. W., *Historical Sketch of Gen. N. P. Banks's Civil and Military Administration in Louisiana* (New York: Privately printed, 1864), 9.

20. McCrary, *Abraham Lincoln and Reconstruction,* 3–18.

21. Herman Belz, *Reconstructing the Union: Theory and Policy during the Civil War* (Ithaca, N.Y.: Cornell University Press for the American Historical Association, 1969), 106; McCrary, *Abraham Lincoln and Reconstruction,* 98–102.

and could you remove from control of public opinion one or two thousand in each of these states, so as to let up from the foundations of political society the mass of common people, you would have a population in all of these States as loyal and true to the Government as the people of any portion of the East or West."[22]

Banks's error was his failure to understand that the average southern workingman shared the racial prejudices of his more privileged neighbor. Furthermore, Banks underestimated the common cause that bound rich and poor together in their fight against Union troops who had invaded their homeland. Nevertheless, he was convinced that he could do more to cultivate "a large share of the small farmers, laborers, mechanics, and a portion of the merchants . . . [who were] truly loyal." All that was required was to get them to take an oath of allegiance and go to the polls to elect loyalist officials.[23]

Banks's goal was particularly difficult to achieve in the rural parishes under Union control. Although a few small farmers did swear allegiance to the United States, the majority remained at arm's length. The wanton destruction of property by Union troops as they moved through these areas alienated many of these men from their "liberators." Others feared the Confederate reprisals that would be sure to follow once Yankees left the vicinity. In addition, many of the provost marshals placed in charge of the occupied areas openly sided with the planters against the small farmers after allowing themselves "to be dined and wined into a blindness to their covert treason."[24]

The situation was different in New Orleans, where a large number of bona fide Unionists resided. Thus, as soon as Mary Banks and the children arrived in New Orleans from Boston in October 1863, Banks en-

22. Louisiana, *Debates in the Convention for the Revision and Amendment of the Constitution of the State of Louisiana, 1864* (New Orleans: W. R. Fish, 1864), 189; Harrington, *Fighting Politician,* 98; *Congressional Globe,* 39th Cong., 1st sess., 1866, 2532–33.

23. *OR,* 30, pt. 3:694–700; Hepworth, *Whip, Hoe, and Sword,* 101; Louisiana, *Debates,* 212; Roger W. Shugg, *Origins of Class Struggle in Louisiana* (Baton Rouge: Louisiana State University Press, 1939), 95–97; Banks to Mary Banks, May 3, 1863, Banks Collection, LC.

24. Hoffman, *Camp, Court, and Siege,* 111; P. W., *Historical Sketch,* 4; Ripley, *Slaves and Freedmen,* 93; Tunnell, *Crucible of Reconstruction,* 29; *OR,* 41, pt. 2:683–84; U.S. Congress, *Report of the Joint Committee on the Conduct of the War: Red River Expedition,* 285–86; *National Anti-Slavery Standard,* July 23, 1864.

listed her help "to dance the fair creoles to loyalty." The general and Mrs. Banks staged dances, concerts, and receptions for local citizens. A new dance, the "Imperial," was introduced at one of the parties and performed with great show at weekly soirees. On these occasions, they decorated their mansion on Coliseum Place with brightly colored Chinese lanterns hanging in the trees. Hundreds of guests, including army generals, foreign consuls, politicians, and prominent Unionists from the local community were entertained in a style the city had not seen since before the war. Although most southern women boycotted the Banks affairs, thinking that these "efforts at gayety seemed a mockery of woe," some did attend and had to admit that their hosts were at least "respectable." Banks's detractors referred to him as the "dancing master" and suggested that he was "disposed to 'toady' to wealthy and aristocratic secessionists wearing the mask of loyalty." Despite the criticism, Banks was convinced that Unionists in New Orleans would provide a foundation upon which Louisiana could be readmitted to the Union.[25]

The foundation that Banks planned to build on had been laid on May 8, 1863, when delegates from the several Unionist clubs in the city, suburbs, and parishes under Federal control assembled in New Orleans to form the "Free State of Louisiana." The chairman of the Free State meeting was Thomas Jefferson Durant. "Tall, thin, sallow, [and] cadaverous," Durant was a Philadelphia native who had come to New Orleans in 1831 as a young man. A powerful orator and shrewd lawyer, Durant had made a name for himself in New Orleans. He had kept a low profile while the secessionists were in charge but let his loyalist sentiments be known after Federal troops arrived. With Flanders and Hahn away in Washington, Durant had become the unchallenged leader of the Unionist movement in New Orleans.[26]

25. Doyle, "Civilian Life in Occupied New Orleans," 232; George L. Andrews to his wife, December 12, 1863, Andrews Papers, LALMVC; Banks to Mary Banks, September 22, November 11, 1863, August 23, 1864, Banks to Mrs. Banks, October 25, 1863, Banks Collection, LC; Samuel M. Quincy to his mother, April 29, 1865, Quincy, Wendell, Holmes, and Upham Papers, LC.

26. *New Orleans Era,* April 26, May 13, 1863; McCrary, *Abraham Lincoln and Reconstruction,* 99, 125, 129–30; Minutes of General Committee of Union Associations, May 19, 1863, New York Historical Society, New York City; Shugg, *Origins of Class Struggle,* 189–90, 196–233; *New Orleans Daily True Delta,* July 14, 1863; Banks to Lincoln, October 23, 1863 (finished but not sent), Banks Collection, LC; [Judge Whitaker], *Sketches of Life and Character in Louisiana* (New Orleans: Ferguson & Crosby, 1847), 23–24; Hans L. Trefousse, *Historical Dictionary of Reconstruction* (New York: Green-

The key to the Free State platform was a call for a constitutional convention to draft a document under which Louisiana could be readmitted to the Union. Shepley was agreeable to the idea and named Durant attorney general with authority to register "all free white male citizens" in preparation for an election of delegates as soon as Banks gave the word.[27]

Lincoln was pleased that supporters of the Free State were ready "to make a new constitution recognizing the emancipation proclamation and adopting emancipation in those parts of the state to which the proclamation does not apply." To expedite the process, Lincoln urged Banks on August 5, 1863, to "confer with intelligent and trusty citizens of the state, among whom I would suggest Messrs. Flanders, Hahn, and Durant." Speed was of paramount importance; Lincoln wanted a new constitution for Louisiana ready by the time Congress convened in December 1863.[28]

Durant was eager to follow through on Lincoln's directive, but Banks was not. In part, Banks was distracted during the fall of 1863 with his grand design to wrest control of Texas from the Confederates by lodging a series of armed enclaves along the coast. But there was more to his hesitancy than the distractions of a military campaign. Nathaniel P. Banks had become disenchanted with Thomas Jefferson Durant.

The reason for Banks's disenchantment was Durant's idea of what the Free State of Louisiana should look like after it was "reconstructed." Durant's view was much more radical than what Banks had in mind. Rather than favoring a state government composed of Unionists drawn from the ranks of the old planter elite, Durant was committed to a complete restructuring of the southern way of life. Such a reconstruction included not only the abolition of slavery but also the right of black men to vote.[29]

Durant went public with his endorsement for free black suffrage in December 1863. Banks was not surprised, for he had distrusted Durant

---

wood Press, 1991), 66; Durant to Butler, February 20, 1865, Benjamin F. Butler Papers, LC.

27. Shepley, Gen. Order No. 24, *New Orleans Daily Picayune,* June 14, 1863; Belz, *Reconstructing the Union,* 144.

28. Lincoln to Banks, August 5, 1863, in Basler, ed., *Collected Works of Abraham Lincoln,* 6:364–66; Belz, *Reconstructing the Union,* 146.

29. Joseph G. Tregle, "Thomas J. Durant, Utopian Socialism, and the Failure of Presidential Reconstruction in Louisiana," *Journal of Southern History* 45 (November 1979): 488–95; McCrary, *Abraham Lincoln and Reconstruction,* 184–85, 228–29; Tunnell, *Crucible of Reconstruction,* 37.

all along and was afraid that a white backlash to Durant's radical ideas would scuttle his plan to coax Louisiana back into the Union. If such an outcome would be unfortunate for the state, it would be disastrous for Banks personally. Banks had his eyes set on the White House, and a failure in Louisiana would seriously undercut his prospects when the Republicans nominated their candidate for president in 1864.[30]

Banks undercut the attorney general's efforts to register loyal white males by refusing to cooperate. His refusal was critical, for Durant did not have funds to carry out the registration on his own and needed transportation and protection of the army, especially in the parishes outside of New Orleans. As a result, the registration of voters for the constitutional convention proceeded slowly.[31]

An exasperated Durant wrote directly to Lincoln on October 1, 1863. "You appear to think that a Registration of voters is going on under my supervision, with the view of bringing on the election of delegates to a Constitutional Convention; but such is not the case," Durant informed the president. "The means of communicating with a large portion of the state are not in our power, and before the commencement of a Registration," he continued, "we ought to have undisputed control of a considerable territory, at least the two congressional districts proclaimed as not being in Rebellion."[32]

Durant knew when he wrote the letter that Banks had tried to discredit him with the president, but he did not realize that someone else had also conspired against him. The pliant Michael Hahn, who was in Washington as one of the state's two "loyal" representatives, had decided to throw in with Banks. Hahn believed that his political future was more

30. Durant announced his support for limited black suffrage at a meeting of the Union National League at the Lyceum Hall on December 3, 1863 (*New Orleans Times*, December 4, 1863). See also Cox, *Lincoln and Black Freedom*, 80; McCrary, *Abraham Lincoln and Reconstruction*, 209, 226–27; Tregle, "Thomas J. Durant," 502–6; Tunnell, *Crucible of Reconstruction*, 36–37, 42–43.

31. Tregle, "Thomas J. Durant," 505; McCrary, *Abraham Lincoln and Reconstruction*, 161–62; Philip D. Uzee, "The Beginnings of the Louisiana Republican Party," *Louisiana History* 12 (Summer 1971): 201.

32. Cox, *Lincoln and Black Freedom*, 65; Tregle, "Thomas J. Durant," 506; Durant to Lincoln, October 1, 1863, Mounting No. 26839, Abraham Lincoln Papers, LC. According to McCrary (*Abraham Lincoln and Reconstruction*, 163), Durant's desire to have a substantial proportion of the electorate represented was not unrealistic. The thirteen parishes participating in the elections for the two congressional seats in December 1862 contained almost half of Louisiana's population.

secure tied to a man with bayonets than one who advocated black suffrage.[33]

Between them, Banks and Hahn systematically distorted what was happening in Louisiana in their reports to Lincoln. "The Union cause is going on gloriously here," Hahn had written to Lincoln after returning to the Crescent City for a visit in May 1863. Banks gave the same optimistic account from Opelousas, where he was engaged in a campaign to penetrate the interior of the state. "It gives me pleasure to say to you that the sentiments of the people, are unexpectedly, and almost universally friendly to the restoration of the Government," he wrote. "Nothing is required but a sufficient force to hold the territory, to secure its immediate return to the Union."[34]

As a result of Banks and Hahn's deception, Durant's letter came as a surprise when it arrived. Lincoln had assumed that the registration of voters was proceeding smoothly. Furthermore, political necessity could not wait for military victories that might not be forthcoming. Lincoln fired off an angry letter to Banks on November 5. He had assumed that Durant "was taking a registry of citizens, preparatory to the election of a constitutional convention," the president began. "I now have his letter, written two months after . . . saying he is not taking registry; and he does not let me know that he personally is expecting to do so. This disappoints me bitterly; yet I do not want to throw blame on you or them. I do however, urge both you and them, to lose no more time."[35]

Banks feigned bewilderment and hurt upon receiving Lincoln's letter. He had not realized that the president was counting on him, he said in a reply drafted on December 6, 1863. Insinuating that Durant and Shepley had rejected his offer to help with the registration of voters, Banks noted that the military governor was in charge. "Had the organization of a *free* state in Louisiana been committed to me under general

33. McCrary, *Abraham Lincoln and Reconstruction*, 173; Tregle, "Thomas J. Durant," 507.

34. Hahn to Lincoln, May 9, 1863, Mounting No. 23388, Lincoln Papers, LC; Banks to Lincoln, May 4, 1863, Mounting No. 23301, ibid. See also McCrary, *Abraham Lincoln and Reconstruction*, 105.

35. Lincoln to Banks, November 5, 1863, in Basler, ed., *Collected Works of Abraham Lincoln*, 7:1–2; also see Cox, *Lincoln and Black Freedom*, 47; McCrary, *Abraham Lincoln and Reconstruction*, 173–74; Nicolay and Hay, *Abraham Lincoln*, 8:422–24; *New Orleans Times*, November 3, 1863; and George S. Boutwell to Banks, December 21, 1863, Banks Collection, LC.

instructions only," he noted, "it would have been complete before this day." Banks promised that he would complete the reorganization of the state government within sixty days, "even in *thirty* days, if necessary," should Lincoln give him the authority to do so.[36]

Even before he received Banks's letter, Lincoln had decided to speed the process along. In his annual address to Congress on December 9, 1863, the president announced a plan for the reconstruction of southern states. According to his plan, Lincoln would recognize the legitimacy of a state government when the number of persons taking an oath of loyalty and voting in a state election exceeded 10 percent of the number of votes cast in the presidential election of 1860.[37]

Durant was ecstatic when he heard of the president's plan and increased pressure on Shepley to order an election. But it was Shepley who hesitated this time, caught between the Free State leader, Durant, and his military commander, Banks. Shepley decided on December 31 to ask Lincoln for permission to call for an election before proceeding. Informing the president that he was "anxious to conform to your views," Shepley asked to be reassured that what Durant proposed was in accord with the president's proclamation on Reconstruction.[38]

Shepley's letter crossed in the mail with one from Lincoln to Banks. Frustrated by the slow pace of Reconstruction in Louisiana and believing Banks's claim that he could get things done, Lincoln wrote the Massachusetts politician on Christmas Eve, apologizing for having wounded Banks's feelings and giving him absolute authority to direct the effort to reconstruct Louisiana. "Give us a free-state organization of Louisiana in the shortest possible time," Lincoln urged.[39]

36. Excerpts from Banks's letter to Lincoln, December 6, 1863, are in Basler, ed., *Collected Works of Lincoln,* 7:90–91; also see Cox, *Lincoln and Black Freedom,* 69. In *Crucible of Reconstruction,* 43, Tunnell opines that Banks was genuinely surprised when he received Lincoln's rebuke.

37. Lincoln, "Proclamation," December 8, 1863, in Basler, ed., *Collected Works of Abraham Lincoln,* 7:55; Cox, *Lincoln and Black Freedom,* 62; McCrary, *Abraham Lincoln and Reconstruction,* 186–91. Fifty thousand votes were cast in Louisiana in the 1860 presidential election.

38. Shepley to Lincoln, December 31, 1863, Mounting No. 29036, Lincoln Papers, LC. See also McCrary, *Abraham Lincoln and Reconstruction,* 195–99.

39. Lincoln to Banks, December 24, 1863, in Basler, ed., *Collected Works of Abraham Lincoln,* 7:89–90; also see Cox, *Lincoln and Black Freedom,* 62–63.

Using his newfound authority, Banks acted swiftly. On January 11, 1864, he issued a proclamation ordering an election on February 22 for governor, lieutenant governor, and several other state offices. Any white male who took an oath of loyalty to the Constitution, laws, and president of the United States would be allowed to vote. In addition, Banks announced that there would be an election on March 28 for a constitutional convention. In the meantime, the state would continue to operate under its constitution of 1852, stripped of its provisions relating to slavery.[40]

Most attention centered on the race for governor. The moderates and the radicals had an advantage because most of the conservative support was off in the Confederate army. Yet the two factions could not agree among themselves and soon went their separate ways. As a result, three Unionist candidates vied for governor: J. Q. A. Fellows, a conservative; the moderate Michael Hahn; and Benjamin F. Flanders, the choice of the radicals.[41]

Banks threw his support behind Hahn, although he was not supposed to endorse any candidate publicly.[42] For his part, Hahn went after workingmen and the foreign vote. He was helped further by Flanders, a slow-thinking politician who fumbled the chances he had. Hahn took advantage of every opportunity to attack Flanders's problack views. He accused Flanders of wanting black suffrage, which was anathema to most white Unionists in Louisiana. Flanders attempted to backtrack by stating that he "had never advocated" black suffrage and "did not deem it practi-

40. Banks's proclamation, "To the People of Louisiana" (January 11, 1864), appeared in several papers, including his own, the *New Orleans Era*. Also see *OR*, Ser. 3, 4:22–23; "The Qualifications of Electors," *New Orleans Daily True Delta*, February 21, 1864; Gilles Vandal, "The New Orleans Riot of 1866: The Anatomy of a Tragedy" (Ph.D. dissertation, College of William and Mary, 1978), 7; and Cox, *Lincoln and Black Freedom*, 58. McCrary (*Abraham Lincoln and Reconstruction*, 207) suggests that Banks ordered the election for state offices first because it would be easier for him to organize his own slate of candidates than to orchestrate the election of almost a hundred convention delegates.

41. McCrary, *Abraham Lincoln and Reconstruction*, 186, 212–36; Harrington, *Fighting Politician*, 145.

42. Hahn was not a newcomer to Louisiana politics. In May 1860, he had joined fifty-five Douglas Democrats calling for an antisecession rally. Although he briefly held a minor post in the local Confederate administration, Hahn decided to cooperate fully with the Federal occupation forces when they arrived (Amos E. Simpson and Vaughn Baker, "Michael Hahn: Steady Patriot," *Louisiana History* 13 [Summer 1972]: 229–33).

cable." Moreover, he added that he had never uttered "one word in favor of negro equality."[43]

Banks worked hard to ensure a large turnout. He ordered regimental bands to play music at Hahn rallies and made election day a holiday. He directed all Louisiana soldiers serving in Union regiments to cast ballots, although in some cases soldiers who were not bona fide residents ended up voting. Banks also allowed Unionists who had fled from areas under Confederate control to cast their ballots in New Orleans. Much to his satisfaction, eleven thousand voters went to the polls on Washington's birthday, February 22. The turnout was twice that required to satisfy Lincoln's 10 percent stipulation. Hahn was victorious, capturing 90 percent of the soldier vote. Flanders polled less than a quarter of the total, finishing far behind Hahn and even trailing Fellows, the conservative.[44]

Although the Banks-Hahn moderates had easily defeated the radicals, Banks was not particularly satisfied with the results. The conservatives had made a good showing, particularly in the plantation districts, while Hahn's strength had been primarily in New Orleans. This reality raised the question of what would happen when the Union army increased its occupation of the rural parishes. Not only that, but if southern sympathizers in the city decided to take the oath and vote in the next election, the conservatives could become dominant.[45]

Disregarding the threat for the time being, Banks turned his attention to plans for Michael Hahn's inauguration on March 4, 1865, as the first governor of the Free State of Louisiana. It was a grand affair with

43. *OR,* Ser. 3, 4:133–34; *New Orleans Era,* February 4, 17, 1864; *New Orleans Times,* February 11, 18, 20, 1864; *New Orleans Daily True Delta,* February 12, 18, 21, 1864. For an extended discussion of the Radicals and black suffrage, see Cox, *Lincoln and Black Freedom,* 89–92, 97–99, 121–29; and Ripley, *Slaves and Freedmen,* 160–68.

44. *OR,* Ser. 3, 4:170–72, 209; Harrington, *Fighting Politician,* 144; McCrary, *Abraham Lincoln and Reconstruction,* 208, 222–23, 234–40; Ripley, *Slaves and Freedmen,* 170; *New Orleans Times,* February 6, 17, 1864; *New Orleans Era,* January 29, 1864. The vote was 6,183 for Hahn, 2,996 for Fellows, and 2,322 for Flanders (Harrington, *Fighting Politician,* 252). Banks's heavy-handed attempt to get Hahn elected provoked a storm of criticism among some Louisiana Unionists (see "Some Remarks upon the Proposed Election of February 22d," Thomas S. Bacon to Francis Lieber, March 5, 1864, Lieber Papers, HL).

45. Denison to Chase, February 19, 1864, in Chase, "Diary and Correspondence," 431; *New York Herald,* March 14, 1864; *New Orleans Daily Picayune,* February 19, 1864.

floats, banners, fireworks, and the music of three hundred musicians aided by an anvil chorus of forty more. A choir of schoolchildren from the New Orleans public schools sang to the crowd of twenty thousand in Lafayette Square. The inauguration was actually Banks's show. When the children sang "Hail to the Chief," they turned to face Banks, not Hahn. Behind the inaugural platform banners read, "Major General Banks, The Hero of Port Hudson" and "Major General Banks, The Noble Citizen and the Dutiful Soldier." And the highlight of the occasion was an address by the major general, in which he spoke of the "receding" Rebel armies, the prospect of a Union victory in the near future, and a bright future for the Free State of Louisiana. Banks was ecstatic. He had "never witnessed such a spectacle," he wrote in his report. There was "no sounder basis for a State government in this country," he proclaimed.[46]

46. *OR*, 34, pt. 2:512–13; Doyle, "Civilian Life in Occupied New Orleans," 209–10; McCrary, *Abraham Lincoln and Reconstruction*, 237–38; *New York Herald*, March 14, 1864; *New Orleans Times*, March 4, 1864; P. S. Gilmore to Banks, March 7, 1864, Banks Collection, LC; Banks to Lincoln, February 25, 1864, *OR*, Ser. 3, 4:133–34; Banks to William Lloyd Garrison, January 30, 1865, *Liberator*, February 24, 1865.

13

The Enemy Retreats before Us

The year 1864 promised to be a good one for Nathaniel P. Banks. On January 11 he issued a proclamation calling for the election of a governor for the Free State of Louisiana and delegates to a constitutional convention. Then he learned that a grateful Congress of the United States had voted on January 28 to thank him and his men for their role in the capture of Port Hudson. But most important, the political general from Waltham, Massachusetts, began the new year preparing for a major military campaign up the Red River.[1]

The campaign had three objectives. The first was to destroy the Confederate army under Richard Taylor. The second, imposed by Washington, was to occupy east Texas. Banks was convinced that his strategy of occupying posts along the Texas coast was superior to a plan to strike into the interior far from the safety of Union warships, but Texas Unionists had convinced Lincoln that he needed to establish a significant presence somewhere else in the Lone Star state. The third objective was closer to Banks's heart. There were thousands of bales of cotton, some thought as many as one hundred thousand, stashed along the banks of the Red River waiting to be confiscated.[2]

1. "To the People of Louisiana," January 11, 1864, in *OR,* Ser. 3, 4:22–23, 96–98, 26, pt. 1:911.

2. Smith and Brady, *Commission on Corrupt Practices,* 43; Johnson, *Red River Campaign,* 5–13, 31–40; Walker, "The War of Secession West of the Mississippi River during the years 1863–4– & 5," 36, typescript, MHI.

Unfortunately, the Red River campaign did not fit into the larger strategic picture. Union troops were needed in the eastern theaters, where the war would eventually be decided. The Trans-Mississippi Department by itself could not survive once Confederate armies east of the river had been defeated. For this reason, the Red River Valley had only slight military value. In fact, Banks himself had initially questioned the wisdom of the operation. He considered Mobile a much more desirable objective. But it did not take long for Banks to change his mind. Although the Free State of Louisiana was taking hold in New Orleans, the state government for Confederate Louisiana was still in session at Shreveport under the able direction of its popular governor, Henry Watkins Allen. As long as Allen remained in power and as long as there were plenty of Rebel troops to enforce Confederate authority, the Free State of Louisiana would be nothing more than a minority alternative. Consequently, Banks began to see the advantage of capturing the Rebel state capital at Shreveport and holding elections in Confederate territory. By making sure that only loyal Unionists could vote, he might add a rural legitimacy to his urban regime. In addition, the Bobbin Boy realized that he could help the textile mills in his home state of Massachusetts if he seized a bunch of cotton in the process.[3]

The operational plan for the Red River campaign originated in the fertile but indecisive mind of the Union army's ranking general, Henry W. Halleck. Banks was to move north along the Bayou Teche through Vermillionville and Opelousas to Alexandria with between fifteen thousand and eighteen thousand men from the Department of the Gulf. Halleck ordered a second force of ten thousand men under Brigadier General Andrew J. Smith detached from Sherman's army at Vicksburg. These troops were to be transported down the Mississippi River and then up the Red River to Alexandria, where they would join Banks for the drive on Shreveport. Finally, Halleck directed Major General Frederick Steele to move his troops from their positions in central Arkansas to link up with Banks and Smith at or near the Confederate state capital. A

3. *OR*, 26, pt. 1:888–90, 34, pt. 2:15–16, 45–47, 133–34, 415, pt. 3:316; but see 30, pt. 3:694–96; John Chipman Gray, *War Letters, 1862–1865, of John Chipman Gray and John Codman Ropes* (Boston: Houghton Mifflin, 1927), 261; U.S. Congress, *Report of the Joint Committee on the Conduct of the War: Red River Expedition*, 3–5; Johnson, *Red River Campaign*, 45–47.

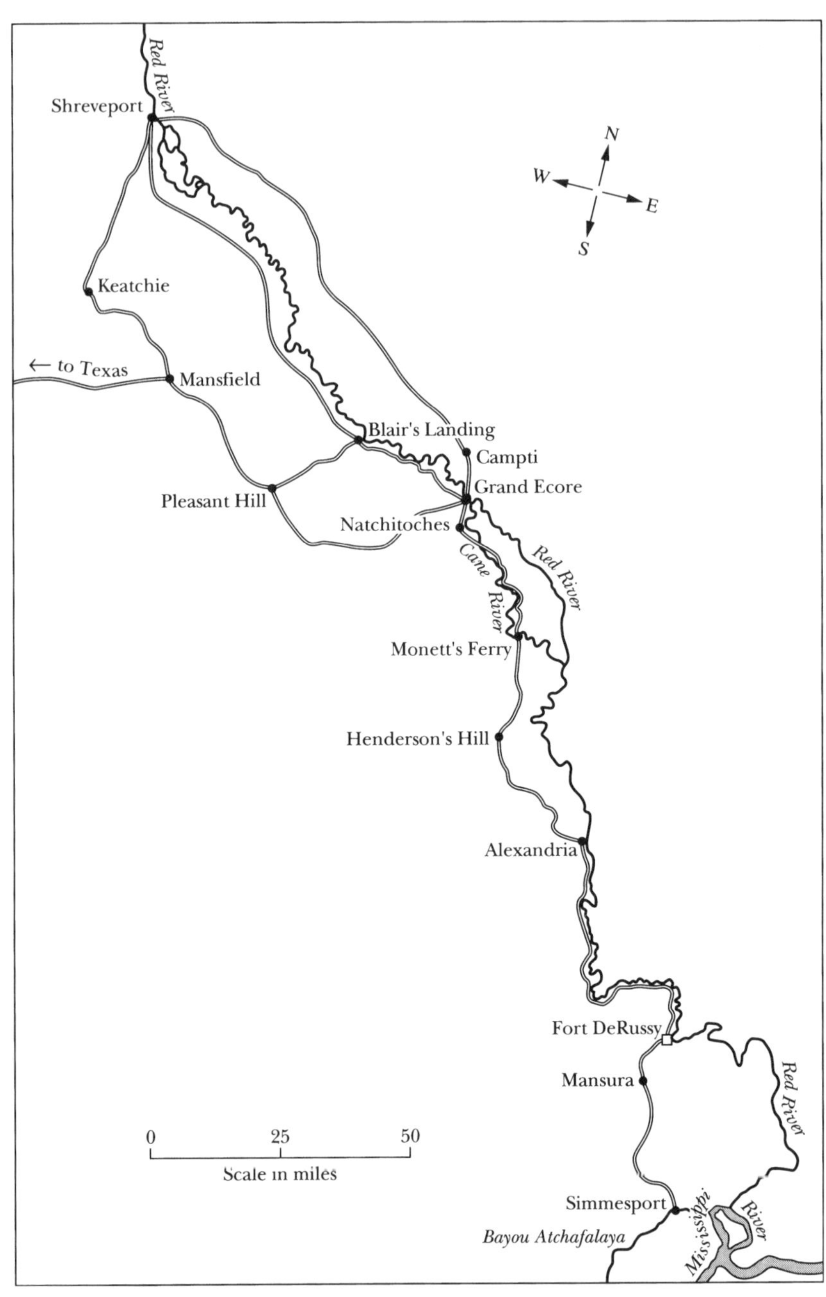

The Red River in 1864

fourth Union force consisted of David Dixon Porter with his fleet of gunboats and transports, which would operate on the Red River.[4]

Halleck's strategy may have worked had it been well coordinated, but he failed to appoint a single commander with authority over the combined force. As Banks remarked after it was over, "The difficulty in regard to this expedition was that nobody assumed to give orders; each commander acted for himself." Halleck complicated the situation further by stipulating that Smith's command had to rejoin Sherman's army no later than April 10. Furthermore, Halleck was so vague in his instructions that Banks, Smith, Steele, and Porter had difficulty determining whether they had received orders or merely suggestions.[5]

For a while, it appeared that Sherman would accompany the detachment from his army. He was familiar with the region, having lived near Alexandria before the war, and he wanted to make sure that his troops would be returned in time for the spring offensive against Atlanta. But Sherman was aware that Banks's commission as major general predated his, which meant that the politician from Waltham might insist on taking overall command of the two forces once they were united. Sherman did not cherish the prospect and decided not to accompany his troops, placing them instead under the command of the able but gloomy A. J. Smith.[6]

Brigadier General Andrew J. Smith was a West Pointer accustomed to serving under professional soldiers like Sherman. Although he was junior in rank to Banks, throughout the campaign he tended to act as though his detachment was not under Banks at all. Furthermore, Smith and his officers were critical of Banks's generalship and sneered at the Gulf Department's eastern troops, whom they thought to be undependable "holiday soldiers." Banks's New England men shot back that Smith's western regiments were filled with "gorillas"—coarse, uncouth, ill-dressed braggarts and chicken thieves. The open antagonism between

4. *OR*, 34, pt. 2:266–67; Johnson, *Red River Campaign*, 99. The detachment from Sherman's army consisted of three divisions, two from the XVI Corps and one from the XVII Corps.

5. *OR*, 34, pt. 2:15–16, 41–42, 55–56, 293–94; U.S. Congress, *Report of the Joint Committee on the Conduct of the War: Red River Expedition*, 19; Flinn, *Campaigning with Banks*, 155–56.

6. *OR*, 34, pt. 2:341, 351, 494, 514–16; M. A. DeWolfe Howe, ed., *Home Letters of General Sherman* (New York: Charles Scribner's Sons, 1909), 284–85.

the two commands did not bode well for a campaign for which cooperation and good communication were essential.[7]

Frederick Steele, the Union commander in Arkansas, also disliked the thought of being under Banks's command and took it upon himself to act more or less independently. As a result, Steele made several decisions that undercut the campaign from the start. Although Banks expected him to provide fifteen thousand soldiers for the expedition, Steele decided that ten thousand were enough. Once the campaign began, Steele pushed south slowly, far behind schedule. As Banks moved closer to Shreveport, Steele remained hundreds of miles away and out of contact.

Rear Admiral David Dixon Porter, who was in charge of the naval component of the Red River expedition, also proved difficult for Banks to work with. The excitable, short-tempered Porter was reluctant to listen to suggestions and, like many navy officers during the war, was disinclined to accept orders from army commanders, especially those who owed their rank to political connections. Porter had a particular dislike for Banks based on the latter's indecisiveness, which Porter had experienced firsthand during the campaign against Port Hudson.[8]

In spite of these obstacles, Banks set out to do what he could to make the campaign a success. On January 25, he dispatched letters to Steele and Sherman asking for a "statement of your position and the concentration of forces that may be possible" for a movement against Shreveport. While he waited for a response, Banks wrote Halleck for clarification regarding who was in command of the Union forces and when the campaign should get under way. The query was not unreasonable, for such decisions fell as a matter of course to the general in chief. But Halleck offered no help. He instructed Banks to "adopt such lines and plans of campaign" as he might think best.[9]

7. J. Cutler Andrews, *The North Reports the Civil War* (Pittsburgh: University of Pittsburgh Press, 1955), 501; Phillip Cuccia, "'Gorillas' and White Glove Gents: Union Soldiers in the Red River Campaign," *Louisiana History* 36 (Fall 1995): 413–30; Gray, *War Letters*, 363; Van Alstyne, *Diary of an Enlisted Man*, 306; Thomas Kilby Smith to Banks, May 26, 1880, Banks Manuscripts, ISHL.

8. *OR*, 34, pt. 3:153–54; U.S. Congress, *Report of the Joint Committee on the Conduct of the War: Red River Expedition*, 270–72; Farragut, *Life of Farragut*, 399; J. T. Woods, *Services of the Ninety-Sixth Ohio Volunteers* (Toledo: Blade Printing & Paper Co., 1874), 77.

9. *OR*, 34, pt. 2:125–28, 149–50, 293–94; Johnson, *Red River Campaign*, 81–82.

There were two reasons why Halleck failed to issue specific directions. First was the tricky problem of determining who should be in command. Sherman would have been the obvious choice, but he had already indicated his unwillingness to participate, which left Halleck in a predicament. Halleck was convinced that Banks was incompetent, but the political ramifications of superseding Banks with Steele were more than Halleck wanted to deal with. Lacking a good alternative, Halleck made no choice at all. A second reason for his reticence was related more to Halleck's personality than Banks's ineptness as a general. Halleck simply did not like to stick his neck out. By leaving these difficult decisions to subordinates in the field, he could avoid assuming responsibility for a failure should it occur. Obviously, this is not the command style Lincoln wanted or needed from the overall commander of Union forces, which was one reason why the president replaced Halleck with someone who was not afraid to make decisions, Ulysses S. Grant, within a month of Halleck's unhelpful response to Banks's inquiry.[10]

A. J. Smith's troops landed at Simmesport on March 12 and began their march up the Red River. The Rebel stronghold on the Red River, Fort De Russy, surrendered two days later. The fall of Fort De Russy meant that the Confederates had to evacuate Alexandria, and Porter's Union flotilla of seventeen gunboats reached the city unopposed the next day.[11]

Smith spent a couple of days razing Fort De Russy before resuming his march. Much to his surprise, Smith discovered when he reached Alexandria that Banks was nowhere to be found. Banks was late because of Michael Hahn's inauguration, and his failure to be on time was the first of several incidents that strained the relationship between Banks and the moody general from the Army of the Tennessee.[12]

While waiting for the tardy Banks, Smith decided to shake up the Confederate cavalry under Colonel William G. Vincent, who had positioned his regiment and a battery of light artillery across the Federal line of advance northwest of Alexandria on Henderson's Hill. Shortly after

10. *OR,* 32, pt. 3:289, 34, pt. 2:293; Johnson, *Red River Campaign,* 41, 81–82. For evidence of Halleck's low opinion of Banks, see Halleck to Francis Lieber, May 21, 1864, January 27, 1867, Lieber Papers, HL.

11. *OR,* 34, pt. 1:304–7, 338–39, 492, 495–96, 574–79; Johnson, *Red River Campaign,* 91–92, 100.

12. U.S. Congress, *Report of the Joint Committee on the Conduct of the War: Red River Expedition,* 190–91, 339.

his arrival, Smith had the good fortune of capturing a courier from Vincent with dispatches for Richard Taylor, from which he learned the Rebel countersign. On the night of March 21 during a heavy storm of rain and hail, a Union raiding party crept around behind the Confederate camp and captured 262 men and officers along with all four artillery pieces. Vincent himself had to escape in slippers. The loss of most of Vincent's regiment denied Taylor the means of obtaining information regarding Federal movements until the arrival of Tom Green with his cavalry from Texas.[13]

Meanwhile, Banks's infantry under Franklin marched along the Teche toward Alexandria. Albert L. Lee with a small division of Union cavalry had started their overland march to Alexandria on March 7. But it was not until March 14, the day Fort De Russy fell, that Franklin's infantry set out from New Iberia. Although Lee's cavalry arrived in Alexandria on March 20, Franklin's troops, slowed by incessant rain and the poor condition of the roads, finally slogged into Alexandria on March 25, seven days late.[14]

Banks arrived at Alexandria the next day and was alarmed to find that Porter and his sailors were busily engaged in grabbing as much cotton as the gunboats and transports could hold. Banks was furious. The navy was interfering with his plan to seize thousands of bales of the staple. Not only were the Confederates under Richard Taylor burning great amounts of the commodity to prevent it from being seized, but the navy, with the advantage of easy transportation by water, was getting most of the cotton that escaped the Rebel torch. Banks complained to Porter, pointing out that it was a great loss to the national treasury. Porter paid no heed.[15]

In fact, Porter was more concerned about Taylor's burning cotton than Banks's displeasure. "The Rebels are retreating before the army, and, as usual, are destroying everything that can fall into our hands, treating public and private property alike," he wrote to Gideon Welles. "This is

13. *OR*, 34, pt. 1:304–12, 501; *New York Daily Tribune*, April 2, 1864; Entry for March 22, 1864, William H. Stewart Diary, SHC; Entry for April 7, 1863, Prince Camille Polignac Diary, MHI.

14. *OR*, 34, pt. 2:1036; U.S. Congress, *Report of the Joint Committee on the Conduct of the War: Red River Expedition*, 6–8; entry for March 16, 1864, Stewart Diary, SHC.

15. *OR*, 34, pt. 2:971–72, 977–78, 982–84; U.S. Congress, *Report of the Joint Committee on the Conduct of the War: Red River Expedition*, iii–xix, 71, 224–25, 285–86, 335–36, 342; H. L. Landers, "Wet Sand and Cotton: Banks's Red River Campaign," *Loui-*

the last hold they will have in this country, and they seem determined to wreak their vengeance on the unoffending inhabitants who have some little cotton to dispose of. Their destructiveness has been a death-blow to the Rebellion in this State, and General Dick Taylor has left a name behind him to be execrated when the Rebellion is long past."[16]

Porter had good reason to speak harshly, for Taylor's success in burning cotton was ruining a prosperous business venture. According to the tenets of naval prize law, property of the Confederate government or of Rebel sympathizers could be seized without compensation, with 50 percent of the selling price going to the sailors who seized it, of which 5 percent went to Porter himself. The remaining 50 percent was paid into a fund for disabled seamen. Thus it would seem that Porter was less concerned for the region's "unoffending inhabitants" than his own financial gain.[17]

The Union sailors were adept in their work. They commandeered wagons and teams of mules and quickly learned how to gin and bale when large stocks of raw cotton were found. To deal with the problem of taking cotton from loyal Union men, the letters "C.S.A." were stenciled on captured cotton, regardless of its origin. Porter knew of the deception and approved of it. Colonel James G. Wilson from Banks's staff reported that the sailors "would go into the country five or six miles, find a lot of cotton and brand it 'C.S.A.' and underneath that 'U.S.N.' I recollect that I asked the admiral one day, when he did me the honor of asking me to dine with him, if he knew what those letters stood for. He said, 'No.' I said they stood for 'Cotton Stealing Association of the United States Navy." Apparently, Porter could afford to take a joke.[18]

Banks found a dispatch from Ulysses S. Grant waiting for him when he reached Alexandria. Grant, who had recently been appointed to replace Halleck as commander in chief of the Union army, informed Banks that

---

siana Historical Quarterly 19 (1936): 166–76; P. W., *Historical Sketch*, 9–10; entry for March 19, 1864, Stewart Diary, SHC.

16. Porter to Welles, March 29, 1864, in Frank Moore, ed., *The Rebellion Record: A Diary of American Events*, 12 vols. (New York: D. Van Nostrand, 1869), 8:520.

17. Robert E. Futrell, "Federal Trade with the Confederate States, 1861–1865, a Study of Governmental Policy" (Ph.D. dissertation, Vanderbilt University, 1950), 122. For Porter's defense of his cotton-gathering activities, see David Dixon Porter, *The Naval History of the Civil War* (New York: Sherman Publishing Co., 1886), 534.

18. U.S. Congress, *Report of the Joint Committee on the Conduct of the War: Red River Expedition*, 81; Thomas Oliver Selfridge, *Memoirs of Thomas O. Selfridge, Jr.*,

"I regard the success of your present move as of great importance in reducing the number of troops necessary for protecting the navigation of the Mississippi River." Nevertheless, he reminded Banks that it was "also important that Shreveport be taken as soon as possible" because A. J. Smith's command must be returned to Sherman by the middle of April, "even if it leads to the abandonment of the main object of your expedition."[19]

Despite Grant's reminder, Banks did not immediately set his troops in motion toward Shreveport. He wanted to organize elections in central Louisiana for delegates to the constitutional convention. To that end, Banks ordered the polls opened in Opelousas, Marksville, Harrisonburg, and Alexandria on Friday, the first day of April. Although the turnout was light (e.g., only three hundred voters in Alexandria), Banks believed that the election would strengthen the Free State government in New Orleans.[20]

A second reason for the delay was that Porter had difficulty getting his large gunboats upriver past the rapids at Alexandria. The annual rise of the Red River, which usually began in December or January, had not occurred for the first time since 1855. Now Banks was faced with the choice of continuing his drive toward Shreveport without the backbone of the Union fleet. Banks urged Porter to do everything he could to get his vessels over the shallows, but Porter was reluctant, telling Banks that if they did go up, it would take a miracle to get them down again. Banks persisted, and Porter, eager to chase more bales of cotton upriver, finally agreed.[21]

After several days and many mishaps, Porter got thirteen gunboats and thirty transports over the rapids. Pleased with the election and reas-

---

Rear Admiral, U.S.N. (New York: G. P. Putnam's Sons, 1924), 96–97; also Andrews, *The North Reports the Civil War,* 503.

19. *OR,* 34, pt. 2:494, 610–11.

20. *OR,* 34, pt. 1:179–80, Ser. 3, 4:170–72, 209; U.S. Congress, *Report of the Joint Committee on the Conduct of the War: Red River Expedition,* 281, 335; Banks to Mary Banks, April 2, 1863, Banks Collection, LC.

21. U.S. Congress, *Report of the Joint Committee on the Conduct of the War: Red River Expedition,* 7–9, 275, 281–83; *OR,* 34, pt. 3:24, 175; *OR (Navy),* 26:50; John G. Belisle, *History of Sabine Parish, Louisiana* (Sabine, La.: Sabine Banner Press, 1912), 159–60; Robert T. Edes to [?], March 6, [1864], Edes to Charlotte, March 6, 30, 1864, Edes to Betsy, March 11, 1864, Robert T. Edes Letters, MAHS (Part VI, Reel no. 6).

sured by the presence of Porter's fleet above the rapids, Banks boarded his headquarters boat, the *Black Hawk,* and steamed upriver toward Grand Ecore on April 2. Porter followed as soon as the last of his ships crossed the rapids on the following day.[22]

Banks arrived at Grand Ecore near Natchitoches the next evening and remained at the little village on bluffs overlooking the river for two days, pondering a tough decision. Up to this point the route along which the army marched had lain near the river, within easy communication with the transports, supply vessels, and Porter's powerful gunboats. At Grand Ecore, however, the road to Shreveport struck off to the west and away from the river toward Pleasant Hill. Twenty-two miles beyond Pleasant Hill, the road converged with several others at Sabine Crossroads near the village of Mansfield. From the crossroads one route turned back north to Shreveport, while another road ran west to Texas.[23]

Banks asked the river pilot accompanying the expedition to indicate the best route to take. The pilot suggested two avenues of advance—the one through Pleasant Hill to Sabine Crossroads and a second on the east side of the river through Campti. Although the road on the east side was in better condition, it also would take the army two or three days longer to reach Shreveport. The pilot made no mention of a third road between Natchitoches and Shreveport along the west bank of the Red River.[24]

Actually, there was a road along the river that wound through a pleasant countryside with plenty of corn and cattle. Porter saw it himself several days later as he steamed upriver. "It struck me very forcibly," the commander wrote to Sherman later, "that this would have been the route for the army, where they could have traveled without all that immense train, the country supporting them as they proceeded along. The roads are good, wide fields on all sides, a river protecting the right flank of the army, and gunboats in company." Although Porter had the benefit of hindsight, Banks did not help matters by refusing to use his cavalry to conduct a reconnaissance. Nor did he avail himself of the services of a

22. Johnson, *Red River Campaign,* 107–8; Banks to Mary Banks, April 2, [1864], Banks Collection, LC.

23. Johnson, *Red River Campaign,* 112–13; U.S. Congress, *Report of the Joint Committee on the Conduct of the War: Red River Expedition,* 33, 35, 80; C. F. Reed, "Army Experiences," 1c, 15–17, MAHS.

24. U.S. Congress, *Report of the Joint Committee on the Conduct of the War: Red River Expedition,* 286–87; Johnson, *Red River Campaign,* 113.

group of draft evaders and deserters from the Confederate army who had joined his army at Natchitoches. Having taken to the woods and swamps to avoid conscription, they were intimately familiar with the area and could have told the general from Massachusetts all he wanted to know. But Banks was not worried. The inability of the Confederates to impede his advance had made Banks confident. "The enemy retreats before [us] & will not fight a battle this side of Shreveport[,] if then," he confided to Mary. He could not have been more wrong.[25]

Banks's opponent during the Red River campaign was Richard Taylor. Taylor had faced Banks in battle before during Stonewall Jackson's Valley campaign in 1862, and he was not impressed. "Banks is cold, timid, easily foiled," Taylor informed his commander, General Edmund Kirby Smith, at Shreveport.[26]

Taylor was having problems of his own. The advantage he had gained as a result of Banks's delay was offset to some degree by Kirby Smith's indecision regarding which of the two Federal columns, Banks's or Steele's, he should concentrate on and defeat first. Taylor naturally saw the needs of his district as paramount and dogged Smith for reinforcements. Now that Banks was at Grand Ecore, he positively bridled with frustration over Kirby Smith's tentativeness and delay. "Action, prompt, vigorous action, is required," Taylor wrote to Smith on April 4. "While we are deliberating the enemy is marching. King James lost three kingdoms for a mass. We may lose three States without a battle."[27]

Kirby Smith finally responded to Taylor's entreaties by ordering Brigadier General Samuel B. Maxey, who commanded Confederate forces in the Indian Territory, to reinforce Major General Sterling Price in Arkan-

25. *OR (Navy)*, 26:60; U.S. Congress, *Report of the Joint Committee on the Conduct of the War: Red River Expedition*, 35; Banks to Mary Banks, April 4, [1864], Banks Collection, LC; also Hoffman, *Camp, Court and Siege*, 87. The belief that the Rebels would not stand and fight was widespread at this point during the campaign (Andrews, *The North Reports the Civil War*, 506; William H. Eastman to his sister, April 5, 1864, Eastman Papers, MAHS; James Matthews to his wife, April 14, 1864, Huntington Manuscripts, HL).

26. *OR*, 34, pt. 1:522.

27. *OR*, 34, pt. 1:512–13, 519, 522–23. Taylor was referring to James II of England, who lost his throne in 1688 to William of Orange (later William III of William and Mary fame) because of his belligerent Catholicism.

sas. The transfer of those troops allowed Price, who was facing Steele's advance in that quarter, to send two small divisions of infantry south to reinforce Taylor. The vanguard of these troops, commanded by Brigadier Generals Mosby M. Parsons and Thomas J. Churchill, arrived in Shreveport on March 24. Smith ordered both divisions to wait there until they could be supplied with ammunition. When they were finally ready to join Taylor on April 3, Kirby Smith sent them only as far as Keatchie, halfway between Mansfield and Shreveport. He still did not believe that Taylor should commit his troops to battle before retreating to Shreveport.[28]

Taylor concentrated his scattered forces while the Federals continued their advance toward Mansfield. His two divisions of infantry under Brigadier General Alfred Mouton and Major General John G. Walker converged on Pleasant Hill before falling back to Mansfield on April 4. Brigadier General Tom Green with a division of cavalry joined them from Texas the next day. Richard Taylor was ready to make a stand. If Banks gained control of the crossroads, he could move in any number of directions. Taylor was also afraid that to retreat further would demoralize his men. Waiting for the Union army to reach Shreveport would be "like the man who admitted the robber into his bed-chamber instead of resisting him at the door." He was tired of retreating and tired of Kirby Smith's Fabian strategy. "It would have been better to lose the State after a defeat," he wrote, "than to surrender it without a fight."[29]

Kirby Smith traveled to Mansfield on Wednesday, April 6, to confer with Taylor in the field. At the meeting Smith indicated that he still preferred to march north to Arkansas with the bulk of the Confederate army to defeat Steele. He also mentioned the possibility of standing siege in Shreveport or even retreating to Texas. Taylor was vehemently opposed to all three alternatives. Smith vacillated in the face of Taylor's opposition and returned to Shreveport without giving Taylor definite instructions.[30]

28. *OR,* 34, pt. 1:479, 493–94, 513, 517–21, 562–63, pt. 2:1056, 1062–63, pt. 3:745, 761; William K. Boggs, *Military Reminiscences of Gen. Wm. R. Boggs,* ed. William K. Boyd (Durham, N.C.: Seeman Printery, 1913), 76.

29. *OR,* 34, pt. 1:515; Odie Faulk, *General Tom Green: "A Fightin' Texan"* (Waco: Texian Press, 1963), 59; Taylor, *Destruction and Reconstruction,* 191, 194.

30. *OR,* 34, pt. 1:480, 485; Smith, "Defense of the Red River," 371; Taylor, *Destruction and Reconstruction,* 190–91.

After Smith left, Taylor positioned his infantry across the main road three miles below Mansfield. Walker's infantry was posted to the right of the Mansfield road with a portion of Green's cavalry division on the right flank. Mouton's infantry covered the left side of the road, with a brigade of cavalry and some unattached troops under James P. Major on Mouton's left. Taylor held the rest of his cavalry in reserve. The infantry from Price's army remained at Keatchie under Kirby Smith's orders.[31]

Banks's army began to leave Grand Ecore on Wednesday morning, April 6. Grover's division of thirty-six hundred men had been left behind in Alexandria to protect supplies. Another twenty-five hundred men from A. J. Smith's command were put aboard transports to accompany Porter's fleet as it steamed up the river. Detachments, illness, and straggling left Banks with between eighteen and nineteen thousand men for his march overland. In contrast, Taylor's force, not including the two divisions at Keatchie, was between eight and nine thousand strong.[32]

Porter's flotilla started for Shreveport on Thursday, April 7. Banks and Porter hoped to effect a junction at Springfield Landing, about forty miles by river north of Grand Ecore. Banks's command stretched out along the road. The cavalry under Lee led the army, followed by three hundred wagons. Next came Franklin with two infantry divisions from the XIII Corps and Emory's division from the XIX Corps. Behind them stretched a wagon train of seven hundred vehicles, followed by the remainder of A. J. Smith's men (two divisions from the XVI Corps). The number of wagons seemed excessive; perhaps they were expected to transport cotton that could be confiscated beyond the reach of Porter's sailors. Whatever the case, the one thousand wagons represented one vehicle for every eighteen men present for duty.[33]

The road over which Banks advanced was so narrow that two wagons could not travel abreast. Sometimes the road resembled nothing more than a sunken path or a deep, broad ditch that wound over hills of red

31. *OR*, 34, pt. 1:563–64; Entry for April 8, 1863, Polignac Diary, MHI.

32. *OR*, 34, pt. 1:167, 572–73; U.S. Congress, *Report of the Joint Committee on the Conduct of the War: Red River Expedition*, vi, 6–8; Taylor, *Destruction and Reconstruction*, 195.

33. *OR*, 34, pt. 1:181, 284, 322, 324, 331, 428, 445; *OR (Navy)*, 26:51; U.S. Congress, *Report of the Joint Committee on the Conduct of the War: Red River Expedition*, 32, 58, 323; Irwin, *History of the Nineteenth Army Corps*, 296.

clay and sand. Thickets of pine pressed from either side like the walls of a corridor. To make matters worse, a hard rain on Thursday afternoon turned the road to rusty mud. The entire column, cavalry, infantry, and wagons together, stretched out for more than twenty miles. The nature of the terrain meant that placing a wagon train directly behind the cavalry effectively blocked the road for either retreat or reinforcement.[34]

Banks was aware that the situation was bad but was still convinced that Taylor would not stand and fight until Federal troops reached Shreveport. An army captain on one of the transports shared his opinion. "There will be no serious fighting . . . on this exped[ition]," he wrote in his diary. "A retreating army and one so demoralized as theirs will not risk a fight even though they have numbers to warrant it." But not everyone thought that the Confederates would give up Louisiana without a fight. A war correspondent for the *New York Herald* traveling with the army reported rumors that "the Rebels are concentrating at Pleasant Hill, about twelve miles from here, where it is expected they will make a vigorous stand, and that there will be a heavy battle."[35]

The lead elements of Banks's column, Albert Lee's cavalry, continued to probe down the road toward Mansfield. Pushing cautiously through Pleasant Hill on Thursday, they encountered little resistance. But several miles north of the village the Union troopers ran up against Major's brigade of Texas cavalry at Wilson's Farm. Lee was growing more and more concerned. He was painfully aware of his exposed position in a strange country before an unseen enemy of unknown strength. On Thursday evening Lee asked Banks for infantry because of his contact with Confederate cavalry. Banks ordered Franklin to reinforce Lee; Franklin sent a small brigade under the command of Colonel William J.

34. *OR,* 34, pt. 1:179–80, 454, 458–59; U.S. Congress, *Report of the Joint Committee on the Conduct of the War: Red River Expedition,* 10, 32, 65–66, 69, 78, 190; Clark, *One Hundred and Sixteenth Regiment,* 152–53; Flinn, *Campaigning with Banks,* 99; Woods, *Services of the Ninety-Sixth Ohio,* 78; W. Simson to Mary Banks, April 6, 1864, Banks Collection, LC; William H. Eastman to his sister, March 6, 23, 1864, Eastman Letters, MAHS.

35. *OR,* 34, pt. 1:324, pt. 3:472–74; U.S. Congress, *Report of the Joint Committee on the Conduct of the War: Red River Expedition,* 30, 32–33, 40, 55–56, 63–64; *New York Herald,* April 16, 24, 1864; *New York Daily Tribune,* April 25, 1864; entry for April 9, 1864, Stewart Diary, SHC. Porter provided Banks with an accurate estimate of Confederate strength around Shreveport in a letter written at Grand Ecore and dated April 6, 1864 (Banks Collection, LC).

Landram to Lee's camp. Landram's men arrived at daybreak on Friday, April 8.[36]

Lee continued to press forward on Friday morning, encountering enough resistance that his troopers had to dismount. Just before noon, the cavalrymen suddenly emerged from the forest into a large clearing, eight hundred yards across and twelve hundred yards from left to right. The high ground in the middle of the clearing was known locally as Honeycut Hill. Unaware that the majority of Taylor's army was in front of him, Lee ordered Landram to clear the line of Confederate skirmishers that held the crest of the hill. The Yankees easily drove the Rebels back and sent their own skirmishers forward half a mile further. There, in the edge of the heavy woods on the far side of the clearing, they saw Confederate infantry and cavalry drawn up in a line of battle.[37]

Lee immediately sent back a request to Franklin for more infantry. Franklin dispatched a second brigade under T. E. G. Ransom. Banks, who had arrived at Franklin's headquarters by eleven o'clock, decided to go to the front himself to see what was happening. Setting off on the heels of Ransom's troops, Banks arrived at Honeycut Hill around one o'clock that afternoon. Lee described the situation. "We must fall back immediately," he urged, "or we must be very heavily reinforced." Lee was certain that he was facing anywhere from fifteen to twenty thousand men. Banks sent a note to Franklin, directing him to move his infantry to the front. Banks then told Lee to hold his position until he could return with infantry that was close at hand, evidently referring to Ransom's troops, whom he had passed on the road. A few minutes later, he sent a second message to Franklin, telling him to push his troops forward as quickly as possible.[38]

The second brigade of Union infantry reached Lee's position at half past three in the afternoon. Initially, the Federals attempted to feel out

36. *OR,* 34, pt. 1:290; U.S. Congress, *Report of the Joint Committee on the Conduct of the War: Red River Expedition,* 29, 58–60, 194–95; Irwin, *History of the Nineteenth Army Corps,* 300–301; Johnson, *Red River Campaign,* 124–27.

37. *OR,* 34, pt. 1:291, 456; U.S. Congress, *Report of the Joint Committee on the Conduct of the War: Red River Expedition,* 60–62; Irwin, *History of the Nineteenth Army Corps,* 302; Taylor, *Destruction and Reconstruction,* 194–95.

38. *OR,* 34, pt. 1:200, 457; U.S. Congress, *Report of the Joint Committee on the Conduct of the War: Red River Expedition,* 10, 60–61; Irwin, *History of the Nineteenth Army Corps,* 303.

the Confederate left flank. To meet this threat, Taylor shifted cavalry to reinforce Major's dismounted troops and moved a brigade of Walker's division to reinforce Mouton. Ransom's command held the center of the Federal line with a brigade from the XIII Corps and Nims's battery to their left. Landram, with parts of two brigades and two batteries, was positioned on their right. Lee's cavalry supported the Federal left and protected the flanks, while another Union brigade was kept in reserve to protect the wagon train in the rear. Together, there were some forty-eight hundred Union troops on the field.[39]

Lee was startled at four o'clock when one of Banks's staff officers rode up to inform him that Banks wanted him to move immediately to Mansfield, three miles on the other side of the Confederate infantry and cavalry to his front. Lee was certain that it was a mistake and sought out Banks to clarify the command. Banks told him that the order was correct; Lee was to occupy Mansfield. Lee argued against the order in strong terms, indicating that he could not advance more than ten minutes without bringing on a general engagement. Banks had second thoughts and agreed to postpone the march. He also sent another staff officer back to bring up more infantry.[40]

While Banks equivocated, Taylor decided to act and ordered Mouton's division to charge the Federal line. Rebel soldiers poured across the field, "yelling like demons," into the face of a heavy barrage of musket fire and canister. "We fired Grape & canister & mowed them down in files but the rebs kept a full front & as fast as they fell others filled their places," wrote one young cannoneer to his mother after the battle. Mouton fell, but the Confederates pressed on and captured three guns from Nims's battery. Other northern guns were trapped in the dense piney woods and captured.[41]

While Mouton's division pressed the center of the line, Green attacked further to the left and succeeded in turning the Federal right

39. *OR*, 34, pt. 1:264, 266, pt. 3:182, 223, 257, 291, 455–59; U.S. Congress, *Report of the Joint Committee on the Conduct of the War: Red River Expedition*, 32, 68, 77; Walker, "War of Secession West of the Mississippi River," 50–51.

40. U.S. Congress, *Report of the Joint Committee on the Conduct of the War: Red River Expedition*, 61.

41. Arceneaux, *Acadian General*, 132; *OR*, 34, pt. 3:127; William H. Eastman to his mother, April 12, 30, 1864, Eastman Letters, MAHS. Federal gunners found that tree limbs prematurely detonated shells fired through the thick woods.

flank. Walker moved into action and drove the Federals before him, even though they tried several times to make a stand. Just as northern reinforcements reached the field, the Union line broke. The new troops checked but could not stop the advancing tide of Taylor's regiments.[42]

The retreating Union soldiers found their way blocked by wagons abandoned by teamsters who had fled to the rear. As the Confederates continued their aggressive attack, the retreating column turned into a "disorganized mob of screaming, sobbing, hysterical, pale, terror-stricken men." Panic-stricken bluecoats broke ranks and fled into the woods, dropping their guns as they ran. Officers left their commands as wagoners and artillerymen abandoned their equipment to join the flight. "Men found themselves swallowed up as it were in a hissing, seething, bubbling whirlpool of agitated men," one soldier recalled. The Confederates closed in on the welter of overturned wagons and captured hundreds of fleeing Union troops, almost all of Lee's artillery, and most of his wagons.[43]

Banks kept his head throughout these dreadful minutes and personally helped reform the shattered line. A correspondent on the field reported that he "rode through the storm of lead as coolly as if at a holiday review, encouraging the men to stand up to the work of death." At another point Banks entreated, "My brave men of the Nineteenth Corps, stand your ground, and we shall win the day."[44]

The rout covered several miles despite Banks's entreaties until the demoralized soldiers reached a ridge called Pleasant Grove, where Emory established a defensive position with a division of the XIX Corps. Emory's men stepped aside to allow the troops to pass through their lines and reform in the rear. "Turn back!" the retreating soldiers screamed at the reinforcements. "The line is broken—all is lost!" But the men under Emory did not panic and formed a new line of battle just as the victorious Confederates arrived.[45]

42. *OR*, 34, pt. 1.257, 273–74, 285, 293, 296; Flinn, *Campaigning with Banks*, 108.

43. Beecher, *Record of the 114th Regiment*, 311; Flinn, *Campaigning with Banks*, 108–9; John G. Glendenning to his brother, June 20, 1864, Banks Collection, LC.

44. *OR*, 34, pt. 1:238–39; Andrews, *The North Reports the Civil War*, 508; Beecher, *Record of the 114th Regiment*, 312; Hoffman, *Camp, Court and Siege*, 92–94; Irwin, *History of the Nineteenth Army Corps*, 313; *New York Herald*, April 24, 1864; John G. Glendenning to his brother, June 20, 1864, Banks Collection, LC.

45. *OR*, 34, pt. 1:182–83, 200–201, 565; U.S. Congress, *Report of the Joint Commit-*

Fortunately for Emory, the Confederate pursuit had become disorganized. In a scene reminiscent of Stonewall Jackson's attack on the wagon train fleeing to Winchester in 1862, the ragged Rebels could not resist the temptation of luxuries they had not seen in months such as liquors, canned goods, and even paper collars. By the time they threw themselves against Emory's position, the Union line held fast. The pressure continued, but Emory refused to budge, and all that the tired Confederates could accomplish before dark was to take possession of a small creek. Of the twelve thousand Union soldiers engaged at Mansfield, nearly twenty-two hundred were killed, wounded, or taken prisoner. In addition, Banks lost a score of artillery pieces and 175 wagons.[46]

---

tee on the Conduct of the War: Red River Expedition, 217–18; Taylor, *Destruction and Reconstruction,* 195–98; Woods, *Services of the Ninety-Sixth Ohio,* 65–66.

46. *OR,* 34, pt. 1:258–59, 263–64, 392, 422–23, 616–17; Clark, *One Hundred and Sixteenth Regiment,* 155–57; Hoffman, *Camp, Court and Siege,* 89; Irwin, *History of the Nineteenth Army Corps,* 306, 311; Johnson, *Red River Campaign,* 280; Taylor, *Destruction and Reconstruction,* 198–99.

14

I Am Alone

Encouraged by the repulse of the Confederates at Pleasant Grove at the end of the day on Friday, Banks decided to hold his ground and ordered A. J. Smith to move his divisions immediately to Pleasant Hill. Franklin did not share Banks's optimism. He did not think that A. J. Smith would arrive in time. Just as important, the Confederates' last attack had given them possession of the creek that ran in front of the Union position, which denied the army water for the thousands of men and animals fatigued from a hard day of fighting. Brigadier General William Dwight joined Franklin in urging Banks to retreat. Not only did he doubt that Smith would arrive in time, he did not think that the badly demoralized XIII Corps could be stopped and reformed short of Pleasant Hill. Banks listened to both officers and decided to issue the order to withdraw at ten o'clock that evening.[1]

Meanwhile, Taylor was doing all he could to follow up his success at Mansfield by hitting the Union army hard the next day. Around midnight he returned to Mansfield from the Confederate lines north of Pleasant Grove to find that Churchill's and Parsons's infantry had arrived from Keatchie. Realizing that he had to move quickly, Taylor ordered Walker to "push him [the enemy] vigorously," while he attempted to get the two divisions from Price's army in motion for Pleasant Grove. Taylor knew

1. *OR,* 34, pt. 1:183–84; U.S. Congress, *Report of the Joint Committee on the Conduct of the War: Red River Expedition,* 77, 179; Hoffman, *Camp, Court and Siege,* 92–93.

the army he was facing. "He has nothing in our front but the troops we beat today, and the 19th Corps—all Yankees whom we have always whipped." Returning to the front in the early morning hours, Taylor found that Banks had retreated fifteen miles further south toward Pleasant Hill.[2]

A. J. Smith had started his men from Grand Ecore on the road to Pleasant Hill on Friday morning, reaching the community by early evening. Around eleven o'clock, a staff officer arrived from Banks's headquarters and confirmed the rumors of the disastrous rout earlier that day. Smith immediately began strengthening his position at Pleasant Hill and had two brigades in place on the high ground commanding the road from Mansfield by nine o'clock the next morning when the first of the Union troops began to pour into his position. Encouraged by the presence of the veterans from Sherman's army, Banks's officers began to reform their disorganized regiments behind Smith's troops. The long wagon train, or what was left of it, continued on the road toward Natchitoches, guarded by the remnant of Lee's cavalry.[3]

Saturday, April 9, was a beautiful spring day. A captain in the 116th New York recalled that "it hardly seemed possible that so much beauty in nature was so soon to see the fierce passions of men engaged in bitter strife." The Union soldiers at Pleasant Hill waited, but the morning passed with no sign of the Confederates. Around eleven o'clock, Banks decided to ride to the front to see what was happening. Other than some sporadic fire toward Mansfield, all was quiet. Returning to his headquarters for lunch, Banks drafted a note to Porter, informing him that the army would resume its advance to Shreveport that evening.[4]

At one o'clock in the afternoon, the lead elements of Price's infantry, which had marched forty-five miles in the last day and a half, reached a point about two miles west of Pleasant Hill. Taylor moved them along a road to the south to a position on the Federal left flank. Given the dis-

2. *OR*, 34, pt. 1:201; Irwin, *History of the Nineteenth Army Corps*, 314; Taylor, *Destruction and Reconstruction*, 198–99; Taylor to John G. Walker, April 9, 1864, John G. Walker Papers, SHC.

3. *OR*, 34, pt. 1:354, 423; U.S. Congress, *Report of the Joint Committee on the Conduct of the War: Red River Expedition*, 12.

4. *OR*, 34, pt. 3:99; U.S. Congress, *Report of the Joint Committee on the Conduct of the War: Red River Expedition*, 176, 218; Clark, *One Hundred and Sixteenth Regiment*, 160.

tance the men had marched, Taylor decided to allow them a two-hour break for a much needed rest.[5]

Taylor's plan of battle was simple. Churchill's and Parsons's divisions were to outflank the Federal left flank. Walker's division was to move forward as soon as he heard Churchill's guns. Brigadier General James P. Major and Colonel Arthur P. Bagby with dismounted cavalry were to fall upon the Federal line of retreat toward Blair's Landing. Finally, Taylor commanded Brigadier General Hamilton P. Bee's cavalry to charge through the town once the Federals became disorganized. He held Mouton's division in reserve. Taylor had approximately 12,500 men, while Banks's troops numbered over 15,000. The Federals also had the advantage of a strong defensive position.[6]

Around 4:30 that afternoon, Taylor ordered his artillery to open fire to divert attention from Churchill's attack. The shelling was effective and forced the Federal artillery to withdraw just as Churchill and Parsons opened their assault on the Federal left at five o'clock. Initially, the Confederate advance was successful, netting three hundred prisoners. In the confusion during the assault, Churchill's right flank was left unprotected, which allowed Union troops to counterattack. The Confederates pressed on, making some headway, but as night began to fall, the Rebel commands became separated from each other and confused. In some cases, it appeared that the Confederates were firing on each other rather than the enemy. Taylor ordered a halt and sought to extricate his troops. Taking advantage of the confusion, the Federals counterattacked, capturing Confederate prisoners and threatening to turn the withdrawal into a rout. Darkness and heavy Union losses were all that saved the Confederate army, which finally halted six miles north of Pleasant Hill.[7]

Banks was excited. "God bless you, general," he said to A. J. Smith, after riding up and shaking his hand as the last Rebels slipped into the darkness. "You have saved the army!" Banks was eager to turn the tables on Taylor by continuing his advance on Shreveport. Smith heartily agreed and rode off to prepare his men for the advance. Soon after,

5. *OR,* 34, pt. 1:527, 566, 605; Taylor, *Destruction and Reconstruction,* 200.

6. Johnson, *Red River Campaign,* 154.

7. Taylor, *Destruction and Reconstruction,* 202–5. One Rebel soldier blamed the Confederates' poor showing toward the end of the day on officers who became intoxicated after the battle (David R. Garrett, *The Civil War Letters of David R. Garrett: Detailing the Adventures of the 6th Texas Cavalry,* ed. Max Lale [Marshall, Tex.: Port Caddo Press, n.d.], 82).

Franklin, Emory, and Dwight arrived at Banks's headquarters to talk him out of resuming the offensive. Almost four thousand Union troops had been lost in the two days of fighting, and, with the supply train far in the rear, the men were low on food and ammunition.[8] The real reason for their trepidation, however, was a loss of confidence in their commander. "From what I had seen of General Banks's ability to command in the field," Franklin testified after he returned to Washington, "I was certain that an operation depending on plenty of troops, rather than upon skill in handling them, was the only one which would have probability of success in his hands, and that, therefore, when we next met the enemy we ought to have all the strength available to us."[9]

The decision to withdraw was ill-advised, for Banks retained a substantial army, while the Confederates, according to one of Kirby Smith's staff officers, were "completely paralyzed by the repulse at Pleasant Hill." Even Banks wrote in his report that "the rout of the enemy was complete." Still, Banks hesitated. At first he sent orders for his wagons to stop their movement toward Natchitoches. Then he decided that it would be better to fall back. Having made the decision, he attempted to retreat in haste. Unfortunately, the ambulances had been sent off with the wagon train, which meant that the army was forced to leave its wounded on the field.[10]

A. J. Smith was not present when his fellow officers convinced Banks to retreat and received the order to withdraw at midnight. He was dumbfounded. Smith had expected to advance, not retreat. Seeking out Banks, he strongly protested the decision. Not only was there no time to bury the dead, but many of his wounded were still on the field. Moreover, a retreat would leave Porter's fleet exposed on the river, vulnerable to Confederate attack. At the very least, Smith argued, the Federals

8. About two thousand of the four thousand were prisoners of war. Taylor's losses had also been severe, especially at Pleasant Hill. Confederate losses for the two days stood at 426 prisoners and approximately 2,500 casualties (*OR*, 34, pt. 1:184, 202–3, 568–69).

9. *OR*, 34, pt. 1:258–61, 309, 313, 603, 605; U.S. Congress, *Report of the Joint Committee on the Conduct of the War: Red River Expedition,* 13, 35, 326–27; Irwin, *History of the Nineteenth Army Corps,* 322–23; Johnson, *Red River Campaign,* 160–62.

10. *OR*, 34, pt. 1:184, 202, 485, 530, 565–69; pt. 3:125; U.S. Congress, *Report of the Joint Committee on the Conduct of the War: Red River Expedition,* 62–63; Belisle, *History of Sabine Parish,* 164; Irwin, *History of the Nineteenth Army Corps,* 323; *New York Daily Tribune,* June 30, 1864.

should hold their strong position at Pleasant Hill until noon the next day so that the wounded could be placed in hospitals and provided for. Banks refused, stating that the lack of water and heavy losses compelled him to order an immediate retreat. At least, Smith argued, keep the troops in position until nine the next morning. No, Banks replied, the withdrawal would begin at once. Banks recalled having delayed his retreat from Winchester in the Shenandoah Valley and was not going to make the same mistake now.[11]

Unfortunately, Banks failed to realize that this time the circumstances were reversed. At Winchester, Stonewall Jackson had outnumbered Banks more than two to one. After Pleasant Hill, Banks's numerical superiority over Taylor was just as great. In addition, Banks's army in the Shenandoah Valley had been demoralized by a hasty and disorderly retreat from Strasburg. In the Red River Valley, it was the Confederate army that had been thrown back and disorganized by Union strength and tenacity.

Banks's retreating troops passed through Natchitoches on Sunday and assumed the defensive position at Grand Ecore on April 11. The retreat added significance to the defeat at Mansfield while diminishing the success gained at Pleasant Hill. As one officer remarked, "Everything has the appearance of a failure in the object of the expedition, provided it had one." On the march, the troops called out derogatorily, "Napoleon P. Banks," as he passed. The cheers of soldiers that had stirred his blood the year before had turned to jeers.[12]

Banks's retreat to Grand Ecore left David Dixon Porter in a fix. Porter's progress up the Red River had been halted a few miles below Shreveport at Loggy Bayou, blocked by the wreck of a large steamboat, the *New Falls City,* which the Rebels had positioned crosswise and sunk in the channel. Porter was making plans to remove the obstacle from the river when he received word of Banks's defeat at Mansfield. Because the Union gunboats were vulnerable to being cut off before they could steam back downriver, Richard Taylor ordered Colonel Arthur P. Bagby to in-

11. *OR,* 34, pt. 1:309; Babcock, "War Commentary," 78–79, MNHS.

12. *OR,* 34, pt. 3:268; John Homans, "The Red River Expedition," in *The Mississippi Valley, Tennessee, Georgia, Alabama, 1861–1864: Papers of the Military Historical Society of Massachusetts,* Vol. 8 (Boston: Military Historical Society of Massachusetts, 1910), 85–86. One such rhyme went as follows: "In 1861 we all skedaddled to Washington, in 1864 we all skedaddled to Grand Ecore."

tercept them. But Bagby was late, and the gunboats had passed down the river by the time he arrived.[13]

Tom Green with a brigade of cavalry did catch up with a portion of Porter's fleet at Blair's Landing on the afternoon of April 12. Green formed his troops in columns of regiments and ordered them to charge a river monitor, the *Osage,* which had run aground. The river was so low that the Union gunners could not see the Rebels from the deck of the gunboat. Nevertheless, the *Osage*'s captain ordered his two eleven-inch guns loaded with canister and elevated just enough to clear the levee along the shore. When the heads of Green's troops appeared over the crest, the guns fired. The battle raged for almost an hour, until the *Osage* had exhausted its stock of grape and canister. Finally, the Union gunners resorted to using shrapnel with fuses cut to one second. In the meantime, the Confederates peppered the gunboat and several transports stranded nearby with hundreds of musket balls. With ammunition running low, a Union gunner aimed one of the *Osage*'s big guns at a Confederate officer mounted on a white horse. The shot took off the top of Tom Green's head, and the death of the charismatic Confederate chieftain caused the dispirited Rebels to withdraw, leaving the *Osage* and the other boats in Porter's flotilla free to continue their retreat to Grand Ecore, where they arrived on April 15.[14]

Unaware that Kirby Smith had stripped Taylor of most of his infantry, Banks thought that more than twenty-five thousand Confederates were waiting to gobble him up with all of his men. Meanwhile, the water level in the Red River was falling, which made maneuvering the gunboats in the channel increasingly difficult. But Banks had other concerns. Shortly after he arrived at Grand Ecore, Brigadier General John M. Corse of Sherman's staff appeared with a message from his commander asking Banks to send the two divisions from the XVI Corps and the XVII Corps detachment to Vicksburg immediately. Banks could not afford to lose these troops and directed A. J. Smith to stay put. On this occasion, Porter supported Banks's decision. He was afraid that if Banks's army was re-

13. *OR,* 34, pt. 1:571, pt. 3:268.

14. Anne J. Bailey, *Between the Enemy and Texas: Parsons's Texas Cavalry in the Civil War* (Fort Worth: Texas Christian University Press, 1989), 171–77; Faulk, *General Tom Green,* 61–62; B. P. Gallaway, *The Ragged Rebel: A Common Soldier in W. H. Parsons' Texas Cavalry, 1861–1865* (Austin: University of Texas Press, 1988), 94–100; Johnson, *Red River Campaign,* 211–12; Selfridge, *Memoirs,* 100–105; Entry for April 12, Stewart Diary, SHC.

duced further, the major general from Massachusetts would pull out of central Louisiana entirely, leaving Porter and his boats to the mercy of the enemy.[15]

For a week the situation at Grand Ecore presented an interesting spectacle of a Federal army of more than twenty-five thousand men cowering in front of a force that could muster scarcely five thousand effectives. But Banks's greatest concern was the Red River, which continued to fall. "The low water of the River threatens to defeat our campaign," he wrote Mary from Grand Ecore, "as it is only by the River that we can get our supplies." Banks believed that he had no alternative than to fall back to Alexandria.[16]

A. J. Smith could not believe that the army was going to retreat again and vented his frustration over Banks's timidity at a meeting with Franklin, Emory, and some officers of lower rank. During the meeting Smith criticized Banks so loudly that one of the staff officers felt obliged to leave. After the officer had gone, Smith made a startling suggestion. "Franklin," he said, "if you will take command of the army, I will furnish a guard and put General Banks in arrest and send him to New Orleans." Emory, who was seated nearby, jumped up and exclaimed, "By God, gentlemen, this is mutiny," and strode out of the tent. And so it was. Sobered by the reminder, Smith dropped his suggestion and spoke no more of the incident.[17]

Meanwhile, in Arkansas, Steele was having troubles of his own. The ravaged land through which he marched made obtaining food and forage for his troops and animals almost impossible, forcing him to depend on large wagon trains for supplies. Realizing that the trains were vulnerable to Confederate attacks, Steele decided to turn his column toward Camden, on the Ouachita River, and, after being resupplied by river, resume

15. *OR*, 32, pt. 3:242–44, 34, pt. 1:186, 191, pt. 3:24; *OR (Navy)*, 26:62, 68–69; U.S. Congress, *Report of the Joint Committee on the Conduct of the War: Red River Expedition*, 245–50; Powers, *Story of the Thirty-Eighth Regiment*, 135–36; Warner, *Generals in Blue*, 94.

16. Johnson, *Red River Campaign*, 220–21; Banks to Mary Banks, April 20, 1864, Banks Collection, LC; Robert T. Edes to Charlotte, April 7, 1864, Edes Letters, MAHS. Although Banks had suffered heavy casualties, he was strengthened at Grand Ecore by the arrival of twenty-five hundred of A. J. Smith's men, who had accompanied Porter up the river.

17. Hoffman, *Camp, Court and Siege*, 96–97; Homans, "Red River Expedition," 86–87.

his advance on Shreveport. This was on April 12, the same day that Porter's gunboats turned back from their attempt to reach Shreveport. On April 18, Rebel cavalry captured one of Steele's wagon trains at Poison Springs, Arkansas, and massacred the detachment of black soldiers who guarded it. The Confederates captured and destroyed a second relief train en route back to Pine Bluff from Camden one week later at Marks' Mills. These events, coupled with Banks's withdrawal to Alexandria, effectively put an end to the offensive phase of the Red River campaign.[18]

In Louisiana, Taylor continued to press Banks during the retreat to Alexandria. Water was scarce along the route, and Banks's men fell out along the way, exhausted. Major General John A. Wharton, who had assumed command of Green's cavalry after the death of that Confederate leader, closed in, sweeping up prisoners in Natchitoches and pressing the rear of the Federal column. The retreat was beginning to degenerate into a headlong flight.[19]

Despite the rapid pace of the march, Federal troops still found time to wreak havoc on the countryside through which they passed. "At night, the burning buildings mark our pathway," one soldier from New York wrote. "As far as the eye can reach, we see in front new fires breaking out, and in our rear the dying embers tell the tale of war. Hardly a building is left unharmed." Most of the destruction was wrought by troops from A. J. Smith's command, who not long before had returned from the Meridian expedition with Sherman in Mississippi, an operation that portended the famous march through Georgia.[20]

Confederate governor Henry Watkins Allen traveled through the desolate country and described what he saw:

> From Mansfield to the Mississippi River the track of the spoiler was one scene of desolation. The fine estates on Cane and Red rivers, on bayous Rapides, Robert, and De Glaize, were all devastated. Houses, gins, mills, barns, and fences were burned, negroes all carried off, horses, cattle, hogs, every living thing, driven away or killed. . . . You can travel for miles, in

18. Johnson, *Red River Campaign*, 170–205; U.S. Congress, *Report of the Joint Committee on the Conduct of the War: Red River Expedition*, 15.

19. *OR*, 34, pt. 1:190–91, pt. 3:782; Beecher, *Record of the 114th Regiment*, 330–31; Clark, *One Hundred and Sixteenth Regiment*, 168; Sprague, *History of the 13th Infantry*, 193; Taylor, *Destruction and Reconstruction*, 220–21.

20. *OR*, 32, pt. 2:498; Elias Porter Pellet, *History of the 114th Regiment, New York State Volunteers* (Norwich, N.Y.: Telegraph & Chronicle Power Press Print, 1866), 225.

> many portions of Louisiana, through a once thickly-settled country, and not see a man, nor a woman, nor a child, nor a four-footed beast. The farm houses have been burned. The plantations deserted. The once smiling fields now grown up in briars and brakes, in parasites and poisonous vines. A painful melancholy, a death-like silence, broods over the land, and desolation reigns supreme.[21]

Taylor did his best to punish the enemy. Although badly outnumbered, he divided his small army and attempted to cut off the retreating Union column at Monett's Ferry on the Cane River about twenty miles northwest of Alexandria. The head of the Federal column reached Monett's Ferry on April 23. Hamilton P. Bee with sixteen hundred Confederate cavalry was posted on the bluffs overlooking the crossing. The column halted and opened fire on Bee's position from a distance. Hearing the firing, Banks rode with his staff to the scene of the action. The large group of mounted men, complete with headquarters flags and orderlies, presented a tempting target for the Rebel gunners. Shells began to burst nearby, but Banks did not move. Presently, a shell burst in the air directly overhead. A shell fragment struck Banks's boot as it fell to the ground. "Hand me that piece of iron, if you please," Banks said calmly to an aide before leading the party back up the road and out of danger.[22]

While Bee engaged the Federals at the head of the column, Taylor made a spirited attack against the tail near Cloutierville with Wharton's cavalry, driving it back some distance. Men in the middle of the column, hearing firing from both the front and rear, became apprehensive. It looked as if "Mr. Banks," as the men in A. J. Smith's division now referred to the commanding general, had gotten them into another jam. But the Union troops forded the river above the ferry, forcing Bee to retire with minor casualties. Although Bee was able to inflict more than three hundred casualties, the Federals continued their march to Alexandria, burning every building, shed, and outhouse in sight.[23]

21. Dorsey, *Recollections of Henry Watkins Allen*, 278–79.

22. Homans, "Red River Expedition," 88; Fredericka Meiners, "Hamilton P. Bee in the Red River Campaign of 1864," *Southwestern Historical Quarterly* 78 (July 1974): 33–36.

23. *OR*, 34, pt. 1:189–91, 439, 580–81, 610–12; Clark, *One Hundred and Sixteenth Regiment*, 170; X. B. Debray, *A Sketch of the History of Debray's (26th) Regiment of Texas Cavalry* (1884; reprint, Suffolk, Va.: Robert Hardy, n.d.), 21–22; Ewer, *Third Massachusetts Cavalry*, 164–66; Hoffman, *Camp, Court and Siege*, 97; Johnson, *Red River Campaign*, 224–33; Meiners, "Hamilton P. Bee in the Red River Campaign," 37–39;

The vanguard of Banks's army arrived at Alexandria on April 25. Meanwhile, Porter continued his efforts to extricate himself from Taylor's trap. Although most of his vessels had reached Alexandria by April 20, Porter's largest gunboat, the *Eastport,* was able to make only twenty miles in six days and grounded six times. The commander finally gave up on saving the big ship and ordered it blown up at Deloach's Bluff on April 26, just as the Confederates prepared to move in for the kill. On the same day, Taylor's troops attacked another gunboat and a transport at the junction of the Cane and Red Rivers. A shot from a Confederate battery on the shore cut the steam pipe, which resulted in the death by scalding of more than one hundred men. A pump boat used to assist the *Eastport* was also burned. Eventually, the remaining boats in the Union fleet reached Alexandria, where low water prevented them from continuing their trip downstream.[24]

Banks dug in at Alexandria as though expecting a siege. Reinforcements joined him from the Texas coast and south Louisiana, giving him over thirty thousand men. Although Taylor had less than one-fifth of that number, Banks believed that he was outnumbered. This perception was aided by Taylor's aggressive tactics around the city. "Compelled to 'eke out the lion's skin with the fox's hide,'" Taylor used deception to help maintain the psychological advantage by "sending drummers to beat calls, lighting camp-fires, blowing bugles, and rolling empty wagons over fence rails." Banks fell for Taylor's stratagem. "The Rebels may concentrate all their forces west of the Mississippi upon us," he wrote to Mary. "They can muster 40,000 men or more." Not surprisingly, Porter was convinced that Banks planned to pull back to the mouth of the Red River and abandon the navy.[25]

Sprague, *History of the 13th Infantry,* 202. Taylor blamed Bee for not holding his position (*Destruction and Reconstruction,* 220–21). Although Bee may have withdrawn prematurely, it is doubtful that he could have prevented the Federals from continuing their retreat (Johnson, *Red River Campaign,* 234).

24. *OR,* 34, pt. 1:583–84; U.S. Congress, *Report of the Joint Committee on the Conduct of the War: Red River Expedition,* 245–50.

25. *OR,* 34, pt. 1:590, pt. 3:296, 369–70; *OR (Navy),* 26:92–95, 130–35; Henry Orr to his sister, May 14, 1864, in John Q. Anderson, *Campaigning with Parsons's Texas Cavalry Brigade, CSA: The War Journals and Letters of the Four Orr Brothers, 12th Texas Cavalry Regiment* (Hillsboro, Tex.: Hill Junior College Press, 1967), 138; John Scott, *Story of the Thirty-Second Iowa Infantry Volunteers* (Nevada, Ia.: Author, 1896), 244; Taylor, *Destruction and Reconstruction,* 229–33; Babcock, "War Commentary," 70, MNHS; Banks to Mary Banks, May 3, 1864, Banks Collection, LC.

Adding to Banks's distress, Taylor ordered his men to disrupt the Union communication and supply links with New Orleans. Taylor knew that fodder for the animals in Banks's army was running short. "We will play the game the Russians played in the retreat from Moscow," Taylor told Kirby Smith. "Forage and subsistence of every kind have been removed beyond the enemy's reach. Rigid orders are given to destroy anything useful that can fall into his hands." To that end, Taylor sent what was left of Vincent's cavalry to the area southwest of New Orleans, where they burned railway bridges east of Berwick Bay. He ordered other troops to the reaches of the Red River, above Fort De Russy, where they captured or sank several transports. In an attempt to obstruct future navigation on the river, the Confederates sank several captured boats in the channel.[26]

Banks huddled with his troops behind his defenses in Alexandria. He was demoralized, and it showed. "Gen Banks is awfully scared," one Union soldier in Alexandria wrote to his sister. Reverting to a habit of younger years by referring to his wife in the third person, Banks poured out his feelings to Mary in a letter. "Thanks to my dear wife, she is a proud woman. I want to see her—to breathe my soul into hers," he confided. "I have nobody to talk to, nobody to embrace," Banks continued. "I am alone."[27]

Banks did not like being cooped up in Alexandria, but he had no choice if he was to save the navy. Low water in the Red River meant that the rapids, which had been difficult to cross on the trip upriver, would be impossible to traverse on the return. Although Porter had boasted that his boats could go "wherever the sand was damp," a dozen of his vessels were trapped above the rapids as a result of record low water levels in the channel.[28]

26. *OR*, 34, pt. 1:582–84, 587, pt. 3:786; U.S. Congress, *Report of the Joint Committee on the Conduct of the War: Red River Expedition*, 269–70; *New Orleans Times*, May 18, 1864.

27. Robert T. Edes to Betsy, April 30, 1864, Edes Letters, MAHS; Banks to Mary Banks, May 13, [1864], Banks Collection, LC.

28. *OR*, 34, pt. 1:189–92, 214–16, pt. 3:169–74; U.S. Congress, *Report of the Joint Committee on the Conduct of the War: Red River Expedition*, 8, 275, 329–30. James B. Eads, the man primarily responsible for building the seven "City Series" gunboats, had originally intended to name them after Union commanders. One boat was to be the *N. P. Banks* (Myron J. Smith, *The U.S. Gunboat* Carondolet, *1861–1865* [Manhattan, Kan.: Sunflower University Press, 1982], 31.) It would have been ironic had the *Carondolet*, trapped above the rapids, borne the name of the general responsible for her rescue.

Lieutenant Colonel Joseph Bailey, an engineer who had helped salvage two mired vessels during the Port Hudson siege, suggested to Banks that he could construct dams to back up the water sufficiently to allow the gunboats to pass. Porter's initial response to the proposal was laughter. "If you can dam better than I can, you must be a good hand at it, for I've been damning all night." Banks thought it was worth a try, and Porter withdrew his objections.[29]

Under Bailey's direction, men in New England regiments who were familiar with lumbering felled trees while other soldiers worked with stone taken from an old quarry. Other troops, including two engineer regiments from the Corps d'Afrique, tore down fences and buildings and seized cotton gin and sugar house machinery. The troops used these materials to build wing dams out from shore, which forced the water to the center of the channel. The navy helped by setting cribs and sinking barges further out in the stream. Sailors worked to lighten the ships by removing all of the guns and stores and as much of the armor as possible. Porter's skepticism disappeared when he saw the river channel rise six and a half feet.[30]

Although Taylor tried to hinder the construction of these dams, there was little he could do. Early on May 9, four vessels passed successfully over the dam, but it gave way before the other boats could follow. Finally, Porter got the remainder of his boats over the rapids on May 12. By the next day, all of the ships were below the falls, marking the success of an operation that Banks believed to be "one of the most remarkable achievements of the war."[31]

29. *OR*, 34, pt. 1:209–10, 402–4; U.S. Congress, *Report of the Joint Committee on the Conduct of the War: Red River Expedition*, 15, 33–34, 40–42; Beecher, *Record of the 114th Regiment*, 341–44; Richard B. Irwin, "The Red River Campaign," in *Battles and Leaders of the Civil War*, 5 vols., ed. Robert U. Johnson and Clarence C. Buel (1884–88; reprint, Secaucus, N.J.: Castle, 1987), 4:358–60; Hoffman, *Camp, Court and Siege*, 100–101; Porter, *Naval History*, 526–27; U. B. Pearsall to Banks, January 13, 1866, Banks Collection, LC.

30. Flinn, *Campaigning with Banks*, 133–35; Johnson, *Red River Campaign*, 260–66; Powers, *Story of the Thirty-Eighth Regiment*, 144–45; Tiemann, *159th Regiment*, 72–73. A full account of Bailey's damming project can be found in E. Cort Williams, *"Recollections of the Red River Expedition," A Paper Read before the Ohio Commandery of the Military Order of the Loyal Legion of the United States* (Cincinnati: H. C. Sherick, 1886), 13–22.

31. *OR*, 34, pt. 1:189–218, 583–89, pt. 3:248–56, 512–13; *OR (Navy)*, 26:130–35; Banks to Mary Banks, May 3, 1864, Banks Collection, LC.

With the fleet safe, Banks was free to resume his retreat down the Red River. Union troops began to evacuate Alexandria at seven o'clock on the morning of May 13. Between eight and nine o'clock, Federal soldiers began setting fires. One soldier, carrying a bucket filled with a mixture of turpentine and camphene, boasted that he was "preparing the place for Hell." The wind scattered sparks and burning debris everywhere, and before long the whole town was in flames. "Cows ran bellowing through the streets. Chickens flew out from yards and fell in the streets with their feathers scorching on them. A dog with his bushy tail on fire ran howling through, turning to snap at the fire as he ran." Looting was widespread, and the property of prominent Unionists, which had remained free from molestation by the Confederates for three years, was put to the torch. A. J. Smith rode through the streets exclaiming, "Hurrah, boys, this looks like war!" Citizens fled to the riverbank to escape the suffocating heat, while the families of local men who had enlisted in the Union army pleaded in vain to go on board the army transports.[32]

Some Federal soldiers, notably Grover's provost guard, Banks's headquarters escort, and officers from his staff, did what they could to help the people fight the fires. But the arsonists had done their work well, setting fires in so many places that nothing could be done to arrest the conflagration. By noon, most of the town had been leveled. Who was responsible? It is clear that Banks did not give orders to burn the town. Most of the evidence implicated A. J. Smith and his troops, which was not too surprising given their eagerness to set fires while marching through the southern countryside. Another possibility was the large group of Confederate deserters and draft evaders who had made their way to the Federal lines. Alarmed at the prospect of the region falling once again under Rebel control, they had sworn to burn Alexandria to the ground rather than turn it over to the Confederates. Whatever the case, Banks was aware of threats to burn Alexandria and could have done more to protect the town.[33]

32. *OR*, 34, pt. 1:428; Van Alstyne, *Diary of an Enlisted Man*, 320–21; Sprague, *History of the 13th Infantry*, 207; G. P. Whittington, "Rapides Parish, Louisiana—A History," *Louisiana Historical Quarterly* 18 (1935): 36–37.

33. U.S. Congress, *Report of the Joint Committee on the Conduct of the War: Red River Expedition*, 335; Henry Watkins Allen, *Official Report Relative to the Conduct of Federal Troops in Western Louisiana, during the Invasions of 1863 and 1864* (1865; reprint, Baton Rouge: Otto Claitor, 1939), 79–85; Babcock, "War Commentary," 75–76,

Leaving the smoldering ruins of Alexandria behind, Banks's army moved toward the security of the Union-controlled territory along the Mississippi River. For the next six days the systematic pillaging and destruction of property continued as the withdrawal degenerated into a disorganized mass of foraging, burning, and looting. The frustration of the retreat was taken out on civilians.[34]

Thousands of slaves joined the retreating column seeking freedom. Black Union soldiers concealed women and children in the wagons to smuggle them to safety within Federal lines, but their white officers searched the wagons on at least two occasions and cleared them of stowaways. In the meantime, officers roamed near and far gathering up horses and mules, as well as recruits for black regiments.[35]

Taylor harassed Banks's army continually, but he was unable to do much damage against the superior force. Wharton's cavalry attempted to block the line of retreat at Mansura on May 16 but was forced to retire after a sharp fight. Two days later at Yellow Bayou, the Confederates tried to inflict as much damage as possible in a final desperate attack before Banks reached Simmesport. Again, they were repulsed with heavy losses. This action effectively ended the Confederate attempt to destroy Banks's army, which crossed the Atchafalaya River on May 20 and 21, leaving almost the whole of Louisiana west of the Mississippi River once again in Confederate hands.[36]

MNHS; Taylor, *Destruction and Reconstruction,* 235; Van Alstyne, *Diary of an Enlisted Man,* 294, 320; Whittington, "Rapides Parish," 25–38.

34. Smith, *Leaves from a Soldier's Diary,* 103–6; Van Alstyne, *Diary of an Enlisted Man,* 320–21; *New York Herald,* June 11, 1864.

35. Glatthaar, *Forged in Battle,* 90–91; Powers, *Story of the Thirty-Eighth Regiment,* 140–41; J. O. Halsey to E. B. Paine, December 10, 1864, in William S. Studley, *Final Memorials of Major Joseph Warren Paine: Remarks at His Funeral, Dec. 29, 1864* (Boston: John Wilson & Son, 1865), 15, 18.

36. *OR,* 34, pt. 1:193, 591–95; U.S. Congress, *Report of the Joint Committee on the Conduct of the War: Red River Expedition,* 397–98; Bailey, *Between the Enemy and Texas,* 186–89; Gallaway, *Ragged Rebel,* 114–22; Johnson, *Red River Campaign,* 273–76; Tiemann, *159th Regiment,* 75–76; Banks to Mary Banks, May 17, [1864], Banks Collection, LC.

15

The Heart of the People

Banks tried to put the best face possible on the Red River campaign. He blamed Lee and Franklin for the defeat at Mansfield and tried to convince Grant that his maneuvers had foiled Confederate plans to invade Missouri. He faulted Steele for failing to execute his part of the operation and even blamed the Red River for failing to rise. No one believed him. Denison wrote Chase that Banks had attempted "to cast the blame on subordinate Generals, but without success, for they only obeyed the orders issued by the Comd'g General. The army would have done better without any Commanding General." Porter, certainly no friend of the major general, wrote, "There is a futile attempt to make a victory out of this, but two or three such victories would cost us our existence." The sentiment was widespread. "The battle of Pleasant Hill is said to have been a great victory for us had he [Banks] not converted it into a defeat by running away," one soldier wrote. "The sooner General Banks goes home," another opined, "the better will it be for the service."[1]

Although they did not know it at the time, events were in the wind that would give Banks's detractors their fondest wish. While Banks was conducting elections for the constitutional convention in Alexandria and

1. *OR*, 34, pt. 1:187–88; Denison to Chase, June 17, 1864, in Chase, "Diary and Correspondence," 438–39; Andrews, *The North Reports the Civil War*, 515–16; Homans, "Red River Expedition," 96–97; Scott, *Story of the Thirty-Second Iowa*, 186; Robert T. Edes to Betsy, April 20, 1864, Edes Letters, MAHS; Banks to Mary Banks, April 18, 1863, Banks Collection, LC.

other towns along the Red River, Grant drafted an order that contained three directives. First, he ordered Banks to turn over the occupation of the region to Steele in the event that he was able to capture Shreveport. Second, Grant directed Banks to evacuate all the positions he had captured along the Texas coast, with the exception of Brownsville. And third, Grant instructed Banks to reduce the number of men holding posts along the Mississippi River and in south Louisiana so that the Department of the Gulf could contribute twenty-five thousand men for operations against Mobile. It was April 18 before Banks received the dispatch, and by then he was firmly entrenched at Grand Ecore. Meanwhile, Steele had already turned aside and was entrenched at Camden.[2]

In Washington, Secretary of War Stanton received news from the navy about Banks's reverse at Mansfield and subsequent "victory" at Pleasant Hill. This ambiguous communication was followed shortly by a newspaper report referring to Banks's "disaster." Stanton forwarded the reports to Grant, who was at Culpeper, Virginia, preparing for the spring offensive against Lee. Upon receiving the news, Grant telegraphed Halleck to suggest that Banks be replaced by Major General Joseph J. Reynolds, then commanding the defenses of New Orleans. Halleck showed the message to President Lincoln, who said only that he must delay acting on it for the present.[3]

Halleck continued to relay information to Grant as more disheartening news made its way back to Washington over the next week. Thoroughly disgusted by Banks's failures in the Red River Valley, Grant decided that an offensive against Mobile was out of the question until the Department of the Gulf could be reorganized "under some good officer." Halleck agreed but appreciated the delicate political nature of the situation. Writing to Grant on Friday, April 29, Halleck informed him that "I think the President will consent to the order [to replace Banks] if you insist upon General Banks's removal as a military necessity, but he will do so very reluctantly, as it would give offense to many of his friends, and probably would be opposed by a portion of his cabinet. Moreover,"

2. *OR*, 34, pt. 1:11, 206.

3. *OR*, 34, pt. 3:211, 220–21, 235, 244, 252–53. For more on conflicting and confusing reports regarding the Red River campaign, see Andrews, *The North Reports the Civil War*, 510–11.

he continued, "what could be done with Banks? He has many political friends who would probably demand for him a command equal to the one he now has."[4]

Halleck was totally disgusted with political generals. "Banks's operations in the West are about what should have been expected from a general so utterly destitute of military education and military capacity," he wrote to William T. Sherman in Nashville on the same day. "It seems but little better than murder," Halleck asserted, "to give important commands to such men as Banks, Butler, McClernand, Sigel, and Lew Wallace, and yet it seems impossible to prevent it."[5]

Halleck waited for Lincoln to digest the information he had given him. The weekend passed without an indication of what the president would do. Halleck sent Grant a confidential letter on May 3 in which he restated the issues he had raised earlier. "General Banks is a personal friend of the President and has strong political supporters in and out of Congress," he reminded the commanding general. "There will undoubtedly be a very strong opposition to his being removed or superseded, and I think the President will hesitate to act unless he has a definite request from you to do so, as a military necessity, you designating his superior or superior in command."[6]

Halleck's cautious tone was more an indication of a reluctance to stick his own neck out than a reflection of Lincoln's inability to make a politically difficult decision. On May 8, Lincoln settled the matter by appointing Major General Edward R. S. Canby to command the newly created Division of West Mississippi, which encompassed the Department of Arkansas and the Department of the Gulf.[7]

Lincoln's action effectively stripped Banks of his military authority. Lincoln regretted having to demote his long-standing political ally, but Banks had failed him once too often. Banks learned of the president's decision when Canby reached Simmesport on May 19, 1864, to assume command.[8]

4. *OR*, 34, pt. 3:331–32; Johnson, *Red River Campaign*, 244–46.

5. Halleck to W. T. Sherman, April 29, 1864, *OR*, 34, pt. 3:333.

6. *OR*, 36, pt. 3:409.

7. *OR*, 34, pt. 1:212, pt. 3:408–9, 490–92.

8. "Oh, ever thus from childhood's hour, I've seen my fondest hopes decay," Lincoln is said to have quoted from Thomas Moore to express his disappointment over Banks's failure to live up to his expectations (entry for May 9, 1864, in Welles, *Diary*, 2:26).

• • •

Although Lincoln's decision to create the Division of West Mississippi effectively terminated Banks's power over military matters, it did not diminish the importance of his role in helping "reconstruct" Louisiana. Central to that effort was the framing of a new constitution that would abolish slavery and address the needs and aspirations of a free society.

Delegates to the constitutional convention had been elected on March 28. Most of the Radicals had boycotted the election, the conservatives refused to cooperate, and many moderates were apathetic. As a result, the voter turnout was so small that it tended to discredit the entire Free State of Louisiana. As one Radical in Boston sneered, "There were more Rebel deserters in the city of New Orleans, who had not taken the oath of allegiance, than the entire vote cast." Nevertheless, Banks was pleased with the outcome. "There were few or none of the old leaders of opinion in public affairs [who were elected]," he assured Lincoln. The delegates represented "the heart of the people," he proclaimed, "and the Constitution will be generously and triumphantly sustained by them."[9]

The constitutional delegates assembled in New Orleans in April to begin their deliberations. They were drawn mostly from the state's middle class—lawyers, medical doctors, educators, and businessmen. But this group differed from earlier legislative bodies in that the planter class, Louisiana's old political elite, was absent. In their place were a fair number of farmers, shopkeepers, and artisans.[10]

The convention quickly gained notoriety for the lavish lifestyle its members adopted during the two and a half months it was in session. Many of the delegates took advantage of their new authority to make a run on the Free State treasury by drawing on public funds for ice, liquor, and cigars. In addition, the convention gave away gifts and lucrative contracts freely, including a $150 pen case presented to Nathaniel P. Banks after his return from the Red River Valley. The Radicals, who had done

9. Louisiana, *Debates,* 300–301, 408; Harrington, *Fighting Politician,* 147; Nicolay and Hay, *Abraham Lincoln,* 8:435–36; *Boston Commonwealth,* March 4, 1865; *New Orleans Daily True Delta,* March 29, 1864; *New Orleans Times,* March 19, 1864; *Carrollton* (Louisiana) *Times,* March 23, 26, 1864.

10. Louisiana, *Debates,* 300–301; Nicolay and Hay, *Abraham Lincoln,* 8:435–36. For a thorough analysis of the convention's membership, see McCrary, *Abraham Lincoln and Reconstruction,* 246–52, 371–72.

poorly in the race for delegates, viewed these excesses with disdain and finally decided that the whole affair was a "grand Convention of Imbeciles."[11]

The convention completed its business by adopting a constitution on July 22, 1864. Although the document was essentially a revised and amended version of the Louisiana constitution of 1853, it abolished slavery and increased the income of New Orleans workingmen by setting minimum wages for public employment. It also gave the labor vote in New Orleans greater value by adopting Banks's plan of representation and relocated the state capital from Baton Rouge to the Crescent City. In addition, the new constitution authorized public education for all persons between the ages of six and eighteen, black and white.[12]

Banks threw what influence and prestige he retained behind getting the new document ratified. He admonished Louisiana citizens in Federal uniforms to cast their ballots, reminding them that "a citizen who refuses to support his government with musket or ballot has but slender claims for its favor or protection." He reminded laborers on public works that they depended on the state government for their jobs and made sure that workingmen in general were aware of the clauses in the constitution that benefited them. Governor Hahn and many of his state officials also worked hard to get out the vote. In addition, Lincoln lent his support by letting it be known that he approved of the document. It is "excellent," Lincoln said, "better for the poor black than [the one] we have in Illinois."[13]

The constitution was ratified by a ratio of two to one on September 5, although the turnout was extremely light. Elections for the legislature, which were held on the same day, drew greater interest. Instead of the twenty thousand voters Banks had hoped for, less than half that total cast their ballots, barely enough to satisfy the 10 percent rule. Nevertheless, the Free State constitution had been adopted. It was "one of the best

11. Smith and Brady, *Commission on Corrupt Practices,* 10–11; *New Orleans Times,* April 17, 21, 29, 1864; *National Anti-Slavery Standard,* October 14, 1865.

12. Louisiana, *Debates,* 598–600, 608–10, 623; McCrary, *Abraham Lincoln and Reconstruction,* 265–67; Cox, *Lincoln and Black Freedom,* 100–102; Shugg, *Origins of Class Struggle,* 200–211.

13. Cox, *Lincoln and Black Freedom,* 102; Harrington, *Fighting Politician,* 149; Ripley, *Slaves and Freedmen,* 176–77; Lincoln to Banks, April 11, 1865, in Nicolay and Hay, *Abraham Lincoln,* 8:435–36; Lincoln to Banks, August 9, 1864, Banks to Joseph Both, September 4, 1864 (printed circular), Banks Collection, LC.

ever penned," Banks proclaimed with his usual hyperbole. "No better constitution has ever been presented to any people on the face of the earth, and there never will be till the end of time." If the U.S. Congress accepted this plan of Reconstruction, Banks predicted, all the problems associated with reuniting the country after the war would be solved.[14]

Despite its several progressive features, the new constitution failed to give blacks the right to vote. Although the mostly middle-class delegates had no objection to outlawing slavery in order to weaken the planter class, they were not about to share their newly won political power with blacks. The new constitution did give the legislature the authority to enfranchise black males, but even then, Banks as well as other moderate Republicans had doubts about the wisdom of universal black suffrage. For one thing, he was concerned that giving the vote to blacks would discourage white Louisianians from participating in the electoral process. If whites chose not to participate, an "exclusively Negro constituency" would be created, Banks argued, which "would not be acceptable to the administration, to congress, nor to the Country."[15]

Banks did not entirely oppose giving blacks the vote. He had used his influence behind the scenes during the constitutional convention to get the delegates to adopt language authorizing the legislature to enfranchise "such other persons" who "may be deemed entitled thereto." But what he had in mind was partial, not universal, black suffrage. More specifically, Banks wanted to limit suffrage to "other persons," that is, blacks, on the basis of military service, taxation, or "intellectual fitness."[16]

14. *Boston Daily Journal,* November 1, 1864; Banks to Mary Banks, August 31, September 6, 1864, October 20, 1871, Lincoln to Banks, August 9, 1864, Banks Collection, LC. It is doubtful that the new constitution was the best "ever . . . presented to any people on the face of the earth," but it was a better document than historians of Reconstruction earlier in this century have claimed. For an example of a revisionist view, see Cox, *Lincoln and Black Freedom,* 102–3.

15. *OR,* Ser. 3, 4:22–23; Louisiana, *Debates,* 212; Denison to Chase, June 17, 1864, in Chase, "Diary and Correspondence," 2:439; Cox, *Lincoln and Black Freedom,* 80; McCrary, *Abraham Lincoln and Reconstruction,* 262–63; Tunnell, *Crucible of Reconstruction,* 36; Banks to William Lloyd Garrison, January 30, 1865, *Liberator,* February 24, 1865; and see Tyler Dennett, ed., *Lincoln and the Civil War in the Diaries and Letters of John Hay* (1939; reprint, Westport, Conn.: Greenwood Press, 1972), 224–45; *New Orleans Daily True Delta,* December 3, 1864. An attempt to enfranchise black voters in Connecticut was soundly defeated during this period (*National Anti-Slavery Standard,* October 14, 1865).

16. Louisiana, *Debates,* 623; George S. Denison to Salmon P. Chase, October 8, No-

Banks believed that one way to achieve partial black suffrage was to ask the United States district court to expand the definition of "white man" to include several thousand persons who had more Caucasian than Negro blood. Neither blacks nor whites warmed to the idea. The *New Orleans Tribune* came out strongly against the proposal because it would split the population into "three casts (white, whitewashed, and black), when it is bad enough to have two (white and colored)." Realizing that his plan would please neither race, Banks quickly dropped it. President Lincoln, however, had also begun to consider the possibility of limited black suffrage, suggesting that the vote might be given to educated blacks and to black soldiers. Chase wrote Banks urging him to take the lead in Louisiana and "let the right to vote be determined not by nativity or complexion, but by intelligence, character, and patriotism." Taking his cue, Banks declared that he favored black "participation in the privileges of citizenship according to the development of intelligence and capacity." Still, most whites would have no part of it. One commentator acceded that Banks was persuasive, but "even he cannot soon remove the prejudices which the poor whites of the state have been acquiring during their whole lives."[17]

Nevertheless, the Radicals continued to clamor for universal suffrage and criticized Banks for his hesitancy to enfranchise all freedmen. Banks stood his ground and continued to argue that the vote be given to blacks who had special qualifications. Although he believed that universal male suffrage would come about eventually, Banks thought that it should be accomplished in the "best and most effective way," which meant after the black man had demonstrated his ability to secure an education and acquire property.[18]

---

vember 25, 1864, in Chase, "Diary and Correspondence," 2:449, 452; Cox, *Lincoln and Black Freedom,* 98; Vandal, "New Orleans Riot," 48–49, 72.

17. Harrington, *Fighting Politician,* 147–49; Tunnell, *Crucible of Reconstruction,* 40; Banks to James McKaye, March 13, 1864, quoted ibid., 115; *New Orleans Tribune,* November 16, 1864, January 17, 1865; Robert B. Warden, *An Account of the Private Life and Public Services of Salmon Portland Chase* (Cincinnati: Wilstach, Baldwin, 1874), 577–78; Louisiana, *Debates,* 247, 547–48; George S. Denison to Salmon P. Chase, November 24, 1864, January 13, 1865, in Chase, "Diary and Correspondence," 452; *OR,* Ser. 3, 4:133–34.

18. Doyle, "Civilian Life in Occupied New Orleans," 293–94; Harrington, *Fighting Politician,* 114–15; Williams, "General Banks and the Radical Republicans," 275–79; *Congressional Globe,* 39th Cong., 1st sess., 1866, 2532; 2d sess., 1867, Appendix, 174–76.

To his credit, Banks did take some steps to hasten the process. Within months of his arrival in Louisiana, he had embarked on an ambitious program to educate former slaves. He started by assigning a white teacher with the rank of lieutenant to each black regiment. The goal was to reduce the high rate of illiteracy among black volunteers, which ranged as high as 90 percent. Although there was a shortage of trained teachers, by June 1864 at least nine military schools in New Orleans were serving on average twenty-four hundred soldier-students a day.[19]

Banks also set up a special Board of Education for the newly freed slaves, which established new schools and consolidated them with those operating independently of the military government, including several started under the auspices of the American Missionary Association. Under the leadership of two officers in the Union army, Major B. Rush Plumly and Lieutenant E. M. Wheelock, ninety-five schools with 162 teachers for black children had been established by the end of 1864. Attendance averaged more than seven thousand a day, and almost half of the black children from ages five to twelve within Union lines were attending school. Thomas W. Conway, who implemented Banks's labor plan, placed the development of this educational system "among the greatest glories of our Emancipation policy . . . the greatest blessing of God which I have witnessed."[20]

Most white Louisianians did not agree. Although some whites realized that an educated labor force was more valuable to them than an uneducated one, the majority felt that the emphasis should be on providing

19. Doyle, "Civilian Life in Occupied New Orleans," 288–92; Gregg, *Life in the Army,* 206, 219; Ripley, *Slaves and Freedmen,* 119–20; *Boston Daily Journal,* November 1, 1864; *New York Tribune,* February 10, 1864; *National Anti-Slavery Standard,* July, 23, 1864.

20. *OR,* 26, pt. 1:704; Patricia Brady, "Trials and Tribulations: American Missionary Association Teachers and Black Education in Occupied New Orleans, 1863–1864," *Louisiana History* 31 (Winter 1990): 13–14; B. Rush Plumly, *Report of the Board of Education for Freedmen, Department of the Gulf, for the Year 1864* (New Orleans: Office of the True Delta, 1865), 6; Ripley, *Slaves and Freedmen,* 131, 144–45; White, *Freedmen's Bureau in Louisiana,* 167–68; Charles Kassel, "Educating the Slave—A Forgotten Chapter of Civil War History," *Open Court* 41 (April 1927): 239–56; Plumly to friend of Banks, June 16, 1864, Banks Collection, LC. A public school system for white pupils in New Orleans had been in place since 1841. It was established after consultation with Horace Mann and was based on the Massachusetts system (Robert C. Reinders, *End of an Era: New Orleans, 1850–1860* [New Orleans: Pelican, 1964], 131).

vocational skills or on teaching freedmen to be good domestic servants. In general, whites considered black schools to be "a farce and humbug" and objected vehemently when provost marshals seized school buildings that had been used for whites, including the Medical College of Louisiana, and turned them over for the education of blacks.[21]

Resistance to black schools was especially strong outside of New Orleans. White instructors from the city were ostracized by being denied board, lodging, and credit at local stores. On occasion, they were pelted with dirt. Southern raiders invaded the school buildings, wrecked furniture, destroyed books, and attempted to make the black schools "untenable by nuisance." The buildings themselves were often in poor condition, with neither floors nor windows. Even provost marshals frequently refused to provide protection or support. "[I] don't believe in nigger teachers," a provost marshal told a white teacher in a black school. "Did'nt 'list to help them."[22]

Both Plumly and Wheelock were abolitionists and did not object to employing blacks as teachers. But black teachers ran even greater risks in the rural parishes. Consequently, white southern women, most of whom were from Unionist families in New Orleans, made up the teaching staffs. They were chosen because men were not readily available and because Banks believed that white southerners understood blacks and could deal more effectively with white opposition. Furthermore, most northern benevolent societies, like the American Missionary Association, were unwilling to send "unacclimated persons to Louisiana during the Sickly Southern Summer."[23]

Banks supported the black educational system by giving good salaries,

21. Louisiana, *Debates,* 493; T. H. Harris, *The Story of Public Education in Louisiana* (New Orleans: Delgado Trades School, 1924), 21–22, 33; Smith and Brady, *Commission on Corrupt Practices,* 137–43.

22. Smith and Brady, *Commission on Corrupt Practices,* 192; Plumly, *Report of the Board of Education for Freedmen,* 7–10; Ripley, *Slaves and Freedmen,* 136–39; White, *Freedmen's Bureau in Louisiana,* 184–85; *New Orleans Tribune,* September 13, 1864; *New Orleans Daily True Delta,* June 24, 1864; *National Anti-Slavery Standard,* December 3, 1864; Wheelock to Banks, August 9, 1864, Banks Collection, LC. For the southern reaction in other areas, see Henry Lee Swint, *The Northern Teacher in the South, 1862–1870* (1941; reprint, New York: Octagon Books, 1967), 94–142.

23. Brady, "Trials and Tribulations," 12; Harrington, *Fighting Politician,* 109; Plumly, *Report of the Board of Education for Freedmen,* 12; White, *Freedmen's Bureau in Louisiana,* 169; Wheelock to Banks, July 30, 1864, Banks Collection, LC.

the money for which was raised partly from a special property tax. Other money was raised through the "hospital fund," which came from taxes levied by the army on cotton, sugar, and molasses. Banks also established a normal school program in which prospective teachers obtained training for one to six weeks before taking their first assignment. "I want it understood that the negro children must be educated," Banks declared, for progress depended on educating the laboring classes.[24]

Despite his good intentions, Banks sacrificed the support of black leaders when he endorsed a new law stating that "white and colored children shall not be taught in the same school; they shall be kept separate and distinct *under all circumstances.*" With astute foresight, the *New Orleans Tribune* realized that such a provision would perpetuate a second-class status for black citizens and "draw a line between two elements of one and the same people, from the cradle itself up to the time of manhood and throughout life."[25]

Nevertheless, Banks believed that he had accomplished much with his support of education. The one issue that remained was permanent funding for the black school system. He was certain that whites would refuse to support black schools with a general property tax if the conservatives regained power. Also, he knew that the freedmen were too poor to support the schools on their own. The only solution was Federal funding for black education. But that prospect was out of the question, and Banks's school system for blacks did not last long after he left New Orleans in September 1865.[26]

There was little left for Banks to do in the lower Mississippi Valley after the adoption of the Free State constitution. General Canby had not only

24. *OR*, 41, pt. 2:869–70; Louisiana, *Debates*, 33, 148–56, 501–2; Harrington, *Fighting Politician*, 109; White, *Freedmen's Bureau in Louisiana*, 174; *National Anti-Slavery Standard*, December 3, 1864. For a critical assessment of Banks's motives, see Keith Wilson, "Education as a Vehicle of Racial Control: Major General N. P. Banks in Louisiana, 1863–64," *Journal of Negro Education* 50 (Spring 1981): 158.

25. John McNair to Banks, August 26, 1864, Nathan Willey to Banks, December 14, 1865, Banks Collection, LC; Oliver Otis Howard, *Autobiography of Oliver Otis Howard, Major General, United States Army*, 2 vols. (New York: Baker & Taylor, 1907), 2:302; *New Orleans Tribune*, February 17, 23, 1865.

26. Harrington, *Fighting Politician*, 108; Ripley, *Slaves and Freedmen*, 186–87; Wilson, "Education as a Vehicle of Racial Control," 168; *New Orleans Tribune*, November 18, 1865; Banks to Mary Banks, July 7, 26, 1865, Banks Collection, LC.

taken command of the army; he had absorbed some of Banks's civil powers as well. Frustrated, Banks welcomed the opportunity in September 1864 to visit Washington on a twenty-day pass from Canby.[27]

After arriving in Washington, Banks met with Lincoln to discuss plans for Reconstruction. Because Mary and the children had left New Orleans and returned to Massachusetts in August, Banks asked for and was granted an extended leave in October. But he did not go to Massachusetts. Lincoln needed him in Washington to help counter the Radicals' efforts in Congress to block his plan for Reconstruction.[28]

Louisiana had been the first state to test Lincoln's strategy for reuniting the nation. The one obstacle that remained was congressional recognition of the Free State of Louisiana. Although there was some sentiment to readmit "reconstructed" states as quickly as possible, the Radicals in Congress were not willing to forgive and forget. Under the leadership of Charles Sumner, Banks's old nemesis from Massachusetts, opponents of quick reunification argued that the new governments in Arkansas and Louisiana were irregular because they had been set up under military rule and they represented only a small minority of the people. The tone of the decrees Banks issued when setting up the Free State of Louisiana did not help. "The fundamental law of the State is martial law," he had proclaimed, thus adding weight to the contention that the Hahn regime was illegitimate.[29]

There was some basis for the Radicals' accusations. The Smith-Brady Commission, which investigated corrupt practices in the Department of the Gulf toward the close of the war, concluded that if the restrictions proscribed in Lincoln's proclamation of December 1863 had been ad-

27. *OR,* 41, pt. 2:619–20; Harrington, *Fighting Politician,* 163; Hoffman, *Camp, Court and Siege,* 108–17; Denison to Chase, July 1, 1864, in Chase, "Diary and Correspondence," 440; *New York Daily Tribune,* July 30, 1864; Plumly to Banks, August 9, October 8, 1864, Banks Collection, LC. Banks left New Orleans on September 24, 1864 (Doyle, "Civilian Life in Occupied New Orleans," 26).

28. Banks to Mary Banks, January 7, 1864[5], Banks's Collection, LC. Mary Banks's departure from New Orleans is established by the August 5, 1864, entry in the Warmoth Diary, Henry Clay Warmoth Papers, SHC. Lincoln extended Banks's leave again on November 14.

29. Belz, *Reconstructing the Union,* 270–71; Cox, *Lincoln and Black Freedom,* 107–8; David Donald, *Charles Sumner and the Rights of Man* (New York: Knopf, 1970), 183; McCrary, *Abraham Lincoln and Reconstruction,* 293–302; Tunnell, *Crucible of Reconstruction,* 47–49; Banks, "To the People of Louisiana," January 11, 1864, *OR,* Ser. 3, pt. 4:23; Banks to Mary Banks, December 22, 1864, Banks Collection, LC.

hered to, "the number of votes polled at the elections above mentioned would have been much less than one tenth of the number defined in the proclamation." Furthermore, they found evidence to suggest that loyalists from New Orleans had been carted to rural areas under Union control to vote so that those parishes could be represented. Perhaps the greatest such charade involved an uninhabitable island in the Gulf twelve miles from Brashear City "where a gang of rowdies from New Orleans, not more than twenty or thirty in number, elected senators and representatives to the State Legislature."[30]

The commission's findings were not known at the time, but rumors of the improprieties documented in its report abounded. Undeterred by the gossip, Banks did what he could to get Congress to recognize the Free State of Louisiana. He met with his old friends in Congress, gave testimony before committees of the House and Senate, and wrote letters. There were some hopeful moments, and it was possible that a majority in the Congress might be willing to go along with the Lincoln-Banks blueprint to reconstruct Louisiana. But Banks met opposition from both sides. Democrats were disinclined to support the Republican plan, and Radicals in his own party opposed Lincoln's more moderate views.[31]

One weapon the Radicals used with success to discredit the administration was the Committee on the Conduct of the War, which had been set up early in the war to investigate administrative irregularities. Although it did not have the power to make policy, the Radicals captured control of the committee and used it as an instrument for pressing their views. As a result, its hearings became a witch-hunt. Witnesses were interrogated without knowing the nature of the allegations against them and were not permitted to have legal counsel present during questioning.[32]

30. *OR,* 34, pt. 2:512–13; Harrington, *Fighting Politician,* 146; McCrary, *Abraham Lincoln and Reconstruction,* 186, 212; Reed, *Life of A. P. Dostie,* 111–13; *New Orleans Daily True Delta,* March 18, 20, May 5, 1864; Denison to Chase, March 5, 1864, in Chase, "Diary and Correspondence," 433–35; Smith and Brady, *Commission on Corrupt Practices,* i, 5, 8–9. Also see "Conservatism against Radicalism," editorial in *New Orleans Daily Picayune,* December 31, 1862; Williams, "General Banks and the Radical Republicans," 271–76.

31. Belz, *Reconstructing the Union,* 268; Banks to Mary Banks, December 29, 1864, January 10, February 5, 15, 24, 1865, Banks Collection, LC.

32. Patrick W. Riddleberger, *George Washington Julian: Radical Republican* (N.p.:

The Committee on the Conduct of the War called Banks to testify on December 14, 1864, about the Red River campaign. Hoping to discredit him, the Radicals in Congress claimed that the expedition was undertaken to strengthen Banks's political aspirations and to benefit cotton speculators. Acknowledging that he did hold some elections, Banks argued that political considerations were not the main reason for the campaign. The question of confiscated cotton was another matter. Banks had wanted to deal with Confederate officers in the cotton trade, but his plan had been foiled. And he had managed to send some cotton to New Orleans, but under new regulations most of the proceeds from the sale of this booty went to the Federal treasury rather than to speculators. There had been some abuses. One very active speculator, William Halliday, traveled on a gunboat under the protection of David Dixon Porter, and the navy had seized all the cotton it could get its hands on. Thus the perception that the expedition had been carried out for personal profit continued to stain Banks's reputation.[33]

After a break for Christmas, the committee continued taking testimony into January and February. Banks appeared before the body a second time on January 13, 1865. In a final effort to lay to rest the allegations that had grown out of the committee's investigation, Banks submitted a statement and supporting documents on March 28. Meanwhile, the Radicals in Congress continued their assault. The Free State of Louisiana, they charged, was riddled with dishonesty and fraud. State officials were referred to as "mere mockeries, these men of straw who represent nobody," and the whole experiment was said to be "absurd, monarchical, and anti-American."[34]

Banks fought back, calling such diatribes "unjustifiable . . . undigni-

---

Indiana Historical Bureau, 1966), 155–56; Williams, "General Banks and the Radical Republicans," 278–79.

33. *OR*, 34, pt. 1:213–14, Ser. 3, 4:170–72, 209; *OR (Navy)*, 26:767–68; Selfridge, *Memoirs*, 95–97; Richard S. West, *The Second Admiral: A Life of David Dixon Porter, 1813–1891* (New York: Coward-McCann, 1937), 248; B. Rush Plumly to Banks, April 7, 1864, Banks Collection, LC. The navy's scheme did not work in the end. Asked to rule on the disposition of sixty thousand bales of cotton expropriated by Porter's men along the Red River, the Federal courts held that the rule of prize did not cover inland seizures (*New York Herald*, March 11, 12, 1865).

34. *Congressional Globe*, 38th Cong., 2d sess., 1865, 1128; Harrington, *Fighting Politician*, 164–65.

fied, disgraceful." But the Radicals won in the end. Although there was support in the Senate for a report from the Judiciary Committee that favored recognition, Sumner was able to keep it from coming to a vote by threatening a filibuster. Finally, Congress adjourned on March 4 without recognizing the Free State of Louisiana.[35]

Banks was not discouraged, for he still enjoyed the support of the president. "I do believe that you, of all men, can best perform the part of advancing the new state government of Louisiana," Lincoln had written Banks in December 1864. He knew that working under Canby placed Banks in a difficult position but urged him to return for one last try. If Canby's policies proved "impractical or personally too disagreeable," Lincoln assured Banks, he would accept his resignation.[36]

Banks started back to Louisiana on April 5. Six days later, in what was to be his last speech, Lincoln signaled a shift in his policy on Reconstruction. Appearing on the balcony of the White House to address a boisterous crowd that had gathered to celebrate Lee's surrender at Appomattox, Lincoln endorsed the idea of limited black suffrage along the lines Banks had proposed during the Louisiana constitutional convention. In large part, Lincoln's announcement was prompted by the criticism in Congress of the Free State regime in Louisiana. By stating publicly what he had been saying privately for more than a year, Lincoln opened the door for a rapprochement with the Radicals in regard to reconstructing the South. Whatever reason he had for making this overture, Lincoln never got a chance to implement his views. Seventy-two hours later he was dead.[37]

Banks was in Cairo, Illinois, when he heard the news of Lincoln's assassination. Shocked and saddened, he rose to the occasion by delivering a touching eulogy. Banks spoke at two more memorials upon reaching New Orleans, giving evidence that his old eloquence and oratorical power had not diminished. Lincoln had been persistent and tenacious in prosecuting the war, but he also believed that "blood cannot restore

35. Belz, *Reconstructing the Union,* 271; Donald, *Charles Sumner and the Rights of Man,* 203–5; McCrary, *Abraham Lincoln and Reconstruction,* 290–304; Merriam, *Life and Times of Samuel Bowles,* 1:419.

36. Lincoln to Banks, December 2, 1864 (printed copy), Banks Collection, LC, also in Basler, ed., *Collected Works of Abraham Lincoln,* 8:131; *New Orleans Era,* December 13, 1864.

37. McCrary, *Abraham Lincoln and Reconstruction,* 3–13.

blood." To the contrary, he had wanted to readmit the former Confederate States with a minimum of disruption to the political process. Several factions opposed Lincoln's plan. Some opponents felt that the South should pay for its acts and make amends for the loss of life suffered by the Union forces in putting down the rebellion. Another group sought the elevation of black men to their rightful place as full citizens of the United States, which included a guarantee of their civil rights and the benefit of total suffrage.[38]

Southerners, however, had no intention of acceding to such an extreme reorganization of their way of life. With surprising ease and rapidity, former Confederates recaptured political control of their respective states and reestablished positions of power similar to those held before the war. They were so successful that, for a while, it appeared that the only change after four years of fighting was the emancipation of the slaves. But even that was not an accomplished fact, for there were many southerners who thought that they could perpetuate black bondage through legal means. Furthermore, little was done to help the former slaves adjust to their newfound freedom. As a result, events following the collapse of the Confederacy transpired to undo much of what Banks had accomplished during his two-year tenure as commander of the Department of the Gulf.[39]

First to unravel was Michael Hahn, who resigned as governor in March 1865 to qualify for a seat in the United States Senate. Although he would never be allowed to occupy the position, his resignation meant that Lieutenant Governor J. Madison Wells assumed the executive post. Both moderates and Radicals had nominated Wells for a spot on the ticket in February 1864, and he had been elected over a conservative opponent. Yet Wells turned his back on both groups and tied in with the conservatives once he became governor. The conversion was not as strange as it first appeared, for Wells was a native-born Louisiana planter, a member of the old slaveholding aristocracy. He never did fit into the Banks-Hahn crowd that drew support from white laborers. Nor did he feel at home with the Radicals, who pressed him vigorously for black suf-

38. *New Orleans Times,* March 6, April 21, 23, 1865; Basler, ed., *Collected Works of Abraham Lincoln,* 7:345; Foner, *Reconstruction,* 230.

39. Ripley, *Slaves and Freedmen,* 156, 182–83; White, *Freedmen's Bureau in Louisiana,* 31.

frage. His nomination as lieutenant governor had been designed to draw votes from Louisiana's upper class, and as governor, he realigned himself with that constituency.[40]

Once in office, the normally quiet Wells went on the offensive. He fired Banks's old friend and political ally Stephen Hoyt as mayor of New Orleans and replaced him with a secessionist newspaper editor, Hugh Kennedy. He made Glendy Burke, a Confederate sympathizer during the war, city superintendent of education, replacing Banks's man, B. Rush Plumly. Wells replaced pro-Banks men with his supporters throughout the various administrative agencies of the city.[41]

Wells implemented most of these changes before Banks reached New Orleans on April 22. But once Banks was back in the department, he used his authority to dismiss Mayor Kennedy and named his own man, Samuel M. Quincy, as acting mayor. Quincy moved quickly to reestablish control over the municipal machine, and moderates flocked back to the jobs they had recently lost. Although the governor fought back by telling the city treasurer not to honor warrants drawn by the acting mayor, Quincy held the upper hand as long as he was supported by Union bayonets.[42]

Lincoln's successor, Andrew Johnson, could easily have thrown his support to Banks and his coalition of middle-class whites, but the new president decided to follow the most expedient means for reestablishing civilian control. In Louisiana, that meant supporting Governor Wells. As

40. *New Orleans Era,* February 2, 1864; *New Orleans Daily True Delta,* May 12, 1864.

41. *OR,* 48, pt. 1:1174–76; Cox, *Lincoln and Black Freedom,* 134–35; Harrington, *Fighting Politician,* 167; Reed, *Life of A. P. Dostie,* 181–83, 190–92; *New Orleans Daily True Delta,* May 11, 1865; *New York Herald,* April 1, 1865. Hoyt's political relationship with Banks dated back to the Rantoul period some twenty years earlier when Banks first attempted to get elected to the Massachusetts House (see Hoyt to Banks, December 9, 14, 1844, November 28, 1845, Banks Manuscripts, ISHL).

42. *OR,* 48, pt. 2:156, 320, 729; Smith and Brady, *Commission on Corrupt Practices,* 13; McCrary, *Abraham Lincoln and Reconstruction,* 311; James A. Padgett, "Some Letters of George Stanton Denison, 1854–1866: Observations of a Yankee on Conditions in Louisiana and Texas," *Louisiana Historical Quarterly* 23 (October 1940): 1221–23; Reed, *Life of A. P. Dostie,* 181–208; *New Orleans Times,* April 23, May 18, 19, 1865; *New Orleans Picayune,* May 9, 10, 1865; *New Orleans Daily True Delta,* May 6, 7, 9, 1865; Samuel M. Quincy to his mother, May 5, 1865, Quincy, Wendell, Holmes, and Upham Family Papers, LC.

a result, Johnson reorganized the military departments of the South on May 17 and thereby stripped Banks of what little authority he retained. Although he was still on the army payroll and was still stationed in New Orleans, Banks had no duties or authority.[43]

The sudden shift in power prompted the Banks-Hahn faction to join hands with the Radicals. Knowing that only with black suffrage could they hope to challenge Wells and the conservatives, Radicals and moderates in Louisiana united forces. The new alliance did not mean that they came to like each other. After all, Banks could hardly be expected to have much affection for those who had prevented Congress from recognizing the Free State of Louisiana. In addition, the two factions continued to disagree over what form the new government should take. Banks hoped to wrest control of the existing administration from the conservatives, while the Radicals favored junking it entirely and starting over with something entirely new.[44]

Despite their disagreements, Radicals and moderates in New Orleans moved closer together during the summer of 1865. The Radicals were particularly pleased with Banks's Fourth of July address at the New Orleans Custom House. Now that "we have crushed, we hope forever, a conspiracy and rebellion," Banks asked, "in whose hands shall political power be vested?" He was willing to allow former Confederates "the opportunities to retrieve shattered fortunes, but their right to resume political power, to control the destinies of the nation, or to decide what questions have been solved by the war," he declared, "I solemnly deny." Instead, Banks proposed to replace Rebel votes with black ones. "Enfranchisement for all!" he proclaimed, indicating publicly for the first time how far he had shifted toward the Radical end of the political spectrum.[45]

43. *OR*, 48, pt. 2:475. Also see *New Orleans Daily True Delta*, May 12, 1865; *New Orleans Times*, May 31, June 3, 1865; *New Orleans Tribune*, June 1, 1865; Samuel M. Quincy to his mother, June 1, 8 (postscript to letter dated June 5, 1865), Quincy, Wendell, Holmes, and Upham Family Papers LC.

44. Foner, *Reconstruction*, 111; Tunnell, *Crucible of Reconstruction*, 41–42; Banks to Mary Banks, July 26, August 12, 1865, Banks Collection, LC.

45. Nathaniel P. Banks, *An Address, Delivered by Major General N. P. Banks, at the Custom-House, New-Orleans, on the Fourth of July, 1865* (New York: Harper & Brothers, 1865), 5, 10, 12, 23. Like Hahn and other Free State officials, Banks had become con-

Banks followed up his Fourth of July oration by attending a meeting of Radicals on July 11 at the Carrollton Railroad Depot. The conclave resulted in the establishment of the National Republican Association, which favored universal black suffrage and economic prosperity for both black and white workers. The Radicals began to see merit in certain aspects of Banks's plan of Reconstruction. Although they would have preferred to confiscate plantations from owners who had served in the Confederate army to divide into one-hundred-acre farms for the freedmen, many Radicals appreciated the progressive steps Banks had taken in setting up his labor system. In a letter to Garrison that was published in the *Liberator*, Wheelock concluded that since the Federal government would not support so drastic a measure, Banks had done "the best thing possible," given that it was "not possible to do the right thing."[46]

Not everyone agreed with Wheelock's assessment. Former secessionists were angered by Banks's attempt to break the back of the slave system by introducing the notion of free labor, and Unionists disliked his conciliatory gestures to their old foes. Thus both sides accused Banks of incompetence.[47] "General Banks's administration in civil as well as military affairs," one of his detractors concluded, "has been a lamentable and prolonged failure."[48]

A correspondent for the *Cincinnati Gazette* who visited New Orleans shortly after the war ended agreed that Banks's tenure in the Crescent City had been a failure. "It was noticeable that General Banks . . . seemed to have gained no popularity by his relaxation of Butler's iron rule," he observed. "The returning Rebels appeared in no way grateful for any of the concessions he was charged with having made to their prejudices," while "the Unionists were in no way grateful for his late conver-

---

vinced by the summer of 1865 that universal black suffrage was the only way the Republican party could survive in the South (Harrington, *Fighting Politician*, 168).

46. McCrary, *Abraham Lincoln and Reconstruction*, 320–21; *New Orleans Times*, July 6, 1865; *National Anti-Slavery Standard*, May 2, 1863; *Liberator*, March 3, 1865; Banks to Mary Banks, July 7, August 2, 1865, October 20, 1871, Banks Collection, LC.

47. For two scurrilous attacks on Banks's character from opposing viewpoints, see "E. W. Vanderhoof to Major-General Banks," July 6, 1864, HNOC, for a Unionist's perspective, and *Private Correspondence—n. p. banks [sic] to E. Kirby Smith*, [1864], HTML, for a satirical piece favoring the Rebel cause.

48. P. W., *Historical Sketch*, 12.

sion to negro suffrage." The correspondent believed that Banks's characteristic tendency to vacillate on important issues had destroyed his credibility.

> When Butler said a thing, they knew precisely what to expect. He might be severe, but they always knew where to find him. Banks, they complained, had done too little for the radical Unionists to command their confidence, and too little for the reconstructing Rebels to command theirs. Possibly a General who should have pleased any one of these parties would have disobeyed his instructions; certainly he would have displeased the rest. But, at the end, the man who marked out his own policy, and inflexibly pursued it, was found commanding a certain sort of respect. All classes, Rebel or Union, expressed it for General Butler. General Banks was less fortunate.[49]

49. Whitelaw Reid, *After the War: A Southern Tour* (New York: Moore, Wilstach & Baldwin, 1866), 266–67. For a more recent but similar view, see Joseph G. Dawson, *Army Generals and Reconstruction: Louisiana, 1862–1877* (Baton Rouge: Louisiana State University Press, 1982), 23.

16

The Destiny of Nations

Stripped of his authority, Nathaniel P. Banks was delighted when his resignation from the army was finally approved on September 6, 1865. Michael Hahn and other friends urged him to stay in New Orleans, suggesting that he could practice law or be appointed district attorney. There would be much work for lawyers following four years of confiscation and conflict with little competition if former Confederates were barred from the Federal courts. Furthermore, the practice of law would enhance his political career and perhaps gain Banks election to the United States Congress as a senator from Louisiana.[1]

Banks considered the possibility and went as far as to win admission to the Federal bar in New Orleans. But ultimately he decided to return to New England. Banks had never done very well in the practice of law, and his political future in Louisiana seemed uncertain as long as Governor Wells remained in power. It was also clear that politics in Louisiana were becoming increasingly polarized. The Radicals continued to gain strength in the National Republican Association, as evidenced by the rapid rise of Henry Clay Warmoth, a young Radical whom Banks heartily disliked. Banks's decision was influenced primarily, however, by the

1. Mrs. Butler to Butler, September 14, 1864, in Butler, *Private and Official Correspondence,* 5:133; George S. Denison to Chase, September 6, 1864, in Chase, "Diary and Correspondence," 445–46; Warner, *Generals in Blue,* 18; *Boston Daily Advertiser,* September 28, 1865; Plumly to Banks, October 8, 1864, Michael Hahn to Banks, June 16, 1865, Banks to Mary Banks, July 22, 26, August 12, September 7, 1865, Banks Collection, LC.

realization that a combination of Johnson's Reconstruction policies and growing resistance by white conservatives would eventually undo all that he had sought to accomplish. "It can no longer be doubted that the President intends to give the Rebels the power of the country," he wrote Mary in August. "It seems incredible and impossible that the blood that has been shed was purposeless and without result."[2]

Unexpectedly, a new opportunity presented itself in Massachusetts when Daniel W. Gooch, a Radical who occupied Banks's old seat in Congress, resigned to assume a lucrative post with the navy for the port of Boston. Banks jumped at the chance and left New Orleans with such haste that there was no time to plan farewell celebrations in honor of the man who had played such an important role in the Free State of Louisiana. The New Orleans moderates were sad to see him go, but former Rebels returning to the Crescent City laughed at his quick departure. "Banks . . . chases office in every latitude. He will pursue it by rail, on horse-back, by still-hunting—or he will take it on the wing."[3]

Banks paid little heed to these parting shots, for he faced a formidable task in his home state. Two Radicals, J. Q. A. Griffin and James M. Stone, faced him in the contest for the Republican nomination. The Radicals enjoyed the support of the political faction that had ruled the state since Banks stepped down as governor in January 1861. Fortunately for Banks, the two most important Radicals in Massachusetts, Senators Charles Sumner and Henry Wilson, considered it expedient to stay out of the fight. Another prominent politician and old friend, George S. Boutwell,

2. *Boston Commonwealth,* October 7, 1865; Banks to Mary Banks, July 7, 16, August 16, 19, 24, 31, September 7, 1865, Banks to Joseph Frémont Banks, July 26, 1865, M. T. Murphy to Banks, December 1, 1865, Plumly to Banks, January 12, 1866, Banks Collection, LC. Several years later, upon learning that Warmoth had been defeated in his race for another term as governor, Banks wrote Mary, "He deserves very little sympathy. Those who come in are as utterly unscrupulous as he has been & will come to that same end" (December 11, 1872, Banks Collection, LC). For Warmoth's postwar career in Louisiana, see Francis Byers Harris, "Henry Clay Warmoth, Reconstruction Governor of Louisiana," *Louisiana Historical Quarterly* 30 (April 1947): 523–653, and Henry Clay Warmoth, *War, Politics and Reconstruction: Stormy Days in Louisiana* (New York: Macmillan, 1930).

3. *Boston Commonwealth,* October 7, 1865; *New Orleans Daily Crescent,* November 3, 1865; *New York Times,* September 16, 1865. Gooch served on the Committee on the Conduct of the War looking into the Red River campaign and wrote a minority report that treated Banks fairly.

threw his weight to Banks. But the rest of the Radical faction was hostile, for they never liked Banks's politics and realized that his bid for office threatened the political monopoly they had enjoyed for four years.[4]

The campaign was bitter, and the Radicals attacked Banks aggressively for his work on Reconstruction in Louisiana. His failure on the Red River also became a point of contention. The Radicals even claimed that Banks had forfeited the right to run because he had abandoned his Massachusetts residency in 1861 when he left to take a position with the Illinois Central Railroad in Chicago. They also charged that he was actually now a resident of Louisiana because he had been admitted to the bar in that state. Banks carried his case to the people and offered a full defense of his Civil War record. To please Radical voters, Banks came out in favor of black suffrage and total reconstruction of the South but stopped short of identifying with the Radical element.[5]

Banks had two advantages in the campaign. First, the Radicals were split between two candidates, Griffin and Stone. Second, Banks had not lost his ability to charm the voters with the magic of his personality. At the Republican nominating convention only two formal ballots were needed. Banks won with seventy-nine votes to Stone's thirty-four and Griffin's twenty-five. He had little to fear in the general election. Democrats did poorly in Massachusetts during the 1860s and their candidate in 1865 was Banks's uncle, the Reverend Thomas J. Greenwood, with whom he had lived when he had started working in the mill many years before. Greenwood's nephew won handily in November by a margin of four to one.[6]

Banks was an outsider when he returned to Washington as a congressman in December 1865. The struggle for control of Reconstruction of the South was in full force. A conciliatory approach had lost its champion

4. *Boston Commonwealth,* October 14, 1865; *Boston Daily Advertiser,* October 5, 10, 26, 1865; *Springfield Daily Republican,* October 14, 1865.

5. *Boston Daily Advertiser,* October 10, 26, 1865; *Boston Daily Journal,* October 19, 1865; *New Orleans Times,* November 2, 1865; Thomas J. Durant to Benjamin F. Butler, October 2, 1865, in Butler, *Private and Official Correspondence,* 5:668.

6. Harrington, *Fighting Politician,* 171; *Boston Daily Advertiser,* October 11, 1865; Mary Banks to daughter Maude, October 11, 1865, Banks's commission from the commonwealth of Massachusetts to fill the unexpired term of Donald W. Gooch, dated November 24, 1865, Banks Collection, LC.

with Lincoln's assassination, and Andrew Johnson had aligned himself with the Democrats, a position that even Banks could not stomach. Banks found himself further isolated after a quarrel with Johnson's secretary of the navy, Gideon Welles, who held the cabinet post Banks had wanted four years earlier.[7]

The quarrel involved control of patronage at the Charlestown Navy Yard. President Johnson supported Welles in the controversy, which forced Banks to line up with the Radicals, but he did so without pleasure, for he still blamed them for rejecting the Reconstruction plan he had initiated in Louisiana. "Had it been left to the people of the State of Louisiana," he argued, "we should have had none of these troubles that now affect us politically or economically. But the power is in the hands of men who have very recently been engaged in a most determined effort to destroy the Government." Banks also had little use for Radical leaders such as Charles Sumner and Benjamin F. Butler, whom he saw as a "coterie of men to whom bloodshed has given temporary power." Nevertheless, he realized where his future lay and, at least publicly, presented himself as having a Radical bent.[8]

This deception did not mean that Banks surrendered all principle to political expediency. In February 1867, he opposed Thaddeus Stevens' bill to place the South under military rule. Of the ten House Republicans who voted against the Stevens measure, only Banks would carry his congressional district in 1868. Banks felt that the measure went too far, for it was a complete rejection of policies he had inaugurated in Louisiana. Banks also realized the futility of such punitive measures. Unlike most of the Radicals in Washington, Banks had lived in the South and had worked closely with southerners. "I am not the enemy of southern men," Banks declared. "I recognize them as brothers, as Americans. I know that we must live together . . . I do not clamor for their punishment."[9]

7. Foner, *Reconstruction,* 179–84, 191; *Boston Post,* April 6, 1868, Banks to Mary Banks, July 26, 1865, Banks Collection, LC.

8. *Congressional Globe,* 39th Cong., 1st sess., 1866, 4255; Banks to Mary Banks, August 16, 24, 1865, Banks Collection, LC; Banks to Mrs. Banks, March 18, 1870, quoted in Harrington, *Fighting Politician,* 172.

9. Richard Nelson Current, *Old Thad Stevens: A Story of Ambition* (Madison: University of Wisconsin Press, 1942), 271; *Springfield Daily Republican,* October 21, 1865, quoted in Harrington, *Fighting Politician,* 172; Joe Gray Taylor, *Louisiana Reconstructed, 1863–1877* (Baton Rouge: Louisiana State University Press, 1974), 128–33.

Banks continued to express this view, even in the face of strong opposition. Speaking on Stevens's military bill in the House of Representatives on February 9, Banks noted that the Radicals claimed that the rebellion had destroyed the rights of southern people and that they, in a sense, had committed suicide or, at least, reverted to a territorial status. This interpretation meant that the South should be considered conquered territory and placed under military rule. Banks argued that because secession had been illegal, the southern states were still in the Union. Instead of military rule, the South should be readmitted to the Union under the leadership of southern Unionists who had reorganized their state governments.[10]

Some in Congress liked Banks's argument, but the Radicals were firmly in control. Stevens ridiculed Banks's reasoning and accused the representative from Massachusetts of being intimate with President Johnson. Although Banks denied the accusation, he saw the handwriting on the wall and decided not to buck the tide. In the end, he voted for the Stevens bill and even opposed changes after it reached the Senate.[11]

Banks's middle-of-the-road views were challenged again in the attempt to impeach Andrew Johnson. Banks dared not risk supporting the unpopular occupant of the White House, although he disapproved of Radical efforts to put the chief executive on trial and declined to participate in the witch-burning speeches against Johnson. The stand may have cost him the cabinet post he had wanted for so long, for one of Johnson's advisers suggested the name of N. P. Banks for secretary of state if the old cabinet resigned en masse in an effort to derail the momentum toward impeachment. In the end, Banks joined other members of his party in voting for the articles of impeachment.[12]

Banks's fence-sitting allowed him to maintain his seat in Congress, but it kept him from regaining the prominence he had enjoyed before the war. The Radicals were now in power, and though Banks would en-

10. *Congressional Globe,* 39th Cong., 2d sess., 1867, Appendix, 174–76.

11. Dennett, ed., *Lincoln and the Civil War,* 268–70; *Springfield Daily Republican,* February 23, 1867; *Boston Weekly Voice,* February 28, 1867; *Congressional Globe,* 39th Cong., 2d sess., 1867, 1104–6, 1208, 1214, 1323, 1328–29; William T. Weston to Banks, February 14, 1867, Banks Manuscripts, ISHL.

12. James Gillespie Blaine, *Twenty Years of Congress: From Lincoln to Garfield,* 2 vols. (Norwich, Conn.: Henry Hill, 1884–86), 2:255; W. G. Moore, "Notes of Colonel W. G. Moore, Private Secretary to President Johnson, 1866–1868," *American Historical Review* 19 (October 1913): 125–26; *Boston Daily Journal,* October 17, 1866.

dorse the Radicals' position to gain reelection, he could not bring himself to champion their cause. Discouraged by the turn of events, Banks considered getting out of politics. What kept him going was the belief that the polarization resulting from the war would soon work its way through, leaving control of the Republican party to the old moderates like himself. For this reason, Banks was pleased with the Democratic gains in the fall election of 1867 and saw them as "a crusher for the wild men." Waiting for the situation to change on the domestic front, Banks cast about for other issues on which to reestablish his popularity.[13]

Most of the choice committee assignments were already taken when Banks took his seat in Thirty-ninth Congress. One exception was the position as chair of the Committee on Foreign Affairs, which was available because of the retirement of Henry Winter Davis. Before the war, the House Committee on Foreign Affairs had been largely ignored because the Senate traditionally played the more important role in effecting foreign policy through its constitutional power to approve treaties with foreign countries. Banks realized, however, that the committee could direct public opinion toward the emergence of the United States as a world power.[14]

Banks's old nemesis, Charles Sumner, was chair of the Senate Committee on Foreign Relations and opposed his appointment. But Banks enjoyed the advantage of a good working relationship with the secretary of state, William H. Seward, who disagreed with Sumner's Radical views and appreciated Banks's more moderate stance. In addition, both Banks and Seward were enthusiastic expansionists, eager to exploit ways the United States might extend its influence. Banks also had the support of an old friend and Speaker of the House, Schuyler Colfax, who saw to it that Banks landed the assignment.[15]

High on Seward's list of priorities was the purchase of Alaska from Russia, which Banks heartily approved. As a young Democrat he had eagerly endorsed the idea of America's manifest destiny. His experience

13. Banks to Mary Banks, October 4, 1866, November 13, 1867, March 17, 1870, Banks Collection, LC.

14. Harrington, *Fighting Politician*, 175.

15. O. J. Hollister, *Life of Schuyler Colfax* (New York: Funk & Wagnalls, 1886), 276, 289; Pierce, *Memoir and Letters of Charles Sumner*, 4:28–29; *New York Daily Tribune*, December 2, 1865.

with the Illinois Central Railroad and trips down the coast of Texas during the war had opened his eyes to the potential for expansion. More important, Banks realized that such a policy would have wide popular appeal, building as it did on the strong sense of nationalism fostered by the Civil War.[16]

Seward negotiated a treaty with the Russians to purchase the territory for $7.2 million, which meant that the measure required a congressional appropriation. As chair of the House Committee on Foreign Affairs, Banks was central to the measure's success.[17]

Banks went to work to bring the members of his committee into line. Using his personality and political skill, he persuaded them that expansionism was emerging as one of the strongest movements of the time. His approach was purely pragmatic, for Banks did not attempt to defend his policies on the basis of an elaborate philosophy of imperialism. To him, the extension of American influence was a natural and irreversible process.[18]

The treaty faced opposition in the House. Some members disliked anything that originated from President Andrew Johnson's administration. Others felt that the territory was not worth the price. Several representatives attempted to block the measure until the tsar settled claims against him arising from the Russian cancellation of an arms contract during the Crimean War. Banks agreed with some of the arguments, but his devotion to imperialism outweighed his reservations.[19]

The fight for the purchase of Alaska began on December 9, 1867,

16. See Banks's speech on the Kansas-Nebraska Bill, *Congressional Globe,* 33d Cong., 1st sess., 1854, Appendix, 880; also *Boston Daily Journal,* June 10, 1854.

17. Thomas A. Bailey, "Why the United States Purchased Alaska," *Pacific Historical Review* 3 (1934): 39–49; Victor J. Farrar, *The Annexation of Russian America to the United States* (Washington, D.C.: W. F. Roberts, 1937), 88–92; Frank A. Golder, "The Purchase of Alaska," *American Historical Review* 25 (April 1920): 411–25.

18. Harrington, *Fighting Politician,* 176–77; *Congressional Globe,* 41st Cong., 2d sess., 1870, Appendix, 504; *Congressional Record,* 44th Cong., 1st sess., 1876, Appendix, 53.

19. Farrar, *Annexation of Russian America,* 85–86, 89; *Congressional Globe,* 40th Cong., 1st sess., 1867, 392, also 37–38; James Morton Callahan, *American Foreign Policy in Canadian Relations* (New York: Macmillan, 1937), 307–8; Dexter Perkins, *Hands Off: A History of the Monroe Doctrine* (Boston: Little, Brown, 1948), 157; Joe Patterson Smith, *The Republican Expansionists of the Early Reconstruction Era* (Chicago: University of Chicago Libraries, 1933), 110–16.

when opponents of the measure tried to get it referred to the appropriations committee. After several sharp exchanges with its chair, Benjamin F. Butler, Banks got the bill referred to his own Committee on Foreign Affairs. When the bill was brought out of committee on May 18, 1868, Banks immediately threw his weight behind it in a series of reports, speeches, and debates. Rising to the best hyperbole of which he was capable, he asserted that whoever owned Alaska would become "the controller of the destiny of nations and the progress of mankind." Lumber, fish, and minerals made the territory worth acquiring, and annexation, after all, was part of America's greater destiny. Alaska was the key to the Pacific, the "great theater of action for the future." Even the Arctic "has a future," Banks declared; "it may be a boundless and glorious future, and it is for us."[20]

Members of the House continued to quarrel over having been excluded from the treaty process. In particular, they objected to the president negotiating a treaty that involved appropriations without first consulting them. To make their point, some representatives planned to vote against the Alaska appropriation bill when it came before the House. Using his skill as a moderator, Banks compromised the House's position in the conference committee. It was not the time to fight President Johnson or insist on House authority in diplomatic matters, he argued. Although some of his colleagues were displeased, a bill providing money for the purchase of Alaska passed and was signed by the president on July 27, 1868.[21]

Banks expected the election of Ulysses S. Grant as president in November 1868 and the appointment of a new secretary of state, Hamilton Fish, to bring increased support for his expansionist policies. He had several reasons for optimism. For one, Seward had been constantly hampered by Johnson's problems with Congress and eventual impeachment. Second, the expansionist talk of the Democrats, who still considered themselves to be the spokesmen of manifest destiny, was becoming more acceptable to Republicans. Even Sumner had labored for the annexation

20. Banks to Mary Banks, March 9, April 14, 1869, Banks Collection, LC; also Appleton, *Russian Life and Society,* 171–72; *New York Herald,* February 22, 1873; *Congressional Globe,* 40th Cong., 2d sess., 1868, 92–95, 1226–27, Appendix, 385–92; 3d sess., 1869, 1557; 41st Cong., 2d sess., 1870, 3628.

21. Farrar, *Annexation of Russian America,* 89–94. For Banks's role, see *Congressional Globe,* 40th Cong., 2d sess., 1868, Appendix, 386–88.

of Alaska and began agitating for the withdrawal of Great Britain from the Western Hemisphere. Finally, Banks believed that the new president favored expansion.[22]

His high expectations meant that Banks was certain to be disappointed. Problems associated with Reconstruction still held most of the public's attention. The few expansionist measures that Grant and Fish did support were isolated initiatives in the Caribbean that bore little relationship to an overall imperialistic policy. Furthermore, Banks distrusted Fish, whom he felt was basically a cold, aristocratic Anglophile with "nothing American in his policy." Banks was convinced that Grant's lukewarm attitude toward expansionism was the result of Fish's influence.[23]

Banks's commitment to the purchase of Alaska was sincere and even visionary. Yet Alaska and Asia ranked somewhat lower on his list of expansionist priorities than an area to the south with which he was already familiar. Banks had been impressed with the importance of Latin America even before the war with Mexico. Until ties to the antislavery movement forced him to modify his stand, Banks had strongly advocated the annexation of Cuba, slaves and all. His two years as commander of the Department of the Gulf had done much to strengthen his earlier impression. Banks wanted to make the Gulf of Mexico "a Sea of the United States" and focused his attention southward during his two terms as chairman of the Committee on Foreign Affairs.[24]

Banks became involved in several Latin American ventures between 1867 and 1870. These included attempting to get the United States government to purchase the Danish West Indies from Denmark, asking the

22. Donald, *Charles Sumner and the Rights of Man,* 308–9; William B. Hesseltine, *Ulysses S. Grant, Politician* (New York: Dodd, Mead, 1935), 19; Allan Nevins, *Hamilton Fish: The Inner History of the Grant Administration,* rev. ed., 2 vols. (New York: Frederick Ungar, 1957), 1:127; Charles Callan Tansill, *The United States and Santo Domingo, 1789–1873: A Chapter in Caribbean Diplomacy* (Baltimore: Johns Hopkins Press, 1938), 338–39; *New York Herald,* January 5, 1871; Banks to Mary Banks, March 9, May 3, 1869, January 14, 1870, Banks Collection, LC.

23. Banks to Mary Banks, June 2, 1871, Banks Collection, LC.

24. Banks to George S. Boutwell, October 15, 1861, in Boutwell, *Reminiscences,* 2:239–40; Banks, *Address, Delivered on the Fourth of July, 1865,* 9–10; *Boston Daily Journal,* June 10, 1854.

government to back a self-centered and unscrupulous adventurer who wanted to annex Santo Domingo (the Dominican Republic), and urging the administration to provide moral and military support to the Cuban insurrection against Spain.[25]

The attempt to get the government to purchase the Danish West Indies died when the Grant administration refused to ratify the treaty before time ran out in October 1869. The government's reluctance to acquire these islands was an indication of the country's lack of interest in expansionist ventures. The plan to annex Santo Domingo met defeat the same year when an unsympathetic House decided against the move by a vote of 63–110. An alternative plan to make the island a protectorate also failed when the shady dealings of the speculators supporting the measure from behind the scenes were revealed. Banks continued to fight, even when his Committee on Foreign Affairs refused to go along. Failing to see anything wrong with the idea, Banks publicly blamed the Grant administration for having "abandoned" Santo Domingo.[26]

In the meantime, insurgents in Cuba had risen against the harsh Spanish rule. The rebellion lasted ten years and caught the attention of politicians in the United States who desired to drive all vestiges of European influence out of the Western Hemisphere. Banks worked energetically in support of the revolt by keeping in touch with its agents and making public statements concerning Spanish cruelty and Spain's stand against the Union in the Civil War. In addition, he worked to secure the release of captured rebels who claimed to be citizens of the United States and got his committee to pass a resolution authorizing the president to recognize the rebel government. In this case, Banks's committee was following rather than leading public opinion, yet Banks drew praise for the skill with which he steered pro-insurrection resolutions through the House in the final days of the Johnson administration and just after Grant's inauguration.[27]

25. Harrington, *Fighting Politician,* 186–96.

26. Ibid., 187–88; Foner, *Reconstruction,* 494–95; Harrington, *Fighting Politician,* 188–89; *Cincinnati Daily Gazette,* October 1, 1872; *Congressional Globe,* 40th Cong., 3d sess., 1869, 769; *New York Herald,* January 5, 1871. For the opposite view, see Banks to Mary Banks, June 9, 1870, Banks Collection, LC.

27. *Congressional Globe,* 40th Cong., 3d sess., 1869, 1819; 41st Cong., 1st sess., 1869, 492, 712; and see *New York Herald,* April 11, 1869; E. Martin to Banks, April 21, 1869, Banks Collection, LC; J. Watson Webb to Banks, April 15, 1870, Francisco Ferrer to Banks, May 19, 1870, Banks Manuscripts, ISHL.

Grant personally sympathized with the Cuban rebels, but both he and Fish objected to the strong language in a report from Banks's committee in June 1870. Banks realized the possible consequences of opposing the Grant administration, but he felt obligated to defend his committee's report.

When the report came before the House on June 14, 1870, Banks delivered a speech that exhibited his native powers of eloquence and his thirty years' experience at oratory. In a clear voice, he impressed both the House and galleries with the strength of his argument. He praised the heroism of the Cuban insurgents and spoke of Spanish atrocities. He reminded his audience that Spain had given the Confederacy legitimacy by recognizing that a state of belligerence existed between the South and the United States. He accused the president of being timid but added that such timidity was understandable given that "Congress has taught the President that it was dangerous for him to entertain an opinion," a veiled reference to the recent impeachment of Andrew Johnson. The audience in the gallery cheered, laughed, stamped, and yelled approval. One admirer called it "glorious," while another said it was "noble." Some renewed the call for Banks to be considered as a presidential nominee, while others referred to his position as a "Banks doctrine." In spite of the excitement, the power of the White House prevailed, and the Cuban resolutions went down two days later by a vote of 77–101. Not only was this outcome a disappointment to Banks, it also meant that he was out of favor with his party.[28]

Banks's thinking on foreign affairs was ahead of his time. The United States purchased Denmark's West Indies (the Virgin Islands) in 1917. The United States also established protectorates over Cuba, Santo Domingo, and Haiti and developed a policy regarding the Panama Canal that Banks would have approved. Although Banks lived to see most of these changes, his strong expansionist views would not find expression until the next generation.

28. *Congressional Globe,* 41st Cong., 2d sess., 1870, 2238, 3770, 3773, 4103, Appendix, 1970, 454, 4506–7; *New York Herald,* June 15, 1870; Lewis Dent to Banks, June 14, 1870, W. O. Bartlett to Banks, June 15, 1870, D. E. Bishop to Banks, June 16, 1870, Charles James to Banks, June 15, 1870, Stephen Hoyt to Banks, June 15, 1870, Banks Collection, LC.

17

I Have Always Been a Republican

Nathaniel P. Banks was almost always chronically short of cash. He and Mary had run up considerable debts, and his income as a congressman did not come close to meeting their expenses. Hence he enthusiastically promoted a bill that would increase congressional pay. The reason he gave, at least publicly, for his support was that low salaries for congressmen threatened the legislative branch of the government with being "thrown into the hands of . . . speculators, monopolists, lobbyists, robbers, and thieves."[1]

Banks knew what he was talking about, for as chair of the House Committee on Foreign Affairs he was in position to help persons with commercial interests in foreign markets. It was not long before rumors emerged that Banks's interest in the Alaskan bill had been based on something more than his belief in America's manifest destiny. Uriah H. Painter, an investigative reporter who wrote for the *New York Sun* and the *Philadelphia Inquirer*, picked up gossip that Banks and others in positions of influence (possibly even Secretary Seward himself) had been given large bribes for their work in getting the Alaskan appropriation bill passed. Suspicion increased when it was discovered that some of the $7.2 million paid for the purchase apparently never made its way to the Russian treasury.[2]

1. *Congressional Globe,* 39th Cong., 1st sess., 1866, 1213, 4286–88; 42d Cong., 3d sess., 1873, 2104; also 41st Cong., 2d sess., 1870, 1196.

2. William A. Dunning, "Paying for Alaska: Some Unfamiliar Incidents in the Pro-

The House decided to investigate the charges through its Committee on Public Expenditures, but the committee members were reluctant to smear their colleagues and exonerated Banks and the others of all charges. Nevertheless, it was clear that the Russian minister, Baron Eduard De Stoeckl, had expended a substantial sum in promoting the measure. Although he spent most of the money on publicity and professional lobbyists, some of it appears to have been ended up in the hands of House members. Old Thaddeus Stevens, who died shortly afterward, was one; Banks was thought to be another. He was said to have received $8,000.[3]

During the war Banks had turned down bribes in New Orleans from persons interested in getting rich with the cotton trade. This decision was no small matter, for the Commission on Corrupt Practices had condemned Banks's predecessor, Benjamin F. Butler, and his replacement as commander of the Department of the Gulf, Stephen A. Hurlbut, for fiscal improprieties. It had even recommended that Hurlbut be court-martialed. Yet the commission found no evidence that Banks had acted improperly in the use of his extensive power, although it did criticize his interference with the state's political process. But Banks's tenure in Louisiana had come when his ambition to be president dictated that he maintain a clean record. Now his hopes for the White House were dim, and he was ready to take "gifts" from businessmen.[4]

Of the many opportunities he had to accept bribes, Banks is known to have accepted at least one. On New Year's Day 1867, Royal E. Robbins of

---

cess," *Political Science Quarterly* 27 (September 1912): 385–98; Farrar, *Annexation of Russian America*, 95–103.

3. U.S. Congress, House, Select Committee, *House Report No. 35: Alaska Investigation*, 40th Cong., 3d sess., 1–5; Current, *Old Thad Stevens*, 298–99, 313–16; Farrar, *Annexation of Russian America*, 100–102; Reinhard H. Luthin, "The Sale of Alaska," *Slavonic Review* 16 (July 1937): 168–82; Benjamin Platt Thomas, *Russo-American Relations, 1815–1867* (Baltimore: John Hopkins Press, 1930), 159–60; Golder, "Purchase of Alaska," 424; John W. Forney to Banks, November 7, 1875, Banks Collection, LC.

4. Smith and Brady, *Commission on Corrupt Practices*, 13–126; Harrington, *Fighting Politician*, 184; Banks to Mary Banks, September 7, 1865, November 22, 1867, R. E. Robbins to Banks, January 1, 1867, N. S. Howe to Banks, January 29, 1869, Banks Collection, LC. The commission's report was so damaging that its publication was suppressed by Stanton, although a portion of it dealing with Butler appeared in the *New Orleans Daily Crescent* under the title "Gen. Butler in New Orleans," on May 17, 1868.

the Waltham Watch Company wrote Banks a letter saying: "On Dec. 7 I took leave to address a note to you inclosing a check, which I hoped you would accept from me as partner in a compliment other friends of yours were about paying you but from which I had been perhaps accidentally excluded. . . . May I inquire what probability there is that the tax on Manufactures will be lowered?"[5]

During this period, Banks also pursued several private ventures for financial gain. The two men with whom he was most involved were Nathan Appleton and Charles B. Norton. Appleton and Norton handled the planning and financial side of these schemes, while Banks served as a public relations manager. As chair of the Committee on Foreign Affairs, Banks was valuable for the influence he could bring to bear on Congress and in the executive branch.[6]

Among the ventures the three men considered were a plan to construct grain elevators in Odessa, Russia, and an option to buy a Swedish formula for extracting alcohol from moss. Their most ambitious project, however, involved the first attempt to build a canal across the isthmus of Panama. Banks had always asserted that "the commerce of the United States—indeed, I may say, of the world—will center ultimately at the isthmus." He even claimed from the floor of the House that Louis Napoleon's venture into Mexico was motivated by his desire to extend French influence over Panama and eventually gain control of this strategically important region.[7]

Intrigued by Banks's interest in the Panama Canal, a banker, Charles Bowles, persuaded Banks and Appleton to attend the opening of the Suez Canal in the fall of 1869. The trip afforded Banks the opportunity to make a grand tour of Europe, something he had always wanted to do. He met Appleton in Paris in mid-September, and the two men traveled to Hamburg, Copenhagen, and Uppsala in Sweden before crossing the Gulf of Finland to arrive at St. Petersburg, where they reviewed the tsar's army. From St. Petersburg they made their way to Moscow, then

5. Robbins to Banks, January 1, 19, 1867, Banks Collection, LC.

6. Harrington, *Fighting Politician,* 193. Appleton was the son of the businessman who had constructed the cotton mill in Waltham at which both Banks and his father had worked.

7. Appleton, *Russian Life and Society,* 207–8; *Congressional Globe,* 40th Cong., 2d sess., 1868, 1220; 41st Cong., 2d sess., 1870, 3627; *New York Herald,* April 29, 1866; Norton to Banks, December 12, 1870; Banks Collection, LC.

Odessa, and finally Constantinople before crossing the Mediterranean to Port Said for the grand ceremony in mid-November.[8]

After numerous celebrations and honors, the two world travelers returned to Paris, where Appleton remained to begin work on forming the Darien Canal Company, a Franco-American venture. Banks returned to Washington to do what he could to promote the scheme with the administration. Among other things, he attempted to get the United States government to make surveys on the isthmus and made inquiries to the Department of State regarding the government's reaction to French investment in the project. He was pleased to cable Appleton that although the "enterprise must be American . . . participation of foreigners was unobjectionable."[9]

In spite of its initial success, the Panama project floundered. With many good investments at home, Wall Street bankers had little interest in taking chances with foreign companies. In addition, the Franco-Prussian War upset the Paris financial markets, making the financing of the Darien Canal Company difficult there. Although Appleton kept trying, Banks dropped out. Not only did he see little chance of personal profit, but after his speech on Cuba, his influence in the White House had waned.[10]

Throughout his life Banks had been a spokesman for the workingman. Now he was faced with a dilemma. The Republican party was beginning to drift away from its working-class roots. Banks realized that the shift in Republican ideology should be a cause for concern, but he had come to

8. Appleton, *Russian Life and Society,* 168–83.

9. *Congressional Globe,* 39th Cong., 2d sess., 1867, 321; 42d Cong., 3d sess., 1873, 719; Harrington, *Fighting Politician,* 194–95; Willis Fletcher Johnson, *Four Centuries of the Panama Canal* (New York: Henry Holt, 1906), 74–75; Banks to Nathan Appleton, January 31, 1870, Appleton to Banks, January 14, 1870, Banks to Mary Banks, October 1869, February 20, 1870, Sten Sternberg to Banks, August 11, 1870, J. B. Stewart to Banks, September 16, 1870, July 2, 1871, Charles B. Norton to Banks, June 3, December 12, 1870, Banks Collection, LC.

10. Harrington, *Fighting Politician,* 195; Nathan Appleton to Banks, December 9, 1875, November 8, 1888, Banks to Ferdinand de Lesseps, February 7, 1881, Banks Collection, LC; *Congressional Globe,* 42d Cong., 2d sess., 1872, 1148–49. For a definitive history of the Panama Canal, see David McCullough, *The Path between the Seas: The Creation of the Panama Canal, 1870–1914* (New York: Simon & Schuster, 1977).

depend on the support of business interests to ensure financial security for himself and his family.[11]

As a congressman, Banks worked energetically to pass legislation that favored business. Proclaiming that the protection of industry was "a national duty," Banks defended "New England Capitalists," who, he argued, were responsible for the region's economic growth. He also attacked the income tax, which chiefly affected the well-to-do, calling it "oppressive" and "unjust." In addition, he favored public grants to railroad promoters and declared that strikes by workingmen were "offensive."[12]

Remarkably, Banks managed to retain his labor following while courting the leaders of American capital. He was able to do this by repeating the oft-told story of the Bobbin Boy who trained at a "college with a water wheel in the basement." He spoke in favor of legislative expenditures that would improve the safety and working conditions of mining jobs. He also continued to arrange for public employment for laborers and made special appeals to Irish workers and Union veterans. He was able to do much of this in the normal course of affairs as a congressman. Many men from his district owed either a job, a pension, or even an artificial limb to Nathaniel P. Banks.[13]

The one pro-labor issue on which Banks equivocated was the movement for shorter working hours. Although he tried to convince a labor delegation that he supported a shorter working day, his comments were met with skepticism. One of the proponents of the eight-hour drive remarked that "in his heart of hearts, General Banks don't care whether the navy yards run ten, eight, or six hours a day. He wants to go to Con-

11. Foner, *Reconstruction,* 233–34, 315, 341, 449, 466–69; Harrington, *Fighting Politician,* 197–98. For examples of the strong working-class ties to the Republican party when it was first formed, see text of speeches given by "the Friends of Mr. Banks" at a banquet held in his honor in February 1856, *Boston Traveller,* February 29, 1856.

12. *Boston Morning Journal,* September 11, 1878; *Boston Daily Journal,* November 22, 1866; *New York Herald,* April 29, 1866; S. P. Hanscom to Banks, June 15, 1868, February 16, 1869, Banks Collection, LC; H. K. Horton to Banks, February 28, 1867, Banks Manuscripts, ISHL.

13. *Boston Herald,* September 2, 1894; *Congressional Globe,* 39th Cong., 1st sess., 1866, 171, 389, 752–53; 2d sess., 1867, 1269; 41st Cong., 2d sess., 1870, 1019–21; 42d Cong., 2d sess., 1872, 1030; 3d sess., 1872, 19–21, 816, Appendix, 85. For examples, see L. W. Barker to Banks, July 10, 1868, W. H. Simmons to Banks, March 2, 1877, John H. Roberts to Banks, November 8, 1877, G. W. M. Hall to Banks, February 15, 1878, Banks Collection, LC.

gress and dont believe Workingmen mean *votes* when they talk. The fact that he was a working man, has no more significance to us than the fact that Benedict Arnold was an American. . . . In General Banks[,] Capital has found an efficient and ambitious ally."[14]

Ever the politician, Banks responded to the charge by promising just before the election to support labor in Congress. The shorter-hour men threw their weight to him at the last minute, and Banks voted for two bills that established the eight-hour day for federal workers. Grant signed the second of these measures into law on June 25, 1868. Gleefully, Banks claimed that passage of the bill was "his own work."[15]

The labor vote ensured Banks's reelection to Congress, even though the Republican party continued to drift toward business. But as his relationship with President Grant soured, Banks began to reconsider whether the Republican party was right for him. Having been passed over repeatedly for either a cabinet post or a foreign mission alienated him further. "[I have] suffered [an] injustice greater than death," Banks complained to Mary.[16]

Banks had another reason to want to distance himself from Grant. Corruption, mismanagement, and continuing conflict over how to proceed with Reconstruction of the southern states caused a widening rift between the administration and elements of the Republican party. This rupture led to speculation that dissatisfied Republicans would try to form a new party that would affiliate with the Democrats. By 1872 the split became a reality with the formation of the Liberal Republican party, which reunited with the Democrats in supporting Horace Greeley for president in the campaign of that year.[17]

14. *Boston Daily Journal,* October 26, 1865. Banks's hesitancy to support the shorter-hour movement some twenty-five years earlier had curtailed his career as a newspaper editor when the *Lowell Democrat* folded (Harrington, *Fighting Politician,* 7).

15. David Montgomery, *Beyond Equality: Labor and the Radical Republicans, 1862–1872* (New York: Knopf, 1967), 244–69; *Congressional Globe,* 40th Cong., 1st sess., 1867, 425; 2d sess., 1868, 334–35; West, *Second Admiral,* 323; *Boston Weekly Voice,* March 22, 1866; Banks to Mary Banks, May 25, 1869, Banks Collection, LC. The victory was made even sweeter because Grant's decision to cut pay had been based on the recommendation of Banks's old foe David Dixon Porter.

16. *New York Daily Tribune,* October 18, 1872; Banks to Mary Banks, March 9, April 14, May 7, 11, 1869, Banks Collection, LC.

17. William S. McFeely, *Grant: A Biography* (New York: Norton, 1974), 380–83; Earle Dudley Ross, *The Liberal Republican Movement* (1910; reprint, Seattle: University of Washington Press, 1970), 129–49; *Boston Morning Journal,* June 13, 1870.

Banks was hesitant to join the new coalition, although he would have been welcomed for his experience and record. But in July Banks announced that he could not support Grant for reelection. The announcement did not receive as much attention as it deserved because it came right behind a similar one by Charles Sumner. Nevertheless, Greeley called Banks's letter the "best thing he had seen." Even Banks's old political antagonist Francis Bird termed it "timely and effective," and the *Boston Post* cried that it was a "rifle shot" that "comes like an earthquake shock to those who were satisfied to follow blindly after the Grant Administration." As expected, Grant was offended and ordered the administration press to assail the turncoat Banks. "A soured, disappointed politician, of inordinate ambition and vanity," the Grant newspapers began calling him.[18]

Despite the calumny, Banks entered the presidential campaign of 1872 with zest. Not since the Frémont race in 1856 had he played such an important role in a presidential contest. His ability as an orator was still one of his greatest assets, and he was much in demand as a speaker. Drawing large, enthusiastic crowds from Maine to Minnesota, Banks struck repeatedly at the Grant administration's corruption and record of high taxation. He wrote bitterly to Mary: "They are all thieves and assassins!" A few days later he again spoke to his wife of the "wickedness of the President & the people who are with him." In his speeches Banks emphasized defects in the Radical program of Reconstruction in the southern states. He also declared that the defeat of Grant would mean "peace, reconciliation with the south, and general prosperity." His speeches were replete with inconsistencies, evasions, and empty phrases, but the crowds loved them. Although Banks expressed some reservations about the candidate in private, publicly he promised that a Greeley administration would be "one of the wisest and most brilliant."[19]

18. Baum, *Civil War Party System,* 168–69; Harrington, *Fighting Politician,* 201; *Boston Post,* August 2, 1872; *New York Herald,* November 6, 1872; *New York Daily Tribune,* August 2, 1872; F. W. Bird to Banks, August 2, 1872, S. P. Hanscom to Banks, August 4, 1872, Banks Collection, LC. Sumner publicly endorsed Greeley on July 29, 1972, in a letter urging black voters in North Carolina to vote against Grant's reelection (Donald, *Charles Sumner and the Rights of Man,* 551–52).

19. *Cincinnati Daily Gazette,* October 1, 1872; *New York Daily Tribune,* September 2, 9, 13, 1872; *Springfield Daily Republican,* September 13, 1872; Banks to Mary Banks, June 28, 1871, October 4, 9, 10, 1872, January 1, 1874, Banks Collection, LC.

Greeley lost the election. Grant carried all but six states with a popular vote of 3.6 million against 2.8 million for Greeley. Among the states swept along by the landslide was Massachusetts, and for the first time in seventeen elections, Banks lost as well. Although he ran two thousand votes ahead of Greeley in his district, Banks was still forty-five hundred behind Daniel W. Gooch, who won.[20]

The loss of his congressional seat in 1872 left Banks without income and with an uncertain future. At the age of fifty-seven, he was too old to start out in the practice of law or to establish a business. To pick up the slack, Banks hit the lecture circuit with the American Literary Bureau and later with James Redpath's famous lyceum agency. His fee was normally $100 per appearance, which kept the family in necessities but did not allow for the repayment of past debts. It did not take long for Banks to decide to try a political comeback.[21]

Banks's defection during the presidential campaign left him with few friends in the Republican party. Grant, Fish, and Gooch were especially hostile and prevented Banks from reestablishing his ties with Republicans. The Democrats would have been glad to have him, but that party was historically weak in New England. Another alternative was to run as an independent, but Banks was hindered in this regard by his support of a pay increase for members of Congress and for having voted for business interests as a congressman. The one thing Banks did have going for him was the continued corruption of the Grant administration. Independents generally do not do well at the polls, but Banks had a way of charming the electorate. As a consequence, liberals, Democrats, and labor reformers all supported him when he ran for the Massachusetts senate in the fall of 1873.[22]

The race had a personal meaning for Banks, for the Republican opponent was George W. Copeland, a law partner of Daniel Gooch. Seven months earlier, Copeland had publicly accused Banks of being drunk at a political rally in Maine. The charge was not true, for Banks had been

20. Baum, *Civil War Party System,* 179; Foner, *Reconstruction,* 502–4, 508; *New York Daily Tribune,* November 7, 1872.

21. For Banks's spending habits and life on the lecture circuit, see miscellaneous bills, advertisements, and itineraries, Banks Collection, LC.

22. *Congressional Globe,* 42d Cong., 3d sess., 1873, 1904, 2104; *New York Herald,* December 5, 1872. See Hugh Smith to Banks, June 23, 1873, George R. Proctor to Banks, July 12, 1873, Banks Collection, LC.

ill and under a doctor's care. Calling Copeland a liar to his face, Banks collected testimony that contradicted affidavits gathered by his accuser. Public sympathy for Banks and reaction to the scandals in the Grant administration gave him a thumping victory.[23]

Banks's triumph attracted a good bit of attention, although his seat in the state senate was relatively minor in comparison to his earlier posts. Freed from the political debts he had accumulated while in the Republican party, Banks came out strongly for the shorter-hour movement. He seemed to rediscover his roots and spoke effectively for the workingman. He also became something of a conservationist by arguing for the preservation of the Old South Church in Boston, which a group of developers proposed to tear down. "I don't know who will be raised up to throw light upon this dark place, but I will stake my life he will not come out of the ranks of [rich] city men who petition us to pass this bill," Banks exhorted. "You must look where God looked for servants for his Son, among the lowly." Old South still stands today, in part because of Banks's eloquent defense.[24]

Banks added to his credentials by speaking out for women's suffrage after a meeting with Elizabeth Cady Stanton. He was also a member of a joint committee that drew up a state law mandating a ten-hour workday. Although "disguised in petticoats" because it applied only to women and children, the measure was a landmark in the shorter-hour movement as the first state statute of its kind.[25]

Fresh from his success as a reform candidate, Banks ran in the congressional off-year election of 1874 against Gooch. Aided by the Democrats, civil service advocates, and labor reformers, he campaigned as "the poor man who is the poor man's friend." Banks was lucky, for the voters

23. Appleton, *Russian Life and Society,* 172; *Boston Daily Advertiser,* October 15, 21, 23, 27, 31, 1873; *Boston Daily Journal,* October 15, 1866; *Boston Post,* December 17, 1866; *Springfield Daily Republican,* October 20, 27, December 15, 1866; William Binney to Banks, October 12, 1866, also congratulatory messages, Banks Collection, LC; L. Barker to Banks, January 4, 1867, Banks Manuscripts, ISHL. Banks's commitment to the temperance movement seems to have been sincere, particularly since it continued after he had gained substantial political success (e.g., *Boston Post,* October 2, 1851).

24. *Boston Daily Advertiser,* February 12, May 15, July 1, 1874; *Boston Daily Globe,* April 24, 1874.

25. Harrington, *Fighting Politician,* 204–5; *Boston Daily Advertiser,* February 11, 13, 14, 27, March 21, 27, 1874.

repudiated the corruption of the Grant administration and expressed their dissatisfaction with the hard times caused by the Panic of 1873, which, rightly or wrongly, they blamed on the administration. "Grantism Judged," read the front-page headline of the deceased Greeley's paper, the *New York Daily Tribune*. "Overwhelming Administration Rout. Even Massachusetts Goes Democratic." As an independent, Banks was helped by the anti-Grant vote, for he carried every town in the district save Gooch's own and won by six thousand votes.[26]

Back in Congress Banks could have become a strong leader of the independent reform movement as "the champion of labor in opposition to monopoly." Supporters urged him to fight the Republican tariff, which they considered to be an indirect tax on the consumer. Banks was so popular that he was mentioned as an independent candidate for Speaker of the House in 1875 and even as a third-party presidential possibility.[27]

Free from the requirements of party discipline that tend to polarize positions, Banks could afford to assume a more moderate stance. This direction was particularly effective in promoting attempts to heal the wounds of the Civil War. As a state senator, Banks had come to the defense of Charles Sumner when the latter advocated the return of captured battle flags to the southern states. As a congressman, Banks participated in a ceremony on June 17, 1875, in which Union veterans presented a battle flag to the surviving members of a Confederate regiment. The occasion provided the opportunity to explore the possibility of a new political party based on the principles of conciliation and composed of veterans from both North and South. Among those who favored such a move was Lucius Q. C. Lamar, the Mississippian who had delivered a gracious speech on the occasion of Sumner's funeral.[28]

26. Foner, *Reconstruction*, 523; *New York Daily Tribune*, November 4, 5, 1874; *Frank Leslie's Illustrated Newspaper*, November 7, 1874 (supplement); Charles Ripley to Banks, September 21, 1874, Banks Collection, LC.

27. Harrington, *Fighting Politician*, 206–7; Ross, *Liberal Republican Movement*, 155; Henry Evans to Banks, February 12, 1876, Banks Manuscripts, ISHL. This was the same tariff issue that had led to South Carolina's doctrine of nullification and the subsequent polarization of the North and South some forty years earlier.

28. George Henry Haynes, *Charles Sumner* (Philadelphia: George W. Jacobs, 1909), 431n; Harrington, *Fighting Politician*, 206; Edward Mayes, *Lucius Q. C. Lamar: His Life, Times, and Speeches* (Nashville: Methodist Episcopal Church, South, 1896), 257; Pierce, *Memoir and Letters of Charles Sumner*, 4:568; M. F. Carr, quoted in J. B. Emerson to Banks, November 11, 1874, Banks to W. P. Aspinwall, November 5, 1874, L. M.

Banks believed that the new party had potential and made a number of conciliatory remarks, which prompted "A Set of old Rebels" from Decatur, Alabama, to write to express their support for him as the next "Democratic President" of the United States. They believed that "a man uttering such sentiments as you used . . . must be an honest man and a Christian gentleman." Stonewall Jackson's adjutant, Henry Kyd Douglas, wrote expressing his support of Banks's comments. The movement made enough progress to justify the convening of a formal conference at the Parker House in Boston in August 1875, which resulted in formation of the National Union party with the motto "Fraternity, Forgiveness, and Peace." Banks publicly stated his sympathy for the party and the aims for which it stood, going so far as to write Jefferson Davis in an attempt to recruit him to the lecture circuit. The idea, which had been suggested initially by Redpath, was "to bring prominent representative men of the North and South together in leading Northern and Southern cities." The result would be beneficial to "a national point of view."[29]

Despite these overtures, Banks realized that the new party lacked both the leadership and the constituency it needed to survive. Furthermore, the memory of his defeat in 1872 and the resultant loss of a steady income was still fresh in his mind. He did not care to risk his job by casting his lot with a fledgling political effort and was tired of the life of an independent. "A man without a party, politically, is without a home," Banks complained as the 1876 congressional races heated up. Because Massachusetts was normally Republican, Banks decided to become a Republican again. "I am a Republican, out and out a Republican," he declared, "and, however much we have differed in the past, I have always been a Republican."[30]

Harris to Banks, December 29, 1874[?], Banks Collection, LC. For opposition, see Burke A. Hinsdale, ed., *The Works of James Abram Garfield* (Boston: James R. Osgood, 1882), 234–39.

29. Harrington, *Fighting Politician,* 206; "A Set of old Rebels," to Banks, January 24, 1876, Banks Collection, LC; Henry Kyd Douglas to Banks, January 17, 1876, Banks Manuscripts, ISHL.

30. See *Congressional Record,* 44th Cong., 1st sess., 1876, 408–10; *Boston Herald,* October 4, 1876; Banks to Jefferson Davis, August 30, 1875, in Dunbar Rowland, ed., *Jefferson Davis, Constitutionalist: His Letters, Papers and Speeches,* 10 vols. (New York: J. J. Little & Ives for the Mississippi Department of Archives and History, 1923), 7:452;

His decision astounded everyone. Democrats and independents were indignant. They saw his defection as another indication that Banks was no more than a slave to political expediency. One disgruntled constituent wrote Banks to express his indignation in rhyme:

> Can you tell me what Strange fascination
> Or mental depression or hallucination
> It is that controls you and forces you back
> To the unenvied fate of an Old Party Hack?
> I had hoped that, as once you [were] safely free from it,
> You would not return, like a dog to his vomit.[31]

Although the Republicans were less than enthusiastic over his return, the old Banks magic still worked. Aided by the fact that his former enemies in the Grant administration were no longer in power, Banks emerged as a Republican nominee for the House of Representatives after a deadlock between the two front-runners. He received the nomination on the twelfth ballot and coasted to election in November 1876, defeating the Democratic party that had supported him just two years before.[32]

Veteran commentators noted that Banks's luck "positively bewilders all calculations and confounds all calculators." As an independent, Banks had denounced businessmen, saying that during the Civil War "the corporationists had gained a foothold, and for fifteen years had fed and fattened upon the public." Now a "Republican, pure and simple," Banks quickly returned to his old ways of assisting merchants and industrialists. Reversing his earlier stand, he fought attempts to cut the tariff as a member of the Ways and Means Committee from 1877 to 1879. He also took the straight Republican position in the presidential contest between Rutherford B. Hayes and Samuel J. Tilden, which resulted in the election of the former. And if all of that was not enough, he set aside his ear-

---

Stephen Hoyt to Banks, January 15, 1876, Banks Collection, LC; Marcus Cook to Banks, June 30, 1876, Banks Manuscripts, ISHL.

31. E. B. Smith to Banks, October 1, 1876, Banks Collection, LC.

32. Worthington Chauncey Ford, ed., *Letters of Henry Adams, 1858–1891,* 2 vols. (1930; reprint, New York: Kraus Reprint Co., 1969), 1:299; Harrington, *Fighting Politician,* 207; *Boston Herald,* October 4, 1876; *New York Daily Tribune,* November 9, 10, 18, 1876.

lier comments regarding reconciliation and returned to sectional appeals, even waving the bloody shirt.[33]

This time his luck ran out. It was clear to everyone by 1878 that Banks was a political chameleon who had changed his colors once too often. Although he went into the Republican nominating convention seeking his tenth congressional term with nearly half the votes, he could not squeeze out a majority. His competition joined forces and sent him down to defeat on the fifteenth ballot, fifty to fifty-one. Although Banks's friends felt that his opponent, S. Z. Bowman, a young railroad attorney, was "all *Gush*—and weak as water," Banks was finished. He was not old by political standards, just sixty-two when he lost to Bowman in November 1878, but he already seemed a member of a bygone generation.[34]

33. Harrington, *Fighting Politician,* 206–8; *Congressional Record,* 44th Cong., 2d sess., 1877, 2014–15; *New York Daily Tribune,* September 16, October 21, 1876; *Boston Morning Journal,* September 11, 1878; *Boston Herald,* October 4, 1876; *Rochester Daily Union and Advertiser,* December 17, 1875; A. F. Davol to Banks, January 29, 1878, Banks Collection, LC.

34. Harrington, *Fighting Politician,* 208; *Boston Morning Journal,* September 11, 1878; *New York Daily Tribune,* October 21, 1876; *New York Times,* October 4, 1878; L. Stetson to Banks, September 3, 1878, Banks Collection, LC. Banks eventually announced support of Bowman in a letter dated October 18, 1878, Banks Manuscripts, ISHL. The national elections of 1878 were not kind to former Union officers in general. The *New Orleans Democrat* reprinted an editorial on January 31, 1879, from a "Republican paper" lamenting that only three senators were former U.S. Army officers while seventeen had been generals in the Confederate service.

18

The General

"The General," as everyone now called Nathaniel P. Banks, surrendered his congressional seat and returned to Waltham in March 1879. Happy to have time to be with his family, he also looked forward to doing some reading that he had put aside in the press of his legislative duties. Although he had offers from several publishers, the General felt no desire to write his memoirs. Instead, he kept his distance from the swirl of printed charges and countercharges that characterized the period and offered no replies to those whose works presented him in a poor light.[1]

Banks's health remained good, although he had put on some weight and was carrying 180 pounds on his five-foot, eight-inch frame. Meanwhile, the three surviving children were grown and situated on their own. Joseph Frémont became a civil engineer and moved west. The youngest daughter, Mary, married an Episcopal clergyman, Paul Ster-

1. Harrington, *Fighting Politician,* 209; *Boston Morning Journal,* August 28, 1886; Banks diary, December 22, 1881, newspaper clipping, January [13], 1886, Banks Collection, LC. For offers to publish his memoirs, see S. Thorndike Rice, editor of the *North American Review,* to Banks, November 8, 1877, Banks Collection, LC, and James Grant Wilson, editor of *Appleton's Dictionary of American Biography,* to Banks, May 8, 1886, Manuscripts and Rare Books Department, College of William and Mary. During this period Banks also refused to allow his name to be used for product endorsements, which may have offered another source of income (E. L. Sweeter, "Florence Sewing Machine Company," to Banks, March 5, 1877, Banks Papers, MAHS; also see Banks's letter of May 6, 1876, and G. M. Savage to Banks, February 4, 1856, both in Banks Papers, ISHL).

ling, and the oldest, Maude, had become an actress in Boston. Clearly, Banks's early flair for the dramatic was in the blood.[2]

In recognition of his long record of service and prominence in the Republican party, President Rutherford B. Hayes appointed Banks United States marshal for the Boston district. This was a job Banks wanted, for the pay was good ($6,000 a year) and the work easy. Banks served as a U.S. marshal for almost ten years. The very fact that he was able to hold on to this patronage appointment so long, even during the Democratic term of Grover Cleveland, was evidence of the high regard with which he was held. As Mary pointed out when she asked President Cleveland to defer his removal in 1885, "His life and his energies have been devoted to his country . . . he has made no provision for the future, & now, almost worn-out with service, he finds he has nothing for himself or for those who are dependent on him."[3]

Cleveland reappointed Banks for two years, but the General had to petition the president again in 1887 for a new appointment. More than 350 of his friends recommended that he be retained in office, and Banks helped his cause by praising the Democratic president publicly. Cleveland gave Banks one more year, but his age was beginning to tell, and Attorney General Augustus H. Garland had reason to believe that Banks should be replaced as soon as possible for the public good.[4]

An investigation by Garland in 1887 found conditions in the marshal's office to be deplorable. Although the examiners concluded that the General's integrity was "unimpeachable," they found that Banks had not adequately supervised the day-to-day operations of the office. More specifically, he had turned over the office to his chief clerk, William D. Pool. It turned out that Pool and three deputies had collected on "false, fraudulent and fictitious" expense account items "for services not performed and travel not made." One deputy, Frederick D. Gallupe, had created

2. Harrington, *Fighting Politician,* 214 n. 45; Maude Banks playbills for performances in Waltham on May 6, 1889, June 1, [18??], WPL. Banks's weight is recorded in his journal for October 1880, Banks Collection, LC. For Maude's career as an actress, see Eugene Tompkins, *The History of the Boston Theater, 1854–1901* (Boston: Houghton Mifflin, 1908).

3. Harrington, *Fighting Politician,* 209; Banks to Thomas Russell, March 31, 1879, Isaac S. Morse to Banks, December 7, 1878, Banks Collection, LC.

4. Harrington, *Fighting Politician,* 210.

paperwork on bogus cases to collect additional fees. There were no standard accounting procedures to ensure the proper management of funds. Banks shrugged off the criticisms, but the Justice Department forced him to fire Pool and two of the deputies. In turn, they sued him for unpaid fees, which involved the General in a legal controversy that plagued him until he died.[5]

Remarkably, Banks's career as a politician was not finished. Redistricting placed Waltham in the Fifth Congressional District in 1888, and its representative, Edgar D. Hayden, chose not to run. After managing to win the Republican nomination over three opponents, Banks went on to face the Democratic candidate, Thomas Wentworth Higginson, in the general election. The Democrats called Banks a "spoilsman" and noted that the General was slipping mentally. The Republicans countered by declaring that Higginson was a "miserable mugwump." As it turned out, both candidates ran even with their tickets, which meant that Banks came out on top in a district that usually went Republican.[6]

Banks stayed in the background during the Fifty-first Congress, for his health, both physical and mental, was failing. When he tried to speak, he wandered so badly that the Democrats circulated a verbatim report of one of his speeches as campaign material against him. With the exception of delivering a few brief eulogies at the funerals of old friends and introducing a joint resolution calling for the publication of a history of black troops in the war, the General sat, listened, and voted with his party.[7]

5. Quoted in Harrington, *Fighting Politician,* 210; Garland to Banks, April 22 (with draft of answer, April 30), 1887, Pool's statement, July 1, 1887, Letters to Banks from L. D. Gallupe and C. H. Snow, December 17, 1887, M. J. Dunham, July 26, 1888, J. Altheus Johnson, February 21, 1889, J. R. Garrison, July 6, September 14, 1891, Banks to O. A. Galvin, March 5, 1891, Owen A. Salvin to George M. Stearns, June 28, 1887, Banks to Editor, *Boston Herald* (draft), June 1888, and other documents, Banks Collection, LC.

6. Harrington, *Fighting Politician,* 211; *Boston Daily Advertiser,* September 19, 1888; *New York Evening Post,* November 3, 6, 1888. Among the many letters of congratulations in the Banks Collection, LC, are ones from John Hay and Henry Cabot Lodge (October 11 and October 15, 1888, respectively). Higginson had been the colonel of the First South Carolina Colored Volunteers during the Civil War and wrote a classic book on his experience *(Army Life in a Black Regiment).*

7. *Boston Daily Advertiser,* September 19, 1888; *Congressional Record,* 51st Cong., 1st sess., 1890, 3564, 6464, 10175; *General Banks on the Surplus,* Speech of October 4,

Banks made a run at the nomination for a second term in 1890, but the infirmities of old age were too evident, and he lost out in the convention. Fortunately, Congress voted him a pension of $100 per month, which helped tide him over. His health declining, Banks performed his last official act in January 1893 when he cast a vote as a presidential elector for Benjamin Harrison.[8]

Although the diagnosis is of more recent origin, the General was probably suffering from Alzheimer's disease. Insidious in onset, the disorder usually follows a progressive, deteriorating course that includes the loss of intellectual abilities such as memory, judgment, and abstract thought. In the early stages, intellectual impairment may be the only apparent deficit, for persons suffering from Alzheimer's disease usually remain neat and well-groomed and behave in socially appropriate ways. In the later stages, there may be changes in personality and behavior. When the sufferer becomes unable to care for himself, death inevitably follows.[9]

At first the outward changes the disorder produced in Banks were hardly noticeable and he was frequently invited to attend public events at which his familiar appearance and dignified bearing added to the occasion. But his failing mental capacity became evident when he engaged in conversation or attempted to make the briefest of remarks. An example of the General's deteriorating condition survives in the form of a reply drafted on the back of an envelope in response to an invitation from the Knights Templar to attend a social function on June 24, 1893:

1888, Banks Collection, LC. But see Banks to Charles Brigham, July 30, 1890 (Banks Manuscripts, ISHL), as an indication that at times his mind was still sharp. Banks was so short of money that his daughter Maude arranged a loan of $100 for the congressman through one of her friends (Mrs. Cook to Maude Banks, February 28, 1889, Banks Collection, LC).

8. Starbuck, *Picturesque Waltham,* 46; *Boston Daily Advertiser,* September 24, 1890, September 1, 3, 1894; *Congressional Record,* 51st Cong., 2d sess., 1891, 1557, 2563–64; Letters to Banks from Nathan Warren, September 6, 24, 1890, Isaac H. Morse, September 17, 1890, E. Winward, September 21, 1890, George D. Robinson to Marcus C. Cook, January 15, 1891, H. L. Dawes to Cook, January 19, 1891, Cook to Banks, January 20, 1891, Copy of the bill awarding Banks his pension, February 18, 1891, Banks Collection, LC.

9. *New York Herald,* September 2, 1894. The formal terminology is Primary Degenerative Dementia of the Alzheimer Type (American Psychiatric Association, *Diagnostic*

> The pressure of personal engagements relating to official and public affairs that could not properly or quite honorably be postponed has prevented my fulfillment of an implied and still pending engagement in regard to as promptly and as satisfactorily to myself & friends here and others in my neighborhood as I desired to make it. Though still embarrassed in regard thereto & not yet absolutely certain of being able to comply with your request I shall take great pleasure in meeting you & the patriotic supporters of [here the draft ends].[10]

Despite his deteriorating health, the General continued to fill his little notebooks with quotations, facts, figures, and other bits of information. On April 18, 1893, he made note of three words, their definitions, and the Latin stem from which all three were derived. The entry was the last one he made, for his mind was failing rapidly. Before long, it was necessary for a member of his family or an attendant to be with him constantly. In one last display of self-reliance, Banks eluded his attendant on the day after Christmas 1893 and rode the trolley to Lynn, Massachusetts, some twenty miles from his home in Waltham. The police in Lynn found him wandering about and returned the General to his home.[11]

The family took Banks to Deer Isle, Maine, in the early summer of 1894, hoping that the change in climate might help. There were no signs of improvement, and his condition continued to worsen. The family brought him home in August, but his behavior became less and less manageable. Finally, they had no choice but to place him in the McLean Asylum for the Insane. After three days there it became evident that he would not survive much longer. By Thursday, August 30, his condition had deteriorated to the point that he could not recognize members of his family, and he was taken to his home on Main Street in Waltham. On Friday evening it seemed that the end was near, but the General rallied, not once but twice. By three o'clock the next morning he was almost comatose. Mary Palmer, his wife of almost half a century, was at his bedside,

---

and Statistical Manual of Mental Disorders, 3d ed., rev. [New York: American Psychiatric Association, 1987], 119–21).

10. Draft on back of an envelope postmarked May 12, 1893, Banks Collection, LC. Banks was made a life member of the Knights Templar on April 11, 1874.

11. *New York Herald*, September 2, 1894; Banks diaries, Banks Collection, LC. The words were "industry," "induviæ," and "indue."

as was his daughter Maude. At eight o'clock Saturday morning, September 1, 1894, Nathaniel P. Banks died. He was seventy-eight years of age.[12]

The General's death made the front page of the evening paper. He was remembered for his "versatility" and organizational skills. The paper termed his retreat before Stonewall Jackson in 1862 "masterful" and duly noted the victory at Port Hudson. It took pains to point out that the Red River campaign "was not of Banks's own planning." His organization of the Corps d'Afrique, by which he allowed the "valor and efficiency of colored men as soldiers" to be recognized, was cited as the "one notable act in Louisiana." His effort to establish the Free State was not mentioned, and his career in Congress after the war was covered only briefly.[13]

In Waltham, signs of mourning were displayed conspicuously in public places. The post office, Asbury Temple, the Grand Army Hall, and several other buildings were hung with draped flags and bunting entwined with crepe. Many shops suspended business, and people crowded the street to pay their last respects. At the Parker House in Boston, Banks's chair was left vacant by the members of the Boston Club when they assembled for their usual Saturday afternoon meeting. Among the many condolences was a letter from President Grover Cleveland. The sculptor William Ordway Partridge took a death mask of the General on Monday evening, just as he had done for Victor Hugo nine years earlier.[14]

Inside the house on Main Street the family admitted a few close personal friends. The body reposed in a coffin covered in black broadcloth and entirely devoid of display, in accordance with the wishes of the family. Episcopal services were conducted at eight o'clock Tuesday morning in the Banks residence by the rector of Christ's Church in Waltham. At nine o'clock, the remains were conveyed to Asbury Temple and placed within a railing in front of the chancel. Until one o'clock that afternoon,

12. *Boston Herald*, April 2, 1894; *New York Herald*, September 2, 1894.

13. *Boston Evening Transcript*, September 1, 1894. See also obituaries in the *Boston Herald*, *New York Herald*, and *New York Times*, September 2, 1894.

14. *Boston Herald*, September 2, 1894; *Boston Evening Transcript*, September 4, 1894; *Waltham Daily Free Press*, September 4, 1894.

a continuous stream of citizens passing up the right aisle and down the left paid their last respects to the General.[15]

George S. Boutwell, Banks's old friend and former governor of Massachusetts, delivered the eulogy, after which the funeral procession marched up Main Street to Newton and then left on Grove to the cemetery. Banks's remains were laid to rest on a hill not far from the graves of his parents and four brothers who had preceded him in death. Mary Theodosia Palmer survived the General by seven years. She died in Waltham on January 31, 1901, eighty-five years and a day after Nathaniel P. Banks was born.[16]

September 16, 1908, was a sunny, bright day in Boston. An American flag covered a statue on the grounds of the statehouse while a large crowd waited in eager anticipation. A band from the Waltham Watch Company entertained the assembly with marches and martial airs. Just after two o'clock a group of more than two dozen officials made their way through the throng to a small platform erected for the occasion. They were here to dedicate a statue of one of Massachusetts's most illustrious sons—Nathaniel P. Banks.[17]

The band struck up the "General Banks March," and Paul Sterling, Jr., the General's young grandson, pulled the cord that held the flag. It fell away, revealing a bronze statue of Banks standing in front of a marble chair as if he had just risen to speak. The acting governor, Eben S. Draper, rose to accept the statue for the commonwealth of Massachusetts. Draper called attention to Banks's long and almost continuous career in public office: election to the Massachusetts legislature, elevation

15. *Boston Evening Transcript,* September 4, 1894.

16. Ibid.; *Waltham Daily Free-Press Tribune,* February 1, 1901. A picture of Asbury Temple draped in mourning for Banks's wake is on page 563 in Petersen, *Waltham Rediscovered.* N. P. Banks, Sr., died on April 24, 1857, Rebecca Greenwood Banks on April 30, 1873. The deceased siblings included Miles Greenwood Banks, who died in infancy, Gardner Banks, who followed Nathaniel to New Orleans and died of heart disease on July 14, 1871, and William Hazlett Banks, who died of "bilious fever" on September 26, 1862. Lieutenant Hiram B. Banks, the fourth brother, was killed at the Battle of Second Bull, but his body was never recovered. Genealogical information furnished by Elizabeth D. Castner, archivist, WPL.

17. *Boston Evening Transcript,* September 16, 1908.

to the governorship of the state, and ten terms of service in the United States Congress. Banks had accomplished all of this in spite of the lack of a formal education and the necessity of going to work in the cotton mills of Waltham while still a young boy. Draper mentioned Banks's service during the Civil War only in passing. When the governor finished, the Reverend Paul Sterling, Sr., Banks's son-in-law, stepped forward to offer an official prayer. The band played "America."[18]

The crowd and dignitaries then moved into the statehouse, where Herbert Parker, secretary of the navy and former attorney general of Massachusetts, delivered an oration in Banks's honor. Parker spoke for almost an hour, during which he declared Banks a born leader who enjoyed none of the fortunes of an advantageous birth. "From his early boyhood the gaining of a livelihood was the first necessity of his thought," Parker informed the audience. "Dominating the limitations of his youth, he gave assurance of that great future which he already grasped in making himself master of opportunities." The oration was a fitting tribute to a man who had served his state and nation well. Banks's "power to sway the minds of men, to lead them wheresoever his voice might call," Parker declared, "was almost without example in New England, and might have raised him to dizziest heights of personal ambition and aggrandizement." But, Parker added, the General "sought no renown, he craved no reward, save that which might be part of the fame and glory of his State and nation, and there his memory is secure."[19]

Banks's statue stood on the corner of the statehouse grounds until 1950, when it was removed to make room for a parking lot. The statue was relocated to Waltham, where it reposed in a peat bog at the rear of the city incinerator for several months until the Waltham City Council approved the funds needed to erect it on a pedestal in the city common. Banks's statue stands there today.[20]

18. *Record of the Dedication of the Statue of Major General Nathaniel Prentiss Banks, September 16, 1908* (Boston: Wright, Potter Printing Co., 1909), 23–26; *Boston Evening Transcript,* September 16, 1908. For more on the statue, including its design and controversy regarding the inscription on its base, see the *Waltham Daily Free Press-Tribune,* July 8, 17, 20, 1908, and the *Boston Herald,* September 17, 1908.

19. *Record of the Dedication,* 29–58.

20. Elizabeth D. Castner, archivist, WPL, to the author, November 6, 1990; also *Waltham News-Tribune,* November 9, 10, 1950.

• • •

Nathaniel P. Banks accomplished much in his lifetime: congressman for ten terms, three times governor of Massachusetts, the first Republican Speaker of the House, and major general of United States Volunteers. These were remarkable achievements for a man who lacked a formal education, the benefit of family connections, or the springboard of a personal fortune. Nevertheless, this "master of opportunities" fell short of his ultimate goal, the White House, and he eventually squandered the promise of his early career.

Reviewing the many twists and turns of Banks's long life, Fred Harvey Harrington blamed expediency for Banks's failure to realize his grand expectations. "Bewildering as these shifts may seem," Harrington asserted, "they all fit into a political pattern of ambition and survival. Banks needed to hold office in order to pay his bills, and he desperately desired to be a famous man. In consequence, he was usually willing to reshape 'principles' to suit the occasion, to deal in compromises and reversals, catch phrases, weasel words, and political tricks."[21]

Harrington was right, as far as he went. But Harrington's analysis fails to explain why a man of exceptional talent and enormous ambition ended his career as a discredited political hack and the inept administrator of a government sinecure.

It is true that Banks was expedient, but his major flaw was an inability to learn from his mistakes. He owed much of his popularity to superficial display, and the more popular Banks became, the more he tended to confuse the appearance of success with hard-earned accomplishment. As a result, he consistently overestimated the importance of his achievements and underestimated the magnitude of his failures.

The mold was cast early. As a founding member of a debating society and an aspiring actor on the Boston stage, Banks learned that the pretense of conviction can be more important than conviction itself. After all, the debater is taught to defend any position, regardless of its merit, and the actor is speaking someone else's truth, not his own.

Banks's early achievements in the political arena—Speaker of the Massachusetts General Court, president of the 1853 Massachusetts constitutional convention, and Speaker of the U.S. House of Representa-

21. Harrington, *Fighting Politician*, viii, 212.

tives—reinforced the initial lesson. Presiding officers rely on tact, verbal skill, and the capacity for compromise, and Banks was perfect in that role, for he looked good, said the right things, and was the king of compromise. In fact, Banks was so adept that he gained the national spotlight without having to defend his beliefs. It is not surprising, therefore, that Banks failed to develop convictions of his own.[22]

The pretense of conviction may be expected, even encouraged, in politics, but the same characteristic can be a serious liability in the military. Such was the case when Banks became a major general in the army and confused the pomp and ceremony of a parade with making hard decisions the exercise of command dictates.[23]

This shortcoming was evident almost from the day he assumed command of the Department of the Shenandoah in 1862. When Stonewall Jackson attacked at Front Royal and sent Banks's men scampering back to Winchester, he rejected the sound advice of one of his most able lieutenants and remained in place. "No sir!" Banks replied to Colonel Gordon's entreaty that he order a withdrawal. "The enemy is not as remorseless as the public!" Banks found out the next day just how wrong he was when Jackson overran his positions around Winchester and sent the Union army reeling toward the Potomac. Although the rout was complete, Banks still could not bring himself to admit that he had been defeated. The retreat from Winchester was "one of the most remarkable [movements] that has occurred or will occur during the war," he boasted.[24]

Neither Banks's luck nor his ability to learn from experience improved after his transfer to Louisiana. An initial success against a greatly outnumbered Rebel army under Richard Taylor in the spring of 1863 prompted Banks to order an all-out assault on the fortifications at Port Hudson when he invested that place several weeks later. Banks's hasty and ill-advised decision resulted in approximately two thousand Union casualties. Blaming the affair on his subordinates rather than accepting

22. The one exception was his vote against the Kansas-Nebraska Bill in 1854, which, as a Democrat, he was expected to support (Harrington, *Fighting Politician,* 19).

23. For an opposing view, which asserts that Banks's experience as a politician served him well as a commanding general, see Williams, *Lincoln Finds a General,* 5:30–31.

24. Gordon, *From Brook Farm to Cedar Mountain,* 225; Banks to Mary Banks, May 28, 1862, Banks Collection, LC.

responsibility himself, Banks ordered another assault eighteen days later with similar results. Combined Federal losses for the two assaults came to approximately 3,750 dead and wounded, as compared to 600 for the Confederates. In no other campaign during the Civil War was there a more disproportionate ratio of casualties between the two sides.[25]

Erroneously believing that the capture of Port Hudson would be remembered as one of the decisive battles of the war, Banks next moved to occupy several backwater outposts along the Texas coast. "I may say for the first time in my life," he wrote his wife after capturing Brownsville, "I believe our success to have one of great importance to the Country." Again, he was wrong. Ulysses S. Grant ordered most of the outposts abandoned as soon as he became general in chief five months later.[26]

Banks's venture up the Red River in 1864 demonstrated conclusively that he was incapable of learning from past mistakes. Making the same errors he had made two years earlier in the Shenandoah Valley, Banks divided his forces, underestimated his opponent, and failed to gather intelligence. Routed at Mansfield, the Union army fell back to Pleasant Hill, where the Rebels themselves were thrown back in confusion. "The rout of the enemy was complete," Banks reported to Washington, but he failed to follow up his advantage and retreated instead to the security of the entrenchments around Alexandria.[27]

When news of Banks's debacle on the Red River reached Washington, Lincoln's secretary of the navy, Gideon Welles, was not surprised. "I am not one of the admirers of Banks," Welles confided in his diary on May 9, 1864. Banks has "a certain degree of offhand smartness, very good elocution and command of the language, with perfect self-possession," Welles observed, "but is not profound. He is a pretender, not a statesman, a politician of . . . great ambition but little fixed principle."[28]

Toward the end of the war Banks had the opportunity to overcome his dismal record as a field commander by taking a lead in Lincoln's plan for Reconstruction. But again he failed, even though this political assignment was one he should have been able to handle with skill. Mistaking

25. *OR*, 26, pt. 1:14, 47, 144, 526–27, 546–49, 554–55.

26. Banks to Mary Banks, November 15, 1863, Banks Collection, LC.

27. *OR*, 34, pt. 1:184, 202, 485, 530, 565–69, pt. 3:125.

28. Welles, *Diary*, 2:26–27.

the superficial show of loyalty for a sincere devotion to the Union, Banks waffled between conservatives and radicals and ended up displeasing both.

Banks's political career after the war took a similar turn. Although he played a pivotal role in effecting the purchase of Alaska, he squandered the opportunity to be recognized as a statesman by taking a bribe for his part in the affair. So it went for the rest of his life. At various times Banks claimed to be a Republican, Democrat, or independent, saying what he thought the voters wanted to hear but destroying his credibility entirely in the process.

Banks was a decent man. He was a good father, a devoted husband, and a loyal patriot. But he never could face reality. As far as Banks was concerned, all of his victories were glorious, all of his accomplishments were grand. But they were too often only the pretense of glory and not the real thing.

Bibliography

Manuscript Sources

American Antiquarian Society, Worcester, Mass.
Banks, Nathaniel P. Correspondence.
Chicago Historical Society, Chicago, Ill.
Banks, Nathaniel P. Collection.
Grant, U. S. Collection.
Rawlins, John A. Collection.
College of William and Mary, Williamsburg, Va.
Wilson, James Grant. Letter.
Historic New Orleans Collection, New Orleans, La.
Gault, Samuel. Diary.
Vanderhoof, E. W. Letter.
Howard-Tilton Memorial Library, Tulane University, New Orleans, La.
Youngman, Charles F. "Historic Sketches of the *Daily Delta* and the *Era* and the *New Orleans Daily Independent* from Oct. 12, 1845 to Jan. 19, 1865." 1939. Typescript.
Huntington Library, San Marino, Calif.
Farragut, David G. Collection.
Huntington Manuscripts (misc.).
Lieber, Francis. Papers.
Illinois State Historical Library, Springfield, Ill.
Banks, N. P. Manuscripts.
Emory, W. H. Papers.
Library of Congress, Washington, D.C.
Banks, Nathaniel P. Collection.
Butler, Benjamin F. Papers.

Hotchkiss, Jedediah. Papers.
Lincoln, Abraham. Papers.
Quincy, Wendell, Holmes, and Upham Family. Papers.

Louisiana and Lower Mississippi Valley Collections, Louisiana State University, Baton Rouge, La.
Andrews, George Leonard. Papers.
Banks, Nathaniel P. Papers.

Massachusetts Historical Society, Boston, Mass.
Andrew, John A. Papers.
Banks, N. P. Papers.
Cary, Richard. Letters.
Eastman, William H. Letters.
Edes, Robert T. Letters. Microfilm.
Goodwin Family. Papers.
Gordon, George H. Papers.
Osborne, James Albert. Diary.
Paine, Charles J. Letters. Microfilm.
Parker, Theodore. Papers.
Reed, C[harles] F[reeman]. Manuscript.
Schouler, William. Papers.

Minnesota Historical Society, Saint Paul, Minn.
Babcock, Willoughby and Family. Papers.

National Archives, Washington, D.C.
Smith, William F., and James T. Brady, *Commission on Corrupt Practices in the Gulf, Final Report, September 23, 1865,* Record Group 94, Records of the Adjutant General's office.

Southern Historical Collection, University of North Carolina, Chapel Hill, N.C.
Brooks, George A. Journal.
Stevens, William H. Papers.
Stewart, William H. Diary.
Walker, John G. Papers.
Warmoth, Henry Clay. Papers.

U.S. Army Military History Institute, Carlisle Barracks, Pa.
Andrews, George L. Papers.
Coco, Gregory A. Collection.
Hayward, William H. Letters.
Polignac, Prince Camille. Diary.
Rust, Henry, Jr. Diary.
Walker, John G. "The War of Secession West of the Mississippi River during the Years 1863–4– & 5." Typescript.

Waltham Public Library, Waltham, Mass.
Local History and Genealogy Records.
William D. McCain Library and Archives, University of Southern Mississippi, Hattiesburg, Miss.
Wilcox, William E. Papers.
William R. Perkins Library, Duke University, Durham, N.C.
Davis, Lois (Wright) Richardson. Papers.
Eltinge-Lord. Papers.
Whitney, Henry B. Papers.

Dissertations

Doyle, Elisabeth Joan. "Civilian Life in Occupied New Orleans, 1862–65." Ph.D. dissertation, Louisiana State University, 1955.

Futrell, Robert E. "Federal Trade with the Confederate States, 1861–1865, a Study of Governmental Policy." Ph.D. dissertation, Vanderbilt University, 1950.

Vandal, Gilles. "The New Orleans Riot of 1866: The Anatomy of a Tragedy." Ph.D. dissertation, College of William and Mary, 1978.

Newspapers

Boston Commonwealth, 1865
Boston Daily Advertiser, 1865–66, 1874, 1888–90
Boston Daily Evening Traveller, 1854–62
Boston Daily Journal, 1845–66
Boston Evening Transcript, 1839–57, 1894, 1908
Boston Globe, 1874–1916
Boston Herald, 1876, 1894
Boston Morning Journal, 1870, 1878, 1886
Boston Post, 1849–58, 1866–68
Boston Weekly Voice, 1866–67
Carrollton (Louisiana) Times, 1864
Cincinnati Daily Gazette, 1872
Frank Leslie's Illustrated Newspaper, 1874
Gloucester (Massachusetts) Telegraph, 1859
Liberator, 1856, 1865
National Anti-Slavery Standard, 1864
New Orleans Daily Crescent, 1865–68
New Orleans Daily Delta, 1863
New Orleans Daily Picayune, 1862–65
New Orleans Daily True Delta, 1862–65

New Orleans Era, 1863–64
New Orleans Times, 1863–65
New Orleans Tribune, 1864–65
New York Evening Post, 1857, 1888
New York Herald, 1852–73, 1894
New York Times, 1856–64, 1878, 1894
New York Tribune, 1855–65, 1872–76
New York World, 1862
Rochester Daily Union and Advertiser, 1875
Springfield Daily Republican, 1865–67
Waltham (Massachusetts) Daily Free Press, 1894, 1901
Waltham (Massachusetts) Sentinel, 1862
Waltham (Massachusetts) News-Tribune, 1950

Government Documents

Louisiana. *Debates in the Convention for the Revision and Amendment of the Constitution of the State of Louisiana, 1864.* New Orleans: W. R. Fish, 1864.

Massachusetts. *Journal of the Constitutional Convention of the Commonwealth of Massachusetts, 1853.* Boston: White & Potter, 1853.

———. *Official Report of the Debates and Proceedings in the State Convention Assembled May 4th, 1853, to Revise and Amend the Constitution of the Commonwealth of Massachusetts.* 3 vols. Boston: White & Potter, 1853.

Official Army Register of the Volunteer Force of the United States Army for the Year 1861, '62, '63, '64, '65. 8 vols. 1865. Reprint. Gaithersburg, Md.: Ron R. Van Sickle Military Books, 1987.

Official Records of the Union and Confederate Navies in the War of the Rebellion. 31 vols. Washington, D.C.: U.S. Government Printing Office, 1894–1927.

U.S. Congress. House. *Congressional Globe.*
33d Cong., 1st sess.
33d Cong., 2d sess.
34th Cong., 1st sess.
35th Cong., 1st sess.
37th Cong., 3d sess.
38th Cong., 2d sess.
39th Cong., 1st sess.
39th Cong., 2d sess.
40th Cong., 1st sess.
40th Cong., 2d sess.
40th Cong., 3d sess.

41st Cong., 1st sess.
41st Cong., 2d sess.
42d Cong., 2d sess.
42d Cong., 3d sess.

U.S. Congress. House. *Congressional Record.*
44th Cong., 1st sess.
44th Cong., 2d sess.
51st Cong., 1st sess.
51st Cong., 2d sess.

U.S. Congress. House. *Executive Document No. 3: Report of the Secretary of the Treasury on the State of Finances for the Year Ending June 30, 1863.* 38th Cong., 1st Sess.

———. *Executive Document No. 68: New Orleans Riots.* 39th Cong., 2d Sess.

———. *Executive Document No. 101: Funds Seized at New Orleans during the Late Civil War.* 49th Cong., 1st sess.

———. Select Committee. *House Report No. 16: Report of the Select Committee on New Orleans Riots.* 39th Cong., 2d Sess. 1867. Reprint. Freeport, N.Y.: Books for Libraries Press, 1971.

———. *House Report No 35: Alaska Investigation.* 40th Cong., 3d sess.

U.S. Congress. Joint Committee. *Report of the Joint Committee on the Conduct of the War, at the Second Session Thirty-Eighth Congress.* Washington, D.C.: U.S. Government Printing Office, 1865.

U.S. Congress. Senate. Select Committee. *Senate Report No. 75: Vessels for the Banks Expedition.* 37th Cong., 3d sess.

———. *Senate Report No. 84: Employment of Transport Vessels.* 37th Cong., 3d sess.

The War of the Rebellion: A Compilation of the Official Records of the Union and Confederate Armies. 70 vols. in 127 and index. Washington, D.C.: U.S. Government Printing Office, 1880–1901.

Articles and Pamphlets

Addresses at the Inauguration of Cornelius Conway Felton, LL.D., as President of Harvard College. Cambridge, Mass.: Sever & Francis, 1860.

Allan, William. "Relative Numbers and Losses at Slaughter's Mountain." *Southern Historical Society Papers* 8 (March 1880): 178–83.

———. "Strength of the Forces under Pope and Lee." In *Papers of the Military Historical Society of Massachusetts,* 2:197–202. Boston: Houghton Mifflin, 1895.

Andrews, George Leonard. "The Battle of Cedar Mountain." In *Papers of the Military Historical Society of Massachusetts,* 2:405–14. Boston: Houghton Mifflin, 1895.

[Bacon, Thomas S.?] "Some Remarks upon the Proposed Election of February 22d." [New Orleans?], 1864.

Bailey, Thomas A. "Why the United States Purchased Alaska." *Pacific Historical Review* 3 (1934): 39–49.

Banks, Nathaniel P. *Address of His Excellency Nathaniel P. Banks, to the Two Branches of the Legislature of Massachusetts, January 7, 1858.* Boston: William White, 1858.

———. *An Address, Delivered by Major-General N. P. Banks, at the Custom-House, New Orleans, on the Fourth of July, 1865.* New York: Harper & Brothers, 1865.

———. *An Oration Delivered before the Neptune and Boyden Fire Companies and the Citizens of Waltham, July 4, 1842.* Boston: H. L. Devereux, 1842.

Barr, Alwyn. "The Battle of Bayou Bourbeau, November 3, 1863: Colonel Oran M. Roberts' Report." *Louisiana History* 6 (Winter 1965): 83–91.

Bean, William G. "Puritan versus Celt, 1850–1860." *New England Quarterly* 7 (March 1934): 70–89.

Beirne, Rosamond Randall, ed. "Three War Letters." *Maryland Historical Magazine* 40 (December 1945): 287–94.

Berry, Mary F. "Negro Troops in Blue and Gray: The Louisiana Native Guards, 1861–1863." *Louisiana History* 8 (Spring 1967): 165–90.

Blassingame, John W. "The Selection of Officers and Non-Commissioned Officers of Negro Troops in the Union Army, 1863–1865." *Negro History Bulletin* 30 (January 1967): 8–11.

Brady, Patricia. "Trials and Tribulations: American Missionary Association Teachers and Black Education in Occupied New Orleans, 1863–1864." *Louisiana History* 31 (Winter 1990): 5–20.

Carman, Harry J., and Reinhard H. Luthin. "Some Aspects of the Know-Nothing Movement Reconsidered." *South Atlantic Quarterly* 39 (April 1940): 213–34.

Carpenter, A. H. "Military Government of Southern Territory, 1861–1865." In *Annual Report of the American Historical Association, the Year 1900,* 1:467–98. Washington, D.C.: U.S. Government Printing Office, 1901.

Celebration of the Centennial of the Birth of General Nathaniel Prentiss Banks: Waltham, Massachusetts, January 30, 1916. Waltham: Mass.: Waltham Publishing Co., [1916].

Chase, Salmon P. "Diary and Correspondence of Salmon P. Chase." In *Annual Report of the American Historical Association, the Year 1902.* Washington, D.C.: U.S. Government Printing Office, 1903.

Copeland, R. Morris. *Statement of R. Morris Copeland.* Boston: Prentiss & Deland, 1864.

Couch, R. Randall. "The Public Masked Balls of Antebellum New Orleans: A

Custom of Masque Outside the Mardi Gras Tradition." *Louisiana History* 35 (Fall 1994): 403–31.

Cuccia, Phillip. "'Gorillas' and White Glove Gents: Union Soldiers in the Red River Campaign." *Louisiana History* 36 (Fall 1995): 413–30.

Curti, Merle E. "Robert Rantoul, Jr., The Reformer in Politics." *New England Quarterly* 5 (April 1932): 264–80.

Dabney, Thomas Ewing. "The Butler Regime in Louisiana." *Louisiana Historical Quarterly* 27 (April 1944): 487–526.

Debray, X. B. *A Sketch of the History of Debray's (26th) Regiment of Texas Cavalry.* 1884. Reprint. Suffolk, Va.: Robert Hardy, n.d.

Dunning, William A. "Paying for Alaska: Some Unfamiliar Incidents in the Process." *Political Science Quarterly* 27 (September 1912): 385–98.

Ellis, Richard N., ed. "The Civil War Letters of an Iowa Family." *Annals of Iowa* 3d ser., 39 (Spring 1969): 561–86.

Farragut, Loyall. "Farragut at Port Hudson." *Putnam's Magazine* 5 (October 1908): 44–53.

Fitts, James Franklin. "The Negro in Blue." *Galaxy* 3 (February 1967): 249–55.

Frazier, Donald S. "Texans on the Teche: The Texas Brigade at the Battle of Bisland and Irish Bend, April 12–14, 1863." *Louisiana History* 32 (Fall 1991): 417–35.

Free Soiler from the Start. *A Review of Mr. Banks's Political History: Designed for the Information of the People of Mass.* N.p., 1855.

Freidel, Frank. "General Orders 100 and Military Government." *Mississippi Valley Historical Review* 32 (March 1946): 541–48.

"General Banks." *Illinois Central Magazine* 2 (July 1913): 13–22.

Golder, Frank A. "The Purchase of Alaska." *American Historical Review* 25 (April 1920): 411–25.

Grosz, Agnes Smith. "The Political Career of Pinckney Benton Stewart Pinchback." *Louisiana Historical Quarterly* 27 (April 1944): 529–610.

Harrington, Fred Harvey. "Frémont and the North Americans." *American Historical Review* 44 (July 1939): 842–48.

———. "A Peace Mission of 1863." *American Historical Review* 46 (October 1940): 76–86.

Harris, Francis Byers. "Henry Clay Warmoth, Reconstruction Governor of Louisiana." *Louisiana Historical Quarterly* 30 (April 1947): 523–653.

Haynes, George H. "The Causes of Know-Nothing Success in Massachusetts. " *American Historical Review* 3 (October 1897): 67–82.

Homans, John. "The Red River Expedition." In *Papers of the Military Historical Society of Massachusetts,* 8:65–97. Boston: Military Historical Society of Massachusetts, 1910.

Howell, Norwood P. "The Negro as a Soldier in the War of the Rebellion." In

Papers of the Military Historical Society of Massachusetts, 13:287–313. Boston: Military Historical Society of Massachusetts, 1913.

Irwin, Richard B. "The Red River Campaign." In *Battles and Leaders of the Civil War,* edited by Robert U. Johnson and Clarence C. Buel, 4:345–62. 5 vols. 1884–88. Reprint. Secaucus, N.J.: Castle, 1987.

Jackson, Crawford M. "An Account of the Occupation of Fort [*sic*] Hudson." *Alabama Historical Quarterly* 18 (Winter 1956): 474–85.

Johnson, Dick. "The Role of Salmon P. Chase in the Formation of the Republican Party." *Old Northwest* 3 (March 1977): 23–38.

Johnson, Howard Palmer. "New Orleans under General Butler." *Louisiana Historical Quarterly* 24 (April 1941): 434–536.

Kassel, Charles. "Educating the Slave—A Forgotten Chapter of Civil War History." *Open Court* 41 (April 1927): 239–56.

———. "The Labor System of General Banks." *Open Court* 42 (January 1928): 35–50.

Kendall, John Smith. "Recollections of a Confederate Officer." *Louisiana Historical Quarterly* 29 (October 1946): 1041–1228.

Landers, H. L. "Wet Sand and Cotton: Banks's Red River Campaign." *Louisiana Historical Quarterly* 19 (1936): 150–95.

Luthin, Reinhard H. "The Sale of Alaska." *Slavonic Review* 16 (July 1937): 168–82.

Meiners, Fredericka. "Hamilton P. Bee in the Red River Campaign of 1864." *Southwestern Historical Quarterly* 78 (July 1974): 21–44.

McGuire, Hunter H. *Address by Dr. Hunter McGuire . . . on 23rd Day of June, 1897.* Lynchburg, Va.: J. P. Bell Co. for the Virginia Military Institute, 1897.

McLure, Mary Lilla. "The Elections of 1860 in Louisiana." *Louisiana Historical Quarterly* 9 (October 1926): 601–702.

Moore, W. G. "Notes of Colonel W. G. Moore, Private Secretary to President Johnson, 1866–1868," *American Historical Review* 19 (October 1913): 98–132.

P. W. *Historical Sketch of Major Gen. N. P. Banks's Civil and Military Administration in Louisiana.* New York: Privately printed, 1864.

Padgett, James A. "Some Letters of George Stanton Denison, 1854–1866: Observations of a Yankee on Conditions in Louisiana and Texas." *Louisiana Historical Quarterly* 23 (October 1940): 1132–1240.

Palfrey, John C. "Port Hudson." In *Papers of the Military Historical Society of Massachusetts,* 8:21–63. Boston: Military Historical Society of Massachusetts, 1910.

Peabody, Charles A. "United States Provisional Court for the State of Louisiana, 1862–1865." In *Annual Report of the American Historical Association, 1892,* 199–210. Washington, D.C.: U.S. Government Printing Office, 1893.

Plumly, B. Rush. *Report of the Board of Education for Freedmen, Department of the Gulf, for the Year 1864.* New Orleans: Office of the True Delta, 1865.

Quincy, Samuel M. "General Halleck's Military Administration in the Summer of 1862." In *Papers of the Military Historical Society of Massachusetts,* vol. 2, edited by Theodore F. Dwight. Boston: Houghton Mifflin, 1895.

Record of the Dedication of the Statue of Major General Nathaniel Prentiss Banks, September 16, 1908. Boston: Wright, Potter Printing Co., 1909.

Roberts, A. Sellew. "The Federal Government and Confederate Cotton." *American Historical Review* 32 (January 1927): 262–75.

Root, William H. "The Experiences of a Federal Soldier in Louisiana in 1863." *Louisiana Historical Quarterly* 19 (July 1936): 635–67.

Sibley, Joel H. "'The First Northern Victory:' The Republican Party Comes to Congress, 1855–1856." *Journal of Interdisciplinary History* 20 (Summer 1989): 1–24.

Simpson, Amos E., and Vaughn Baker. "Michael Hahn: Steady Patriot." *Louisiana History* 13 (Summer 1972): 229–52.

Smith, E. Kirby. "The Defense of the Red River." In *Battles and Leaders of the Civil War,* edited by Robert U. Johnson and Clarence C. Buel, 4:369–74. 5 vols. 1884–88. Reprint. Secaucus, N.J.: Castle, 1987.

Smith, George Winston. "The Banks Expedition of 1862." *Louisiana Historical Quarterly* 26 (April 1943): 341–60.

Smith, M. J., and James Freret. "Fortifications and Siege of Port Hudson." *Southern Historical Society Papers* 14 (1886): 305–48.

Steiner, Bernard C. "James Alfred Pearce." *Maryland Historical Magazine* 19 (March 1924): 13–29.

Stone, Eben F. "Sketch of John Albion Andrew." *Essex Institute Historical Collections* 27 (1890): 1–30.

"The Story of the Illinois Central Lines during the Civil Conflict 1861–5: General Banks." *Illinois Central Magazine* 2 (August 1913): 13–18.

Strother, David Hunter. "Personal Recollections of the War." *Harper's New Monthly Magazine* 34 (March 1867): 423–49; and (May 1867): 714–34.

Tanner, Linn. "Port Hudson Calamities—Mule Meat." *Confederate Veteran* 17 (October 1909): 512.

Taylor, Robert M. "Reverend Lyman Whiting's Test of Faith." *Historical Journal of Massachusetts* 12 (June 1984): 90–103.

Tregle, Joseph G. "Thomas J. Durant, Utopian Socialism, and the Failure of Presidential Reconstruction in Louisiana." *Journal of Southern History* 45 (November 1979): 485–512.

Uzee, Philip D. "The Beginnings of the Louisiana Republican Party." *Louisiana History* 12 (Summer 1971): 197–211.

Wallis, S. Teackle. *Correspondence between S. Teackle Wallis, Esq. of Balti-*

more, and the Hon. John Sherman of the U.S. Senate, Concerning the Arrest of Members of the Maryland Legislature. Baltimore: N.p., 1863.

Wesley, Charles H. "The Employment of Negroes as Soldiers in the Confederate Army." *Journal of Negro History* 4 (July 1919): 239–53.

Whittington, G. P. "Rapides Parish, Louisiana—A History." *Louisiana Historical Quarterly* 18 (1935): 5–39.

Williams, E. Cort. *"Recollections of the Red River Expedition." A Paper Read before the Ohio Commandery of the Military Order of the Loyal Legion of the United States.* Cincinnati: H. C. Sherick, 1886.

Williams, T. Harry. "General Banks and the Radical Republicans in the Civil War." *New England Quarterly* 12 (June 1939): 268–80.

Wilson, Keith. "Education as a Vehicle of Racial Control: Major General N. P. Banks in Louisiana, 1863–64." *Journal of Negro Education* 50 (Spring 1981): 156–70.

Woodbury, Charles Levi. "Some Personal Recollections of Robert Rantoul, Junior." *Historical Collections of the Essex Institute* 34 (December 1898): 195–206.

Books

Ackerman, William K. *Historical Sketch of the Illinois-Central Railroad.* Chicago: Fergus Printing Co., 1890.

Adams, Charles Francis. *Richard Henry Dana: A Biography.* 2 vols. Boston: Houghton Mifflin, 1891.

Alden, Carroll Storrs. *George Hamilton Perkins, Commodore, U.S.N.: His Life and Letters.* Boston: Houghton Mifflin, 1914.

Allan, William. *The Army of Northern Virginia in 1862.* Boston: Houghton Mifflin, 1892.

———. *History of the Campaign of Gen. T. J. (Stonewall) Jackson in the Shenandoah Valley of Virginia.* 1912. Reprint. Dayton, Ohio: Morningside, 1987.

Allen, Henry Watkins. *Official Report Relative to the Conduct of Federal Troops in Western Louisiana, during the Invasions of 1863 and 1864.* 1865. Reprint. Baton Rouge: Otto Claitor, 1939.

American Psychiatric Association. *Diagnostic and Statistical Manual of Mental Disorders,* 3d ed., rev. New York: American Psychiatric Association, 1987.

Anderson, John Q. *Campaigning with Parsons's Texas Cavalry Brigade, CSA: The War Journals and Letters of the Four Orr Brothers, 12th Texas Cavalry Regiment.* Hillsboro, Tex.: Hill Junior College Press, 1967.

Andrews, J. Cutler. *The North Reports the Civil War.* Pittsburgh: University of Pittsburgh Press, 1955.

Andrus, Onley. *The Civil War Letters of Sergeant Onley Andrus,* Illinois Studies in the Social Sciences, edited by Fred Albert Shannon, vol. 28, no. 4. Urbana: University of Illinois Press, 1947.

Appleton, Nathan. *Russian Life and Society.* Boston: Murray & Emery, 1904.

Arceneaux, William. *Acadian General: Alfred Mouton and the Civil War.* Lafayette, La.: Center for Louisiana Studies, 1981.

Ashby, Thomas A. *The Valley Campaigns.* New York: Neale, 1914.

Babcock, Willoughby M. *Selections from the Letters and Diaries of Brevet-Brigadier General Willoughby Babcock of the Seventy-Fifth New York Volunteers.* Albany: University of the State of New York, 1922.

Bacon, Edward. *Among the Cotton Thieves.* 1867. Reprint. Bossier City, La.: Everett, 1989.

Bailey, Anne J. *Between the Enemy and Texas: Parsons's Texas Cavalry in the Civil War.* Fort Worth: Texas Christian Press, 1989.

Ballard, Colin R. *The Military Genius of Abraham Lincoln.* Cleveland: World, 1965.

Baringer, William Eldon. *A House Dividing: Lincoln as President Elect.* Springfield, Ill.: Abraham Lincoln Association, 1945.

———. *Lincoln's Rise to Power.* 1937. Reprint, St. Clair Shores, Mich.: Scholarly Press, 1971.

Bartlett, Ruhl Jacob. *John C. Frémont and the Republican Party.* Columbus: Ohio State University Press, 1930.

Basler, Roy P., ed. *The Collected Works of Abraham Lincoln.* 9 vols. New Brunswick, N.J.: Rutgers University Press for the Abraham Lincoln Association, 1953–55.

Bates, Edward. *Diary of Edward Bates, 1859–66.* Edited by Howard Kennedy Beale. Washington, D.C.: U.S. Government Printing Office, 1933.

Baum, Dale. *The Civil War Party System: The Case of Massachusetts, 1848–1876.* Chapel Hill: University of North Carolina Press, 1984.

Bearss, Edwin Cole. *The Campaign for Vicksburg.* Vol. 1, *Vicksburg Is the Key.* Dayton, Ohio: Morningside, 1985.

Beecher, Harris H. *Record of the 114th Regiment, N.Y.S.V.: Where It Went, What It Saw, and What It Did.* Norwich, N.Y.: J. F. Hubbard, Jr., 1866.

Belisle, John G. *History of Sabine Parish, Louisiana.* Sabine, La.: Sabine Banner Press, 1912.

Belz, Herman. *Reconstructing the Union: Theory and Policy during the Civil War.* Ithaca, N.Y.: Cornell University Press for the American Historical Association, 1969.

Benedict, G. G. *A History of the Part Taken by the Vermont Soldiers and Sailors in the War for the Union, 1861–65.* Burlington, Vt.: Free Press Association, 1888.

Berlin, Ira, Joseph P. Reidy, and Leslie S. Rowland. *Freedom: A Documentary*

History of Emancipation, 1861–1867. 2d ser. *The Black Military Experience.* New York: Cambridge University Press, 1982.

Beveridge, Albert J. *Abraham Lincoln, 1809–1858.* 2 vols. Boston: Houghton Mifflin, 1928.

Bigelow, John. *Retrospections of an Active Life.* 4 vols. New York: Baker & Taylor, 1909.

Billington, Ray Allen. *The Protestant Crusade, 1800–1860: A Study of the Origins of American Nativism.* New York: Macmillan, 1938.

Binney, Charles James Fox. *The History of the Prentice, or Prentiss Family.* 2d ed. 1883. Reprint, as part of John K. Prentice, "Descendants of Rev. Amos Prentice [1804–1849]." Barrington, Ill., 1942, mimeograph.

Blackford, Charles Minor. *Letters from Lee's Army.* New York: Charles Scribner's Sons, 1947.

Blaine, James Gillespie. *Twenty Years of Congress: From Lincoln to Garfield.* 2 vols. Norwich, Conn.: Henry Hill, 1884–86.

Blassingame, John W. *Black New Orleans, 1860–1880.* Chicago: University of Chicago Press, 1973.

Boggs, William K. *Military Reminiscences of Gen. Wm. R. Boggs,* Edited by William K. Boyd. Durham, N.C.: Seeman Printery, 1913.

Boutwell, George S. *Reminiscences of Sixty Years in Public Affairs.* 2 vols. 1902. Reprint. New York: Greenwood Press, 1968.

Boyce, Charles William. *A Brief History of the Twenty-Eighth Regiment, New York State Volunteers.* Buffalo: Matthews-Northup, 1896.

Brown, George William. *Baltimore and the Nineteenth of April, 1861: A Study of the War.* Studies in Historical and Political Science, vol. 3. Baltimore: Johns Hopkins University, 1887.

Brown, William Wells. *The Negro in the American Rebellion: His Heroism and His Fidelity.* 1867. Reprint, New York: Johnson Reprint Corp., 1968.

Bryant, Edwin E. *History of the Third Regiment of Wisconsin Veteran Volunteer Infantry.* Madison: Veteran Association, 1891.

Butler, Benjamin F. *Butler's Book: Autobiography and Personal Reminiscences of Major-General Benj. F. Butler.* Boston: A. M. Thayer, 1892.

———. *Private and Official Correspondence of Gen. Benjamin F. Butler during a Period of the Civil War.* 5 vols. Edited by Jessie Ames Marshall. Norwood, Mass.: Plimpton Press, 1917.

Callahan, James Morton. *American Foreign Policy in Canadian Relations.* New York: Macmillan, 1937.

Camper, Charles, and J. W. Kirkley. *Historical Record of the First Regiment Maryland Infantry.* 1871. Reprint. Baltimore: Butternut & Blue, 1990.

Carman, Harry James, and Reinhard Harry Luthin. *Lincoln and the Patronage.* New York: Columbia University Press, 1943.

Carter, Dan T. *When the War Was Over: The Failure of Self-Reconstruction in the South, 1865–1867.* Baton Rouge: Louisiana State University Press, 1985.

Clark, George Faber. *History of the Temperance Reform in Massachusetts, 1813–1883.* Boston: Clarke & Carruth, 1888.

Clark, Orton S. *The One Hundred and Sixteenth Regiment of New York State Volunteers.* Buffalo: Matthews & Warren, 1868.

Clark, Victor S. *History of Manufactures in the United States.* 3 vols. New York: McGraw-Hill, 1929.

Cole, Arthur Charles. *The Era of the Civil War, 1848–1870.* Springfield, Ill.: Illinois Centennial Commission, 1919.

Congdon, Charles T. *Reminiscences of a Journalist.* Boston: James R. Osgood, 1880.

Conway, Moncure Daniel. *Autobiography, Memories and Experiences of Moncure Daniel Conway.* 2 vols. Boston: Houghton Mifflin, 1904.

Copeland, Melvin T. *The Cotton Manufacturing Industry of the United States.* New York: Augustus M. Kelley, 1966.

Cornish, Dudley Taylor. *The Sable Arm: Negro Troops in the Union Army, 1861–1865.* New York: Norton, 1966.

Cowley, Charles. *History of Lowell.* 2d ed. Boston: Lee & Shepard, 1868.

Cox, LaWanda. *Lincoln and Black Freedom: A Study in Presidential Leadership.* Columbia: University of South Carolina Press, 1981.

Cunningham, Edward. *The Port Hudson Campaign, 1862–1863.* Baton Rouge: Louisiana State University Press, 1963.

Current, Richard Nelson. *Old Thad Stevens: A Story of Ambition.* Madison: University of Wisconsin Press, 1942.

Curtis, Francis. *The Republican Party: A History of Its Fifty Years' Existence and a Record of Its Measures and Leaders.* 2 vols. New York: G. P. Putnam's Sons, 1904.

Dabney, Robert L. *Life and Campaigns of Lieut.-Gen. Thomas J. Jackson.* New York: Blelock, 1866.

Dargan, James F. *My Experiences in Service; or, A Nine Months Man.* Los Angeles: California State University, Northridge, Libraries, for the Bibliographic Society of California State University, Northridge, 1974.

Darling, Arthur Burr. *Political Changes in Massachusetts, 1824–1848: A Study of Liberal Movements in Politics.* New Haven: Yale University Press, 1925.

Dawson, Joseph G. *Army Generals and Reconstruction: Louisiana, 1862–1877.* Baton Rouge: Louisiana State University Press, 1982.

Dawson, Sarah Morgan. *A Confederate Girl's Diary.* Boston: Houghton Mifflin, 1913.

De Forest, John William. *A Volunteer's Adventures: A Union Captain's Record of the Civil War.* Edited by James H. Croushore. New Haven: Yale University Press, 1946.

Dennett, Tyler ed. *Lincoln and the Civil War in the Diaries and Letters of John Hay.* 1939. Reprint, Westport, Conn.: Greenwood Pres, 1972.

Donald, David. *Charles Sumner and the Coming of the Civil War.* New York: Knopf, 1960.

———. *Charles Sumner and the Rights of Man.* New York: Knopf, 1970.

Dorsey, Sarah A. *Recollections of Henry Watkins Allen: Brigadier General, Confederate States Army; Ex-Governor of Louisiana.* New York: M. Doolady, 1866.

Douglas, Henry Kyd. *I Rode with Stonewall.* Chapel Hill: University of North Carolina Press, 1940.

Dow, Neal. *The Reminiscences of Neal Dow: Recollections of Eighty Years.* Portland, Me.: Evening Press Publishing Co., 1898.

Drake, Samuel Adams. *History of Middlesex County, Massachusetts.* Boston: Estes & Lauriat, 1880.

Drayton, Percival. *Naval Letters of Captain Percival Drayton, 1861–1865.* New York: New York Public Library, 1906.

Duganne, A. J. H. *Camps and Prisons: Twenty Months in the Department of the Gulf.* New York: J. P. Robens, 1865.

Dumond, Dwight Lowell. *The Secession Movement, 1860–1861.* New York: Macmillan, 1931.

Dwight, Wilder. *Life and Letters of William Dwight.* Edited by Elizabeth Amelia Dwight. 1868; 2d ed., Boston: Little, Brown, 1891.

Dyer, Frederick Henry. *A Compendium of the War of the Rebellion.* 1908. Reprint. New York: Thomas Yoseloff, 1959.

Edmonds, David C. *The Guns of Port Hudson.* 2 vols. Lafayette, La.: Acadiana Press, 1983–84.

———. *Yankee Autumn in Acadiana: A Narrative of the Great Texas Overland Expedition through Southeastern Louisiana, October–December 1863.* Lafayette, La.: Acadiana Press, 1979.

English Combatant. *Battle-fields of the South: From Bull Run to Fredericksburg.* New York: J. Bradburn, 1864.

Ewer, James K. *Third Massachusetts Cavalry in the War for the Union.* Maplewood, Mass.: Wm. G. J. Perry Press for the Historical Committee of the Regimental Association, 1903.

Farragut, Loyall. *The Life of David Glasgow Farragut, First Admiral of the United States Navy.* New York: D. Appleton, 1907.

Farrar, Victor J. *The Annexation of Russian America to the United States.* Washington, D.C.: W. F. Roberts, 1937.

Faulk, Odie. *General Tom Green: "A Fightin' Texan."* Waco: Texian Press, 1963.

Flinn, Frank M. *Campaigning with Banks in Louisiana, in '63 and '64, and with Sheridan in the Shenandoah Valley in '64 and '65.* Lynn, Mass.: Thos. P. Nichols, 1887.

Follett, Mary Parker. *The Speaker of the House of Representatives.* New York: Longmans, Green, 1896.

Foltz, Charles S. *Surgeon of the Seas: The Adventurous Life of Surgeon General Jonathan M. Foltz in the Days of Wooden Ships.* Indianapolis: Bobbs-Merrill, 1931.

Foner, Eric. *Reconstruction: America's Unfinished Revolution, 1863–1877.* New York: Harper & Row, 1988.

Foner, Philip S. *Business and Slavery: The New York Merchants and the Irrepressible Conflict.* Chapel Hill: University of North Carolina Press, 1941.

Ford, Worthington Chauncey, ed. *Letters of Henry Adams, 1858–1891.* 2 vols. 1930. Reprint. New York: Kraus Reprint Co., 1969.

Forney, John W. *Anecdotes of Public Men.* 2 vols. New York: Harper & Brothers, 1873.

Foulke, William Dudley. *Life of Oliver P. Morton, Including His Important Speeches.* 2 vols. Indianapolis: Bowen-Merrill, 1899.

Freeman, Douglas Southall. *Lee's Lieutenants: A Study in Command.* 3 vols. New York: Charles Scribner's Sons, 1942–44.

Frothingham, Louis Adams. *A Brief History of the Constitution and Government of Massachusetts.* Cambridge, Mass.: Harvard University Press, 1916.

Fuess, Claude M. *The Life of Caleb Cushing.* 2 vols. New York: Harcourt, Brace, 1923.

Gallaway, B. P. *The Ragged Rebel: A Common Soldier in W. H. Parsons' Texas Cavalry, 1861–1865.* Austin: University of Texas Press, 1988.

Garrett, David R. *The Civil War Letters of David R. Garrett: Detailing the Adventures of the 6th Texas Cavalry.* Edited by Max Lale. Marshall, Tex.: Port Caddo Press, n.d.

Gates, Paul W. *The Illinois Central Railroad and Its Colonization Work.* Cambridge, Mass.: Harvard University Press, 1934.

Gerteis, Louis S. *From Contraband to Freedman: Federal Policy toward Southern Blacks, 1861–1865.* Westport, Conn.: Greenwood Press, 1973.

Gienapp, William E. *Origins of the Republican Party, 1852–1856.* New York: Oxford University Press, 1987.

Glatthaar, Joseph T. *Forged in Battle: The Civil War Alliance of Black Soldiers and White Officers.* New York: Free Press, 1990.

Gordon, George H. *From Brook Farm to Cedar Mountain: In the War of the Great Rebellion, 1861–62.* Boston: James R. Osgood, 1883.

———. *History of the Campaign of the Army of Virginia.* Boston: Houghton, Osgood, 1880.

Gould, John M. *History of the First-Tenth-Twenty-ninth Maine Regiments.* Portland, Me.: Stephen Berry, 1871.

Gray, John Chipman. *War Letters, 1862–1865, of John Chipman Gray and John Codman Ropes.* Boston: Houghton Mifflin, 1927.

Greeley, Horace. *Recollections of a Busy Life.* 1868. Reprint. New York: Arno Press, 1970.

Gregg, John Chandler. *Life in the Army, in the Departments of Virginia, and the Gulf, Including Observations in New Orleans.* Philadelphia: Perkinpine & Higgins, 1866.

Grimsley, Daniel A. *Battles in Culpeper County, Virginia, 1861–1865.* Culpeper, Va.: Raleigh Travers Green, 1900.

Gurowski, Adam. *Diary.* 3 vols. Boston: Lea & Shepard, 1862–66.

Hall, Henry, and James Hall. *Cayuga in the Field: A Record of the Nineteenth N.Y. Volunteers and Third New York Artillery.* Auburn, N.Y.: Truair, Smith, 1873.

———. *Cayuga in the Field: A Record of the 75th N.Y. Volunteers.* Auburn, N.Y.: Truair, Smith, 1873.

Hall, James E. *Diary of a Confederate Soldier.* Edited by Ruth Woods Dayton. Philippi, W.Va.: Editor, 1961.

Hamlin, Charles Eugene. *Life and Times of Hannibal Hamlin.* 2 vols. 1899. Reprint. Port Washington, N.Y.: Kennikat Press, 1971.

Handlin, Oscar. *Boston's Immigrants: A Study in Acculturation.* Cambridge, Mass.: Harvard University Press, 1959.

Hargrove, Handon B. *Black Union Soldiers in the Civil War.* Jefferson, N.C.: McFarland, 1988.

Harrington, Fred Harvey. *Fighting Politician: Major General N. P. Banks.* Philadelphia: University of Pennsylvania Press, 1948.

Harris, T. H. *The Story of Public Education in Louisiana.* New Orleans: Delgado Trades School, 1924.

Hart, Albert Bushnell. *Commonwealth History of Massachusetts.* 5 vols. New York: States History Co., 1930.

Hattaway, Herman, and Archer Jones. *How the North Won: A Military History of the Civil War.* Urbana: University of Illinois Press, 1983.

Haynes, George Henry. *Charles Sumner.* Philadelphia: George W. Jacobs, 1909.

Henderson, G. F. R. *Stonewall Jackson and the American Civil War.* 1898. Reprint. New York: Longmans, Green, 1961.

Hennessy, John J. *Return to Bull Run: The Campaign and Battle of Second Manassas.* New York: Simon & Schuster, 1993.

Hepworth, George H. *The Whip, Hoe, and Sword; or, The Gulf-Department in '63.* Boston: Walker, Wise, 1864.

Hesseltine, William B. *Ulysses S. Grant, Politician.* New York: Dodd, Mead, 1935.

Hewitt, Lawrence Lee. *Port Hudson, Confederate Bastion on the Mississippi.* Baton Rouge: Louisiana State University Press, 1987.

Higginson, Thomas Wentworth. *Army Life in a Black Regiment.* Boston: Fields, Osgood, 1870.

Hinsdale, Burke A., ed. *The Works of James Abram Garfield.* Boston: James R. Osgood, 1882.

Hoar, George F. *Autobiography of Seventy Years.* New York: Charles Scribner's Sons, 1903.

Hoffman, Wickham. *Camp, Court and Siege: A Narrative of Personal Adventure and Observation during Two Wars, 1861–1865, 1870–71.* New York: Harper & Brothers, 1877.

Hollandsworth, James G., Jr. *The Louisiana Native Guards: The Black Military Experience during the Civil War.* Baton Rouge: Louisiana State University Press, 1995.

Hollister, O. J. *Life of Schuyler Colfax.* New York: Funk & Wagnalls, 1886.

Holzman, Robert S. *Stormy Ben Butler.* New York: Macmillan, 1954.

Hosmer, James K. *The Color-Guard: Being a Corporal's Notes of Military Service in the Nineteenth Army Corps.* Boston: Walker, Wise, 1864.

Houzeau, Jean-Charles. *My Passage at the New Orleans "Tribune": A Memoir of the Civil War Era.* Edited by David C. Rankin, and translated by Gerard F. Denault. Baton Rouge: Louisiana State University Press, 1984.

Howard, McHenry. *Recollections of a Maryland Confederate Soldier and Staff Officer under Johnston, Jackson and Lee.* 1914. Reprint, Dayton, Ohio: Morningside, 1975.

Howard, Oliver Otis. *Autobiography of Oliver Otis Howard, Major General, United States Army.* 2 vols. New York: Baker & Taylor, 1907.

Howe, M. A. DeWolfe, ed. *Home Letters of General Sherman.* New York: Charles Scribner's Sons, 1909.

Hurd, D. Hamilton. *History of Middlesex County, Massachusetts.* 4 vols. Philadelphia: J. W. Lewis, 1890.

Irwin, Richard B. *History of the Nineteenth Army Corps.* 1892. Reprint. Baton Rouge: Elliott's Book Shop Press, 1985.

Jackson, Joseph Orville, ed. *"Some of the Boys . . . ": The Civil War Letters of Isaac Jackson, 1862–1865.* Carbondale: Southern Illinois University Press, 1960.

Jimerson, Randall C. *The Private Civil War: Popular Thought during the Sectional Conflict.* Baton Rouge: Louisiana State University Press, 1988.

Johns, Henry T. *Life with the Forty-Ninth Massachusetts Volunteers.* Pittsfield, Mass.: C. A. Alvord, 1864.

Johnson, Ludwell H. *Red River Campaign: Politics and Cotton in the Civil War.* 1958. Reprint, Gaithersburg, Md.: Butternut Press, 1986.

Johnson, Willis Fletcher. *Four Centuries of the Panama Canal.* New York: Henry Holt, 1906.

Josephy, Alvin M. *The Civil War in the American West.* New York: Knopf, 1991.

Julian, George Washington. *Political Recollections, 1840 to 1872.* Chicago: Jansen, McClurg, 1884.

Kerby, Robert L. *Kirby Smith's Confederacy: The Trans-Mississippi South, 1863–1865.* New York: Columbia University Press, 1972.

Kirkland, Edward Chase. *The Peacemakers of 1864.* 1927. Reprint. New York: AMS Press, 1969.

Knox, Thomas W. *Camp-Fire and Cotton-Field: Southern Adventures in Time of War.* 1865. Reprint, New York: Da Capo Press, 1969.

Krick, Robert K. *Stonewall Jackson at Cedar Mountain.* Chapel Hill: University of North Carolina Press, 1990.

Krout, John Allen. *The Origins of Prohibition.* New York: Knopf, 1925.

LeGrand, Julia. *The Journal of Julia LeGrand, New Orleans, 1862–63,* edited by Kate Mason Rowland and Mrs. Morris L. Croxall. Richmond: Everett Waddey, 1911.

Lowe, Richard. *The Texas Overland Expedition of 1863.* Fort Worth, Tex.: Ryan Place, 1996.

Luthin, Reinhard H. *The First Lincoln Campaign.* Cambridge, Mass.: Harvard University Press, 1944.

McCall, Samuel W. *The Life of Thomas Brackett Reed.* Boston: Houghton Mifflin, 1914.

McCrary, Peyton. *Abraham Lincoln and Reconstruction: The Louisiana Experiment.* Princeton: Princeton University Press, 1978.

McCullough, David. *The Path between the Seas: The Creation of the Panama Canal, 1870–1914.* New York: Simon & Schuster, 1977.

McDonald, Archie P., ed. *Make Me a Map of the Valley: The Civil War Journal of Stonewall Jackson's Topographer.* Dallas: Southern Methodist University Press, 1973.

McDonald, Cornelia. *A Diary with Reminiscences of the War and Refugee Life.* Nashville: Hunter McDonald, 1934.

McDonald, William N. *A History of the Laurel Brigade.* Baltimore: Sun Job Printing Office, 1907.

McFeely, William S. *Grant: A Biography.* New York: Norton, 1974.

Mackay, Alexander. *The Western World; or, Travels in the United States in 1846–47.* Philadelphia: Lea & Blanchard, 1849.

McPherson, James M. *Abraham Lincoln and the Second American Revolution.* New York: Oxford University Press, 1991.

———. *The Negro's Civil War: How American Negroes Felt and Acted During the War for the Union.* New York: Pantheon Books, 1965.

Marshall, Albert O. *Army Life; From a Soldier's Journal.* Joliet, Ill.: Author, 1883.

Marshall, Thomas B. *History of the Eighty-Third Ohio Volunteer Infantry, the Greyhound Regiment.* Cincinnati: Eighty-Third Ohio Volunteer Infantry Association, 1912.

Martin, David G. *Jackson's Valley Campaign: November 1861–June 1862.* New York: W. H. Smith, 1988.

Martineau, Harriet. *Society in America.* 2 vols. New York: Saunders & Otley, 1837.

Marvin, Edwin E. *The Fifth Connecticut Volunteers.* Hartford, Conn.: Wiley, Waterman & Eaton, 1889.

Mayes, Edward. *Lucius Q. C. Lamar: His Life, Times, and Speeches.* Nashville: Methodist Episcopal Church, South, 1896.

Memorial of Lt. Daniel Perkins Dewey, of the Twenty-Fifth Regiment, Connecticut Volunteers. Hartford, Conn.: Press of Cage, Lockwood, 1864.

Merriam, George S. *The Life and Times of Samuel Bowles.* 2 vols. New York: Century, 1885.

Milton, George Fort. *Eve of Conflict: Stephen A. Douglas and the Needless War.* 1934. Reprint. New York: Octagon Books, 1963.

Montgomery, David. *Beyond Equality: Labor and the Radical Republicans, 1862–1872.* New York: Knopf, 1967.

Moore, Frank, ed. *The Rebellion Record: A Diary of American Events.* 12 vols. New York: D. Van Nostrand, 1869.

Moors, J. F. *History of the Fifty-second Regiment, Massachusetts Volunteers.* Boston: George H. Ellis, 1893.

Nash, Howard P. *Stormy Petrel: The Life and Times of General Benjamin F. Butler, 1818–1893.* Rutherford, N.J.: Fairleigh Dickinson University Press, 1969.

Neely, Mark E. *The Abraham Lincoln Encyclopedia.* New York: Da Capo Books, 1982.

Nelson, Charles A. *Waltham, Past and Present.* Cambridge, Mass.: Thomas Lewis, 1879.

Nevins, Allan. *Frémont: Pathmarker of the West.* Lincoln: University of Nebraska Press, 1992.

———. *Hamilton Fish: The Inner History of the Grant Administration.* Rev. ed. 2 vols. New York: Frederick Ungar, 1957.

Nichols, Roy Franklin. *The Democratic Machine, 1850–1854.* Studies in History, Economics and Public Law, Whole Number 248. New York: Columbia University, 1923.

———. *Franklin Pierce: Young Hickory of the Granite Hills.* 2d ed. Philadelphia: University of Pennsylvania Press, 1958.

Nicolay, John G., and John Hay. *Abraham Lincoln: A History.* 10 vols. New York: Century, 1914.

Palfrey, Francis Winthrop. *Memoir of William Francis Bartlett.* Boston: Houghton Mifflin, 1881.

Parker, William B. *Life and Public Service of Justin Smith Morrill.* 1924. Reprint, New York: Da Capo Press, 1971.

Parks, Joseph H. *General Edmund Kirby Smith, C.S.A.* Baton Rouge: Louisiana State University Press, 1954.

Parrish, T. Michael. *Richard Taylor: Soldier Prince of Dixie.* Chapel Hill: University of North Carolina Press, 1992.

Parton, James. *General Butler in New Orleans: History of the Administration of the Department of the Gulf in the Year 1862.* New York: Mason Brothers, 1864.

Pearson, Henry Greenleaf. *The Life of John A. Andrew, Governor of Massachusetts, 1861–1865.* 2 vols. Boston: Houghton Mifflin, 1904.

Pease, Theodore Calvin, and James G. Randall, eds. *The Diary of Orville Hickman Browning,* 2 vols., Collections of the Illinois State Historical Library, vol. 20. Springfield: Illinois State Historical Library, 1925.

Pellet, Elias Porter. *History of the 114th Regiment, New York State Volunteers.* Norwich, N.Y.: Telegraph & Chronicle Power Press Print, 1866.

Perkins, Dexter. *Hands Off: A History of the Monroe Doctrine.* Boston: Little, Brown, 1948.

Perkins, George Hamilton. *Letters of Geo. Hamilton Perkins, U.S.N.* Edited by George E. Belknap. Concord, N.H.: Rumford Press, 1901.

Petersen, Kristen A. *Waltham Rediscovered: An Ethnic History of Waltham, Massachusetts.* Waltham: Peter E. Randall, 1988.

Phillips, Ulrich Bonnell, ed. *The Correspondence of Robert Toombs, Alexander H. Stephens, and Howell Cobb.* 1913. Reprint. New York: Da Capo Press, 1970.

Pierce, Edward L. *Memoir and Letters of Charles Sumner.* 4 vols. 2d ed. 1894. Reprint. New York: Arno Press, 1969.

Pike, James Shepherd. *First Blows of the Civil War.* New York: American News Co., 1879.

Plummer, Albert. *History of the Forty-Eighth Regiment M.V.M. during the Civil War.* Boston: New England Druggist Co., 1907.

Porter, David Dixon. *Incidents and Anecdotes of the Civil War.* New York: D. Appleton, 1885.

———. *The Naval History of the Civil War.* New York: Sherman, 1886.

Powers, George Whitfield. *The Story of the Thirty-Eighth Regiment of Massachusetts Volunteers.* Cambridge, Mass.: Dankin & Metcalf, 1866.

Pyne, Henry R. *The History of the First New Jersey Cavalry (Sixteenth Regiment, New Jersey Volunteers).* Trenton, N.J.: J. A. Beecher, 1871.

Quarles, Benjamin. *The Negro in the Civil War.* Boston: Little, Brown, 1963.

Quint, Alonzo Hall. *The Potomac and the Rapidan.* Boston: Crosby & Nichols, 1864.

Rable, George C. *But There Was No Peace: The Role of Violence in the Politics of Reconstruction.* Athens: University of Georgia Press, 1984.

Randall, J. G. *Lincoln, the President.* 2 vols. New York: Dodd, Mead, 1945.

Rantoul, Robert, Jr. *Memoirs, Speeches and Writings.* Boston: John P. Jewett, 1854.

Raphael, Morris. *The Battle in the Bayou Country.* Detroit: Morris Raphael Books, 1975.

Reed, Emily Hazen. *Life of A. P. Dostie; or, The Conflict in New Orleans.* New York: Wm. P. Tomlinson, 1868.

Reid, Whitelaw. *After the War: A Southern Tour.* New York: Moore, Wilstach & Baldwin, 1866.

Reinders, Robert C. *End of an Era: New Orleans, 1850–1860.* New Orleans: Pelican, 1964.

Richards, Laura E., ed. *Letters and Journals of Samuel Gridley Howe.* 2 vols. Boston: Dana Estes, 1909.

Riddleberger, Patrick W. *George Washington Julian: Radical Republican.* N.p.: Indiana Historical Bureau, 1966.

Riley, Elihu S. *"The Ancient City," a History of Annapolis in Maryland, 1649–1887.* Annapolis: Record Printing Office, 1887.

Ripley, Charles P. *Slaves and Freedmen in Civil War Louisiana.* Baton Rouge: Louisiana State University Press, 1976.

Robinson, William Stevens. *"Warrington" Pen-Portraits.* Edited by Mrs. W. S. Robinson. Boston: Lee & Shepard, 1877.

Roland, Charles P. *Louisiana Sugar Plantations during the American Civil War.* Leiden, Netherlands: E. J. Brill, 1957.

Ross, Earle Dudley. *The Liberal Republican Movement.* 1910. Reprint. Seattle: University of Washington Press, 1970.

Rowland, Dunbar, ed., *Jefferson Davis, Constitutionalist: His Letters, Papers and Speeches.* 10 vols. New York: J. J. Little & Ives, Co. for the Mississippi Department of Archives and History, 1923.

Savage, John. *Our Living Representative Men.* Philadelphia: Childs & Peterson, 1860.

Scharf, J. Thomas. *The Chronicles of Baltimore.* Baltimore: Turnbull Brothers, 1874.

Scott, John. *Story of the Thirty-Second Iowa Infantry Volunteers.* Nevada, Iowa: Author, 1896.

Sears, Lorenzo. *Wendell Phillips: Orator and Agitator.* 1909. Reprint. New York: Benjamin Bloom, 1967.

Selfridge, Thomas Oliver. *Memoirs of Thomas O. Selfridge, Jr., Rear Admiral, U.S.N.* New York: G. P. Putnam's Sons, 1924.

Sherman, John. *Recollections of Forty Years in the House, Senate and Cabinet: An Autobiography.* 3 vols. Chicago: Werner, 1895.

Shugg, Roger W. *Origins of Class Struggle in Louisiana.* Baton Rouge: Louisiana State University Press, 1939.

Simpson, Harold B., and Marcus J. Wright. *Texas in the War, 1861–1865.* Hillsboro, Tex.: Hill Junior College Press, 1965.

Slaughter, Philip. *A Sketch of the Life of Randolph Fairfax.* 2d ed. Richmond: Tyler, Allegre & McDaniel, Enquirer Job Office, 1864.

Smith, George Gilbert. *Leaves from a Soldier's Diary: The Personal Record of Lieutenant George G. Smith, Co. C, 1st Louisiana Regiment Infantry Volunteers [White].* Putnam, Conn.: George G. Smith, 1906.

Smith, Joe Patterson. *The Republican Expansionists of the Early Reconstruction Era.* Chicago: University of Chicago Libraries, 1933.

Smith, Myron J. *The U.S. Gunboat* Carondolet, *1861–1865.* Manhattan, Kan.: Sunflower University Press, 1982.

Southwood, Marion. *"Beauty and Booty," The Watchword of New Orleans.* New York: M. Doolady, 1867.

Sprague, Homer B. *History of the 13th Infantry Regiment of Connecticut Volunteers during the Great Rebellion.* Hartford, Conn.: Case, Lockwood, 1867.

Starbuck, Walter F. *Picturesque Features of the History of Waltham.* Waltham, Mass.: Waltham Publishing Co., 1917.

Stearns, Frank Preston. *The Life and Public Services of George Luther Stearns.* Philadelphia: J. B. Lippincott, 1907.

Stedman, Laura, and George M. Gould. *Life and Letters of Edmund Clarence Stedman.* 2 vols. New York: Moffat, Yard, 1910.

Stevens, William B. *History of the Fiftieth Regiment of Infantry, Massachusetts Volunteer Militia in the Late War of the Rebellion.* Boston: Griffith-Stillings Press, 1907.

Stevenson, B. F. *Letters from the Army.* Cincinnati: W. E. Dibble, 1884.

Strother, David Hunter. *A Virginia Yankee in the Civil War: The Diaries of Da-*

vid Hunter Strother. Edited by Cecil D. Eby. Chapel Hill: University of North Carolina Press, 1961.

Studley, William S. *Final Memorials of Major Joseph Warren Paine: Remarks at His Funeral, Dec. 29, 1864.* Boston: John Wilson & Son, 1865.

Swint, Henry Lee. *The Northern Teacher in the South, 1862–1870.* 1941. Reprint. New York: Octagon Books, 1967.

Tanner, Robert G. *Stonewall Jackson in the Valley: Thomas J. "Stonewall" Jackson's Shenandoah Valley Campaign, Spring 1862.* Garden City, N.Y.: Doubleday, 1976.

Tansill, Charles Callan. *The United States and Santo Domingo, 1789–1873: A Chapter in Caribbean Diplomacy.* Baltimore: Johns Hopkins Press, 1938.

Taylor, Joe Gray. *Louisiana Reconstructed, 1863–1877.* Baton Rouge: Louisiana State University Press, 1974.

Taylor, Richard. *Destruction and Reconstruction: Personal Experiences of the Late War.* Edited by Richard Harwell. New York: Longmans, Green, 1955.

Thayer, William Makepeace. *The Bobbin Boy: or, How Nat Got His Learning.* 1860. Reprint. Boston: Lee & Shepard, 1863.

Thomas, Benjamin Platt. *Russo-American Relations, 1815–1867.* Baltimore: John Hopkins Press, 1930.

Thompson, D. G. Brinton. *Ruggles of New York: A Life of Samuel B. Ruggles.* New York: Columbia University Press, 1946.

Tiemann, William F. *The 159th Regiment Infantry, New-York State Volunteers.* Brooklyn: Author, 1891.

Tompkins, Eugene. *The History of the Boston Theater, 1854–1901.* Boston: Houghton Mifflin, 1908.

Townsend, Luther T. *History of the Sixteenth Regiment, New Hampshire Volunteers.* Washington, D.C.: Norman T. Elliott, 1897.

Trefousse, Hans L. *Ben Butler: The South Called Him BEAST!* New York: Twayne, 1957.

———. *Historical Dictionary of Reconstruction.* New York: Greenwood Press, 1991.

Tunnell, Ted. *Crucible of Reconstruction: War, Radicalism, and Race in Louisiana, 1862–1877.* Baton Rouge: Louisiana State University Press, 1984.

Van Alstyne, Lawrence. *Diary of an Enlisted Man.* New Haven: Tuttle, Morehouse & Taylor, 1910.

Vital Records of Waltham Massachusetts, to the Year 1850. Boston: New-England Historic Genealogical Society, 1904.

Warden, Robert B. *An Account of the Private Life and Public Services of Salmon Portland Chase.* Cincinnati: Wilstach, Baldwin, 1874.

Ware, Edith Ellen. *Political Opinion in Massachusetts during Civil War and*

Reconstruction. Studies in History, Economics and Public Law, vol. 74. New York: Columbia University, 1916.

Warmoth, Henry Clay. *War, Politics and Reconstruction: Stormy Days in Louisiana.* New York: Macmillan, 1930.

Warner, Ezra J. *Generals in Blue: Lives of the Union Commanders.* Baton Rouge: Louisiana State University Press, 1964.

Weed, Thurlow. *Life of Thurlow Weed, Including His Autobiography and a Memoir.* Edited by T. W. Barnes. 2 vols. Boston: Houghton Mifflin, 1883–84.

Weiss, John. *Letters and Correspondence of Theodore Parker.* 2 vols. 1864. Reprint. New York: Da Capo Press, 1970.

Welles, Gideon. *Diary of Gideon Welles: Secretary of the Navy under Lincoln and Johnson.* Edited by Howard K. Beale. 3 vols. New York: Norton, 1960.

West, Richard S. *Lincoln's Scapegoat General: A Life of Benjamin F. Butler, 1818–1893.* Boston: Houghton Mifflin, 1965.

———. *The Second Admiral: A Life of David Dixon Porter, 1813–1891.* New York: Coward-McCann, 1937.

Whipple, George Chandler. *State Sanitation: A Review of the Work of the Massachusetts State Board of Health.* Cambridge, Mass.: Harvard University Press, 1917.

[Whitaker, Judge]. *Sketches of Life and Character in Louisiana.* New Orleans: Ferguson & Crosby, 1847.

White, Howard A. *The Freedmen's Bureau in Louisiana.* Baton Rouge: Louisiana State University Press, 1970.

Wiley, Bell Irvin. *Southern Negroes, 1861–1865.* New Haven: Yale University Press, 1965.

Williams, Charles Richard. *The Life of Rutherford B. Hayes, Nineteenth President of the United States.* 2 vols. Boston: Houghton Mifflin, 1914.

Williams, George W. *A History of the Negro Troops in the War of the Rebellion, 1861–1865.* 1888. Reprint. New York: Kraus Reprint Co., 1969.

Williams, Kenneth P. *Lincoln Finds a General: A Military Study of the Civil War.* 5 vols. New York: Macmillan, 1949–59.

Williams, T. Harry. *Lincoln and His Generals.* New York: Knopf, 1952.

———. *Lincoln and the Radicals.* Madison: University of Wisconsin Press, 1941.

Willis, Henry A. *The Fifty-third Regiment Massachusetts Volunteers.* Fitchburg, Mass.: Blanchard & Brown, 1889.

Wilson, Henry. *History of the Rise and Fall of the Slave Power in America.* 4 vols. Boston: J. R. Osgood, 1875–77.

Winters, John D. *The Civil War in Louisiana.* Baton Rouge: Louisiana State University Press, 1963.

Winthrop, Robert Charles. *A Memoir of Robert C. Winthrop*. Boston: Little, Brown, 1897.

Woods, J. T. Woods. *Services of the Ninety-Sixth Ohio Volunteers*. Toledo: Blade Printing & Paper Co., 1874.

Woodworth, Steven E. *Jefferson Davis and His Generals: The Failure of Confederate Command in the West*. Lawrence: University of Kansas Press, 1990.

Worsham, John H. *One of Jackson's Foot Cavalry*. New York: Neale, 1912.

Index